Managing Behavior in Organizations

in Organizations

Science in Service to Practice

Jerald Greenberg

The Ohio State University

Prentice Hall
Upper Saddle River, N. J. 07458

Library of Congress Cataloging-in-Publication Data

Greenberg, Jerald.
   Managing behavior in organizations: science in service to
practice / Jerald Greenberg.
      p.   cm.
   Includes index.
   ISBN 0-205-16322-X
   1. Organizational behavior.   I. Title
HD58.7.G7176   1995
658.3—dc20   95-26126
                                                       CIP

Acquisitions editor: Natalie Anderson
Production manager: Maureen Wilson
Associate editor: Lisamarie Brassini
Buyer: Ken Clinton
Marketing manager: JoAnn DeLuca
Cover designer: Donna Wickes
Interior design: Donna Wickes
Design director: Patricia Wosczyk
Cover illustration: Paul Schulenburg

© 1996 by Prentice-Hall, Inc.
A Division of Simon & Schuster
Upper Saddle River, NJ 07458

Printed in the United States of America
10   9   8   7   6   5   4   3   2   1

ISBN 0-205-16322-X

Prentice-Hall International (UK) Limited, *London*
Prentice-Hall of Australia Pty. Limited, *Sydney*
Prentice-Hall Canada, Inc., *Toronto*
Prentice-Hall Hispanoamericana, S.A., *Mexico*
Prentice-Hall of India Private Limited, *New Delhi*
Prentice-Hall of Japan, Inc., *Tokyo*
Simon & Schuster Asia Pte. Ltd., *Singapore*
Editora Prentice Hall do Brasil Ltda., *Rio de Janeiro*

BK
32.50

To Carolyn, my best pal.

Contents

CHAPTER
4

WORK-RELATED ATTITUDES: FEELINGS ABOUT OUR JOBS, ORGANIZATIONS, AND COWORKERS   94

CHAPTER
5

JOINING UP AND FITTING IN: SOCIALIZATION, CULTURE, AND CAREERS   122

PART III   GROUP PROCESSES

CHAPTER
6

ORGANIZATIONAL COMMUNICATION AND SOCIAL INFLUENCE   151

CHAPTER
7

GROUPS AND TEAMS IN ORGANIZATIONS   178

List of Special Features

GROUP EXERCISES

Preface

A NEW KIND OF OB TEXT:
SHORT, SWEET, AND PRACTICAL

When it comes to organizations there seem to be two distinct camps—people who work in them, and people who study people who work in them. Unfortunately, these two groups don't get together as often as you might imagine. As a result, much of what goes on in organizations occurs in the absence of sound scientific knowledge about people at work. At the same time, much of what scientists study about the workplace never finds its way back to organizations in ways that help them operate more effectively.

Why does the gap occur? I would venture to guess that it is not due to lack of interest. Rather, the main reason why scientists and practitioners often don't learn from each other is that each knows little about what the other is doing. Each fails to see the connections between what actually goes on in the workplace and the scientific theories and research that help explain "what makes people tick." However, to truly understand behavior in organizations it is essential to bridge this gap. That's what this book is all about.

In this regard, this is no ordinary textbook on organizational behavior (OB). Traditional OB texts focus almost exclusively on research and theory as an end in itself. Although this is a highly legitimate orientation (indeed, I have co-authored one such book myself!), the real benefit of learning about OB comes from the insight it provides about creating effective workplaces—ones in which both employees and the organizations that employ them thrive. With this in mind, this book is quite different. Here, I review all the major theories and research findings in the field of OB, but do so from a perspective that sheds light on actual organizational practices. In so doing, OB is presented as a "science in service to practice," not coincidentally the subtitle of this book.

A BRIEF NOTE ABOUT BREVITY

In addition to its applied orientation, the nontraditional nature of this book is also reflected by its size. Indeed, it is some 400 pages shorter in length and several inches smaller in dimension than the standard text. Not surprisingly, it does not describe every nook and cranny of OB. It does not intend to. Instead,

I have written this book to cover only the highlights of the field—those aspects of OB that students most need to know. Thus, it is a succinct guide to understanding OB, its current theories and their value in understanding modern organizational practices.

With this in mind, I have kept references to a minimum, citing only major sources and direct quotes. To have been more thorough could easily have doubled the length of the book. And, with my underlying mission of keeping it simple, direct, lively, and practical, this would have been out of the question.

WHO SHOULD READ THIS BOOK?

A growing number of today's management and OB professors are seeking an alternative to the traditional 700-page text. Instead of relying on a single book crammed with all the latest research and theoretical advances, they prefer to expose their students to a variety of materials from several sources, including cases, exercises, and articles. In such classes, students still need to read about the basics of OB—those topics that they *really* have to know. This book is designed to fill this need.

But, as I noted above, this book goes beyond simply presenting an abridged overview of the field. With an eye toward highlighting the usefulness of OB concepts, this book illustrates *how* these concepts are put to use in today's organizations. As such, the book is designed for three major audiences: undergraduate students with little or no background in the social sciences, MBA students, and executives being trained in organizational skills. Undergraduates will appreciate the clear and succinct presentation of the theories. MBA students and executives will relate to the book's many practical applications. And all will benefit from this book's efforts to develop the rapprochement between the two.

SPECIAL FEATURES

With an eye toward highlighting the applied nature of the field of OB, I have scoured hundreds of professional books and magazines, and report current examples of actual organizational practices that illustrate key points made in the text. These are integrated throughout the body of the text.

I also have included several *special features* that further bring out the practical side of the field of OB. These include:

- **Winning Practices**—A close-up examination of particularly noteworthy organizational practices that illustrate a key point in the text.
- **Self-Assessment Exercise**—A self-assessment tool designed to provide insight into an aspect of your own individual behavior in organizations.
- **Group Exercise**—A hands-on experience requiring the joint efforts of classmates to help illustrate an important organizational phenomenon.
- **Putting It to Use**—An applications-oriented summary of each chapter's main points.

•**You Be the Consultant**   A chapter-closing exercise that asks you to apply key concepts from the chapter to a hypothetical situation.

ACKNOWLEDGMENTS

Several people have been extremely helpful in preparing this book. First, I wish to thank my colleagues who provided valuable suggestions and comments after reading various drafts of this book. These include:

Richard Grover, University of Southern Maine

Jeffrey Miles, University of Illinois

Michael Buckley, University of Oklahoma

Second, I wish to thank my editor, Natalie Anderson. Without her constant support and encouragement, this book would not have been possible. Third, I gratefully acknowledge the tireless, behind-the-scenes work of Maureen Wilson and Prentice Hall's outstanding production team, including copyeditor Donna Mulder. These talented people are responsible for the beautiful book you have before you, and I am indebted to them.

Finally, I wish to acknowledge the family of the late Irving Abramowitz for their generous endowment to The Ohio State University, which provided invaluable support during the writing of this book.

To all these truly outstanding people, and to many others too, I express my warm personal regards.

CHAPTER 1

What Is Organizational Behavior and How Do We Learn About It?

PREVIEW OF CHAPTER HIGHLIGHTS

Organizational behavior (OB) is the field that seeks knowledge of behavior in organizational settings by systematically studying individual, group, and organizational processes.

Today's OB adopts a **Theory Y** philosophy, believing that people are basically interested in working hard under the right conditions. It also adopts a **contingency approach,** believing that organizational behavior is the complex result of individual, social, organizational, and environmental factors.

Almost a century ago, the **scientific management** school emphasized that work can be designed so as to perform it in a highly efficient manner. In contrast, the **human relations movement** emphasized the importance of social determinants of work performance.

Classical **organizational theory** advocated that there is one best way to design organizations.

Today's OB scientists rely on the use of **survey research,** in which questionnaires are used to determine the degree to which variables are **correlated** with each other.

To draw conclusions about the cause-and-effect relationships between variables, organizational scientists rely on the use of **experimental research,** as well as **qualitative research** (e.g., **observational research** and **case studies**).

What image comes to mind when you think of an organization? For most, it's a huge building, such as a tall office tower or a sprawling factory decked with smokestacks. Although these edifices are certainly important when it comes to housing where work is done, the most important component of organizations themselves is *people*.

This sentiment was expressed clearly by Max DePree, the retired chief executive officer (CEO) of Herman Miller, Inc. (the Michigan-based office furniture company), who said:

> *Our people and our values—these are exactly the things most fragile and important in our corporation . . . we should be more involved in principles and relationships than in numbers.*[1]

There can be no organizations without people. So, no matter how sophisticated a company's mechanical equipment may be, and how healthy its bottom line, people problems can bring an organization down very quickly. By contrast, organizations in which people work happily and effectively can benefit greatly. Hence, it makes sense to realize that the human side of work is critical to the effective functioning—and basic existence—of organizations. It is this people-centered orientation that is taken in the field of *organizational behavior*—the topic of this book.

This chapter will introduce you to the field of organizational behavior—its characteristics, its history, and the tools it uses to learn about the behavior of people in organizations. We will begin by formally defining the field, describing exactly what it is and what it seeks to accomplish. In so doing we will emphasize how the field is oriented toward understanding individuals, groups, and entire organizations, and how these all interact with each other. We also will emphasize the fact that the field of organizational behavior is concerned with applying scientific knowledge to applied organizational problems. Following this, we will summarize the history of the field of organizational behavior, tracing its roots from its origins to its emergence as a modern science. Finally, we will discuss the research methods scientists use to learn about the behavior of people in organizations.

WHAT IS THE FIELD OF ORGANIZATIONAL BEHAVIOR ALL ABOUT?

As we have been alluding, the field of **organizational behavior** (or, **OB**, as it is commonly called) deals with human behavior in organizations. Formally, organizational behavior may be defined as *the field that seeks knowledge of behavior in organizational settings by systematically studying individual, group, and organiza-*

tional processes. This knowledge is used *both* by scientists interested in understanding human behavior, and by practitioners interested in enhancing organizational effectiveness and individual well-being. Our orientation in this book will highlight both these purposes, focusing on how scientific knowledge has been—or may be—used for these practical purposes.

OB APPLIES THE SCIENTIFIC METHOD TO PRACTICAL MANAGERIAL PROBLEMS

The definition of OB refers to seeking knowledge and to studying behavioral processes. Although not as sophisticated as the study of physics or chemistry (nor as mature as these fields), the orientation of the field of OB is still scientific in nature. Thus, like other scientific fields, OB seeks to develop a base of knowledge by using an empirical, research-based approach. As such, it relies on systematic observation and measurement of the phenomena of interest.

Why is it so important to learn about behavior in organizational settings? To social scientists, learning about human behavior on the job—"what makes people tick" in organizations—is valuable for its own sake. After all, scientists are interested in the generation of knowledge—in this case, insight into the effects of organizations on people and the effects of people on organizations. This is not to say, however, that such knowledge has no value outside of scientific circles. Far from it! OB specialists also apply knowledge from scientific studies, putting it to practical use. As they seek to improve organizational functioning and the quality of life of people working in organizations, they rely heavily on knowledge derived from OB research. Thus, there are both scientific and applied facets of the field of OB—aspects that not only coexist, but complement each other.

OB FOCUSES ON THREE LEVELS OF ANALYSIS: INDIVIDUALS, GROUPS, AND ORGANIZATIONS

To best appreciate behavior in organizations, OB specialists cannot focus exclusively on individuals acting alone. After all, in organizational settings people frequently work together in groups. Furthermore, people—alone and in groups—both influence and are influenced by their work environments. Considering this, it should not be surprising to learn that the field of OB focuses on three distinct levels of analysis—individuals, groups, and organizations.

The field of OB recognizes that all three levels of analysis must be considered to fully comprehend the complex dynamics of behavior in organizations. Careful attention to all three levels of analysis is a central theme in modern OB and will be fully reflected throughout this text. For example, we will be describing how OB specialists are concerned with individual perceptions, attitudes, and motives. We also will be describing how people communicate with each other and coordinate their activities among themselves in work groups. Finally, we will examine organizations as a whole—the way they are structured and operate in their environments, and the effects of their operations on the individuals and groups within them.

OB SEEKS TO IMPROVE THE QUALITY OF LIFE AT WORK

In the early part of the twentieth century, as railroads opened up the western portion of the United States and the nation's population rapidly grew (it doubled from 1880 to 1920!), the demand for manufactured products was great. New manufacturing plants were built, attracting waves of new immigrants in search of a living wage and laborers lured off farms by the employment prospects factory work offered. These men and women found that factories were gigantic, noisy, hot, and highly regimented—in short, brutal places in which to work. Bosses demanded more and more of their employees, and treated them like disposable machines, replacing those who quit or who died from accidents with others who waited outside the factory gates.

Clearly, the managers of a century ago held very negative views of employees. They assumed that people were basically lazy and irresponsible, and treated them with disrespect. This very negativistic approach, which has been with us for many years, reflects the traditional view of management called a **Theory X** orientation. This philosophy of management assumes that people are basically lazy, dislike work, need direction, and will only work hard when they are pushed into performing.

Today, however, if you asked corporate officials to describe their views of human nature, you'd probably find some more optimistic beliefs. Although some of today's managers still think that people are basically lazy, many others would disagree, arguing that it's not that simple. They would claim that most individuals are just as capable of working hard as they are of "goofing off." If employees are recognized for their efforts (such as by being fairly paid) and are given an opportunity to succeed (such as by being well trained), they may be expected to work very hard without being pushed. Thus, employees may put forth a great deal of effort simply because they want to. Management's job, then, is to create those conditions that make people want to perform as desired.

Theory Y philosophy runs so deep at J. M. Smucker, the largest U.S. jam maker, that managers are viewed as working for their staffs, and not the other way around. Prospective employees must meet the approval of all others with whom they will be working. With an approach like that, "it's got to be good."

The approach that assumes that people are not intrinsically lazy, but that they are willing to work hard when the right conditions prevail is known as the **Theory Y** orientation. This philosophy assumes that people have a psychological need to work and that they seek achievement and responsibility. In contrast to the Theory X philosophy of management, which essentially demonstrates distrust for people on the job, the Theory Y approach is strongly associated with improving the quality of people's work lives. (For a summary of the differences, see Table 1-1.)

The Theory Y perspective prevails within the field of organizational behavior today. It assumes that people are highly responsive to their work environments, and that the ways they are treated will influence the ways they will act. In fact, OB scientists are very interested in learning exactly what conditions will lead people to behave most positively—that is, those conditions that make work both productive for organizations and enjoyable for the people working in them. (Do your own assumptions about people at work more closely match a Theory X or Theory Y perspective? To find out, complete the **Self-Assessment Exercise** on p. 6.)

OB RECOGNIZES THE DYNAMIC NATURE OF ORGANIZATIONS

Thus far, our characterization of the field of OB has focused more on behavior than on organizations. Nonetheless, it is important to point out that both OB scientists and practitioners do pay a great deal of attention to the nature of organizations themselves. Under what conditions will organizations change? How are organizations structured? How do organizations interact with their environments? Questions such as these are of major interest to specialists in OB. But before we can consider them (as we will do in Chapters 10 and 11), we must first clarify exactly what we mean by an organization.

Formally, we define an **organization** as *a structured social system consisting of groups and individuals working together to meet some agreed-upon objectives.* In other words, organizations consist of structured social units, such as individuals

■ *Table 1-1 Theory X Versus Theory Y: A Comparison*

The traditional *Theory X* orientation toward people is far more negativistic than the more contemporary *Theory Y* approach—the one accepted by modern OB. Differences between these approaches with respect to four key variables are summarized here.

Dimension	Theory X	Theory Y
Orientation toward people	Distrusting	Accepting, seeks to improve the quality of working life
Assumptions about people	Basically lazy	Need to achieve and be responsible
Interest in working	Disinterested	Highly interested
Conditions under which people will work hard	Work when pushed	Work when appropriately trained and recognized

SELF-ASSESSMENT EXERCISE

Testing Your Assumptions About People at Work: Theory X or Theory Y?

What assumptions do you make about human nature? Are you inclined to think of people as primarily lazy and disinterested in working (a Theory X approach) or that they are willing to work hard under the right conditions (a Theory Y approach)? This exercise is designed to give you some insight into this question.

DIRECTIONS

For each of the following eight pairs of statements, select the one that best reflects your feelings by marking the letter that corresponds to it.

1. (a) If you give people what they need to do their jobs, they will act very responsibly.

   (b) Giving people more information than they need will lead them to misuse it.

2. (c) People naturally want to get away with doing as little work as possible.

   (d) When people avoid working, it's probably because the work itself has been stripped of its meaning.

3. (e) It's not surprising to find that employees don't demonstrate much creativity on the job because people tend not to have much of it to begin with.

   (f) Although many people are, by nature, very creative, they don't show it on the job because they aren't given a chance.

4. (g) It doesn't pay to ask employees for their ideas because their perspective is generally too limited to be of value.

   (h) When you ask employees for ideas, you are likely to get some useful suggestions.

5. (i) The more information people have about their jobs, the more closely their supervisors have to keep them in line.

(j) The more information people have about their jobs, the less closely they have to be supervised.

6. (k) Once people are paid enough, they tend to care less about being recognized for a job well done.

(l) The more interesting work is for people, the less likely it is that they care about their pay.

7. (m) Supervisors lose prestige when they admit that their subordinates may have been right, while they were wrong.

(n) Supervisors gain prestige when they admit that their subordinates may have been right, while they were wrong.

8. (o) When people are held accountable for their mistakes, they raise their standards.

(p) Unless people are punished for their mistakes, they will lower their standards.

SCORING

1. Give yourself one point for having selected b, c, e, g, i, k, m, and p. The sum of these points is your Theory X score.

2. Give yourself one point for having selected a, d, f, h, j, l, n, and o. The sum of these points is your Theory Y score.

QUESTIONS FOR DISCUSSION

1. Which perspective did this questionnaire indicate that you more strongly endorsed, Theory X or Theory Y? Is this consistent with your own intuitive conclusion?

2. Do you tend to manage others in ways consistent with Theory X or Theory Y ideas?

3. Can you recall any experiences that may have been crucial in defining or reinforcing your Theory X or Theory Y philosophy?

and/or work groups, who strive to attain a common goal. Typically, we think of making a profit as the primary goal of an organization—and indeed, for most business organizations, it is. However, different organizations may be guided by different goals. For example, charitable organizations may focus on the objective of helping people in need, political parties may be interested in electing candidates with certain ideas, and religious organizations may strive to save souls. Regardless of the specific goals sought, the structured social units working together toward them may be considered organizations.

In studying organizations, OB scientists recognize that organizations are not static but dynamic and ever-changing entities. In other words, they recognize that organizations are **open systems**—that is, self-sustaining systems that use energy to transform resources from the environment (such as raw materials) into some form of output (for example, a finished product).[2] Figure 1-1 summarizes some of the key properties of open systems.

As this diagram makes clear, organizations receive input from their environments and continuously transform it into output. This output gets transformed back into input, and the cyclical operation continues. Consider, for example, how organizations may tap the human resources of the community by hiring and training people to do jobs. These individuals may work to provide a product in exchange for wages. They then spend these wages, putting money

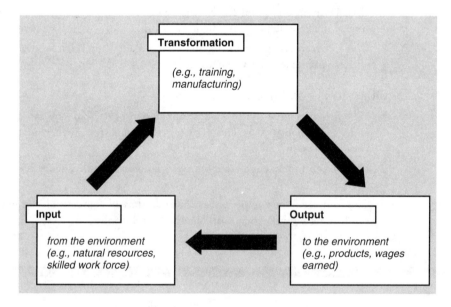

■ *Figure 1-1   Organizations as Open Systems*

The *open systems* approach assumes that organizations operate in a self-sustaining manner. They transform inputs into outputs in continuous fashion. (*Source:* Based on suggestions by Katz & Kahn, 1978; see Note 2.)

back into the community, allowing more people to afford the company's products. This in turn creates the need for still more employees, and so on. If you think about it this way, it's easy to realize that organizations are dynamic and constantly changing.

The dynamic nature of organizations can be likened to the operations of the human body. As people breathe, they take in oxygen and transform it into carbon dioxide. This in turn sustains the life of green plants, which in turn emit oxygen for people to breathe. The continuous nature of the open system characterizes not only human life but the existence of organizations as well.

OB ASSUMES THERE IS NO "ONE BEST" APPROACH

What's the most effective way to motivate people? What style of leadership works best? Should groups of individuals be used to make important organizational decisions? Although these questions are quite reasonable, there is a basic problem with all of them. Namely, they all assume that there is a simple, unitary answer—that is, one best way to motivate, to lead, and to make decisions.

Specialists in the field of OB today agree that there is no one best approach when it comes to such complex phenomena. To assume otherwise is not only overly simplistic and naive but, as you will see, grossly inaccurate. When it comes to studying human behavior in organizations, there are no simple answers. Instead, OB scholars recognize that behavior in work settings is the complex result of many interacting forces. This fact is recognized in what is known as the **contingency approach,** an orientation that is a hallmark of modern OB. Consider, for example, how an individual's personal characteristics (e.g., personal attitudes and beliefs) in conjunction with situational factors (e.g., an organization's climate, relations between coworkers) may all work together when it comes to influencing how a particular individual is likely to behave on the job.

Explaining OB phenomena often requires saying, "it depends." As our knowledge of work-related behavior becomes increasingly complex, it is difficult to give "straight answers." Rather, it is usually necessary to say that people will do certain things "under some conditions," or "when all other factors are equal." Such phrases provide a clear indication that the contingency approach is being used. In other words, a certain behavior occurs "contingent upon" the existence of certain conditions—hence, the name.

THE FIELD OF ORGANIZATIONAL BEHAVIOR: HISTORICAL BACKGROUND

The importance of understanding the behavior of people at work has not always been as recognized as it is today. In fact, it was not until the early part of the twentieth century that the idea first developed, and only during the last few decades that it has gained widespread acceptance. So that we can appreciate how the field of OB got to where it is today, we will now briefly outline its history and describe some of the most influential forces in its development.

SCIENTIFIC MANAGEMENT: THE ROOTS OF ORGANIZATIONAL BEHAVIOR

The earliest attempts to study behavior in organizations came out of a desire by industrial efficiency experts to improve worker productivity. Their central question was straightforward: What could be done to get people to do more work in less time? It's not particularly surprising that attempts to answer this question were made at the turn of the century. After all, this was a period of rapid industrialization and technological change in the United States. As engineers attempted to make machines more efficient, it was a natural extension of their efforts to work on the human side of the equation—making people more productive too. Given this history, it should not be too surprising that the first people we now credit for contributions to OB were actually industrial engineers.

Frederick Winslow Taylor worked most of his life in steel mills, starting as a laborer and working his way up to the position of chief engineer. In the 1880s, while a foreman at Philadelphia's Midvale Steel Company, Taylor became aware of some of the inefficient practices of the employees. Noticing, for example, that laborers wasted movements when shifting pig iron, Taylor studied the individual components of this task and identified a set of the most efficient motions needed to perform it. A few years later, while at Pittsburgh's Bethlehem Steel, Taylor similarly redesigned the job of loading and unloading rail cars so that they could be done as efficiently as possible. On the heels of these experiences, Taylor published his ground-breaking book, *Scientific Management.* In this work, he argued that the objective of management is "to secure the maximum prosperity for the employer, coupled with the maximum prosperity of each employee."[3]

Beyond identifying ways in which manual labor jobs can be performed more efficiently, Taylor's **scientific management** approach was unique in its focus on the role of employees as individuals. Taylor advocated two ideas that hardly seem special today but were quite new at the beginning of the twentieth century. First, he recommended that employees be carefully selected and trained to perform their jobs. Second, he believed that increasing workers' wages would raise their motivation and make them more productive. Although this idea is unsophisticated by today's standards—and not completely accurate (as we will see in Chapter 3)—Taylor may be credited with recognizing the important role of motivation in job performance.

It was contributions like these that stimulated further study of behavior in organizations and created an intellectual climate that eventually paved the way for the development of the field of OB. Acknowledging these contributions, management theorist Peter Drucker has described Taylor as "the first man in history who did not take work for granted, but who looked at it and studied it."[4]

The publication of *Scientific Management* stimulated several other scientists to pick up on and expand Taylor's ideas. Among the most strongly influenced were the industrial psychologists Frank and Lillian Gilbreth. This husband-and-wife team pioneered an approach known as **time-and-motion study,** a type of applied research designed to classify and streamline the individual movements needed to perform jobs, with the intent of finding "the one best way" to perform them. Although this approach appears to be highly mechanical and dehumanizing, the Gilbreths, parents of 12 children, practiced "Taylorism" with a human face in their personal lives. In fact, you may even recall the story of how the Gilbreths applied the principles of scientific management to the operation of their household as told in the classic film, *Cheaper by the Dozen.*

THE HUMAN RELATIONS MOVEMENT
AND THE HAWTHORNE STUDIES

Although scientific management did a good job of highlighting the importance of the efficient performance of work, it did not go far enough in directing our attention to the wide variety of factors that might influence work behavior. In fact, many experts rejected Taylorism, favoring instead an approach that focused on employees' own views and emphasized respect for individuals. At the forefront of this orientation was Elton W. Mayo, an organizational scientist and consultant widely regarded as the founder of what is called the **human relations movement.** This management philosophy rejects the primarily economic orientation of scientific management, and focuses instead on the noneconomic, social factors operating in the workplace. Mayo and other proponents of the human relations movement recognized that task performance was greatly influenced by the social conditions that existed in organizations— that is, the way employees were treated by management, and the relationships they had with each other.

In 1927 a series of studies was begun at Western Electric's Hawthorne Works outside Chicago. The researchers were interested in determining several things, including the effects of illumination on worker productivity. In other words, how brightly or dimly lit should the work environment be for people to produce at their maximum level? Two groups of female employees took part in the study. One group, the control room condition, did their jobs without any changes in lighting; the other group, the test room condition, worked while the lighting was systematically varied, sometimes getting brighter, and sometimes getting dimmer. The results were puzzling: productivity increased in both locations. Just as surprising, there was no clear connection between illumination and performance. In fact, output in the test room remained high even when the level of illumination was so low that workers could barely see what they were doing!

In another study conducted at the company's Bank Wiring Room, male members of various work groups were observed during regular working conditions and were interviewed at length after work. In this investigation, no attempts were made to alter the work environment. What Mayo found here also was surprising. Namely, instead of improving their performance, employees deliberately restricted their output. Not only did the researchers actually see the men stopping work long before quitting time, but in interviews, the men admitted that they easily could have done more if they desired.

Why did this occur? Eventually, Mayo and his associates recognized that the answer resided in the fact that organizations are social systems. How effectively people worked depended, in great part, not only on the physical aspects of the working conditions experienced, but also the social conditions encountered. In the Hawthorne studies, Mayo noted, productivity rose simply because people responded favorably to the special attention they received. Knowing they were being studied made them feel special and motivated them to do their best. Hence, it was these social factors more than the physical factors that had such profound effects on job performance.

The same explanation applied in the Bank Wiring Room study as well. Here the employees feared that because they were being studied, the company would eventually raise the amount of work they were expected to do. So as to guard against the imposition of unreasonable standards (and, hopefully, to keep their jobs!), the men agreed among themselves to keep output low. In other words, informal rules (known as norms) were established about what constituted acceptable levels of job performance. (We will discuss this topic more thoroughly in Chapter 7.) These social forces at work in this setting proved to be much more potent determinants of job performance than the physical factors studied.

This conclusion, based on the surprising findings of the Hawthorne studies, is important because it ushered in a whole new way of thinking about behavior at work. It suggests that to understand behavior on the job, we must fully appreciate people's attitudes and the processes by which they communicate with each other. This way of thinking, so fundamental to modern OB, may be traced back to Elton Mayo's pioneering Hawthorne studies. Although the research was flawed in some important ways (e.g., conditions in the study rooms were not carefully controlled), what they revealed about the importance of human needs, attitudes, motives, and relationships in the workplace was quite influential and novel for its time.

CLASSICAL ORGANIZATIONAL THEORY

During the same time that proponents of scientific management got people to begin thinking about the interrelationships between people and their jobs, another approach to managing people emerged. This perspective, known as **clas-**

sical organizational theory, focused on the efficient structuring of overall organizations. This is in contrast, of course, to scientific management, which sought to effectively organize the work of individuals.

Several different theorists are identified with classical organizational theory. Among the first was Henri Fayol, a French industrialist who attributed his managerial success to various principles he developed. Among these are the following:

- A division of labor should be used because it allows people to specialize, doing only what they do best.

- Managers should have authority over their subordinates, the right to order them to do what is necessary for the organization.

- Lines of authority should be uninterrupted; that is, a clear chain of command should connect top management to the lowest-level employees.

- There should exist a clearly defined unity of command, such that employees receive directions from only one other person so as to avoid confusion.

- Subordinates should be allowed to formulate and implement their own plans.

Although many of these principles are still well accepted today, it is widely recognized that they should not always be applied in exactly the same way. For example, whereas some organizations thrive on being structured according to a unity of command, still others require that some employees take directions from several different superiors. We will have more to say about this subject when we discuss various types of organizational designs in Chapter 10. For now, suffice it to say that current organizational theorists owe a debt of gratitude to Fayol for his pioneering and far-reaching ideas.

Although we tend to think of bureaucracies as being inefficient, **United Parcel Service (UPS)** *has prospered by adhering to many of the tenets of bureaucratic structure.*

Probably the best known classical organizational theorist is the German sociologist, Max Weber. Among other things, Weber is known for proposing a form of organizational structure familiar today—the **bureaucracy.** Weber's idea was that the bureaucracy is the one best way to efficiently organize work in all organizations—much as proponents of scientific management searched for the ideal way to perform a job. The elements of an ideal bureaucracy are summarized in Table 1-2.

When you think about bureaucracies, negative images probably come to mind of lots of inflexible people getting bogged down in lots of red tape. Weber's "universal" view of bureaucratic structure lies in contrast to the more modern approaches to organizational design (see Chapter 10) in which it is recognized that different forms of

■ *Table 1-2 Bureaucracy: Its Ideal Characteristics*

According to Max Weber, bureaucracies must possess certain characteristics. Here are the major characteristics that define bureaucratic organizations.

Characteristic	Description
Formal rules and regulations	Written guidelines are used to control all employees' behaviors.
Impersonal treatment	Favoritism is to be avoided, and all work relationships are to be based on objective standards.
Division of labor	All duties are divided into specialized tasks and are performed by individuals with the appropriate skills.
Hierarchical structure	Positions are ranked by authority level in clear fashion from lower-level to upper-level ones.
Authority structure	The making of decisions is determined by one's position in the hierarchy; people have authority over those in lower-ranking positions.
Lifelong career commitment	Employment is viewed as a permanent, lifelong obligation on the part of the organization and its employees.
Rationality	The organization is committed to achieving its ends (e.g., profitability) in the most efficient manner possible.

organizational structure may be more or less appropriate under different situations. Although the bureaucracy may not have proven to be the perfect structure for organizing all work, many of Weber's ideas are still considered viable today.

Despite differences between Fayol's and Weber's principles for organizing work, both approaches assume that there is a single most effective way to structure organizations. Although, as noted earlier, such approaches seem simplistic by modern standards, we are indebted to Fayol, Weber, and other classical management theorists for calling our attention to the important effects that the design of organizations can have.

ORGANIZATIONAL BEHAVIOR
IN THE MODERN ERA

The pioneering contributions noted thus far set the stage for the emergence of the modern science of organizational behavior. Although the first doctoral degrees in OB were granted in the 1940s, the field's early growth was uneven. It was not until the late 1950s and early 1960s that OB became a going concern. By that time, active programs of research were going on, including investigations of such key processes as motivation and leadership, and the impact of organizational structure on productivity.

Stimulated by a report by the Ford Foundation in the 1960s, advocating that students trained in business receive firm grounding in the social sciences, the field of OB rapidly grew into one that borrowed heavily from other disciplines. In fact, the field of OB as we know it today may be characterized as a hybrid science that draws from many social science fields. For example, studies of motivation and work-related attitudes, dealing as they do with the processes of learning and perception, draw on psychology. Similarly, the study of group dynamics and leadership relies heavily on sociology. The topic of organizational communication, obviously, draws on research in the field of communication. And OB scientists look to the field of management science to understand the design of organizational hierarchies and other structural arrangements. Taken together, it is clear that modern OB is truly a multifaceted field.

In recent years, the study of OB has added a few new characteristics worth noting. Although there are too many new developments to mention, a few current trends deserve to be pointed out.

- The field of OB has been paying increased attention to the *cross-cultural aspects of business,* recognizing that our understanding of organizational phenomena may not be universal. Today research that considers the international generalizability of OB phenomena is considered key to understanding organizational competitiveness in a global society.

- The study of *(un)ethical behavior in organizations* is considered more important than ever before. Indeed, OB scientists are fascinated by understanding the factors that lead people to make ethical or unethical decisions, and by their willingness to engage in such antisocial behaviors as lying, cheating, stealing, and acting violently.

- Today's OB scientists and practitioners recognize the importance of the *external environment* on organizational behavior. That is, they do not consider organizational behavior in a vacuum. Instead, they investigate how factors such as laws, governmental regulations, and international affairs affect behavior in organizations.

- The traditional emphasis on manufacturing has been expanded to include studies of the *service and information sectors* of business. As more people move into these lines of work, the study of OB follows right behind them.

- Few developments have changed the world of work more than *advances in technology.* Many people do different jobs and perform them in different ways than they did just a few years ago. Naturally, such developments are important to the field of OB.

Paying Attention to People Pays Off Big on the Bottom Line

We can safely say that organizational officials are generally well aware of the importance of properly maintaining equipment, machinery, and financial investments. However, too many take for granted the need to properly maintain organizations' most important resources of all—its people. Unfortunately, some companies make their employees' lives miserable (e.g., providing uncomfortable or unsafe working conditions, paying them unfairly low wages, and treating them with disrespect), creating abusive conditions under which employees will have little reason to channel their energies toward making the organization better. Fortunately, most of today's organizational leaders take a more enlightened approach. They recognize that there's more to be gained by creating a more positive workplace, an environment in which people care about the company's success and strive to contribute toward it. In other words, they practice the suggestions for good management that follow from research in organizational behavior.

Companies that mistreat people are not making the most of their human resources. In contrast, people-oriented companies that fully develop and nurture these resources stand to benefit financially. You want proof? Consider these facts and figures.[5]

- A survey of over 1,000 New York Stock Exchange companies found that 75 percent of companies reported that human resource programs (e.g., employee training and development) not only lowered costs but also improved productivity.

Be assured that as you read this book you will learn more about not only the traditional interdisciplinary nature of OB, but also these rapidly developing topics. (For all its changes, the study of organizational behavior has always been based on the assumption that it can help make organizations operate more effectively—hence, profitably. Evidence presented in the **Winning Practices** section above explicitly supports this claim.)

- A study of over 100 industrial firms compared those that used participative management techniques (e.g., giving workers a say in important organizational decisions) with those that did not. Not only did the firms using participation have lower rates of turnover and absenteeism (which can be costly), but also more impressive showings on financial indices such as earnings per share and net profits.

- A book called *The 100 Best Companies to Work for in America* identifies those organizations that treat employees best with respect to such key factors as pay/benefits, opportunities, job security, friendliness, fairness, and pride in the company. These companies (e.g., Hallmark Cards, Procter & Gamble, J. M. Smucker, Polaroid), on average, are twice as profitable (based on earnings per share and stock appreciation) as the Standard & Poor's 500 companies.

- A human resources consultant found that companies with highly people-oriented cultures (e.g., ones in which good benefits and friendly conditions existed) had profit margins averaging 5.3 percent, compared to only 3.3 percent for those organizations that were less people-oriented.

It is one thing to claim that effective management of people is wise, and quite another to demonstrate that it pays off on an organization's bottom line. The conclusion is clear: Good people management is good business—and OB holds the key.

LEARNING ABOUT BEHAVIOR IN ORGANIZATIONS: RESEARCH METHODS

Because, as we have already noted, organizational behavior is a science, it should not be surprising to learn that the field relies heavily upon the scientific method. OB uses the tools of science to achieve its goals—to learn about orga-

Typically, scientists conduct organizational research. However, companies such as the training and development consulting firm, Honeycott and Associates, also have conducted their own studies to answer questions vital to their own operations. GM Europe has hired consultants to conduct research to help them address organizational issues as well.

nizations and the behavior of people working in them. With this in mind, it is essential to understand the tools scientists use to learn about behavior in organizations. In this section we will briefly describe some of these techniques.

SURVEY RESEARCH: THE CORRELATIONAL METHOD

The most popular approach to conducting research in OB involves giving people questionnaires in which they are asked to report how they feel about various aspects of themselves, their jobs, and organizations. Such questionnaires, also known as **surveys,** make it possible for organizational scientists to delve into a broad range of issues. This research technique is so very popular because it is applicable to studying a wide variety of topics. After all, you can learn a great deal about how people feel by asking them a systematic series of carefully worded questions. Moreover, questionnaires are relatively easy to administer (be it by mail, phone, or in person), and—as we will note shortly—they are readily quantifiable and lend themselves to powerful statistical analyses. These features make survey research a very appealing option to OB scientists.

Three major steps are used in survey research. First, the researcher must identify the variables of interest. These may be various aspects of people (e.g., their attitudes toward work), organizations (e.g., the pay plans they use), or the environment in general (e.g., how competitive the industry is). They may be suggested from many different sources, such as a theory, previous research, or even hunches based on casual observations. Second, these variables are measured as precisely as possible. As you might imagine, it isn't always easy to tap precisely people's feelings about things (especially if they are uncertain about those feelings or reluctant to share them). As a result, researchers must pay a great deal of attention to the way they word the questions they use. For some examples of questions designed to measure various work-related attitudes, see Figure 1-2.

Finally, after the variables of interest have been identified and measured, scientists must determine how—if at all—they are related to each other. With this in mind, scientists analyze their survey findings using a variety of different statistical procedures. For example, let's say that a researcher is interested in learning the relationship between how fairly people believe they are paid and various work-related attitudes, such as their willingness to help their coworkers and their interest in quitting. Based on various theories and previous research (which we will describe in Chapters 3 and 4), a researcher may suspect that the more people believe they are unfairly paid, the less likely they will be

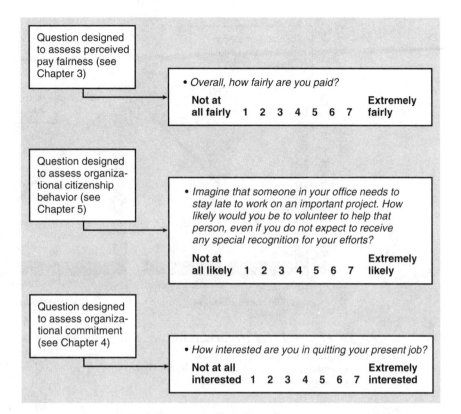

Question designed to assess perceived pay fairness (see Chapter 3)

• *Overall, how fairly are you paid?*

**Not at
all fairly** 1 2 3 4 5 6 7 **Extremely
fairly**

Question designed to assess organizational citizenship behavior (see Chapter 5)

• *Imagine that someone in your office needs to stay late to work on an important project. How likely would you be to volunteer to help that person, even if you do not expect to receive any special recognition for your efforts?*

**Not at
all likely** 1 2 3 4 5 6 7 **Extremely
likely**

Question designed to assess organizational commitment (see Chapter 4)

• *How interested are you in quitting your present job?*

**Not at all
interested** 1 2 3 4 5 6 7 **Extremely
interested**

■ *Figure 1-2 Organizational Survey Questions: Some Examples*
Items such as these may be used to measure attitudes toward various aspects of the work experience.

to help their coworkers and the more likely they will be to desire new jobs. These predictions constitute the researcher's **hypothesis**—the as of yet untested prediction the researcher wishes to investigate. After developing an appropriate questionnaire measuring these variables, the researcher would have to administer it to a large number of people so that the hypothesis can be tested.

Interpreting Surveys Using Correlations.   Once the data are collected, the investigator must statistically analyze them and compare the results to the hypothesis. Suppose a researcher obtains results like those shown in the left side of Figure 1-3. In this case, the more fairly employees believe they are paid, the more willing they are to help their coworkers. In other words, the variables are related to each other such that the more one variable increases, the more

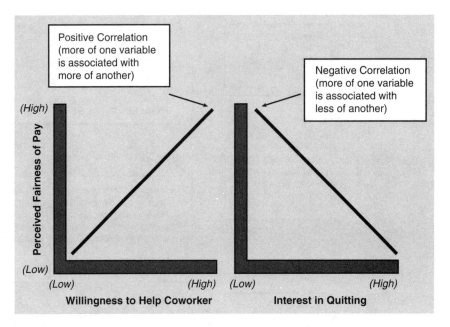

■ *Figure 1-3 Interpreting Positive and Negative Correlations*

Positive correlations (left panel) exist when more of one variable is associated with more of another variable. *Negative correlations* (right panel) exist when more of one variable is associated with less of another variable.

the other variable also increases. Any variables described in this way are said to have a **positive correlation.** Now imagine what will be found when the researcher compares the sample's perceptions of pay fairness with their interest in quitting their jobs. If the experimenter's hypothesis is correct, the results will look like those shown on the right side of Figure 1-3. In other words, the more people believe their pay is fair, the less interested they are in looking for a new job. Any such case—in which the more one variable increases, the more another decreases—is said to have a **negative correlation.**

Although the examples we've been using involve the relationship between only two variables at a time, organizational researchers are frequently interested in the interrelationships between many different variables at once. For example, an employee's intent to quit may be related to several variables besides the perceived fairness of one's pay—such as satisfaction with the job itself or liking for one's immediate supervisor. Researchers may make predictions using several different variables at once (using a sophisticated statistical technique known as *multiple regression*). Using this approach, researchers may be able to tell the extent to which each of several different variables contributes to predicting the behavior in question. In our example, they would be able to learn the degree to which the several variables studied, together and individually, are related to the intent to quit one's job. Given the complex nature of human behavior on the job and the wide range of variables likely to influence it, it should not be surprising to learn that this approach is very popular among OB researchers.

Despite the fact that the analysis of surveys using correlational techniques such as multiple regression can be so very valuable, conclusions drawn from correlations are limited in a very important way. Namely, *correlations do not reveal anything about causation.* In other words, although correlations tell us about how variables are related to each other, they don't provide any insight into their cause-and-effect relationships. So, in our example, although we may learn that the less employees feel they are fairly paid the more interested they are in quitting, we cannot tell why this is the case. In other words, we cannot tell whether or not employees want to quit because they believe they are unfairly paid. Might this be the case? Yes, but it also might be the case that people who believe they are unfairly paid tend to dislike the work they do, and it is this that encourages them to find a new job. Another possibility is that people believe they are unfairly paid because their supervisors are too demanding—and it is this that raises their interest in quitting. Our point is simple: Although all these possibilities are reasonable, knowing only that variables are correlated does not permit us to determine their causes.

EXPERIMENTAL RESEARCH: THE LOGIC OF CAUSE AND EFFECT

Scientists and practitioners alike not only want to know about the relationships between variables, but also whether or not one variable causes another. With this purpose in mind, the **experimental method** is also popular in OB. The more we know about the causal connections between variables, the better we can explain the underlying causes of behavior and seek to change them as desired to help individuals and organizations.

Studying Work Behavior Experimentally: An Example. To illustrate how experiments work, let's consider an example. Suppose we're interested in determining the effects of social density (the number of people per unit of space) on the job performance of clerical employees—that is, the degree to which the crowdedness of working conditions in an office influences how well word processing operators do their jobs. Although this topic might be studied in many different ways, imagine that we do the following. First, we select at random a large group of word processing operators working in a variety of different organizations—the participants in our study. Then we prepare a specially designed office—the setting for the experiment. Throughout the study, we would keep the design of the office and all the working conditions (e.g., temperature, light, and noise levels) alike with one exception—we would systematically vary the number of people working in the office at any given time.

For example, we could have one condition (the "high-density" condition) in which 50 people are put into a 500-square-foot room at once (allowing 10 square feet per person). In another condition (the "low-density" condition) we could put five people into a 500-square-foot room at once (allowing 100 square feet per person). Finally, we can have a "moderate-density" condition in which we put 25 people into a 500-square-foot room (allowing 20 square feet per person). Say we have several hundred people participating in the study and we assign them at random to each of these three conditions. Each word processing operator is given the same passage of text to type over two hours. After this period, the typists are dismissed, and the researcher counts the number of words accurately typed by each typist, noting any possible differences between performance in the various conditions. Suppose that we obtain the results summarized in Figure 1-4.

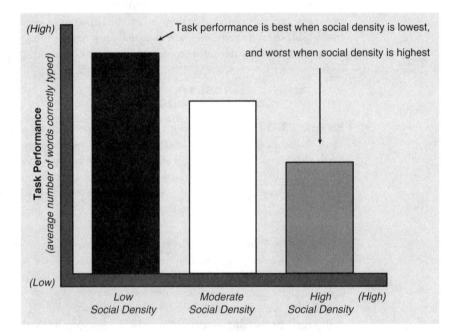

■ *Figure 1-4 Hypothetical Experimental Results*

In our hypothetical example, word processing operators were assigned to rooms that differed with respect to a single variable—social density. The results summarized here show that subjects performed best under conditions of low density and worst under high density.

Rationale Behind the Experimental Method.   To understand the logic of the experimental method, let's analyze what was done in this simple hypothetical experiment. First, recall that we selected participants from the population of interest and assigned them to conditions on a random basis. This means that each of the participants had an equal chance of being assigned to any one of the three conditions. This is critical because it's possible that differences between conditions could result from having many fast operators in one condition and slow ones in another. So, to safeguard against this possibility, it is important to assign people to conditions at random. When this is done, we can assume that the effects of any possible differences between people would equalize over conditions. Thus, by assigning people to conditions at random, we can be assured that there will be just as many fast operators and slow operators in each group. As a result, there is no reason to believe that any differences in productivity that may be noted between conditions can be attributed to systematic differences in the skills of the participants. Given "the luck of the draw," such differences can be discounted, thereby enhancing our confidence that differences are solely the result of the social density of the rooms. This is the logic behind random assignment. Although it is not always feasible to use random assignment when conducting experiments in organizations, it is highly desirable whenever possible.

Now recall that operators were assigned to conditions that differed with respect to only the variable of interest—in this case, social density. We can say that the experimenter manipulated this aspect of the work environment, systematically changing it from condition to condition. A variable altered in this way is called an **independent variable.** An independent variable is that variable which is systematically manipulated by the experimenter so as to determine its effects on the behavior of interest. In our example, the independent variable is social density. Specifically, it may be said to have three different levels—that is, degrees of the independent variable: high, moderate, and low.

The variable that is measured, the one influenced by the independent variable, is known as the **dependent variable.** A dependent variable is the behavior of interest that is being measured—the behavior that is dependent upon the independent variable. In this case, the dependent variable was word processing performance, the quantity of words typed. Besides studying this, we could have studied other dependent variables, such as satisfaction with the work, or the perceived level of stress encountered. In fact, it would be quite likely for OB researchers to study several dependent variables in one experiment. The matter of which particular independent variables and dependent variables are being studied is one of the most important decisions researchers make. Often they base these decisions on suggestions from previous research (other experiments suggesting that certain variables are important) and existing theory (conceptualizations suggesting that certain variables may be important).

The basic logic behind the experimental method is quite simple. In fact, it involves only two major steps. First, some variable of interest (the independent variable) must be systematically varied. Second, the effects, if any, of such variations must be measured. The underlying idea is that if the independent variable does indeed influence behavior, then people exposed to different amounts of it should behave differently. In our example, we can be certain that social density caused differences in processing performance because when all other factors were held constant, different amounts of density led to different levels of performance. Although our experiment is fabricated, it follows the same basic logic of all experiments—namely, it is designed to reveal the effects of the independent variables on the dependent variables.

For the conclusions of experiments to be valid, it is critical for them to hold constant all factors other than the independent variable. Then, if there are differences in the dependent variable, we can assume that they are the result of the effects of the independent variable. By assigning participants to conditions at random we already took an important step to ensure that one key factor—differences in the ability levels of the participants—would be equalized. But there are other possible factors that also may affect the results. For example, it would be essential also to hold constant environmental conditions that might influence word processing speed. In this case, more people would generate more heat, so to make sure that the results are influenced only by density—and not heat—it would be necessary to air condition the work room so as to keep it the same temperature in all conditions at all times. If you think about it, our simple experiment is really not that simple at all—especially if it is conducted with all the care needed to permit valid conclusions to be drawn. Thus, experiments require all experimental conditions to be kept identical with respect to all variables except the independent variable so that its effects can be determined unambiguously—something that is often easier said than done.

Where to Conduct Experiments: Laboratory or Field?   How simple it is to control the effects of extraneous variables (i.e., factors not of interest to the experimenter) depends, in large part, on where the experiment is conducted. In the study of OB, there are generally two options available: Experiments can be conducted in naturalistic organizational settings referred to as the *field*, or in settings specially created for the study itself, referred to as the *laboratory* (or, *lab* for short).

Let's consider the trade-offs involved with conducting research in each setting. The study in our example was a lab experiment. It was conducted in carefully controlled conditions specially created for the research. The great amount of control possible in such settings improves the chances of creating the conditions needed to allow valid conclusions to be drawn from experiments. At the same time, however, lab studies suffer from a lack of realism. Although the working conditions can be carefully controlled, they may be relatively unrealistic, not carefully simulating the conditions found in actual organizations. As a result, it may be difficult to generalize the findings of lab studies to settings outside the lab, such as the workplace.

However, if we conducted our experiment in actual organizations, there would be many unknowns, many uncontrollable factors at work. To conduct such a study we would have to distinguish between those who worked in offices differing with respect to social density and later compare people's performance. If we did this, we would be sure that the conditions studied were realistic. However, there would be so little control over the setting that many different factors could be operating. For example, because people would not be assigned to conditions at random, it might be the case that people work in those settings they most desire. Furthermore, there would be no control over such factors as distractions and differences in environmental conditions (e.g., noise and temperature).

In short, field experiments, although strong in the level of realism they offer, are weak with respect to the level of control they provide. By contrast, lab experiments permit a great deal of control but tend to be unrealistic. In view of these complementary strengths and weaknesses, it should be clear that experiments should be conducted in *both* types of sites. As researchers do so, our confidence can be increased that valid conclusions will be drawn about behavior in organizations.

QUALITATIVE RESEARCH: NATURALISTIC OBSERVATION AND THE CASE METHOD

In contrast to the highly empirical approaches to research we have been describing thus far, OB researchers also rely on less empirical approaches. Probably the most obvious ways of learning about behavior in organizations are to observe it firsthand and to describe it after it occurs. Organizational scientists have a long tradition of studying behavior using these nonempirical, descriptive techniques, relying on what is known as **qualitative research.** The qualitative approach to research relies on preserving the natural qualities of the situation being studied, attempting to capture the richness of the context while disturbing naturalistic conditions only minimally, if at all. The two major qualitative methods used by OB scientists are *naturalistic observation* and the *case method*.

Naturalistic Observation. There's probably no more fundamental way of learning about how people act in organizations than simply to observe them — a research technique known as **naturalistic observation.** Suppose, for example, that you wanted to learn how employees behave in response to layoffs. One thing you could do would be to visit an organization in which layoffs will be occurring and systematically observe what the employees do and say both before and after the layoffs occur. Making comparisons of this type may provide very useful insights into what's going on. As a variation of this technique, you could take a job in the organization, and make your observations as an insider actually working there—giving you a perspective you might not otherwise gain. This technique, often used by anthropologists, is known as **participant observation.**

It's not too difficult to think of the advantages and disadvantages of observational research. Its major advantage is that it can be used without disrupting normal routines, allowing behavior to be studied in its natural state. Moreover, almost anyone—including people already working in the host organization—can be trained to use it. Observational research also suffers from several important limitations. First, the potential for subjectivity among researchers is considerable. Even among the most diligent of researchers, it's inevitable that different people will make different observations of the same

---

Putting Your Common Sense About OB to the Test

Even if you already have a good intuitive sense about behavior in organizations, some of what you think may be inconsistent with established research findings (many of which are noted in this book). So that you don't have to rely on your own judgments (which may be idiosyncratic), working with others in this exercise will give you a good sense of what our collective common sense has to say about behavior in organizations. You just may be enlightened.

DIRECTIONS

Divide the class into groups of about five. Then within these groups discuss the following statements, reaching a consensus as to whether each is true or false. Spend approximately 30 minutes on the entire discussion.

1. People who are satisfied with one job tend to be satisfied with other jobs too.
2. Because "two heads are better than one," groups make better decisions than individuals.
3. The best leaders always act the same, regardless of the situations they face.
4. Specific goals make people nervous; people work better when asked to do their best.
5. People get bored easily, leading them to welcome organizational change.

events. Second, being involved in the daily functioning of an organization will make it difficult for observers to be impartial. Researchers interpreting organizational events may be subject to bias due to their feelings about the people involved. Finally, because most of what goes on in an organization is fairly dull and routine, it's very easy for researchers to place a great deal of emphasis on unusual or unexpected events, possibly leading to inaccurate conclusions. Given these limitations, most OB scientists consider observational research to be more useful as a starting point for providing basic insight into behavior than as a tool for acquiring definitive knowledge about behavior.

The Case Method. Suppose that we conducted our hypothetical study of reactions to layoffs differently. Instead of observing behavior directly, we might fully describe the company's history leading up to the event and some

6. Money is the best motivator.
7. Interpersonal conflict is likely in a highly diverse work force.
8. People generally shy away from challenges on the job.

SCORING
Give your group one point for each item you scored as follows: 1 = true, 2 = false, 3 = false, 4 = false, 5 = false, 6 = false, 7 = false, and 8 = false. (Should you have questions about these answers, information bearing on them appears in this book as follows: 1 = Chapter 4; 2 = Chapter 9; 3 = Chapter 8; 4 = Chapter 3; 5 = Chapter 11; 6 = Chapter 3; 7 = Chapter 4; 8 = Chapter 3.)

QUESTIONS FOR DISCUSSION
1. How well did your group do? Were you stumped on a few?
2. Comparing your experiences to those of other groups, did you find that there were some questions that proved trickier than others (i.e., ones where the scientific findings were more counterintuitive)? If you did poorly, don't be frustrated. These statements are a bit simplistic and need to be qualified to be fully understood. Have your instructor explain the statements that the class found most challenging.
3. Did this exercise give you a better understanding of the sometimes surprising (and complex) nature of behavior in organizations?

statistics summarizing its aftermath (e.g., how long people were unemployed, how the company was restructured after downsizing, and the like). We might even include some interviews with people affected by the event and quote them directly. Such an approach is known as the **case method.** More often than not, the rationale behind the case method is not to teach us about a specific organization per se, but to learn what happened in that organization as a means of providing cues as to what may be going on in other organizations. The case method is similar to naturalistic observation in that it relies on descriptive accounts of events. However, it is different in that it often involves using post hoc accounts of events from those involved as opposed to firsthand observations by scientists.

As you might imagine, a great deal can be learned by detailed accounts of events in organizations summarized in the form of written cases. However, to the extent that the organization studied is unique, it may not be possible to generalize what is learned to others. To get around this limitation, some researchers have recommended that multiple cases should be used to test theories. Another problem with the case method—a limitation it shares with naturalistic observation—is that the potential for bias is relatively high. As a result, many scientists believe that the case method is better used as a valuable source of hypotheses about behavior on the job rather than as a way of testing those hypotheses.

CONCLUSION: DON'T LET COMMON SENSE BE YOUR ONLY GUIDE!

Experiences you may have had in organizations will doubtlessly lead you to know something about the behavior of people on the job. This isn't surprising given that we can all observe a great deal about people's behavior in organizational settings just by paying casual attention. So, whether you're the CEO of a *Fortune* 500 firm or a part-time pizza delivery driver, you probably have a few ideas about how people behave on the job. For example, you may believe that happier employees tend to be more productive. And most people would probably agree, saying, "Yes, of course, it's only logical." However, despite what you may believe, this is generally *not* true. (In fact, as we will see in Chapter 4, research has shown that people who are satisfied with their jobs tend to be no more productive than those who are dissatisfied with their jobs.)

It is important to realize that this contradiction of common sense is not an isolated example. In fact, OB researchers have uncovered many things about human behavior that you might find surprising. (To see how well your own common sense squares with established research findings, see the **Group Exercise** on pp. 26–27.) Moreover, even if some of what researchers find can be predicted in advance, the research is likely to reveal complexities that never could have been expected—let alone, understood—without careful scientific investigation. Our conclusion is clear: When it comes to predicting and understanding behavior in organizations, careful scientific investigation is the best guide.

SUMMARY:
PUTTING IT TO USE

Organizational behavior (OB) is the field that seeks knowledge of behavior in organizational settings by systematically studying individual, group, and organizational processes. The field may be characterized as applying the scientific method to practical managerial problems, focusing on three levels of analysis (individuals, groups, and organizations), interested in improving the quality of people's lives at work, recognizing the dynamic nature of organizations, and acknowledging that there is no one best solution to solving organizational problems.

Traditionally, management practitioners espoused a *Theory X* philosophy, assuming that people are disinterested in working hard and will only do so when goaded into performing. However, contemporary theorists and practitioners adopt a *Theory Y* approach, believing instead that people are interested in working hard and will do so under the right conditions. In addition, modern OB accepts a *contingency approach* to the field, acknowledging that behavior in organizations is the result of complex combinations of both individual characteristics and a wide variety of situational factors.

The earliest approach to OB was Frederick W. Taylor's *scientific management*. This perspective focused on ways of doing work as efficiently as possible. Extending Taylor's ideas, the Gilbreths developed *time-and-motion study*, a technique for finding and standardizing the one most efficient way to perform various jobs.

Rejecting the overly mechanical approach to work espoused by scientific management, Elton Mayo advanced the *human relations movement*. This approach to OB acknowledged that job performance is influenced by the social conditions existing within organizations. Mayo and his associates conducted a series of well-known organizational investigations known as the *Hawthorne studies*. Among other things, this research found that social factors, such as group pressure, affect work performance even more so than physical conditions.

Classical organizational theory, including work by Fayol, suggested that the route to organizational success involved designing organizations in certain highly specific ways (e.g., having clear lines of authority). Similarly, Weber's concept of *bureaucracy* advances a single best way of designing organizations (e.g., having rigid rules and a strict division of labor). By contrast, modern OB recognizes that there may be many effective ways to design the way work is done in organizations. Today's field of OB is interdisciplinary in nature, drawing on many different social science fields, and focusing on a very broad array of topics (including cross-cultural issues, ethics, technology, and others).

Survey research (using questionnaires) is the most popular way of learning about OB phenomena today. Surveys allow us to examine the interrelationships between variables—that is, the extent to which they are *correlated*. However, they do not allow us to draw conclusions about the extent to which one variable causes another.

Understanding cause-and-effect relationships requires the use of *experimental research*. This technique requires that investigators select research participants at random (if at all possible), and subjects them to systematically different conditions. In the ideal experiment, only the variable of interest—the *independent variable*—is manipulated, whereas all others are held constant. OB research may be conducted in both the lab (in which control is great, but realism is poor) and the field (in which control is poor, but realism is great).

In contrast to these empirical approaches, some OB research is *qualitative* in nature. The major qualitative techniques include *systematic observation* in which researchers observe and systematically take notes about human behavior. Also used are *case studies* in which after-the-fact accounts of organizational events are written up in great detail. The highly subjective nature of qualitative research makes it better suited to coming up with ideas for empirical research rather than for testing hypotheses directly.

You Be the Consultant

A large publishing company hires you to help design a new suite of offices in which proofreaders will be working. Your task is to determine the level of illumination that helps the proofreaders work most effectively. Answer the following questions relevant to this situation based on the material in this chapter.

1. What would be the advantages and disadvantages of using survey research for this purpose? How would you go about preparing an appropriate questionnaire?

2. What would be the advantages and disadvantages of using an experiment for this purpose? How would you go about designing and conducting one?

3. What would be the advantages and disadvantages of using some type of qualitative research for this purpose? How would you go about doing so?

4. What would be your overall recommendation about the most appropriate type (or types) of research designed to shed light on the question? Explain your answer.

CHAPTER 2

Basic Psychology in Organizations: Social Perception, Learning, and Personality

PREVIEW OF
CHAPTER HIGHLIGHTS

Social perception is the process of integrating and interpreting information about others so as to accurately understand them. It involves the process of **attribution**—judging what people are like and why they behave as they do.

Kelley's theory of causal attribution explains why people judge the causes of others' behavior to **internal** (under their own influence) or **external** (beyond their control) sources.

Perceptions of others are often biased such that we attribute others' behavior to internal causes (the **fundamental attribution error**). Also we tend to judge people on the basis of the characteristics we associate with the groups to which they belong (**stereotypes**).

Learning is a relatively permanent change in behavior occurring as a result of experience. In organizations, the main forms of learning are **operant conditioning,** based on the systematic administration of rewards and punishments, and **observational learning,** based on imitating others.

Learning is applied in organizations in the form of **training, organizational behavior modification,** and **discipline.**

Personality is the unique and relatively stable pattern of behavior, thoughts, and emotions shown by individuals. The personality characteristics that have been found to be associated with organizational behavior include the **Type A** personality, **self-efficacy, self-esteem, Machiavellianism,** and **achievement motivation.**

To understand why people act as they do on the job—one of the major objectives of the field of OB—it makes sense to begin by examining some of the underlying processes that guide behavior in *any* setting. As such, we must consider several basic aspects of human psychology. Although there are likely to be many psychological processes responsible for behavior in organizations, three in particular—*social perception, learning,* and *personality*—appear to be most central. As we describe these processes in this chapter, relevance to OB will become apparent.

Despite our emphasis on individual determinants of organizational behavior in this chapter, it is important to keep in mind that individuals don't work in a vacuum. Fully understanding organizational behavior requires knowledge about groups and organizations, as well as individuals—and the interrelationships between them. Indeed, we will have more to say about these factors later in this book. For now, however, given the fundamental importance of basic psychological processes to the world of OB, we will focus our attention on them alone. Specifically, we will examine three sets of processes: those by which we come to judge and understand others (i.e., social perception), those by which we acquire new skills and adapt to the world around us (i.e., learning), and those by which we develop our uniqueness as individuals (i.e., personality).

SOCIAL PERCEPTION:
UNDERSTANDING AND JUDGING OTHERS

What do the following organizational situations have in common? (1) You are interviewing a prospective employee for a new position in your company. (2) You apologize profusely after spilling a cup of coffee on your boss. (3) You complete a form asking you to rate the strengths and weaknesses of your subordinates.

If you don't immediately see the connection, it's probably because these situations all involve a phenomenon that is so automatic that you probably have never thought about it before. The answer is that they all involve understanding and evaluating others, figuring out what they are like: You judge the applicant's qualifications, you make sure your boss's opinion of you is not negative, and you assess the extent to which your employees are doing their jobs properly. In all these instances, you are engaging in **social perception**—*the process of integrating and interpreting information about others so as to accurately understand them.* As these examples illustrate, social perception is a very important process in a wide variety of organizational situations.[1] To better understand social perception, we will examine the way the process works.

ATTRIBUTION: JUDGING WHAT PEOPLE ARE LIKE AND WHY THEY DO WHAT THEY DO

A question we often ask about others is "why?" Why did the manager use the wrong data in his report? Why did the CEO develop the policy she did? When we ask such questions, we're attempting to get at two different types of information: (1) What is someone really like, and (2) what made the person behave as he or she did? People attempt to answer these questions in different ways.

Making Correspondent Inferences: Using Acts to Judge Dispositions. Situations frequently arise in organizations in which we want to know what someone is like. Is your new boss likely to be tough or kind-hearted? Are your coworkers prone to be punctual or late? The more you know about what people are like, the better equipped you are to know what to expect and how to deal with them. How, then, do we go about identifying another's traits?

Generally speaking, the answer is that we infer others' traits based on what we are able to observe of their behavior. The judgments we make about what people are like based on what we have seen them do are known as **correspondent inferences.** Simply put, correspondent inferences are *judgments about people's dispositions—their traits and characteristics—that correspond to what we have observed of their actions.*

At first blush, this process seems deceptively simple. A person with a disorganized desk may be thought of as sloppy. Someone who slips on the shop floor may be considered clumsy. Such judgments might be accurate, but not necessarily! After all, the messy desk actually may be the result of a coworker rummaging through it to find some important documents. Similarly, the person who slipped could have encountered oily conditions under which anyone, even the least clumsy individual, would have fallen. In other words, it is important to recognize that the judgments we may make about someone may be inaccurate because there are many possible causes of behavior. For this reason, correspondent inferences may not always be accurate.

Another reason why this is so has to do with the tendency for people to conceal some of their traits—especially when they may be viewed as negative. So, for example, a sloppy individual may work hard in public to appear to be organized. Likewise, the unprincipled person may talk a good show about the importance of being ethical. In other words, people often do their best to disguise some of their basic traits. Not surprisingly, this makes the business of forming correspondent inferences risky at best.

Causal Attribution of Responsibility: Answering the Question "Why?" Imagine finding out that your boss just fired one of your fellow employees. Naturally, you'd ask yourself, "Why did he do that?" Was it because your coworker violated the company's code of conduct? Or was it because the boss is a cruel and heartless person? These two answers to the question "why?" represent two major classes of explanations for the causes of someone's behavior: *internal* causes, explanations based on actions for which the individual is responsible, and *external* causes, explanations based on situations over which the individual has no control. In this case, the internal cause would be the person's violation of the rules, and the external cause would be the boss's cruel and arbitrary behavior.

Generally speaking, it is very important to be able to determine whether an internal or an external cause is responsible for someone's behavior. Knowing why something happened to someone else might better help you prepare for what might happen to you. For example, in this case, if you believe that your colleague was fired because of something for which she was responsible herself, such as violating a company rule, then you might not feel as vulnerable as you would if you thought she was fired because of the arbitrary, spiteful nature of your boss. In the latter case, you might decide to take some precautionary actions, to do something to protect yourself from your boss, such as staying on your boss's good side, or even giving up and finding a new job—before you are forced to. The key question of interest to social scientists is: How do people go about judging whether someone's actions were caused by internal or external causes?

An answer to this question is provided by **Kelley's theory of causal attribution.** According to this conceptualization, we base our judgments of internal and external causality on three types of information.[2] These are as follows:

- *Consensus*—the extent to which other people behave in the same manner as the person we're judging. If others do behave similarly, consensus is considered high; if they do not, consensus is considered low.

- *Consistency*—the extent to which the person we're judging acts the same way at other times. If the person does act the same at other times, consistency is high; if he or she does not, then consistency is low.

- *Distinctiveness*—the extent to which this person behaves in the same manner in other contexts. If he or she behaves the same way in other situations, distinctiveness is low; if he or she behaves differently, distinctiveness is high.

According to the theory, after learning about these three factors, we combine this information to make our attributions of causality. Here's how. If we learn that other people act like this one (consensus is high), this person behaves in the same manner at other times (consistency is high), and that this person does not act in the same manner in other situations (distinctiveness is high), we are likely to conclude that this person's behavior stemmed from *external* causes. In contrast, imagine learning that other people do not act like this one (consensus is low), this person behaves in the same manner at other times (consistency is high), and that this person acts in the same manner in other situations (distinctiveness is low). In this case, we will probably conclude that this person's behavior stemmed from *internal* causes.

Because this explanation is highly abstract, let's consider an example that helps illustrate how the process works. Imagine that you're at a business lunch with several of your company's sales representatives when the sales manager makes some critical remarks about the restaurant's food and service. Further imagine that no one else in your party acts this way (consensus is low), you have heard her say the same things during other visits to the restaurant (consistency is high), and you have seen her acting critically in other settings, such as the regional sales meeting (distinctiveness is low). What would you conclude in this situation? Probably that her behavior stems from internal causes. In other words, she is a "picky" person, someone who is difficult to please.

Now imagine the same setting but with different observations. Suppose that several other members of your group also complain about the restaurant (consensus is high), that you have seen this person complain in the same restaurant at other times (consistency is high), but that you have never seen her complain about anything else before (distinctiveness is high). By contrast, in this case, you probably would conclude that the sales manager's behavior stems from external causes: The restaurant really *is* inferior. For a summary of these contrasting conclusions and an example, see Figure 2-1 on p. 36.

THE BIASED NATURE OF SOCIAL PERCEPTION

As you might imagine, people are far from perfect when it comes to making judgments of others. In fact, researchers have noted that there are several important types of biases that interfere with making completely accurate judgments of others.

The Fundamental Attribution Error. Despite what Kelley's theory says, people are *not* equally predisposed to reach judgments regarding internal and external causality. Rather, they are more likely to explain others' actions in terms of internal rather than external causes. In other words, we are prone to assume that others' behavior is due to the way they are, their traits and dispositions (e.g., "she's that kind of person"). So, for example, we are more likely to assume that someone who shows up for work late does so because she is lazy rather than because she got caught in traffic. This tendency is so strong that it has been referred to as the **fundamental attribution error.**

This phenomenon stems from the fact that it is far easier to explain someone's actions in terms of his or her traits than to recognize the complex

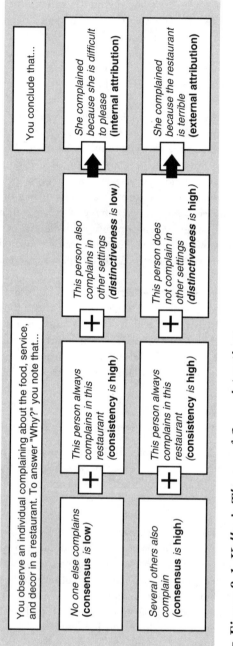

■ Figure 2-1 Kelley's Theory of Causal Attribution

In determining whether others' behavior stems mainly from internal or external causes, we focus on the three types of information illustrated here.

pattern of situational factors that may have affected their actions. As you might imagine, this tendency can be quite damaging in organizations. Specifically, it leads us to prematurely assume that people are responsible for the negative things that happen to them (e.g., "he wrecked the company car because he is careless"), without considering external alternatives, ones that may be less damning (e.g., "another driver hit the car"). And this can lead to inaccurate judgments about people.

Stereotypes: Fitting People into Categories. Inaccurate judgments about people can also stem from the preconceived ideas we hold about certain groups. Here we are referring to **stereotypes**—beliefs that all members of specific groups share similar traits and behaviors. Expressions of stereotypes usually take the form: "People from group X possess characteristic Y." For example, what comes to mind when you think about people who wear glasses? Are they studious? Eggheads? Although there is no evidence of such a connection, it is interesting that for many people, such an image lingers in their minds.

Deep down inside many of us know, and can articulate, that not all people from a specific group possess the characteristics—either negative or positive—we associate with them. In other words, most of us accept that the stereotypes we use are at least partially inaccurate. After all, not *all X*'s are *Y*; there are exceptions (maybe even quite a few!). If so, then why are stereotypes so prevalent? Why do we use them?

To a great extent, the answer lies in the fact that people tend to do as little cognitive work as possible when it comes to thinking about others. That is, we tend to rely on mental shortcuts. If assigning people to groups allows us to assume that we know what they are like and how they may act, then we can save the tedious work of having to learn about them as individuals. After all, we come into contact with so many people that it's impractical—if not impossible—to learn everything about them we need to know. So we rely on readily available information—such as someone's age, race, gender, or job type—as the basis for organizing our perceptions in a coherent way. If you believe that members of group X tend to have trait Y, then simply observing that someone falls into category X becomes the basis for your believing something about that individual (in this case, that he or she possesses Y). To the extent that the stereotype applies in this case, then the perception will be accurate. But in that case we are just lucky. More likely than not, such mental shorthand will lead us to judgments about people that are inaccurate—the price we pay for using stereotypes. (We will discuss the implications of this more fully in Chapter 4.)

It is easy to imagine how the use of stereotypes can have powerful effects on the kinds of judgments people make in organizations. For example, if a personnel officer believes that members of certain groups are lazy, then he or she purposely may avoid hiring anyone belonging to those groups. The personnel officer may firmly believe that he or she is using good judgment—gathering all

Identifying Occupational Stereotypes

Although we usually reserve our concern over stereotypes to women and members of racial and ethnic minorities, the simple truth is that people can hold stereotypes toward members of just about *any* group. And in organizations people are likely to hold stereotypes about people based on a variable whose importance cannot be downplayed—the occupational groups to which they belong. What we expect of people and the way we treat them are likely to be affected by stereotypes about their professions. This exercise will help you better understand this phenomenon.

DIRECTIONS

Divide the class into groups of approximately five to eight students, and gather each group in a circle. Then, working together, rate each of the following occupational groups with respect to how much of the characteristics listed they tend to show. Use this scale:

1 = not at all   4 = a great amount
2 = a slight amount   5 = an extreme amount
3 = a moderate amount

Accountants   *Professors*   *Lawyers*
_____ interesting   _____ interesting   _____ interesting
_____ generous   _____ generous   _____ generous

the necessary information and listening to the candidate carefully. Still, without being aware of it, the stereotypes the personnel officer holds may influence the way he or she judges people. The result, of course, is that the fate of the individual in question is sealed in advance—not necessarily because of anything he or she may have done or said, but by the mere fact that he or she belongs to a certain group. In other words, even people who are not being intentionally bigoted still may be influenced by the stereotypes they hold. The effects of stereotypes may be quite subtle and unintentional. (To give you a feel for some of the stereotypes people hold toward members of certain occupational groups, complete the above **Group Exercise**.)

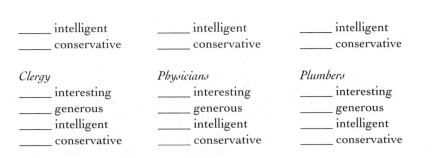

_____ intelligent	_____ intelligent	_____ intelligent
_____ conservative	_____ conservative	_____ conservative

Clergy   *Physicians*   *Plumbers*

_____ interesting	_____ interesting	_____ interesting
_____ generous	_____ generous	_____ generous
_____ intelligent	_____ intelligent	_____ intelligent
_____ conservative	_____ conservative	_____ conservative

QUESTIONS FOR DISCUSSION

1. How easy was it for your group to form a consensus? Did members of your group generally agree or disagree on the ratings?

2. What professions were generally easiest to rate? Which were most difficult?

3. Did the various groups agree or disagree with each other? In other words, how strongly held were the stereotypes overall?

4. To what extent were your group's responses based on specific people that group members knew? How did knowledge, or lack of knowledge, of members of the various occupational groups influence your group's ratings?

5. To what extent do you believe that exposing these stereotypes will (a) perpetuate them, or (b) help you refrain from behaving in accord with them?

OVERCOMING BIAS IN SOCIAL PERCEPTION: SOME GUIDELINES

For the most part, people's biased perceptions of others are not the result of any malicious intent to inflict harm. Instead, biases in social perception tend to occur because we, as perceivers, are imperfect processors of information. We assume that people are internally responsible for their behavior because we cannot be aware of all the possible situational factors that may be involved—hence, we make the fundamental attribution error. Further, it is highly impractical to be able to learn everything about someone that may guide our reactions—hence, we use stereotypes. This does not mean, however, that we cannot minimize the impact of these biases. Indeed, there are several steps that can be taken to help promote the accurate perception of others in the workplace.

- *Do not overlook external causes of others' behavior.* The fundamental attribution error leads us to discount the possibility that people's poor performance may be due to conditions beyond their control. As a result, we may ignore legitimate explanations for poor performance. Ask yourself if anyone else may have performed just as poorly under the same conditions. If the answer is yes, then you should not automatically assume that the poor performer is to blame. Good managers need to make such judgments accurately so that they can decide whether to focus their efforts on developing employees or changing work conditions.

- *Identify and confront your stereotypes.* Let's face it, we all rely on stereotypes—especially when it comes to dealing with new people. Although this is natural, erroneous perceptions are bound to result—and quite possibly, at the expense of someone else. For this reason, it's good to identify the stereotypes you hold. Doing so will help you become more aware of them, taking a giant step toward minimizing their impact on your behavior. After all, unless you are aware of your stereotypes, you may never be able to counter them. (You will find the **Group Exercise** on pp. 38–39 useful in this regard.)

- *Evaluate people based on objective factors.* The more objective the information you use to judge others, the less your judgments will be subjected to perceptual distortion. People tend to bias subjective judgments in ways that are self-serving (such as positively evaluating the work of those we like and negatively evaluating the work of those we dislike). To the extent that evaluations are based on objective information, this is less likely to occur.

*Employees at **DEC's** Customer Support Center regularly appraise each other's performance. Because they work together closely, they are motivated to avoid bias and give highly accurate evaluations of each other's work.*

- *Avoid making rash judgments.* It is human nature to jump to conclusions about what people are like, even when we know very little about them. Take the time to get to know people better before convincing yourself that you already know all you need to know about them. What you learn just may make a big difference in your opinion.

We realize that many of these tactics are far easier to say than to do. However, to the extent that we conscientiously try to apply these suggestions to our everyday interaction with others in the workplace, we stand a good chance of perceiving people more accurately. And this is a fundamental ingredient in the recipe for managerial success.

LEARNING: ADAPTING TO THE WORLD OF WORK

Question: What process is so broad and fundamental to human behavior that it may be said to occur in organizations—and throughout life, in general—continuously? The answer: *learning.* This process is so basic to our lives that you probably have a good sense of what learning is—but you may find it difficult to define. So, to make sure that we clarify exactly what it is, we formally define learning as *a relatively permanent change in behavior occurring as a result of experience.*

Several aspects of this definition bear pointing out. First, it's clear that learning requires that some kind of change occurs. Second, this change must be more than just temporary. Finally, it must be the result of experience—that is, continued contact with the world around us. Given this definition, we cannot say that short-lived performance changes on the job, such as those due to illness or fatigue, are the result of learning. Learning is a difficult concept for scientists to study because it cannot be directly observed. Instead, it must be inferred on the basis of relatively permanent changes in behavior. We will now consider two of the most prevalent forms of learning that occur in organizations—*operant conditioning* and *observational learning.*

OPERANT CONDITIONING: LEARNING THROUGH REWARDS AND PUNISHMENTS

Imagine you are a chef working at a catering company where you are planning a special menu for a fussy client. If your dinner menu is accepted and the meal is a hit, the company stands a good chance of adding a huge new account. You work hard at doing the best job possible and present your culinary creation to the skeptical client. Now, how does the story end? If the client loves your meal, your grateful boss gives you a huge raise and a promotion. However, if the client hates it, your boss asks you to turn in your chef's hat. Regardless of which of these outcomes occur, one thing is certain: Whatever you did in this situation, you will be sure to do it again *if* it was successful, or to avoid doing it again *if* it failed.

This situation nicely illustrates an important principle of **operant conditioning** (also known as **instrumental conditioning**)—namely, that our behavior produces consequences and that how we behave in the future will depend on what those consequences are. If our actions have pleasant effects, then we will be more likely to repeat them in the future. If, however, our actions have unpleasant effects, we are less likely to repeat them in the future. This phenomenon, known as the **law of effect,** is fundamental to operant conditioning.

Our knowledge of this phenomenon comes from the work of the famous social scientist B. F. Skinner.[3] Skinner's pioneering research has shown us that it is through the connections between our actions and their consequences that we learn to behave in certain ways. We summarize this process in Figure 2-2.

A great deal of behavior is learned because of the pleasurable outcomes that we associate with it. In organizations, for example, people usually find it pleasant and desirable to receive monetary bonuses, paid vacations, and various forms of recognition. The process by which people learn to perform acts leading to such desirable outcomes is known as **positive reinforcement.** Whatever behaviors led to the positive outcomes are likely to occur again, thereby strengthening that behavior. For a reward to serve as a positive reinforcer, it must be made contingent on the specific behavior sought. So, for example, if a sales representative is given a bonus after landing a huge account, the bonus will only reinforce the person's actions *if* he or she associates it with the landing of the account. When this occurs, the individual will be more inclined in the future to do whatever it was that helped get the account.

Sometimes we also learn to perform acts because they permit us to avoid undesirable consequences. Unpleasant events, such as reprimands, rejection, probation, and termination, are some of the consequences faced for certain negative actions in the workplace. The process by which people learn to perform acts leading to the avoidance of such undesirable consequences is known

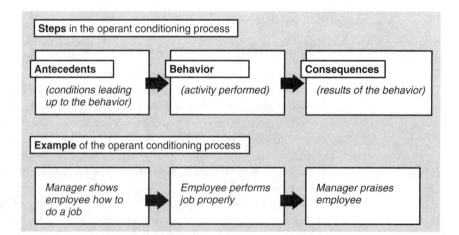

■ *Figure 2-2 The Operant Conditioning Process*

The basic premise of *operant conditioning* is that people learn by associating the consequences of their behavior with the behavior itself. In this example, the manager's praise increases the subordinate's tendency to perform the job properly in the future.

as **negative reinforcement,** or **avoidance.** Whatever response led to the termination of these undesirable events is likely to occur again, thereby strengthening that response. For example, you may stay late at the office one evening to revise a sales presentation because you believe that the boss will "chew you out" if it's not ready in the morning. You learned how to avoid this type of aversive situation and behaved accordingly.

Thus far, we have identified responses that are strengthened—either because they lead to positive consequences, or the termination of negative consequences. However, the connection between a behavior and its consequences is not always strengthened; such links also may be weakened. This is what happens in the case of **punishment.** Punishment involves presenting an undesirable or aversive consequence in response to an unwanted behavior. A behavior accompanied by an undesirable outcome is less likely to recur if the person associates the negative consequences with the behavior. For example, if you are chastised by your boss for taking excessively long coffee breaks, you are considered punished for this action. As a result, you will be less likely to take long breaks again in the future.

The link between a behavior and its consequences also may be weakened by withholding reward—a process known as **extinction.** When a response that was once rewarded is no longer rewarded, it tends to weaken and eventually die out—or be *extinguished.* Let's consider an example. Suppose for many months you brought boxes of donuts to your weekly staff meetings. Your colleagues always thanked you as they gobbled them down. You were positively reinforced by their approval, so you continued bringing the donuts. Now, after several months of eating donuts, your colleagues have found it necessary to begin dieting. So, although tempting, your donuts go uneaten. After several months of no longer being praised for your generosity, you will be unlikely to continue bringing donuts. Your once-rewarded behavior will die out; it will be extinguished.

The various relationships between a person's behavior and the consequences resulting from it—*positive reinforcement, negative reinforcement, punishment,* and *extinction*—are known collectively as **contingencies of reinforcement.** They represent the conditions under which rewards and punishments will either be given or taken away. The four contingencies we discussed are summarized in Table 2-1 on p. 44. As we will see later in this chapter, administering these contingencies can be an effective tool for managing behavior in organizations.

OBSERVATIONAL LEARNING: LEARNING BY IMITATING OTHERS

Although operant conditioning is based on the idea that we engage in behaviors for which we are directly reinforced, many of the things we learn on the job are *not* directly reinforced. Suppose, for example, on your new job you see many of your coworkers complimenting your boss on his attire. Each time

■ Table 2-1 Contingencies of Reinforcement

The four reinforcement contingencies may be defined in terms of the presentation or withdrawal of a pleasant or unpleasant stimulus. Positively or negatively reinforced behaviors are strengthened; punished or extinguished behaviors are weakened.

Stimulus Presented or Withdrawn	Desirability of Stimulus	Name of Contingency	Strength of Response	Example
Presented	Pleasant	Positive reinforcement	Increases	Praise from a supervisor encourages continuing the praised behavior
	Unpleasant	Punishment	Decreases	Criticism from a supervisor discourages enacting the punished behavior
Withdrawn	Pleasant	Extinction	Decreases	Failing to praise a helpful act reduces the odds of helping in the future
	Unpleasant	Negative reinforcement	Increases	Future criticism is avoided by doing whatever the supervisor wants

someone says something flattering, the boss stops at his or her desk, smiles, and acts friendly. By complimenting the boss, they are reinforced by being granted his social approval. Chances are, after observing this several times, you too will eventually learn to say something nice to the boss. Although you may not have directly experienced the boss's approval, you would expect to receive it based on what you have observed from others. This is an example of a kind of learning known as **observational learning,** or **modeling.** It occurs when someone acquires new knowledge *vicariously*—that is, by observing what happens to others.

A great deal of what is learned about how to behave in organizations can be explained as the result of the process of observational learning. On the job, observational learning is a key part of many formal job instruction training programs. As we will explain in the next section, trainees given a chance to observe experts doing their jobs, followed by an opportunity to practice the desired skills, and given feedback on their work, tend to learn new job skills quite effectively. Observational learning also occurs in a very informal, uncalculated manner. For example, people who experience the norms and traditions of their organizations and who subsequently incorporate these into their own behavior may be recognized as having learned through observation.

Finally, it is important to note that people learn not only what to do by observing others, but also what *not* to do. Specifically, research has shown that people observing their coworkers getting punished for behaving inappropriately on the job tend to refrain from engaging in those same actions themselves. As you might imagine, this is a very effective way for people to learn how to behave—and without ever experiencing any displeasure themselves.

APPLICATIONS OF LEARNING IN ORGANIZATIONS

The principles of learning we have discussed thus far are used in organizations in many different ways. We will now discuss three systematic approaches to incorporating learning in organizations: *training, organizational behavior management,* and *discipline.*

> *Top executives at **Bacardi**, a leading manufacturer of rum, receive classroom training focusing on ways of improving the company's competitiveness in a global market.*

Training: Learning and Developing Job Skills.   Probably the most obvious use to which principles of learning may be applied in organizations is **training**—that is, the process through which people systematically acquire and improve the skills and knowledge needed to better their job performance. Just as students learn basic educational skills in the classroom, employees must learn job skills. Training is used not only to prepare new employees to meet the challenges of the jobs they will face, but also to upgrade and refine the skills of existing employees. In fact, according to the American Society for Training and Development, American companies spend over $44 billion on training annually.

In view of this staggering investment, it is important to consider ways of enhancing the effectiveness of employee training. Four major principles may be identified.

1.   **PARTICIPATION.** People not only learn more quickly but also retain the skills longer when they have actively participated in the learning process. This applies to the learning of both motor tasks as well as cognitive skills. For example, when learning to swim, there's no substitute for actually getting in the water and moving your arms and legs. In the classroom, students who listen attentively to lectures, think about the material, and get involved in discussions tend to learn more effectively than those who just sit passively.

2.   **REPETITION.** If you know the old adage "Practice makes perfect," you are already aware of the benefits of repetition on learning. Perhaps you learned the multiplication table, or a poem, or a foreign language phrase by going over it repeatedly. Scientists have not only established the benefits of repetition on learning but have shown that these effects are even greater when practice is spread out over time than when it is lumped together. After all, when practice periods are too long, learning can suffer from fatigue, whereas learning a little bit at a time allows the material to sink in.

Employee Training: Learning From the Best

Despite the obvious importance of training human resources to meet the ever-growing technical demands of today's workplace, job training remains the exception rather than the rule in most organizations. In fact, only five companies out of 1,000 (a mere 15,000) account for 90 percent of all the training done in the United States. Among these are several companies, both large and small, that devote considerable resources to training their employees and that benefit greatly as a result.

At the top of the list is Motorola, a company that spent $120 million on employee education in 1992 alone (a year in which its sales reached a record $13.3 billion). That same year, the company's training arm, known as "Motorola University," delivered 102,000 training days to its employees, customers, and suppliers at its branches in Phoenix, Arizona, and Austin, Texas. According to the university's president, William Wiggenhorn, "When you buy a piece of equipment, you set aside a percentage for maintenance. Shouldn't you do the same for people?"[4] Indeed, the company does just that. Motorola uses engineers, scientists, and former managers to teach most of its courses. These range from coverage of people-related skills (e.g., communication and teamwork) to technical skills (e.g., advanced statistical techniques). Company officials credit Motorola's training investment for much of its recent success. Specifically, it has been calculated that each dollar Motorola spends on training brings $30 in increased productivity over three years. In the words of materials manager Karney Yakmalian, "Other companies talk about quality, but Motorola gives you the tools."[5]

A very different but equally effective approach is taken by Corning at its Erwin, New York ceramics plant. Here, employees are trained in the class-

3.   **TRANSFER OF TRAINING.** As you might imagine, for training to be most effective, what is learned during training must be applied to the job. In general, the more closely a training program matches the demands of a job, the more effective that training will be. A good example is the elaborate simulation devices used to train pilots and astronauts. More down to earth is the equipment used in many technical schools for people to learn skilled trades such as welding, computer repair, and radiation technology.

4.   **FEEDBACK.** It is extremely difficult for learning to occur in the absence of feedback—that is, knowledge of the results of one's actions. Feedback

room and on the job in formal apprentice programs in which they become certified as specialists in working with Celcor, a clay-based product used in cat-
alytic converters. To reach that stage takes about two years of training (with
the equivalent of one day per week in the classroom) and demonstrated com-
petency on a series of tests. Upon being certified, employees receive increases
of 20 percent in their hourly pay. Training director Everett Larson explains
that "There's a heavy up-front cost in training, but the payback is quite impressive." That benefit has come to Corning in the form of increased productivity
and reduced waste as well as a 38 percent drop in product defects in 1992
alone.

It would be misleading to leave you with the impression that training occurs only within large companies. Consider, for example, Chicago's Wm.
Dudek Manufacturing Co., a family-owned business of 35 employees that
makes small clips and clasps used in manufacturing appliances and automobiles. Although Dudek employees knew how to operate their machines, most
of them are immigrants who lack skills in basic English and math. Working
with instructors at a local college, Dudek began training its work force to develop these skills so they could learn what they needed to know to meet specifications and fill out order forms.

Training, whether in basic skills or more advanced knowledge, is critical
to the success of organizations—especially in these competitive times when resources are tight. In the words of W. J. Conaty, an official at General Electric's Aircraft Engine division, "When an industry is in turmoil, productivity
and people become the name of the game. That's where we get our edge."[6]
Clearly, training is the steel that hones this edge.

provides information about the effectiveness of one's training. Of course, unless you learn what you already are doing well and what behaviors you need to
correct, you will probably be unable to improve your skills. For example, it is
critical for people being trained as word processing operators to know exactly
how many words they correctly entered per minute if they are to be able to
gauge their improvement.

In sum, these four principles—*participation, repetition, transfer of training,*
and *feedback*—are key to the effectiveness of any training program. The most

effective training programs are those that incorporate as many of these principles as possible. (Given the importance of training in today's competitive business environment, several companies are going beyond most others in the training they do. For a closer look at some particularly impressive examples, see the **Winning Practices** section on pp. 46–47.)

ORGANIZATIONAL BEHAVIOR MANAGEMENT: POSITIVELY REINFORCING DESIRABLE ORGANIZATIONAL BEHAVIORS

Earlier, in describing operant conditioning, we noted that the consequences of our behavior determine whether we repeat it or abandon it. Behaviors that are rewarded tend to be strengthened and repeated in the future. With this in mind, it is possible to administer rewards selectively to help reinforce behaviors that we wish repeated in the future. This is the basic principle behind **organizational behavior management** (also known as **organizational behavior modification,** or more simply, **OB Mod**). Organizational behavior management may be defined as *the systematic application of positive reinforcement principles in organizational settings for the purpose of raising the incidence of desirable organizational behaviors.*

Organizational behavior management programs have been used successfully to stimulate a variety of behaviors in many different organizations (see summary in Table 2-2).[7] For example, a particularly interesting and effective

■ *Table 2-2 Organizational Behavior Management Programs: Some Success Stories*

Although not all organizational behavior management programs are as successful as the ones summarized here, many have been extremely effective in bringing about improvements in desired behaviors. (Based on material appearing in Frederiksen, 1982; see Note 7.)

Company	*Reinforcers Used*	*Results*
General Electric	Praise and constructive reinforcement	Productivity increased, cost savings resulted.
Weyerhaeuser	Contingent pay, and praise or recognition	Productivity increased in most work groups (by 18–33 percent).
B. F. Goodrich Chemical	Praise and recognition	Production increased more than 300 percent.
Connecticut General Life Insurance	Time off based on performance	Chronic absenteeism and lateness were drastically reduced.
General Mills	Praise and feedback for meeting objectives	Sales increased.

program has been used in recent years at Diamond International, the Palmer, Massachusetts company of 325 employees that manufactures Styrofoam egg cartons. In response to sluggish productivity, a simple but elegant reinforcement was put into place. Any employee working for a full year without an industrial accident is given 20 points. Perfect attendance is given 25 points. Once a year, the points are totaled. When employees reach 100 points, they get a blue nylon jacket with the company's logo on it and a patch identifying their membership in the "100 Club." Those earning still more points receive extra awards. For example, at 500 points, employees can select any of a number of small household appliances. These inexpensive prizes go a long way toward symbolizing to employees the company's appreciation for their good work.

This program has helped improve productivity dramatically at Diamond International. Compared to before the OB Mod program began, output improved 16.5 percent, quality-related errors dropped 40 percent, grievances decreased 72 percent, and time lost due to accidents was lowered by 43.7 percent. The result of all of this has been over $1 million in gross financial benefits from the company—and a much happier work force. Needless to say, this has been a very simple and effective organizational behavior management program. Although not all such programs are equally successful, evidence suggests that they are generally quite beneficial.

DISCIPLINE: ELIMINATING UNDESIRABLE ORGANIZATIONAL BEHAVIORS

Just as organizations systematically may use rewards to encourage desirable behavior, they also may use punishment to discourage undesirable behavior. Problems such as absenteeism, lateness, theft, and substance abuse cost companies vast sums of money, situations many companies attempt to manage by using **discipline**—the systematic administration of punishment.

By administering an unpleasant outcome (e.g., suspension without pay) in response to an undesirable behavior (e.g., excessive tardiness), companies seek to minimize the undesirable behavior. In one form or another, using discipline is a relatively common practice. Survey research has shown, in fact, that 83 percent of companies use some form of discipline, or at least the threat of discipline, in response to undesirable behaviors. But, as you might imagine, disciplinary actions taken in organizations vary greatly. At one extreme, they may be very formal, such as written warnings that become part of the employee's permanent record. At the other extreme, they may be informal and low-key, such as friendly reminders and off-the-record discussions between supervisors and their problem subordinates.

The trick to disciplining effectively is to know how to administer punishment in a way that is considered fair and reasonable. Fortunately, research and theory have pointed to principles that may be followed to maximize the effectiveness of discipline in organizations. We will now consider several of these.

1. **DELIVER PUNISHMENT IMMEDIATELY AFTER THE UNDESIRABLE RESPONSE OCCURS.** The less time that passes between the occurrence of an undesirable behavior and the administration of a negative consequence, the more strongly people will make the connection between them. When people make this association, the consequence is likely to serve as a punishment, thereby reducing the probability of the unwanted behavior. Thus, it is best for managers to talk to their subordinates about their undesirable behaviors immediately after subordinates commit them. Expressing disapproval after several days or weeks have gone by will be less effective, because the passage of time will weaken the association between behavior and its consequences.

2. **GIVE MODERATE LEVELS OF PUNISHMENT—NOTHING TOO HIGH OR TOO LOW.** If the consequences for performing an undesirable action are not very severe (e.g., rolling one's eyes as a show of disapproval), then it is unlikely to serve as a punishment. After all, it is quite easy to live with such a mild response. In contrast, consequences that are overly severe might be perceived as unfair and inhumane. When this occurs, not only might the individual resign, but also a strong signal will be sent to others about the unreasonableness of the company's actions.

3. **PUNISH THE UNDESIRABLE BEHAVIOR, NOT THE PERSON.** Effective punishment is impersonal in nature and focuses on the individual's actions rather than his or her personality. So, for example, when addressing an employee who is repeatedly caught taking excessively long breaks it is unwise to say, "You're lazy and have a bad attitude." Instead, it would be better to say, "By not being at your desk when expected, you're making it more difficult for all of us to get our work done on time." Responding in this manner will be less humiliating for the individual. Additionally, focusing on exactly what people can do to avoid such disapproval (taking shorter breaks, in this case) increases the likelihood that they will attempt to alter their behavior in the desired fashion. By contrast, the person who feels personally attacked might not only "tune out" the message, but also not know exactly how to improve.

4. **USE PUNISHMENT CONSISTENTLY—ALL THE TIME, FOR ALL EMPLOYEES.** Sometimes managers attempting to be lenient turn a blind eye to infractions of company rules. Doing this may cause more harm than good insofar as it inadvertently reinforces the undesirable behavior (by demonstrating that one can get away with breaking the rules). As a result, it is considered most effective to administer punishment after each occurrence of an undesirable behavior. Similarly, it is important to show consistency in the treatment of all employees. In other words, everyone who commits the same infraction should be punished the same way, regardless of the person administering the

punishment. When this occurs, supervisors are unlikely to be accused of showing favoritism.

5. **CLEARLY COMMUNICATE THE REASONS FOR THE PUNISHMENT GIVEN.** Making clear exactly what behaviors lead to what disciplinary actions greatly facilitates the effectiveness of punishment. Clearly communicated expectations help strengthen the perceived connection between behavior and its consequences. Wise managers use their opportunities to communicate with subordinates to make clear that the punishment being given does not constitute revenge, but an attempt to eliminate an unwanted behavior (which, of course, it is).

If, after reading all this, you are thinking that it is truly difficult to properly administer rewards and punishments in organizations, you have reached the same conclusion as experts in the field of organizational behavior. Indeed, one of the key skills that makes some managers so effective is their ability to influence others by properly administering rewards and punishments.

PERSONALITY: WHAT MAKES US UNIQUE

If our experience with other people tells us anything, it is that they are all in some way *unique*, and at least to a degree, they are all *consistent*. That is, we each possess a distinct pattern of traits and characteristics not found in anyone else, and these are generally stable over time. Thus, if you know someone who is courteous and outgoing today, he or she probably showed these traits in the past and will likely continue to show them in the future. Moreover, this person will tend to show them in different situations over time.

Together, these two facts form the basis for our definition of **personality**—*the unique and relatively stable pattern of behavior, thoughts, and emotions shown by individuals.* In short, personality refers to the lasting ways in which any one person is different from all others. And, as you might imagine, personality characteristics can be very important when it comes to organizational behavior.[8] With this in mind, we will review five key personality dimensions that are most relevant to OB.

THE TYPE A BEHAVIOR PATTERN: THE FRENZIED PERSONALITY

Think about the people you know. Can you identify someone who always seems to be in a hurry, is extremely competitive, and is often irritable? Now try to name one who shows the opposite pattern—someone who is relaxed, not very competitive, and easygoing. The people you have in mind represent extremes on one key dimension of personality. The first individual would be labeled **Type A,** and the second, **Type B.** People categorized as Type A show high levels of competitiveness, irritability, and time urgency (they are always in a hurry). In addition, they demonstrate certain stylistic patterns, such as using loud and exaggerated speech, and a tendency to respond very quickly (e.g., speaking before others are through). People classified as Type B show the opposite pattern; they are much calmer and laid-back.

Do people who are Type A or Type B differ with respect to job performance? Given their high level of competitiveness, it seems reasonable to expect that Type A's would work harder at various tasks than Type B's and, as a result, perform at higher levels. In fact, however, the situation turns out to be more complex. On the one hand, Type A's *do* tend to work faster on many tasks than Type B's, even when no pressure or deadline is involved. Similarly, they are able to get more done in the presence of distractions. In addition, Type A's often seek more challenges in their work than do Type B's.

Despite these differences, Type A's do not *always* perform better than Type B's. For example, Type A's frequently do poorly on tasks requiring patience or careful, considered judgment. For the most part, they are simply in too much of a hurry to complete such work in an effective manner. A study comparing Type A and Type B nurses suggests why this may be so. Although Type A's were significantly more involved in their jobs and invested greater effort, they also were more overloaded (e.g., took on too much to do) and experienced more conflict with respect to the various required aspects of the job. It is easy to understand how differences such as these may well interfere with any possible improvements in performance that may derive from effort alone.

Consistent with this idea are surveys revealing that most top executives are Type B's rather than Type A's. Several factors probably contribute to this pattern. First, it is possible that Type A's simply do not last long enough on their jobs to rise to the highest management levels; the health risks they face (especially coronary heart disease—a serious illness often linked to the Type A behavior pattern) may remove such individuals from contention before they're experienced enough to advance. Second, the impatient, always-in-a-hurry style of Type A's is generally incompatible with the deliberate, carefully studied decision style required of top managers. Finally, it is possible that the impatient, hostile style of Type A's may irritate the people around them so much that it interferes with their chances for promotion. For these reasons, Type A's may be hard to find in top managerial ranks.

Taken together, these findings suggest that neither pattern has the overall edge when it comes to task performance. Although Type A's may excel on tasks involving time pressure or solitary work, Type B's have the advantage when it comes to tasks involving complex judgments and accuracy as opposed to speed.

SELF-EFFICACY:
THE "CAN DO" FACET OF PERSONALITY

Suppose that two individuals are assigned the same task by their supervisor, and suppose that one is confident of his or her ability to carry it out successfully, whereas the other has some serious doubts on this score. Which person is more likely to succeed? Assuming that all other factors (e.g., differences in their ability and motivation) are held constant, it is reasonable to predict that the first will do better. Such an individual has higher amounts of **self-efficacy**—the belief in one's own capacity to perform a task. Based on both direct and vicarious experiences, people acquire general expectations about their ability to perform a wide range of tasks in many different contexts. Such generalized beliefs about self-efficacy are stable over time and reflect a key personality variable.

Self-efficacy has been found to be a good predictor of people's success on the job. For example, in a study of university professors, it was found that self-efficacy was positively correlated with research productivity; that is, such key indices as number of publications increased as self-efficacy increased. In addition, it has been found that unemployed people who are trained in ways of enhancing their self-efficacy perceptions are more likely to look for jobs and, therefore, more likely to become re-employed. Clearly, when it comes to behavior in organizations, self-efficacy is an important aspect of personality.

SELF-ESTEEM:
THE IMPORTANCE OF SELF-EVALUATIONS

Beliefs about one's ability to perform specific tasks are an important part of the *self-concept*—individuals' conceptions of their own abilities, traits, and skills. Yet, they are only a small part. Another important aspect concerns **self-esteem**—the extent to which people hold positive or negative views about themselves. People high in self-esteem evaluate themselves favorably, believing they possess many desirable traits and qualities. In contrast, people low in self-esteem evaluate themselves unfavorably, believing they are lacking in important respects and that they have characteristics that others consider unappealing.

Self-esteem is very important when it comes to organizational behavior. For example, people who are low in self-esteem tend to be less successful in their job searches than those who are high in self-esteem. In addition, when people with low self-esteem are eventually employed, they tend to be attracted to positions in larger organizations, ones in which it is more difficult for them to be noticed and call attention to themselves.

Once on the job, what can be expected of people who are low in self-esteem? Research has shown that the lower an employee's self-esteem, the less

SELF-ASSESSMENT EXERCISE

Checking Out Your Self-Esteem

To objectively measure self-esteem—and most other personality variables—scientists rely on paper-and-pencil questionnaires. This scale, adapted from one actually used to measure self-esteem, may give you some interesting insight into this important aspect of your personality.[9] It is important to caution, however, that this measure is *not* definitive, and that personality assessment is a complex process requiring the work of trained professionals. Still, you should find it interesting to see what the scale suggests.

DIRECTIONS

For each of the following items, indicate whether you: *strongly disagree (SD), disagree (D), agree (A)*, or *strongly agree (SA)* by marking the space provided.

_____   1.   I believe I am a worthwhile person, who is as good as others.

_____   2.   I have several positive qualities.

_____   3.   For the most part, I consider myself a failure.

_____   4.   Generally speaking, I can do things as well as others.

_____   5.   I cannot be proud of too many things about myself.

_____   6.   My feelings about myself are quite positive.

_____   7.   I am very pleased with myself, in general.

likely he or she is to take any active steps to solve problems confronted on the job. As a result, their performance tends to suffer. By contrast, employees with high levels of self-esteem are more inclined to actively attempt to acquire the resources needed to cope with work problems, and to use their skills and abilities to their fullest—and, as a result, to perform at higher levels. Interestingly, people with low self-esteem tend to be aware of their tendency to perform poorly. Research has shown that they are predisposed to evaluate themselves quite negatively (especially when ambiguity exists concerning their performance), and to believe that they are inherently responsible for their poor per-

_____ 8. I really don't have a lot of self-respect.

_____ 9. There are times when I feel useless.

_____ 10. Sometimes I don't think I'm very good at all.

SCORING

1. For items 1, 2, 4, 6, and 7, assign points as follows: $SD = 1$; $D = 2$; $A = 3$; $SA = 4$.

2. For items 3, 5, 8, 9, and 10, assign points as follows: $SD = 4$; $D = 3$; $A = 2$; $SA = 1$.

3. Add the number of points in 1 and 2. This should range from 10 to 40. Higher scores reflect greater degrees of self-esteem.

QUESTIONS FOR DISCUSSION

1. Based on this questionnaire, how high or low is your self-esteem?

2. Does your score make sense to you? In other words, does the questionnaire tell you something you already believed, or did it provide new insight?

3. Why do you think items 1, 2, 4, 6, and 7 are scored opposite from 3, 5, 8, 9, and 10?

4. Do you think the techniques outlined in Table 2-3 on p. 56 may help raise your self-esteem?

formance. (To get a sense of how your self-efficacy rates, complete the **Self-Assessment Exercise** above.)

Although our comments sound a discouraging note with respect to the fate of people with low self-esteem, there is good news: Low self-esteem can be changed. Formal approaches are available, requiring the skills of psychiatrists, although these can be very time-consuming. Fortunately, however, there are some things that can be done on an everyday basis in organizations to help minimize the degree to which feelings of low self-esteem may emerge. For a summary of these, see Table 2-3 on p. 56.

■ *Table 2-3 Boosting Low Self-Esteem: Some Suggestions*

Although it is difficult to completely change key aspects of personality, such as self-esteem, without intensive psychological help, there are several things that organizations can do to boost and maintain the self-esteem of their employees.

Suggestion	*Description*
• Make people feel uniquely valuable.	Create opportunities for people to feel accepted by finding ways to make use of their unique skills and experiences.
• Make people feel competent.	Recognize the good things that people do and praise them accordingly. That is, "catch someone in the act of doing something right."
• Make people feel secure.	Employees' self-esteem will be enhanced when managers make their expectations clear and are forthright with them.
• Make people feel empowered.	People given opportunities to decide how to do their jobs feel good about themselves and their work.

MACHIAVELLIANISM: USING OTHERS ON THE WAY TO SUCCESS

In 1513 the Italian philosopher Niccolo Machiavelli published a book entitled *The Prince,* in which he outlined a ruthless strategy for seizing and holding political power now known as **Machiavellianism.** The essence of his approach was straightforward: People can be readily controlled by sticking to a few basic rules. These include: (a) never show humility; arrogance is far more effective, (b) morality and ethics are for the weak; powerful people do whatever it takes to suit their purpose, and (c) it is better to be feared than loved.

The philosophy Machiavelli promoted almost 500 years ago is still very much with us today. In fact, it is readily visible in the many popular "get to the top at all costs" books that outline similar self-centered strategies for achieving power and success. As you know from your experiences, some people (known as high Machs) are more Machiavellian in nature than others.

If high Machs are willing to do whatever it takes to succeed, you would expect that they would be rather successful at whatever jobs they perform. But are they? Research has shown that whether or not highly Machiavellian people will succeed at their jobs depends on the nature of the organizational setting faced. In contexts in which work is highly regulated, with lots of rules and tight supervision, high Machs have no advantage. In fact, they have little or no opportunities to exercise the skills that make them so unique, leading them to become apathetic and disinterested in their work, and their perfor-

mance suffers as a result. However, when the work setting is loosely structured and imposes few rules, high Machs are well equipped to take advantage
of the opportunities existing in such contexts, and they perform exceptionally
well.

   As you might imagine, high Machs can be very difficult to have around
in one's work environment. Because they are attracted to situations in which
they can use their devious skills and show little regard for others, they can be
wily adversaries indeed. Although you cannot always restructure work situations so as to stymie high Machs, there are several strategies you can use to
protect yourself from them. Table 2-4 summarizes several key suggestions.

ACHIEVEMENT MOTIVATION: STRIVING FOR SUCCESS

You probably know some people who yearn for success, concentrating on
doing what it takes to achieve it. However, others are far less concerned about
success; if it comes fine, but if not, that's okay too. These individuals differ
with respect to an important personality dimension known as **achievement
motivation**—the strength of an individual's desire to excel, to succeed at difficult tasks, and to do them exceptionally well.

■ *Table 2-4 Tips for Protecting Yourself From High Machs*

Because most organizations have some people in them who are highly Machiavellian,
it may be useful to follow some of the guidelines for not falling prey to them
summarized here.

Suggestion	*Description*
• Expose high Machs to others.	Once high Machs' actions are made public within an organization, others may be on guard, making it harder for high Machs to use, and get away with, their manipulative tactics in the future.
• Pay attention to what others do, not what they say.	High Machs are prone to be masters of deception, so concentrate on people's deceptive and ruthless actions more than on their handy excuses for them.
• Avoid situations that give high Machs an edge.	High Machs succeed when emotions run high, and people are uncertain about how to proceed. Under these conditions people are unlikely to recognize that they are being manipulated, opening the door for high Machs.

Although Sam Walton, the late founder and CEO of Wal-Mart, *was always driven to achieve success, he did not open his first Wal-Mart store (in Bentonville, Arkansas) until he was 44 years old.*

People high in achievement motivation may be characterized as having a highly task-oriented outlook: They are more concerned with getting things done than they are with having good relationships with others. Also, because they are so interested in achieving success, people who have a high amount of achievement motivation tend to seek tasks that are moderately difficult and challenging. After all, a too difficult task is likely to lead to failure, and a too easy task doesn't offer sufficient challenge to suit them. By contrast, people who are low on achievement motivation are just the opposite; they strongly prefer extremely difficult or extremely easy tasks. This is because success is almost guaranteed if the task is easy enough, and failure

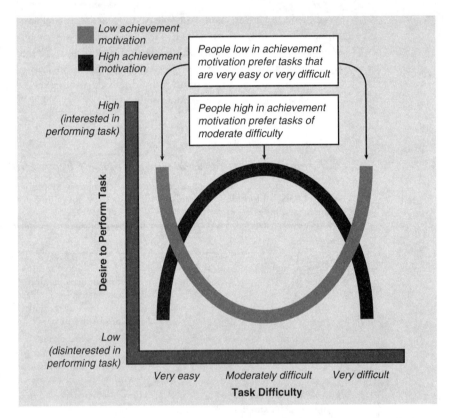

■ *Figure 2-3 Achievement Motivation and Attraction to Tasks: The General Relationship*

People who are high in achievement motivation are attracted to tasks of moderate difficulty, whereas people who are low in achievement motivation are attracted to tasks that are very easy or very difficult.

can readily be justified by attributing it to external sources (i.e., the extreme difficulty of the task) if the task is difficult (see Figure 2-3).

As you might imagine, people who are high in achievement motivation strongly desire feedback on their performance. This allows them to adjust their aspirations (i.e., to shoot for easier or more difficult goals) and to determine when they have succeeded, allowing them to attain the good feelings about their accomplishments that they crave. As part of this tendency, people who are high and low in achievement motivation are not likely to be attracted to the same kinds of jobs. People with a high achievement motivation prefer jobs in which they receive feedback that tells them how well they do, whereas those with a low achievement motivation have little such interest. Not surprisingly, people high in achievement motivation prefer jobs in which pay is based on merit, whereas those low in achievement motivation prefer jobs in which pay is based on seniority.

SUMMARY:
PUTTING IT TO USE

Social perception is the process of integrating and interpreting information about others so as to accurately understand them. It involves the process of *attribution*—judging what people are like and what makes them behave as they do. Judgments about what people are like based on observations of their behavior are known as *correspondent inferences*. Although they may be inaccurate, correspondent inferences are widely used.

Judgments about the underlying causes behind people's behavior may be based on either internal reasons (e.g., one's own characteristics) or external reasons (e.g., the situation). The extent to which we attribute the causes of people's behavior to internal or external causes is explained by *Kelley's theory of causal attribution.* According to this theory, such judgments depend on three types of information: *consensus* (whether others act in a similar manner), *consistency* (whether the individual previously acted this way in the same situation), and *distinctiveness* (whether this person acted similarly in different situations).

Our perceptions of others tend to be biased. For example, we are likely to explain others' behavior in terms of internal explanations rather than external ones. This is known as the *fundamental attribution error.* Our judgments of others are also biased by *stereotypes*—beliefs that all members of specific groups share similar traits. Stereotypes are responsible for inaccurate judgments about others that may be very harmful. Fortunately, there are several ways of overcoming these biases in social perception.

Learning is a relatively permanent change in behavior occurring as a result of experience. Much learning in organizations occurs as a result of *operant conditioning,* learning based on the association between behavior and its consequences. According to the *law of effect,* behaviors are repeated when they lead to positive consequences, such as the presentation of desirable outcomes *(positive reinforcement)* or the removal of undesirable outcomes *(negative reinforcement).* It also states that behaviors are not repeated when they lead to negative consequences, such as the presentation of undesirable outcomes *(punishment)* or the removal of positive outcomes *(extinction).* Learning also occurs indirectly, through observing what happens to others, and imitating their behavior. This is known as *observational learning.*

The process of learning is essential to organizational *training,* the systematic acquisition of new job skills. Training is enhanced by requiring participation; repeating the desired behaviors, particularly under conditions similar to those found on the job; and providing feedback. In organizations, systematic attempts at applying principles of reinforcement, known as *organizational behavior modification,* have led to improvements in performance. Undesirable forms of organizational behavior may be eliminated by applying punishment, the practice of *discipline.* For discipline to be effective, it is useful to: (1) deliver punishment immediately after the undesirable response occurs, (2) administer only moderate levels of punishment, (3) punish the undesirable behavior instead of the person, (4) use punishment consistently, and (5) clearly communicate the reasons for the punishment given.

Personality is the unique and relatively stable pattern of behavior, thoughts, and emotions shown by individuals. Several personality traits are important in organizations. The *Type A* personality is characterized by high levels of competitiveness, irritability, and time urgency, whereas the *Type B* personality is just the opposite. Type A's work harder than Type B's, but Type A's perform more poorly on tasks requiring care and patience.

Self-efficacy is the belief in one's ability to perform a task. In general, higher degrees of self-efficacy are associated with greater levels of task success. *Self-esteem* is the extent to which people hold positive views about themselves. The task performance of people with low self-esteem tends to suffer. However, several techniques can be used to raise self-esteem.

People who are highly *Machiavellian* are willing to manipulate others and to do whatever it takes to get what they want. They tend to succeed in organizational settings that are loosely structured and have few rules, as opposed to ones involving high degrees of regulation and tight supervision.

People's general interest in attaining success is reflected in a personality trait known as *achievement motivation.* People with high amounts of achievement motivation prefer tasks of intermediate difficulty (challenging, but not too difficult). However, people with low amounts of achievement motivation prefer tasks of very low difficulty (where success is assured) and very high difficulty (where failure can be excused).

You Be the Consultant

You are asked to consult the vice president of human resources of a large broadcasting company with respect to three key issues for which she is responsible—employee selection, training, and performance appraisal. Answer the following questions relevant to this situation based on the material in this chapter.

1. When it comes to judging and appraising employees' performance, what types of biases and inaccuracies may be expected? And what can be done to minimize their impact?

2. The company invests a great deal of money in employee training. What specific steps can the company take to improve the effectiveness of its training programs?

3. In preparing the employee manual, the vice president wants to carefully formulate the company's policies regarding employee discipline. What can you recommend the company do to use discipline effectively?

4. Naturally, the company is interested in selecting employees whose personalities most strongly predispose them to being successful, and to avoid those who are likely to be unproductive and/or to cause problems. What personality characteristics would you recommend that the company seeks to find in its prospective employees? Which ones should it seek to avoid? Explain your answers.

CHAPTER 3

What Motivates People to Work?

**PREVIEW OF
CHAPTER HIGHLIGHTS**

Motivation is defined as the process of arousing, directing, and maintaining behavior toward a goal.

The motivational value of fulfilling human needs on the job is described by **need hierarchy theory.** This approach identifies five basic needs that people are motivated to satisfy.

Equity theory explains that people seek fairness with respect to the rewards they receive relative to the contributions they make. The motivation to reduce inequitable conditions strongly influences work behavior.

According to **expectancy theory** people are motivated by the belief that their effort will lead to performance for which they will receive valued rewards. Motivation is just one determinant of job performance.

People work hard to attain performance goals that are specific and difficult but not impossible to reach. **Goal setting** is enhanced when feedback about goal attainment is provided.

Motivation can be enhanced by designing jobs that are **enlarged** by giving people more tasks to perform at the same level, or **enriched** by giving them more responsibility over a broader range of tasks. The **job characteristics model** identifies specific ways in which jobs can be enriched.

Would you continue working if you already had enough money on which to live? Although many might say "no," for even more, the answer appears to be "yes." Surveys have found that most Americans would continue to work even if they didn't need the money, suggesting that people are motivated by more than just a paycheck. The quest to achieve success on the job and to perform interesting work are also goals toward which people strive. And this appears to be the case all around the world, making the motivation to work a universal phenomenon.

But exactly what does it take to motivate today's workers? This question has been the focus of a great deal of attention among both practicing managers and organizational scientists. Our attempt to answer this question will examine five different approaches. Specifically, we will focus on motivating by: (1) meeting basic human needs, (2) rewarding people fairly, (3) enhancing beliefs that desired rewards can be attained, (4) setting goals, and (5) designing jobs so as to make them more desirable. Before we turn our attention to these specific orientations we must first consider a very basic matter—exactly what is meant by motivation.

WHAT IS MOTIVATION? A DEFINITION

Scientists have defined **motivation** as *the process of arousing, directing, and maintaining behavior toward a goal.* As this definition suggests, motivation involves three components. The first component, *arousal,* has to do with the drive or energy behind our actions. For example, when we are hungry we are driven to seek food. The *direction* component involves the choice of behavior made. A hungry person may make many different choices—eat an apple, have a pizza delivered, go out for a burger, and so on. The third component, *maintenance,* is concerned with people's persistence, their willingness to continue to exert effort until a goal is met. The longer you would continue to search for food when hungry the more persistent you would be.

Putting it all together, it may help to think of motivation by using the analogy of driving a car. In this manner, arousal may be likened to the energy generated by the car's engine and fuel system. The direction it takes is dictated by the driver's turning of the steering wheel. And finally, maintenance may be thought of as the driver's determination to stay on course until the final destination is reached.

Despite this simple analogy, motivation is a highly complex concept. This is reflected by the fact that people often are motivated by many things at once, sometimes causing conflicts. For example, a factory worker may be motivated to make a positive impression on a supervisor by doing a good job, but at the same time maintain friendly relations with coworkers by not making them look bad. This example has to do with job performance, and indeed, motivation is a key determinant of performance. However, it is important to note that motivation is not synonymous with performance. In fact, as we will explain later, even the most highly motivated employee may fall short of achieving success on the job—especially if he or she lacks the required skills or works under poor conditions. Clearly, although motivation does not completely account for job performance, it is a key determinant. Importantly, it is something that managers can do something about. With this in mind, we are prepared to launch into our discussion of different approaches to motivating people on the job.

MOTIVATING BY MEETING BASIC HUMAN NEEDS: MASLOW'S NEED HIERARCHY THEORY

As our definition suggests, people are motivated to fulfill their needs—whether it's a need for food, as in our example, or other needs, such as the need for social approval. Companies that help their employees in this quest are certain to reap the benefits. In fact, this is one of the premises of Robert H. Waterman, Jr.'s, recent bestseller, *What America Does Right: Learning From Companies That Put People First.*[1] Waterman, an organizational consultant, claims that companies that strive to meet the needs of their employees attract the best people and motivate them to do excellent work. Some insight into how this may come about is provided by Maslow's **need hierarchy theory.**[2]

Maslow's basic idea was simple: People will not be healthy and well-adjusted unless their needs are met. This idea applies whether we're talking about becoming a functioning member of society, Maslow's original focus, or a productive employee of an organization, a later application of his work. Specifically, Maslow identified five different types of needs which, he claimed, are activated in a specific order, starting at the lowest, most basic needs, and working upward to higher-level needs (hence, a hierarchy). Furthermore, these needs are not aroused all at once or in random fashion. Rather, each need is triggered after the one directly beneath it in the hierarchy has been satisfied. The specific needs and the hierarchical order in which they are arranged are summarized in Figure 3-1. You may find it useful to refer to this overview as we describe each of Maslow's five categories of needs.

PHYSIOLOGICAL NEEDS

The lowest-order needs involve satisfying fundamental biological drives, such as the needs for air, food, water, and shelter. These *physiological needs*, as they are called, are surely the most basic needs because unless they are met people will become ill and suffer. For this reason, they are depicted at the base of the triangle in Figure 3-1.

There are many things that companies do to help their employees meet basic physiological needs. Probably the simplest involves paying them a living

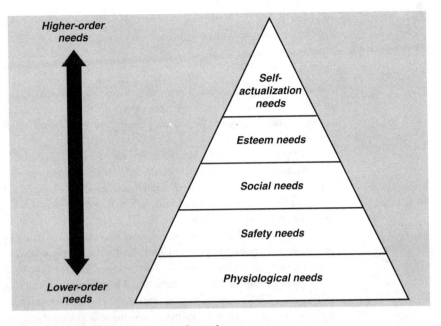

■ *Figure 3-1 Need Hierarchy Theory*

Maslow's need hierarchy specifies that the five needs shown here are activated in order, from lowest to highest. Each need is triggered after the one immediately below it in the hierarchy is satisfied.

wage, money that can be exchanged for food and shelter. But there's more to satisfying physiological needs than simply giving employees a paycheck. There are also coffee breaks and opportunities to rest. Even the cruelest, slave-driving bosses know the importance of giving workers time to relax and recharge their systems.

Staying physically healthy involves more than just resting; it also requires exercise, something that the sedentary nature of many of today's technologically advanced jobs does not permit. With this in mind, thousands of companies are providing exercise facilities for their employees. By keeping the work force healthy and fit they are paving the way for people to become productive. Some companies, such as Southern California Edison and Hershey Foods, have taken this thinking to the extreme. They offer insurance rebates to employees who live healthy lifestyles (e.g., physically fit nonsmokers) and raise the premiums of those at greater risk for illness. In this manner, not only are the insurance burdens distrib-

Although it's commonly said that "there's no such thing as a free lunch," this is not so at **Northwestern Mutual Life, Hewitt Associates, and J.P. Morgan.** *These companies help meet their employees' physiological needs by providing lunches to their employees absolutely free of charge.*

uted fairly, but the incentives encourage wellness activities that promise to benefit both employers and employees.

SAFETY NEEDS

After physiological needs have been satisfied, the next level of needs is triggered—*safety needs*. These are concerned with the need to operate in an environment that is physically and psychologically safe and secure, one free from threats of harm.

Organizations help satisfy their employees' safety needs in several ways. For example, they protect shop workers from hazards in the environment by fitting them with goggles and hard hats. Even seemingly safe work settings, such as offices, can be riddled with safety hazards. This is why efforts are made to spare office workers from eye strain, wrist injuries (such as the increasingly prevalent carpal tunnel syndrome), and back pain, by using specially designed computer monitors, desks, and chairs. Physical safety also may involve such basic services as security and fire prevention. In contrast to the "sweat shops" (hot, poorly ventilated, uncomfortable factories) in which garment workers toiled in the 1940s, today's organizations show considerable interest in protecting the safety of their employees. Although government regulations dictate many safety practices, it is safe to say that employers independently recognize the motivational benefits realized by providing safe work environments.

We are referring to not only physical safety but psychological safety as well. Although you probably haven't given it much thought, psychological security is an important concern in the workplace. For example, by providing tenure, educational institutions offer teachers a high level of psychological security. However, tenure is an exception, and concerns over layoffs and cutbacks can be considerable in an era in which organizations are restructuring and getting smaller (as we will see in Chapter 11). With this in mind, some organizations have incorporated policies that promise employees that they will be retrained for new jobs within the company should their present jobs be eliminated. Sometimes, however, it isn't always possible to offer lifetime guarantees of employment, and layoffs are inevitable. In these instances, some companies, such as AT&T and Wang Labs, have attempted to soften the blow by offering counseling and assistance in finding new jobs to their laid-off employees. Although it may be better not to get laid off at all, there is surely some degree of psychological security provided by knowing that the company will offer help if needed.

SOCIAL NEEDS

Once people's physiological and safety needs have been satisfied, Maslow claims, *social needs* are activated. These refer to the need to be affiliative—that is, to be liked and accepted by others. As social animals we want to be with others and to have them approve of us.

Organizations do much to satisfy these needs when they sponsor social events, such as office parties and company picnics. For example, by holding its annual "Family Day" picnic near its Armonk, New York headquarters, IBM employees enjoy good opportunities to socialize with their coworkers and their families. Similarly, joining a company's bowling team or softball team also provides good opportunities to meet social needs within an organization. While discussing physiological needs we noted that many companies provide health club facilities for their employees. Besides keeping employees healthy, it's easy to see how such opportunities also help satisfy social needs. "Playing hard" with those with whom we also "work hard" provides good opportunities to fulfill social needs on the job.

ESTEEM NEEDS

Not only do we need to be liked by others socially, but we also need to gain their respect and approval. In other words, we have a need for *self-esteem*— that is, to achieve success and have others recognize our accomplishments. Consider, for example, reserved parking spots or plaques honoring the "employee of the month." Both are ways of demonstrating esteem for employees. So too are awards banquets in which worthy staff members' contributions are recognized. The same thing is frequently done in print by recognizing one's organizational contributions on the pages of a corporate newsletter. For example, employees of Merck, the large pharmaceutical company, enjoyed the recognition they received for developing Proscar (a highly successful drug treatment for prostate enlargement) when they saw their pictures in the company newsletter. In fact, it meant more to Merck employees to have their colleagues learn of their success than it did to have their accomplishments touted widely, but to an anonymous audience, on the pages of *The New York Times.*

The practice of awarding bonuses to people making suggestions for improvement is another highly successful way to meet employees' esteem needs. Companies have used a variety of different rewards in this regard. For example, GTE Data Services awards a four-day first-class vacation, $500 in cash, and a plaque to the employee who develops the most effective way to improve customer satisfaction. Less extravagant small prizes, such as VCRs and computers, are used routinely by companies such as Shell Oil, Campbell Soup, AT&T, and American Airlines to reward a wide range of special contributions. However, few companies have taken the practice of rewarding contributions to the same high art as Mary Kay Cosmetics. Not only are lavish banquets staged to recognize modest contributions to this company's bottom line, but top performers are awarded the most coveted prize of all—a pink Cadillac. As founder Mary Kay Ash put it, "There are two things people want more than sex and money . . . recognition and praise."[3]

Importantly, recognition may involve nothing more than a heartfelt "thank you." Or, as Mark Twain said, "I can live for two months on a good

A Honey of a Way to Recognize "Great Performers" at Honeywell

A few years ago, the Electro-Optics Division of Honeywell, Inc. (the Minneapolis-based manufacturer of thermostatic controls) was suffering financial difficulties that were made worse by poor morale. Something had to be done to turn things around, but the bleak financial picture limited options. A creative solution was called for, and a good one was found by Electro-Optics manager, Deborah van Rooyen.

One day, she got to thinking that throughout history there were many individuals who ultimately became successful when they worked hard to overcome obstacles. With this in mind, she launched the "Great Performers" program—a way to recognize successful employees by celebrating their accomplishments alongside those of their more famous counterparts. Her idea was simple: Inspire the division's employees to put forth their best efforts by showing them that the company appreciates their contributions. As van Rooyen said:

> *We wanted to convey the idea that every job is important. For example, we wanted to encourage secretaries to type a letter only once, and to encourage employees in the shipping department to be careful enough that nothing would get broken, and so forth.*[4]

To get things going, van Rooyen and her staff developed and circulated within the company a diverse list of celebrity Great Performers, along with explanations as to what made them so great. Next, the employees were given a chance to nominate their own Great Performers from among their colleagues at Electro-Optics. Each nominee was given a pin shaped like the letter G, signifying "great." From among those nominated, a committee selected five winners who best exemplified the spirit of greatness embodied in the celebrities.

The winners were then treated like the celebrities themselves—for each, a poster was created in which their photo was featured along with a quote and a brief description of their special achievements. Overnight, the Great Performers became company celebrities, and everyone wanted to be one. Each month, five new Great Performers were selected, making even more local celebrities. As the company's public relations manager, Chuck Madaglia, put it, "The posters were a visible way to help boost self-esteem. The idea was to catch employees doing something right and get them feeling good about themselves."[5] Soon employee moral improved dramatically, and after six months, the company became profitable once again. No one associated with the program would argue that the boost to employees' self-esteem was anything less than a major determinant of this turnaround. The Great Performers program clearly helped turn the Electro-Optics Division into a great performer itself.

compliment." Some companies are highly creative in the forms they take to show their recognition. For a close-up look at one such ingenious approach, see the **Winning Practices** section on p. 68

SELF-ACTUALIZATION NEEDS

What happens after all an employee's lower-order needs are met? According to Maslow, people will strive for *self-actualization*—that is, they will work to become all they are capable of being. When people are self-actualized they perform at their maximum level of creativity and become extremely valuable assets to their organizations. For this reason, companies are interested in paving the way for their employees to self-actualize by meeting their lower-order needs.

As this discussion clearly suggests, Maslow's theory provides excellent guidance with respect to the needs that workers are motivated to achieve. Indeed, many organizations have taken actions that are directly suggested by the theory and have found them to be successful. For this reason, the theory remains popular with organizational practitioners. Scientists, however, have noted that specific elements of the theory—notably, the assertion that there are only five needs, and that they are activated in a specific order—have not been supported. Despite this shortcoming, the insight that Maslow's theory provides into the importance of meeting human needs in the workplace makes it a valuable approach to motivation.

EQUITY THEORY: THE IMPORTANCE OF BEING FAIR

There can be little doubt about the importance of money as a motivator on the job. However, it would be overly simplistic and misleading to say that people only want to earn as much money as possible. Even the highest-paid executives, sports figures, and celebrities sometimes complain about their pay despite their multimillion-dollar salaries. Are they being greedy? Not necessarily. Often the issue is not the actual amount of pay received, but rather, pay fairness, or *equity*.

Not surprisingly, people are very concerned about maintaining fairness on the job. In fact, workers frequently rebel when they believe they are operating under a pay system that treats them unfairly. In 1985, for example, pilots at United Airlines went on strike when the company proposed a new pay plan that would slash by 50 percent the amount that veteran DC-10 pilots could earn. Nine years later, in 1994, United's reservation agents were up in arms when a similar plan was proposed for them. To save costs, new agents would hit a permanent ceiling of $18,000 annually, whereas their colleagues hired only six months earlier could earn up to $34,000 after ten years. Such *two-tier pay structures*, as they are known, can wreck havoc on motivation. In the words of one employee of the Giant Food supermarket chain, in which such a plan was instituted in the mid-1980s, "it stinks."[6]

Organizational scientists have been actively interested in the difficult task of explaining exactly what constitutes fairness on the job, and how people respond when they believe they have been unfairly treated. The major conceptualization that addresses these issues is known as **equity theory.**[7]

BALANCING OUTCOMES AND INPUTS

Equity theory proposes that people are motivated to maintain fair, or equitable, relationships between themselves and others, and to avoid those relationships that are unfair or inequitable. To make judgments of equity, people compare themselves to others by focusing on two variables: *outcomes* —what we get out of our jobs (e.g., pay, fringe benefits, prestige), and *inputs* —the contributions made (e.g., time worked, effort exerted, units produced). It helps to think of these judgments in the form of ratios—that is, the outcomes received relative to the inputs contributed (e.g., $500 per week in exchange for working 40 hours). It is important to note that equity theory deals with outcomes and inputs as they are perceived by people, not necessarily objective standards. As you might imagine, well-intentioned people sometimes disagree about what constitutes equitable treatment.

According to equity theory, people make equity judgments by comparing their own outcome/input ratios to the outcome/input ratios of others. This so-called "other" may be someone else in one's work group, another employee in the organization, an individual working in the same field, or even oneself at an earlier point in time—in short, almost anyone against whom we compare ourselves. As shown in Figure 3-2, these comparisons can result in any of three different states: *overpayment inequity, underpayment inequity,* or *equitable payment.*

Let's consider an example. Imagine that Andy and Bill work together as copywriters in an advertising agency. Both men have equal amounts of experience, training, and education, and work equally long and hard at their jobs. In other words, their inputs are equivalent. But suppose Andy is paid an annual salary of $30,000 while Bill is paid only $25,000. In this case, Andy's ratio of outcomes/inputs is higher than Bill's, creating a state of *overpayment inequity* for Andy (since the ratio of his outcomes/inputs is higher), but *underpayment inequity* for Bill (since the ratio of his outcomes/inputs is lower). According to equity theory, Andy, realizing that he is paid more than an equally qualified person doing the same work, will feel *guilty* in response to his *overpayment.* By contrast, Bill, realizing that he is paid less than an equally qualified person for doing the same work, will feel *angry* in response to his *underpayment.* Guilt and anger are negative emotional states that people are motivated to change. As a result, they will seek to create a state of *equitable payment* in which their outcome/input ratios are equal, leading them to feel *satisfied.*

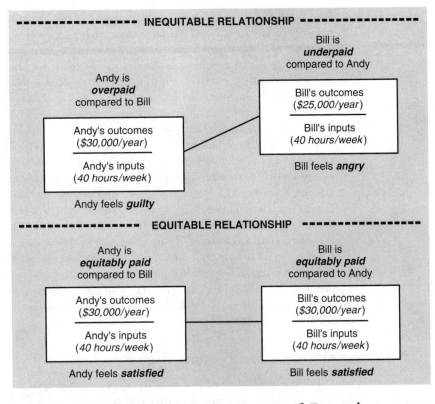

■ *Figure 3-2 Equity Theory: A Summary and Example*

People make judgments of equity or inequity by comparing the ratios of their out-comes/inputs to the corresponding ratios of others. People are motivated to change in-equitable relationships (such as the one shown on top) to equitable ones (such as the one shown on the bottom).

How can inequitable states be turned into equitable ones? The answer lies in adjusting the balance of outcomes and/or inputs. Among people who are underpaid, equity can be created by lowering one's outcomes and/or raising one's inputs. Likewise, those who are overpaid may either raise their inputs or lower their outcomes. In both cases, either action would effectively make the two outcome/input ratios equivalent. For example, the underpaid person, Bill, might lower his inputs by slacking off, arriving at work late, leaving early, tak-ing longer breaks, doing less work or lower-quality work—or, in an extreme case, quit his job. He also may attempt to raise his outcomes, such as by asking for a raise, or even taking home company property, such as tools or office sup-plies. By contrast, the overpaid person, Andy, may do the opposite—raise his inputs or lower his outcomes. For example, he might put forth much more effort, work longer hours, and try to make a greater contribution to the company. He also might lower his outcomes, such as by working while on a paid vacation, or not taking advantage of fringe benefits the company offers.

These are all specific *behavioral* reactions to inequitable conditions—that is, things people can *do* to turn inequitable states into equitable ones. However, people may be unwilling to do some of the things necessary to respond behaviorally to inequities. In particular, they may be reluctant to steal from their employers, or unwilling to restrict their productivity, for fear of getting caught "goofing off." In such cases, people may attempt to resolve inequity *cognitively*, by changing the way they think about the situation. As noted earlier, because equity theory deals with perceptions, inequitable states may be redressed by altering one's thinking about one's own and others' outcomes and inputs. For example, underpaid people may rationalize that others' inputs are really higher than their own (e.g., "I suppose they really *are* more qualified than me"), thereby convincing themselves that their higher outcomes are justified. Similarly, overpaid people may convince themselves that they really *are* better, and deserve their relatively higher pay. So, by changing the way they see things, people can come to perceive inequitable situations as equitable, thereby effectively relieving their feelings of guilt and anger, and transforming them into feelings of satisfaction.

RESPONDING TO INEQUITIES ON THE JOB

There is a great deal of evidence to suggest that people are motivated to redress inequities at work, and that they respond much as equity theory suggests. Consider two examples from the world of sports. Research has shown that professional basketball players who are underpaid (i.e., ones who are paid less than others who perform as well or better) score fewer points than those who are equitably paid.[8] Similarly, among baseball players, those paid less than others who play comparably well tend to change teams or even leave the sport when they are unsuccessful at negotiating higher pay. Cast in terms of equity theory, the underpaid players may be said to have lowered their inputs.

We also know that underpaid workers attempt to raise their outcomes. For example, in an organization studied by the author, workers at two manufacturing plants suffered an underpayment created by the introduction of a temporary pay cut of 15 percent.[9] During the ten-week period under which workers received lower pay company officials noticed that theft of company property increased dramatically, approximately 250 percent. However, in another factory in which comparable work was done by workers paid at their normal rates, the theft rate remained low. This pattern suggests that employees may have stolen property from their company in order to compensate for their reduced pay. Consistent with this possibility, it was found that when the normal rate of pay was reinstated in the two factories, the theft rate returned to its normal, low level. These findings suggest that companies that seek to save money by lowering pay may merely be encouraging their employees to find other ways of making up for what they believe is rightfully theirs.

Consider the examples we've given. First, airline employees went on strike when a two-tier wage system threatened to pay some pilots less than others doing the same work. Second, professional athletes performed worse, or even quit, when they received salaries that were not commensurate with their performance. And third, factory workers stole from their employers while they received lower pay than usual. Together, these examples clearly illustrate a key point explained by equity theory—namely, that people are highly motivated to seek equity and to redress the inequities they face on the job.

EXPECTANCY THEORY: BELIEVING YOU CAN ACHIEVE WHAT YOU WANT

Beyond seeking fair treatment on the job, people are also motivated by the belief that they can expect to achieve certain desired rewards by working hard to attain them. If you've ever put in long hours studying in the hopes of receiving an "A" in one of your classes, then you know what we mean. Believing that there may be a carrot dangling at the end of the stick, and that it may be attained by putting forth the appropriate effort, can be a very effective motivator. This is one of the basic ideas behind the popularity of pay systems known as *merit pay plans*, or *pay-for-performance plans*, which formally establish links between job performance and rewards. However, a recent survey found that only 25 percent of employees see a clear link between good job performance and their pay raises. Clearly, companies are not doing all that they can to take advantage of this form of motivation. To better understand this process, let's take a look at a popular theory of motivation that addresses this issue—**expectancy theory.**

THREE COMPONENTS OF MOTIVATION

In general, expectancy theory claims that people will be motivated to exert effort on the job when they believe that doing so will help them achieve the things they want.[10] Expectancy theory characterizes people as rational beings who think about what they have to do to be rewarded and how much the reward means to them before they perform their jobs. Specifically, the theory views motivation as the result of three different types of beliefs that people have. These are: *expectancy*—the belief that one's effort will affect performance, *instrumentality*—the belief that one's performance will be rewarded, and *valence*—the perceived value of the expected rewards. For a summary of these components and their role in the overall theory, see Figure 3-3 on p. 74.

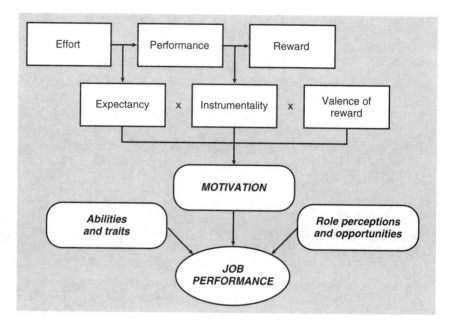

■ *Figure 3-3 Overview of Expectancy Theory*

Expectancy theory claims that motivation is the combined result of the three components identified here—expectancy, instrumentality, and valence of reward. It also recognizes that motivation is only one of several determinants of job performance.

Expectancy.   Sometimes people believe that putting forth a great deal of effort will help them get a lot accomplished. However, in other cases, people do not expect that their efforts will have much effect on how well they do. For example, an employee operating a faulty piece of equipment may have a very low *expectancy* that his or her efforts will lead to high levels of performance. Someone working under such conditions probably would not continue to exert much effort. After all, there is no good reason to go on trying to fill a bucket riddled with holes. Accordingly, good managers will do things that help their subordinates believe that their hard work will lead them to do their jobs better. With this in mind, training employees to do their jobs better can be very effective in helping enhance expectancy beliefs (recall our discussion of training in Chapter 2). Indeed, a large part of working more effectively involves making sure that one's efforts will pay off.

  Some companies have taken a more direct approach by soliciting and following their employees' suggestions about ways to improve their work efficiency. For example, United Electric Controls (a manufacturer of industrial temperature and pressure controls located in Watertown, Massachusetts) routinely asks its employees for ways to do their jobs more effectively. Since instituting this approach, not only have individual employees become more effective, but so too has the company. In fact, important indicators revealed that the company's performance improved dramatically after it began following its employees' suggestions (e.g., on-time deliveries rose from 65 percent to 95 percent). By improving organizational effectiveness, workers' beliefs were enhanced that their hard work would pay off.

Instrumentality. Even if an employee performs at a high level, motivation may suffer if that performance is not appropriately rewarded—that is, if the performance is not perceived as *instrumental* in bringing about the rewards. So, for example, an extremely productive employee may be poorly motivated if he or she has already reached the top level of pay given by the company. Recognizing this possibility, several organizations have crafted pay systems that explicitly link desired performance to rewards. For example, rather than receiving raises tied to seniority, which rewards "staying around" more than "doing something," employees at Procter & Gamble's fabric softener plant in Lima, Ohio are formally rewarded for the skills they possess (e.g., knowing the intricacies of making Downy fabric softener). To receive raises, technicians must demonstrate that they have mastered a certain set of skills. As a result, employees are motivated to perform in ways that not only reward themselves but also help the company.

The same can be said about a newly instituted pay plan for IBM's 30,000 sales representatives. Previously, most of the pay these reps received was based on flat salary; their compensation was not linked to how well they did. Now, however, their pay is carefully tied to two factors that are essential to the company's success—profitability and customer satisfaction. So, instead of receiving commissions on the amount of the sale, as so many salespeople do, 60 percent of IBMers' commissions are tied to the company's profit on that sale. As a result, the more the company makes, the more the reps make. And, to make sure that the reps don't push only high-profit items that customers might not need, the remaining 40 percent of their commissions are based on customer satisfaction. Checking on this, customers are regularly surveyed about the extent to which their sales representatives helped them meet their business objectives. The better the reps have done in this regard, the greater their commissions. Since introducing this plan in late 1993, IBM has been effective in reversing its unprofitable trend. Although there are certainly many factors responsible for this turnaround, experts are confident that this practice of clearly linking desired performance to individual rewards is a key factor.

Valence. Thus far, we have been assuming something that needs to be made explicit—namely, that the rewards the organization offers in exchange for desired performance are themselves desirable. In other words, using terminology from expectancy theory, they should have a positive *valence*. This is no trivial

> *If money is a positively valent reward,* **Microsoft** *employees must be quite content: One out of five is a millionaire.*

point if you consider that rewards are not equally desirable to everyone. For example, whereas a bonus of $200 may not be seen like much of a reward to a multimillionaire CEO, it can be quite valuable to a minimum-wage employee struggling to make ends meet. Valence is not just a matter of the amount of reward received, but what that reward means to the person receiving it.

These days, with a highly diverse work force, it would be erroneous to assume that employees are equally attracted to the same rewards. Some (e.g., single, young employees) might recognize the incentive value of a pay raise, whereas others (e.g., those taking care of families) might prefer additional vacation days, improved insurance benefits, and day-care or elder-care facilities. So, how can an organization find out what its employees want? Some companies have found a simple answer—ask them. For example, executives at PKF-Mark III (a construction company in Newton, Pennsylvania) have recently done just this. They put together a committee of employees representing a broad cross section of the company and allowed them to select exactly what fringe benefits they wanted most. This led to a package of fringe benefits that was highly desirable to the employees.

Many more companies have taken a completely individualized approach, introducing *cafeteria-style benefit plans*—incentive systems allowing employees to select their fringe benefits from a menu of available alternatives. Given that fringe benefits represent almost 40 percent of payroll costs, more and more companies are recognizing the value of administering them flexibly. In fact, a recent survey found that such plans are in place in as many as half of all large companies (those employing over 5,000) and 22 percent of smaller companies (those with under 1,000 employees). For example, Primerica has had a flexible benefit plan in use since 1978—one that almost all of the employees believe is extremely beneficial to them. Many of today's companies are doing creative things to ensure that their employees can achieve rewards that have value to them. For a summary of some of these practices, see Table 3-1. To help recognize those sources of reward that are currently most valuable to you personally, complete the **Self-Assessment Exercise** on p. 78.

THE ROLE OF MOTIVATION IN PERFORMANCE

Thus far, we have discussed the three components of motivation identified by expectancy theory. However, expectancy theory views motivation as just one of several determinants of job performance. As shown on the right side of Figure 3-3, motivation combines with a person's skills and abilities, role perceptions, and opportunities to influence job performance.

It's no secret that the unique characteristics, special skills, and abilities of some people predispose them to perform their jobs better than others. For example, a tall, strong, well-coordinated person is likely to make a better pro-

■ *Table 3-1 Going "Beyond the Fringe" in Benefits: Especially Creative Reward Practices*

Although all companies pay their employees and provide the usual array of fringe benefits, some offer more unusual forms of reward. (Based on material in Nelson, 1994; see Note 4.)

Company	Reward
• Apple Computer	Stock purchase options
• Publix Super Markets	Partial ownership in the company
• Advanta Corporation	Opportunity to help train new employees
• Westin Hotels	Free meals while on the job
• Worthington Industries	Haircuts for $2 while at work
• *Reader's Digest*	Fridays off during the month of May
• Pitney Bowes	Courses in real estate, golf, painting, photography, and cake decorating
• Steelcase	Access to camping facilities and equipment
• Delta Airlines	Free airline travel for employees and spouses

fessional basketball player than a very short, weak, uncoordinated one—even if the shorter person is highly motivated to succeed. Recognizing this, it would be a mistake to assume automatically that someone performing poorly is poorly motivated. Instead, some poor performers may be very highly motivated but lack the knowledge or skills needed to succeed. With this in mind, companies often make big investments in training employees to ensure that they have what it takes to succeed (see Chapter 2) regardless of their levels of motivation.

Expectancy theory also recognizes that job performance will be influenced by people's *role perceptions*—that is, what they believe is expected of them on the job. To the extent that there are uncertainties about what one's job duties may be, performance may suffer. For example, a shop foreman who believes his primary job duty is to teach new employees how to use the equipment may find that his performance is downgraded by a supervisor who believes he should be spending more time doing routine paperwork instead. In this case the foreman's performance wouldn't suffer due to any deficit in motivation, but because of misunderstandings regarding what the job entails.

Finally, expectancy theory also recognizes the role of *opportunities to perform* one's job. Even the best employees may perform at low levels if their opportunities are limited. For example, a highly motivated salesperson may perform poorly if opportunities are restricted, such as if the territory is having a financial downturn, or if the available inventory is limited.

What Rewards Do You Value?

According to expectancy theory, companies can motivate employees by giving rewards that have positive valence to them. What work-related rewards have the greatest value to you? Completing this questionnaire will help you answer this question.

DIRECTIONS

Following are ten work-related rewards. For each, circle the number that best describes the value that particular reward has for you personally. Use the following scale to express your feelings: 1 = no value at all, 2 = slight value, 3 = moderate value, 4 = great value, 5 = extremely great value.

Reward	*Personal Value*				
Good pay	1	2	3	4	5
Prestigious title	1	2	3	4	5
Vacation time	1	2	3	4	5
Job security	1	2	3	4	5
Recognition	1	2	3	4	5
Interesting work	1	2	3	4	5
Pleasant conditions	1	2	3	4	5
Chances to advance	1	2	3	4	5
Flexible schedule	1	2	3	4	5
Friendly coworkers	1	2	3	4	5

QUESTIONS TO ASK YOURSELF

1. Based on your answers, which rewards do you value most? Which do you value least? Do you think these preferences will change as you get older and perform different jobs? If so, how?

2. To what extent do you believe that you will be able to attain each of these rewards on your job? Do you expect that the chances of receiving these rewards will improve in the future? Why or why not?

3. Do you believe that the rewards you value most are also the ones valued by other people? Are these reward preferences likely to be the same for all people everywhere, or at least for all workers performing the same job in the same company?

4. Do you ever find yourself thinking about these rewards while on the job? Are you aware of these rewards most of the time, or do they only come to your attention when they are not received?

In conclusion, expectancy theory has done a good job of sensitizing managers to several key determinants of motivation, variables that frequently can be controlled. Beyond this, the theory clarifies the important—but not unique—role that motivation plays in determining job performance.

GOAL SETTING: TAKING AIM
AT PERFORMANCE TARGETS

Suppose that you are a word processing operator. You are performing quite well, but your boss believes that you can do even better. She asks you to try to type 70 words per minute (wpm) from now on instead of the 60 wpm you've been doing all along. Would you work hard to meet this goal, or would you simply give up? Organizational scientists have found that under certain conditions **goal setting** can lead to marked improvements in performance.[11] Specifically, it has been found that improvements result under three conditions— when goals are: (1) specific; (2) difficult, but reasonable; and (3) accompanied by feedback.

ASSIGN SPECIFIC GOALS

In our word processing example, the supervisor set a goal that was very specific (70 wpm) and also somewhat difficult to attain (10 wpm faster than current performance). Would you perform better under these conditions than if the supervisor merely said something general like "do your best to improve"? Decades of research on goal setting suggests that the answer is "yes."

Indeed, we know that people perform at higher levels when asked to meet specific high-performance goals than when they are directed simply to "do your best," or when no goal at all is assigned. People tend to find specific goals quite challenging and are motivated to try to meet them—not only to fulfill management's expectations, but also to convince themselves that they have performed well. Scientists have explained that attaining goals enhances people's beliefs in their *self-efficacy*—that is, their assessments of themselves as being competent and successful. And, when they believe that they can, in fact, succeed at a task, they will be motivated to work hard at it. For this reason people will be motivated to pursue specific goals, ones that readily enable them to define their accomplishments, enhancing their self-efficacy beliefs.

To demonstrate this principle, let's consider a classic study conducted at an Oklahoma lumber camp owned by Weyerhaeuser, a major producer of paper products.[12] The initial step in the paper-making process involves cutting down the trees and hauling them to the sawmill, where they are ground into pulp. For some time, the company was plagued by a problem: The loggers were only loading the trucks to about 60 percent of their maximum capacity. As a result, there were many wasted trips, adding considerably to the company's costs. To help solve this problem a goal-setting program was introduced. A specific goal was set: The loggers were challenged to load the trucks to 94 percent of their capacity before returning to the mill.

How effective was this goal in raising performance? The results summarized in Figure 3-4 show that the goal was extremely effective. In fact, not only was the specific goal effective in raising performance to the goal level in just a few weeks, but the effects were long-lasting as well. In fact, the loggers were found to sustain this level of performance as long as seven years later! The resulting savings logged in by the company has been considerable, a classic goal-setting success story.

Importantly, these dramatic effects are not unusual, nor are they limited to this special setting. Rather, this study is just one of many that highlight the effectiveness of setting specific, challenging performance goals in a variety of organizational contexts. For example, specific goals also have been used to

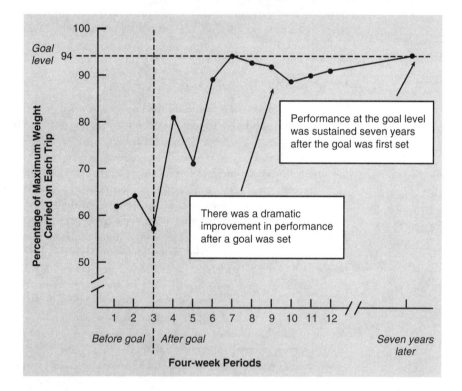

■ *Figure 3-4 Goal Setting in a Logging Camp: An Impressive Demonstration*

After a specific goal was set, loggers did a better job of loading trucks to their maximum limits before returning to the mill. (Adapted from Latham & Baldes, 1975; see Note 12.)

help improve many other kinds of organizational behaviors, such as reducing absenteeism and lowering the occurrence of industrial accidents.

ASSIGN DIFFICULT, BUT ACCEPTABLE, PERFORMANCE GOALS

The goal set at the logging camp was successful not only because it was specific, but also because it pushed crew members to a higher standard. Obviously, a goal that is too easy to attain will *not* bring about the desired increments in performance. For example, if you already type 60 wpm, a goal of 50 wpm, although specific, would probably *lower* your performance. The key point is that a goal must be difficult as well as specific for it to raise performance. At the same time, however, people will work hard to reach challenging goals so long as these are within the limits of their capability. As goals become too difficult, performance suffers because people reject the goals as unrealistic and unattainable. For example, you may work much harder as a student in a class that challenges your ability than in one that is very easy. At the same time, you would probably give up trying if the only way of passing was to get perfect scores on all exams—a standard you would reject as being unacceptable. In short, specific goals are most effective if they are set neither too low nor too high.

The same phenomenon occurs in organizations. For example, Bell Canada's telephone operators are required to handle calls within 23 seconds, and Federal Express's customer service agents are expected to answer customers' questions within 140 seconds. Although both goals were initially considered difficult when they were imposed, the employees of both companies eventually met—or exceeded—these goals, and enjoyed the satisfaction of knowing they succeeded at this task. At a General Electric manufacturing plant, specific goals were set for productivity and cost reduction. Those goals that were perceived as challenging but possible led to improved performance, whereas those thought to be unattainable led to decreased performance.

In recent years, several companies faced with stiff competition and financial pressures, such as Boeing, CSX, 3M, and Mead, have introduced what they call *stretch targets*—goals that are considerably more difficult than those that have been imposed before. For example, at 3M, there was a long-standing tradition to derive 25 percent of the company's revenues from products introduced within the past five years. Then, in 1991, faced with lackluster growth, CEO L. D. DeSimone introduced a difficult new standard: 30 percent of sales were to come from products introduced in the past four years. A large part of the problem was that new products were taking too long to go from the initial development stage to store shelves, often five years. According to one observer, "The goal sent tremors through 3M's campuslike headquarters in St. Paul."[13] By encouraging executives to focus on those products with the greatest commercial potential and rushing them to market, over 25 new products

were introduced the very next year, yielding higher sales and profitability figures than in the recent past. Among these products was the Scotch-Brite
Never Rust soap pad, a web of plastic fibers (made from recycled plastic bot-
tles) coated with fine abrasives, which, unlike steel wool pads, will not rust or
splinter. Not only was this product the fastest one to be introduced in company history, but also one of the most successful. In great part, the extremely
difficult new goal was responsible for this success. As one management consultant put it, "If you don't demand something out of the ordinary, you won't get
anything but ordinary results."[14]

How, then, should goals be set in a manner that strengthens employees'
commitment to them? One obvious way of enhancing goal acceptance is to involve employees in the goal-setting process. Research on workers' participation in goal setting has demonstrated that people better accept goals that they
have been involved in setting than goals that have been assigned by their supervisors—and they work harder as a result.[15] Participation in the goal-setting
process may have these beneficial effects for several reasons. For one, people
are more likely to better understand and appreciate goals they had a hand in
setting themselves than those that are merely presented to them. In addition,
people are likely to be committed to attaining such goals, in large part because
they must psychologically rationalize their decisions to set those goals. (After
all, one can hardly justify setting a specific goal and then not work to attain it.)
Finally, because workers often have more direct knowledge about what it
takes to do a job than their supervisors, they are in a good position to come up
with goals that are acceptably high but not unreasonable. Further capitalizing
on workers' experiences, executives generally agree that it is a good idea to let
employees figure out the best way to meet new goals. In the words of John
Snow, CEO of the large railroad company, CSX, "It's people in the field who
find the right path."[16]

PROVIDE FEEDBACK
CONCERNING GOAL ATTAINMENT

The final condition for setting effective goals appears to
be glaringly obvious, although it is not followed in practice as often as you might expect: Provide feedback about
the extent to which goals have been met. Just as golfers
interested in improving their games need feedback about
where their balls are going, so do workers benefit by feedback about how closely they are approaching their performance goals. Extending our golf analogy, when it comes
to setting work goals effectively, "hooks" and "slices" need
to be corrected.

A recent study of the performance of work crews in
the U.S. Air Force illustrates the importance of using
feedback in conjunction with goal setting.[17] A standard-

*The entrance to **Kellogg's**
cereal plant in Battle Creek,
Michigan displays a sign
indicating the company's
share of the cereal market.
Such feedback is meaningful
inasmuch as a single
percentage of market share
represents annual revenues of
$40 million.*

ized index of job performance was used to measure five different groups repeatedly over a two-year period. During the first nine months, a baseline measure of effectiveness was taken that was used to compare the relative impact of feedback and goal setting. Then the groups received feedback for five months (reports detailing how well they performed on various performance measures). After five months of feedback, the goal-setting phase of the study was begun. During this period, the crew members set goals for themselves with respect to their performance on various measures. Then, for the final five months, in addition to the feedback and goal setting, an incentive (time off from work) was made available to crew members who met their goals.

It was found that feedback and goal setting dramatically increased group effectiveness. Group feedback improved performance approximately 50 percent over the baseline level. The addition of group goal setting improved it 75 percent over baseline. These findings show that the combination of goal setting and feedback helps raise the effectiveness of group performance. Groups that know how well they're doing and have a target goal to shoot for tend to perform very well. Providing incentives, however, improved performance only negligibly. The real incentive seems to be meeting the challenge of performing up to the level of the goal.

In sum, goal setting is a very effective tool managers can use to motivate people. Setting a specific, acceptably difficult goal and providing feedback about progress toward that goal greatly enhance job performance. To demonstrate the effectiveness of goal setting in your own behavior, complete the **Group Exercise** on pp. 84–85.

DESIGNING JOBS THAT MOTIVATE

As you may recall from Chapter 1, Frederick W. Taylor's approach to stimulating work performance was to design jobs so that people worked as efficiently as possible. No wasted movements and no wasted time added up to efficient performance, or so Taylor believed. However, Taylor overlooked one thing: The repetitive machinelike movements required of his workers were highly routine and monotonous. And, not surprisingly, people became bored with such jobs and frequently quit. Fortunately, today's organizational scientists have found several ways of designing jobs that may not only be performed very efficiently, but are also highly pleasant and enjoyable. This is the basic principle behind **job design,** to create jobs that people desire to perform because they are so inherently appealing.

JOB ENLARGEMENT: DOING MORE OF THE SAME KIND OF WORK

If you've ever purchased a greeting card, chances are good that you've picked up at least one made by American Greetings, one of the largest U.S. greeting card companies. What you might not know is that this Cleveland, Ohio-based

Demonstrating the Effectiveness of Goal Setting

The tendency for specific, difficult goals to enhance task performance is very well established. The following exercise is designed to help you demonstrate this effect yourself. All you need is a class of students willing to participate and a few simple supplies.

DIRECTIONS

1. Select a page of text from a book and make several photocopies. Then carefully count the words, and number each word on one of the copies. This will be your score sheet.

2. Find another class of 30 or more students who don't know anything about goal setting. (We don't want their knowledge of the phenomenon to bias the results.) On a random basis, divide the students into three equal-size groups.

3. Ask the students in the first group ("baseline" group) to copy as much of the text as they can onto another piece of paper, giving them exactly one minute to do so. Direct them to work at a fast pace. Using the score sheet created in step 1, identify the highest number of words counted by any one of the students. Then multiply this number by 2. This will be the specific, difficult goal level.

4. Ask the students in another group ("specific goal" group) to count the number of words on the same printed page for exactly one minute. Tell them to try to reach the specific goal number identified in step 3.

5. Repeat this process with the third group ("do your best" group) but instead of giving them a specific goal, direct them to "try to do your best at this task."

organization recently redesigned some 400 jobs in its creative division. Now rather than always working exclusively on say Christmas cards, employees will be able to move back and forth between different teams, such as those working on birthday ribbons, humorous mugs, and Valentine's Day gift bags. Similarly, employees at the Blue Ridge, Georgia plant of Levi Strauss & Co. used to perform the same task all day on the assembly line, but now they have been trained to handle three different jobs. Employees at American Greetings and Levi Strauss reportedly enjoy the variety, as do those at RJR Nabisco,

6. Compute the average number of words copied in the "difficult goal" group and the "do your best" group. Have your instructor compute the appropriate statistical test (a *t*-test, in this case) to determine the statistical significance of the difference between the performance levels of the groups.

QUESTIONS FOR DISCUSSION

1. Was there, in fact, a statistically significant difference between the performance levels of the two groups? If so, did students in the "specific goal" group outperform those in the "do your best" group, as expected? What does this reveal about the effectiveness of goal setting?

2. If the predicted findings were not supported, why do you suppose this happened? What was it about the procedure that may have led to this failure? Was the specific goal (twice the fastest speed in the "baseline" group) too high, making the goal unreachable? Or was it too low, making the specific goal too easy?

3. What do you think would happen if the goal was lowered, making it easier, or raised, making it more difficult?

4. Do you think it would have helped to provide feedback about goal attainment (e.g., someone counting the number of words copied, and calling this out to the performers as they worked)?

5. For what other kinds of tasks do you believe goal setting may be effective? Specifically, do you think you can use goal setting to improve your own performance on something you do? Explain this possibility.

Corning, and Eastman Kodak, other companies that have recently allowed employees to make such lateral moves.

Scientists have referred to what these companies are doing as **job enlargement**—the practice of giving employees more tasks to perform at the same level. There's no higher responsibility involved, nor any greater skills, just a wider variety of the same types of tasks. The idea behind job enlargement is simple: You can decrease boredom by giving people a greater variety of jobs to do.

Do job enlargement programs work? To answer this question, consider the results of a recent study comparing the job performance of people doing enlarged and unenlarged jobs.[18] In the unenlarged jobs different employees performed separate paperwork tasks such as preparing, sorting, coding, and keypunching various forms. The enlarged jobs combined these various functions into larger jobs performed by the same people. Although it was more difficult and expensive to train people to perform the enlarged jobs than the separate jobs, important benefits resulted. In particular, employees expressed greater job satisfaction and less boredom. And, because one person followed the whole job all the way through, greater opportunities to correct errors existed. Not surprisingly, customers were satisfied with the result.

In a follow-up investigation of the same company conducted two years later, however, it was found that not all the beneficial effects continued.[19] Notably, employee satisfaction leveled off, and the rate of errors went up, suggesting that as employees got used to their enlarged jobs they found them less interesting and stopped paying attention to all the details. Hence, although job enlargement may help improve job performance, its effects may be short-lived. It appears that the problem with enlarging jobs is that after a while, people get bored with them, and they need to be enlarged still further. Because it is impractical to continue enlarging jobs all the time, the value of this approach is rather limited.

JOB ENRICHMENT: INCREASING REQUIRED SKILLS AND RESPONSIBILITIES

As an alternative, consider another approach taken to redesigning jobs. For many years, big companies like Procter & Gamble (P&G) manufactured items such as detergent by having large numbers of people perform a series of narrow tasks. Then, in the early 1960s, realizing that this rigid approach did little to utilize the full range of skills and abilities of employees, P&G executive David Swanson introduced a new way to make detergent in the company's Augusta, Georgia plant. The technicians worked together in teams (see Chapter 7) to take control over large parts of the production process. They set production schedules, hired new coworkers, and took responsibility over evaluating each others' performance, including the process of deciding who was going to get raises. In short, they not only performed more tasks, but ones at higher levels of skill and responsibility. The general name given to this approach is **job enrichment.**

One of the best-known job enrichment programs was the one developed by Volvo, the Swedish auto manufacturer. In response to serious dissension among its work force in the late 1960s, the company's president at that time, Pehr Gyllenhammar, introduced job enrichment in its Kalmar assembly plant. Cars were assembled by 25 groups of approximately 20 workers who were each responsible for one part of the car's assembly (e.g., engine, electrical system). In contrast to the usual assembly-line method of manufacturing cars used in Detroit, Volvo's work groups are set up so employees can freely plan, organize, and inspect their own work. In time, workers became more satisfied with their jobs and the plant experienced a significant reduction in turnover and absenteeism.

Although job enrichment programs also have been successful at other organizations, several factors limit their popularity. First, there is the difficulty of implementation. Redesigning existing facilities so that jobs can be enriched is often prohibitively expensive. Moreover, the technology needed to perform certain jobs makes it impractical for them to be redesigned. Another impediment is the lack of universal employee acceptance. Although many relish it, some people do *not* desire the additional responsibility associated with performing enriched jobs. In fact, when a group of American auto workers was sent to Sweden to work in a Saab engine assembly plant where jobs were highly enriched, five out of six indicated that they preferred their traditional assembly-line jobs. As one union leader put it, "If you want to enrich the job, enrich the paycheck."[20] Clearly, enriched jobs are not for everyone.

THE JOB CHARACTERISTICS MODEL

Thus far, we have failed to specify precisely *how* to enrich a job. What elements of a job need to be enriched for it to be effective? An attempt to expand the idea of job enrichment, known as the **job characteristics model,** provides an answer to this important question.[21]

Basic Elements of the Job Characteristics Model.   This approach assumes that jobs can be designed to help people get enjoyment out of their jobs and care about the work they do. The model identifies how jobs can be designed to help people feel that they are doing meaningful and valuable work. In particular, it specifies that enriching certain elements of jobs alters people's psychological states in a manner that enhances their work effectiveness. Specifically, the model identifies five *core job dimensions* that help create three *critical psychological states,* leading in turn to several beneficial *personal and work outcomes* (see Figure 3-5 on p. 88).

The five critical job dimensions are *skill variety, task identity, task significance, autonomy,* and *feedback.* Let's take a closer look at these.

Employees at the **Land's End** *mail-order house can move between different jobs in different departments so as to keep things interesting for them.*

- *Skill variety* is the extent to which a job requires using several different skills and talents that an employee has. For example, a restaurant manager with high skill variety will perform many different tasks (e.g., maintaining sales records, handling customer complaints, scheduling staff, supervising repair work, and the like).

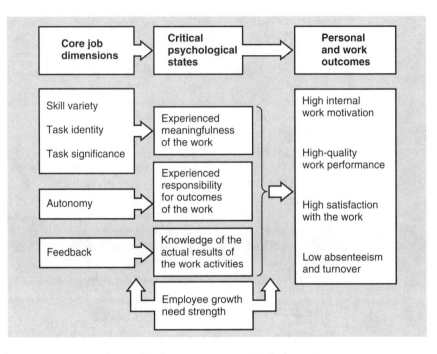

■ *Figure 3-5 The Job Characteristics Model*

According to the job characteristics model, five core job dimensions listed create three critical psychological states, which in turn influence the personal and work outcomes shown. The model also acknowledges that these relationships are strongest among those individuals highest in growth need strength. (Adapted from Hackman & Oldham, 1980; see Note 21.)

- *Task identity* is the degree to which a job requires doing a whole task from beginning to end. For example, tailors will have high task identity if they do everything associated with making an entire suit (e.g., measuring the client, selecting the fabric, cutting and sewing it, and altering it to fit).

- *Task significance* is the amount of impact a job is believed to have on others. For example, medical researchers working on a cure for a deadly disease surely recognize the importance of their work to the world at large. Even more modest contributions to the company can be recognized as being significant to the extent that employees understand the role of their jobs in the overall mission of the organization.

- *Autonomy* is the extent to which employees have the freedom and discretion to plan, schedule, and carry out their jobs as desired. For example, in 1991 a team of Procter & Gamble employees was put in charge of making all the arrangements necessary for the building of a new $5 million facility for making concentrated Downy.

- *Feedback* is the extent to which the job allows people to have information about the effectiveness of their performance. For example, telemarketing representatives regularly receive information about how many calls they make per day and the monetary values of the sales made.

The job characteristics model specifies that these various job dimensions have important effects on certain critical psychological states. Specifically, skill variety, task identity, and task significance jointly contribute to a task's *experienced meaningfulness*. A task is considered to be meaningful insofar as it is experienced as being highly important, valuable, and worthwhile. Jobs that provide a great deal of autonomy are said to make people feel *personally responsible and accountable for their work*. When they are free to decide what to do and how to do it, they feel more responsible for the results, whether good or bad. Finally, effective feedback is said to give employees *knowledge of the results of their work*. When a job is designed to provide people with information about the effects of their actions, they are better able to develop an understanding of how effectively they have performed—and such knowledge improves their effectiveness.

The job characteristics model specifies that the three critical psychological states affect various personal and work outcomes—namely, people's feelings of motivation, the quality of work performed, satisfaction with work, absenteeism, and turnover. The higher the experienced meaningfulness of work, responsibility for the work performed, and knowledge of results, the more positive the personal and work benefits will be. When they perform jobs that incorporate high levels of the five core job dimensions, people should feel highly motivated, perform high-quality work, be highly satisfied with their jobs, be absent infrequently, and be unlikely to resign from their jobs.

We should also note that the model is theorized to be especially effective in describing the behavior of individuals who are high in *growth need strength*—that is, people who have a high need for personal growth and development. People not particularly interested in improving themselves on the job are not expected to experience the theorized psychological reactions to the core job dimensions, nor consequently to enjoy the beneficial personal and work outcomes predicted by the model. By introducing this variable, the job characteristics model recognizes the important limitation of job enrichment noted earlier—not everyone wants and benefits from enriched jobs.

Assessing the Motivating Potential of Jobs.   Based on the proposed relationship between the core job dimensions and their associated psychological reactions, the model claims that job motivation will be highest when the jobs performed rate high on the various dimensions. To assess this, a questionnaire known as the Job Diagnostic Survey (JDS) has been developed to measure the degree to which job incumbents recognize that various characteristics are present in a particular job. Based on responses to the JDS, we can make predictions about the degree to which a job motivates people who perform it. This is done by using an index known as the *motivating potential score (MPS)*, computed as follows:

$$\text{MPS} = \frac{\text{Skill variety} + \text{Task identity} + \text{Task significance}}{3} \times \text{Autonomy} \times \text{Feedback}$$

The MPS is a summary index of a job's potential for motivating people. The higher the score for a given job, the greater the likelihood of experiencing the personal and work outcomes specified by the model. Knowing a job's MPS helps one identify jobs that might benefit by being redesigned.

The job characteristics model has been the focus of many empirical tests, most of which are supportive of many aspects of the model. One study conducted among a group of South African clerical workers found particularly strong support.[22] The jobs of employees in some of the offices in this company were enriched in accordance with techniques specified by the job characteristics model. Specifically, employees performing the enriched jobs were given opportunities to choose the kinds of tasks they perform (high skill variety), do the entire job (high task identity), receive instructions regarding how their job fit into the organization as a whole (high task significance), freely set their own schedules and inspect their own work (high autonomy), and keep records of their daily productivity (high feedback). Another group of employees, equivalent in all respects except that their jobs were not enriched, served as a control group.

After employees performed the newly designed jobs for six months, comparisons were made between them and their counterparts in the control group. With respect to most of the outcomes specified by the model, individuals performing redesigned jobs showed superior results. Specifically, they reported feeling more internally motivated and more satisfied with their jobs. Lower rates of absenteeism and turnover were also found among employees performing the enriched jobs. The only outcome predicted by the model that was not found to differ was actual work performance; people performed equally well in enriched and unenriched jobs. Considering the many factors that are responsible for job performance (as discussed in connection with expectancy theory), this finding should not be too surprising.

Suggestions for Enhancing the Motivating Potential of Jobs. The job characteristics model specifies several ways in which jobs can be designed to enhance
their motivating potential. For example, instead of using several workers, each
of whom performs a separate part of a whole job, it would be better to have
each person perform the entire job. Doing so helps provide greater skill variety
and task identity. For example, Corning Glass Works in Medford, Massachusetts redesigned jobs so that people who assembled laboratory hot plates put
together entire units instead of contributing a single part to the assembly
process.

The job characteristics model also suggests that jobs should be set up so
that the person performing a service (such as an auto mechanic) comes into
contact with the recipient of the service (such as the car owner). Jobs designed
in this manner will not only help the employee by providing feedback, but also
by enhancing skill variety (e.g., talking to customers in addition to fixing cars),
and by building autonomy (by giving people the freedom to manage their own
relationships with clients). This suggestion has been implemented at Sea-Land
Service, the large containerized ocean-shipping company. After this company's
mechanics, clerks, and crane operators started meeting with customers, they
became much more productive. Having faces to associate with the once-
abstract jobs they did clearly helped employees take their jobs more seriously.

Another implication of the job characteristics model is that jobs should
be designed so as to give employees as much feedback as possible. The more
people know how well they're doing (be it from customers, supervisors, or
coworkers), the better equipped they are to take appropriate corrective action
(recall our discussion in Chapter 2 about the importance of feedback). Sometimes cues about job performance can be clearly identified as people perform
their jobs (as we noted in conjunction with goal setting). In the best cases,
open lines of communication between employees and managers are so strongly
incorporated into the corporate culture—as has been reported to exist at Boise
Cascade's paper products group—that feedback flows without hesitation. As a
case in point, Childress Buick Co., a Phoenix, Arizona auto dealership, once
suffered serious customer dissatisfaction and employee retention problems before owner, Rusty Childress, began encouraging his employees to use their
own judgment and initiative. Sometimes, long-autocratic managers are
shocked when they see how hard people work when they are allowed to make
their own decisions. Bob Freese, CEO of Alphatronix Inc., in Research Triangle Park, North Carolina is among them. "We let employees tell us when they
can accomplish a project and what resources they need," he says. "Virtually always they set higher goals than we would ever set for them."[23]

SUMMARY:
PUTTING IT TO USE

Need hierarchy theory specifies that people are motivated to fulfill a series of needs, arranged in hierarchical fashion from the lowest to highest. Most basic are physiological needs, which employers can help meet by paying workers enough to satisfy their basic needs for food and shelter. The next level, safety needs, can be met by providing workplaces that are free from both physical and psychological harm. Social needs are often met by giving employees opportunities to socialize with each other, such as by engaging in athletic pursuits. Programs honoring special contributions, such as "employee of the month" awards, are useful in helping satisfy esteem needs. When all of these needs have been met, the theory says, people will strive to self-actualize — that is, to become all they are capable of being. Insofar as self-actualized employees work at their maximum creative potential they are valued employees of the organizations in which they work.

The basic premise of *equity theory* is that people are motivated to redress inequities in the workplace, both overpayment and underpayment, and to establish equitable relationships with others. This involves making sure that people are paid the same as others doing comparable work. When people believe that this is not the case, they frequently attempt to change conditions — working less hard, or seeking higher pay — to help restore equity. Insofar as employees who feel inequitably treated have been known to respond in extreme ways, such as by going on strike and stealing from their employers, managers should work hard to make sure that employees believe that they are being treated fairly.

A broader approach to motivation is taken by *expectancy theory*. This approach specifies that people will be motivated to work hard when they believe that their efforts will lead them to perform well, their performance will be suitably rewarded, and when the rewards they receive are valued. As such, it is considered useful to make sure that workers are trained well enough to have their efforts pay off, are rewarded in a manner commensurate with their performance (e.g., a merit pay system), and receive rewards that they truly value (such as by allowing them to select fringe benefits from a list of options). Expectancy theory recognizes that motivation is necessary but not sufficient for good performance to result. Employees also must have the skills and abilities needed to succeed (such as those provided by training and natural talent) as well as opportunities to succeed (e.g., the necessary sales tools and customer base).

The process of *goal setting* has also been used effectively to stimulate high levels of performance. To be successful, goals must meet three characteristics. First, they must be highly specific, identifying exactly the level of performance that is expected. Second, they must be difficult but not impossible to attain. Finally, feedback helps people understand the adjustments in their behavior needed to reach their goals.

Finally, workers' motivation can be enhanced by the process of *job design*—making jobs so inherently appealing that people will be motivated to do them. One major approach has been *job enlargement*, giving people more jobs to do at the same level. Although this works temporarily, people soon become bored with their jobs, requiring even more enlargement. *Job enrichment* is considered a more successful approach. This involves giving people not only more jobs to do, but ones with greater levels of responsibility. The *job characteristics model* specifies that jobs should be enriched by adding to the number of skills required, allowing people to perform entire tasks, helping them understand the significance of their work, giving them the freedom and discretion to do their jobs as they wish, and regularly sharing information about the effectiveness of their work.

You Be the Consultant

Suppose that you were just hired by executives of a large manufacturing company to help resolve problems of poor morale that have been plaguing the work force. Turnover and absenteeism are high, and performance is at an all-time low. Answer the following questions relevant to this situation based on the material in this chapter.

1. Suppose, after interviewing the workers, you found that they believed that no one cared how well they were doing. What theories could help explain this problem? Applying these approaches, what would you recommend the company does to resolve this situation?

2. Company officials tell you that the employees are well paid, adding to their surprise about the low morale. However, your interviews reveal that the employees themselves feel otherwise. Theoretically, why is this a problem? What could be done to help?

3. "I'm bored with my job," an employee tells you, and you believe he speaks for many within the company. What could be done to make the jobs more interesting to those who perform them? What are the limitations of your plan? Would it work equally well for all employees?

CHAPTER 4

Work-Related Attitudes: Feelings About Our Jobs, Organizations, and Coworkers

PREVIEW OF CHAPTER HIGHLIGHTS

An **attitude** is defined as a relatively stable cluster of feelings, beliefs, and behavioral predispositions toward some specific target.

Job **satisfaction** is explained by **two-factor theory** (which claims that job satisfaction and dissatisfaction are caused by different factors), and **value theory** (which claims that job satisfaction is based on discrepancies between what people have and what they want). High levels of dissatisfaction have important consequences (e.g., absenteeism and voluntary turnover), although several steps can be taken to promote job satisfaction.

Organizational **commitment** has three distinct forms: **continuance commitment** (based on the costs of leaving), **affective commitment** (based on agreement with the organization), and **normative commitment** (based on social pressure). Highly committed employees are likely to remain in their organizations and to help them be successful. Several techniques can be used to promote organizational commitment.

Negative attitudes toward others, **prejudices,** are frequently based on **stereotypes,** judgments about people based on their group membership. Major victims of prejudice include workers who are young or old, have disabling conditions, are gay or lesbian, belong to ethnic minorities, and are women. Both **affirmative action programs** and **diversity management programs** have attempted to reduce prejudice in the workplace.

How do you feel about your job? Is it pleasant, or pure drudgery? How about your organization? Do you want to continue working there, or are you considering quitting? What do you think of your coworkers? Do they know what they're doing, or would the company be better off without them? Such questions are likely to elicit strong opinions. Indeed, people tend to have definite feelings about everything related to their jobs, whether it's the work itself, superiors, coworkers, subordinates, or even the food in the company cafeteria. Feelings such as these, and many others, are referred to as **work-related attitudes,** the topic of this chapter.

As you might imagine, these attitudes can be very important in organizations. Not only do we want to feel good about our work for its own sake, but such feelings may have important effects on how we do our jobs and the functioning of organizations. Our examination of work-related attitudes will focus on three major targets—attitudes toward the job (known as *job satisfaction*), attitudes toward the organization (known as *organizational commitment*), and attitudes toward our coworkers (including a special kind of negative attitude known as *prejudice*). Before reviewing these attitudes and their impact on organizations, we will begin with the very basic, but important, task of formally defining attitudes.

WHAT IS AN ATTITUDE? A DEFINITION

As noted previously, we all hold definite views about things and people—feelings referred to as attitudes. Formally, we define an **attitude** as *a relatively stable cluster of feelings, beliefs, and behavioral predispositions (i.e., intentions) toward some specific target.* If we examine this definition more closely, we find that attitudes consist of three major components: an evaluative component, a cognitive component, and a behavioral component.

Our example has focused on the most obvious component of attitudes, how we feel about something. This aspect of an attitude, its *evaluative component,* refers to our liking or disliking of any particular target—be it a person, thing, or event (what might be called the *attitude object,* the focus of the attitude). You may, for example, feel positively or negatively toward your boss, your coworkers, or the company logo. In fact, anything can be an attitude object. Please note that our definition refers to "relatively stable" feelings toward attitude objects. Temporary shifts in feelings about something may not reflect changes in attitudes. Rather, attitudes are more enduring. So, for example, although people sometimes change their membership in political parties, their endorsement of a particular party's philosophy is generally consistent over time. Hence, the attitude toward it is stable.

Attitudes involve more than feelings, however; they also involve knowledge—things you know about an attitude object. For example, you might believe that your company just lost an important contract, or that a coworker doesn't really know what he or she is doing. These beliefs may be completely accurate or inaccurate, but they still comprise the personal knowledge that contributes to your attitude. Such beliefs are referred to as the *cognitive component* of attitudes.

Naturally, what you believe about something and the way you feel about it will influence the way you are predisposed to behave. For example, if you believe that your boss is a crook, and you dislike this, you may be inclined to report him or her to the authorities and to begin looking for a new job. What we are saying is that attitudes have a *behavioral component*—a predisposition to act in a certain way. It is very important to caution that a predisposition may not perfectly predict one's behavior. In our example, although you may dislike your unethical boss, you might not take action against him or her for fear of retaliation, and you might not take a new position if a better one isn't available. Hence, your intention to act a certain way may or may not dictate how you will actually behave. Indeed, as we shall see, attitudes are not perfect predictors of behavior.

Now that we have formally defined attitudes, we are prepared to begin exploring various attitudes that come into play on the job. The first one we will consider is job satisfaction.

JOB SATISFACTION: FEELINGS ABOUT OUR WORK

Do people generally like their jobs? Despite what you may hear in the news about dissatisfied workers going on strike or even acting violently toward their supervisors, overall people are quite satisfied with their jobs. In fact, surveys have found that the percentage of people reporting satisfaction with their jobs averages between 80 and 90 percent. These feelings, reflecting attitudes toward one's job, are known as **job satisfaction.** Insofar as job satisfaction plays an important role in organizations, it makes sense to ask: What factors contribute to job satisfaction? As we will point out, a great deal of research, theory, and practice bears upon this question.

THEORIES OF JOB SATISFACTION AND THEIR IMPLICATIONS

There is no more direct way to find out what causes people's satisfaction and dissatisfaction with their jobs than to ask them. Some 30 years ago Frederick Herzberg did just this. He assembled a group of accountants and engineers and asked them to recall incidents that made them feel especially satisfied and especially dissatisfied with their jobs.[1] His results were surprising: Different factors accounted for satisfaction and dissatisfaction. Rather than finding that the presence of certain variables made people feel satisfied and that their absence made them feel dissatisfied, as you might expect, Herzberg found that satisfaction and dissatisfaction stemmed from two different sources. For this reason, his approach is widely referred to as the **two-factor theory of job satisfaction.**

What are the two factors? In general, people were satisfied with aspects of their jobs that had to do with the work itself or to outcomes directly resulting from it. These included things such as chances for promotion, opportunities for personal growth, recognition, responsibility, and achievement. Because these variables were associated with high levels of satisfaction, Herzberg referred to them as *motivators*. However, dissatisfaction was associated with conditions surrounding the job, such as working conditions, pay, security, relations with others, and so on, rather than the work itself. Because these variables prevent dissatisfaction when present, they are referred to as *hygiene factors* (or *maintenance factors*). So, rather than a single continuum anchored at one end by satisfaction and at the other by dissatisfaction, Herzberg conceived of satisfaction and dissatisfaction as separate variables. Motivators, when present at high levels, contribute to job satisfaction, but when absent, do not lead to job dissatisfaction—just less satisfaction. Likewise, hygiene factors only contribute to dissatisfaction when present, but not to satisfaction when absent. You may find the diagram in Figure 4-1 helpful in summarizing these ideas.

> *To keep working conditions enjoyable, managers and support staff for the* **Los Angeles Dodgers** *have offices with glass windows overlooking the stadium. This allows them to watch their team in action on game days.*

This theory has important implications for managing organizations. Specifically, managers would be well-advised to focus their attention on factors known to promote job satisfaction, such as opportunities for personal growth. Indeed, several of today's companies have realized that satisfaction within their work forces is enhanced when they provide opportunities for their employees to develop their repertoire of professional skills on the job. For example, front-line service workers at Marriott Hotels, known as "guest services associates," are hired to perform a variety of tasks, including checking guests in and out, carrying their bags, and so on. Instead of doing just one job, this approach enables Marriott employees to call upon and develop many of their talents, thereby adding to their level of job satisfaction. (If you are thinking that this sounds like an example of *job enrichment,* described in Chapter 3, you are correct. Indeed, two-factor theory was greatly responsible for the development of the job enrichment approach to motivation.)

Two-factor theory also implies that steps should be taken to create conditions that help avoid dissatisfaction—and it specifies the kinds of variables required to do so (i.e., hygiene factors). For example, creating pleasant working conditions may be quite helpful in getting people to avoid being dissatisfied with their jobs. Specifically, research has shown that dissatisfaction is great under conditions that are highly overcrowded, dark, noisy, have extreme tem-

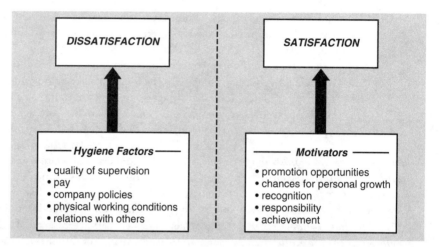

■ *Figure 4-1 Herzberg's Two-Factor Theory*

According to Herzberg's *two-factor theory*, job satisfaction and dissatisfaction are not opposite ends of the same continuum but independent dimensions. Some examples of *hygiene factors*, which lead to dissatisfaction, and *motivators*, which lead to satisfaction, are presented here.

peratures, and poor air quality. These factors, associated with the conditions under which work is performed, but not directly linked to the work itself, contribute much to the levels of job dissatisfaction encountered.

Another approach to job satisfaction, known as **value theory,** takes a broader look at the question of what makes people satisfied. This theory argues that almost any factor can be a source of job satisfaction so long as it is something that people value. The less people have of some aspect of the job (e.g., pay, learning opportunities) relative to the amount they want, the more dissatisfied they will be—especially for those facets of the job that are highly valued. Thus, value theory focuses on discrepancies between what people have and what they want: the greater those discrepancies, the more dissatisfied they will be.

This approach to job satisfaction implies that an effective way to satisfy workers is to find out what they want and, to the extent possible, give it to them. Believe it or not, this is sometimes easier said than done. In fact, organizations sometimes go through great pains to find out how to satisfy their employees. With this in mind, a growing number of companies, particularly big ones, have been systematically surveying their employees. For example, FedEx is so interested in tracking the attitudes of its employees that it has started using a fully automated on-line survey. The company relies on information gained from surveys of its 68,000 U.S.-based employees as the key to

_____ 11. I would be quite pleased to spend the rest of my life working for this organization.

_____ 12. I stay on my job because people would think poorly of me for leaving.

SCORING

1. Add the scores for items 1, 4, 7, and 10. This reflects your degree of *continuance commitment*.

2. Add the scores for items 2, 5, 8, and 11. This reflects your degree of *affective commitment*.

3. Add the scores for items 3, 6, 9, and 12. This reflects your degree of *normative commitment*.

QUESTIONS TO ASK YOURSELF

1. Which form of commitment does the scale reveal you have most? Which do you have least? Are these differences great, or are they highly similar?

2. Did the scale tell you something you didn't already know about yourself, or did it merely reinforce your intuitive beliefs about your own organizational commitment?

3. To what extent is your organizational commitment, as reflected by this scale, related to your interest in quitting your job and taking a new position?

4. How do your answers to these questions compare to those of your classmates? Are your responses similar to theirs or different from them? Why do you think this is?

ted to them demonstrate a great willingness to share and make sacrifices required for the organization to thrive. For example, years ago when Chrysler Corp. was in serious financial trouble, CEO Lee Iacocca demonstrated his commitment to help the company through its difficult period by reducing his annual pay to only $1. Although this move was clearly symbolic of the sacrifices the company wanted all employees to make, there is no doubt that Iacocca's actions cost him a great deal of real money. Had he been less committed to saving Chrysler, a company that is now highly successful, there would have been little incentive for him to be so generous. In fact, a less strongly committed CEO may have been expected to bail out altogether. This example should not be taken as an indication that only highly magnanimous gestures result from commitment. In fact, small acts of good organizational citizenship are also likely to occur among people who are highly committed to their organizations. This makes sense if you consider that it would take people who are highly committed to their organizations to be willing to make the investment needed to give of themselves for the good of the company.

In view of these benefits of organizational commitment, it makes sense for organizations to take the steps necessary to enhance commitment among its employees. We will now describe various ways of doing this.

APPROACHES TO DEVELOPING ORGANIZATIONAL COMMITMENT

Some determinants of organizational commitment fall outside of managers' spheres of control, giving them few opportunities to enhance these feelings. For example, commitment tends to be lower when the economy is such that employment opportunities are plentiful. An abundance of job options will surely lower continuance commitment, and there's not too much a company can do about it. However, although managers cannot control the external economy, they can do several things to make employees want to stay working for their company—that is, to enhance affective commitment.

First, commitment may be enhanced by *enriching jobs*. In other words, people tend to be highly committed to their organizations to the extent that they have a good chance to take control over the way they do their jobs and are recognized for making important contributions. This approach worked well for the Ford Motor Company. In the early 1980s, Ford confronted a crisis of organizational commitment in the face of budget cuts, layoffs, plant closings, lowered product quality, and other threats. In the words of Ernest J. Savoie, the director of Ford's Employee Development Office:

> *The only solution for Ford, we determined was a total transformation of our company ... to accomplish it, we had to earn the commitment of all Ford people. And to acquire that commitment, we had to change the way we managed people.*[6]

With this in mind, Ford instituted its *Employee Involvement* program, a systematic way of involving employees in many aspects of corporate decision making. They not only got to perform a wide variety of tasks but also enjoyed considerable autonomy in doing them (e.g., freedom to schedule work, and to stop the assembly line if needed). By 1985, Ford employees were more committed to their jobs—so much so, in fact, that the acrimony that usually resulted at contract renewal time had all but vanished. Although employee involvement may not be the cure for all commitment ills, it was clearly highly effective in this case.

Another way of effectively enhancing employee commitment is by *align-*

ing the interests of the company with those of the employees. Many companies do this quite directly by introducing **profit-sharing plans**—that is, incentive plans in which employees receive bonuses in proportion to the company's profitability. Such plans are often quite effective in enhancing organizational commitment, especially when they are perceived to be administered fairly. For example, the Holland, Michigan auto parts manufacturer, Prince Corporation, gives its employees yearly bonuses based on several indices: the company's overall profitability, the employee's unit's profitability, and each individual's performance. Similarly, workers at Allied Plywood Corporation (a wholesaler of building materials in Alexandria, Virginia) receive cash bonuses based on company profits, but these are distributed monthly as well as yearly. The monthly bonuses are the same size for all, whereas the annual bonuses are given in proportion to each employee's individual contributions to total profit, days worked, and performance. These plans are good examples of some of the things companies are doing to enhance commitment. Although the plans differ, their underlying rationale is the same: By letting employees share in the company's profitability, they are more likely to see their own interests as consistent with those of their company. And, when these interests are aligned, commitment is high.

Third and finally, organizational commitment may be enhanced by starting at the very beginning—that is, *recruiting and selecting newcomers whose values closely match those of the organization.* The better the match, the higher the organizational commitment that may be expected. Recruiting is not only important insofar as it provides opportunities to find people whose values fit those of the organization, but also because of the dynamics of the recruitment process itself. In this connection, research has shown that the more an organization invests in someone by working hard to lure him or her to the company, the more that individual is likely to return the same investment of energy by expressing commitment toward the organization. In other words, companies that show their employees they care enough to work hard to attract them are likely to find strong commitment among those who are so actively courted.

In conclusion, it is useful to think of organizational commitment as an attitude that may be influenced by managerial actions. Not only might people be selected who are predisposed to be committed to the organization, but also various measures can be taken to enhance commitment in the face of indications that it is suffering.

NEGATIVE ATTITUDES TOWARD OUR COWORKERS: PREJUDICE

Thus far, our discussion has focused on two different attitude objects, jobs and organizations. However, we also develop attitudes toward another important element of the work environment—other people. Such attitudes are highly problematic when they are negative, especially when these feelings are based on misguided beliefs and prompt harmful behavior. **Prejudice** is the term used to refer to attitudes of this type. Prejudicial attitudes often hold people back, creating an invisible barrier to success commonly known as the **glass ceiling.**

Because prejudicial attitudes can have devastating effects on both people and organizations, we will closely examine them in this section of the book. To give you a feel for how serious prejudices can be, we will describe specific targets of prejudice in the workplace and the special nature of the problems they confront. We will then follow up on this by describing various strategies that have been used to overcome prejudice in the workplace. Before doing this, however, we will describe exactly what is meant by prejudice and distinguish it from related concepts.

ANATOMY OF PREJUDICE: BASIC DISTINCTIONS

To understand prejudice it is useful to examine the three components of attitudes described earlier—the cognitive component, the evaluative component, and the behavioral component. As you may recall, the cognitive component refers to things we believe about an attitude object, whether or not they are accurate. In the case of prejudice, we tend to rely on beliefs about people based on the groups to which they belong. So, to the extent that we believe that people from certain groups possess certain characteristics, knowing that someone belongs to a group will lead us to believe certain things about them. Beliefs of this type are referred to as **stereotypes.**

As you surely realize, stereotypes, whether positive or negative, are generally inaccurate. If we knew more about someone than that which we would assume based on his or her membership in various groups, we would probably make more accurate judgments. However, to the extent that we often find it difficult or inconvenient to learn everything we need to know about someone, we frequently rely on stereotypes as a kind of mental shortcut. So, for example, if you believe that individuals belonging to group X are lazy, and that person A belongs to group X, you would be predisposed to believe that person A is lazy too. Although this may be logical, engaging in such stereotyping runs the risk of misjudging person A. After all, he or she might not be lazy at all despite the fact that you assumed so based on the stereotype.

Nonetheless, assume you believe person A to be lazy. How do you feel about lazy people? Chances are that you don't like them—that is, your evaluation of person A would be negative. Would you want to hire a lazy individual, such as A, for your company? Probably not. Thus, you would be predisposed against hiring A. Your prejudicial attitude toward person A is clear. Such attitudes are particularly harmful when the behavioral predispositions turn into actual behaviors. In such instances, people become the victims of others' prejudices—that is, **discrimination.** If prejudice is an attitude, then you can think

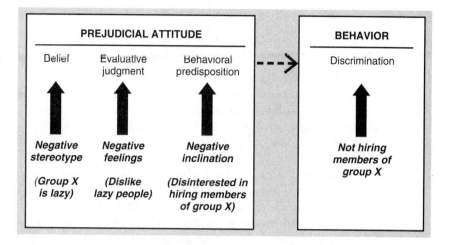

■ *Figure 4-3 Prejudice Versus Discrimination*

Prejudice is an attitude consisting of negative beliefs known as *stereotypes*, negative feelings about those beliefs, and negative predispositions toward people described by those stereotypes. These attitudes may or may not lead to behavior consistent with it—that is, *discrimination*.

of discrimination as the behavior consistent with that attitude. (For a summary of this process, and this example, see Figure 4-3.)

Completing our example, you might refrain from hiring person *A*, or giving him or her a positive recommendation. By acting this way, you would be behaving consistently with your attitude. Logical? Perhaps, but not in the best interest of the individual involved. After all, your behavior may be based on an attitude formed on the basis of inaccurate stereotypes. For this reason, it is important to identify ways of overcoming the natural tendency to base our attitudes on stereotypes and to unfairly discriminate between people on this basis. Later in this chapter we will outline some strategies shown to be effective in this regard. Before doing so, however, it would be useful to give you a feel for the seriousness of prejudicial attitudes in organizations today.

EVERYBODY IS A VICTIM OF PREJUDICE!

Unfortunate as it may be, we are all potential victims of prejudicial attitudes. Indeed, no matter what personal characteristics we may have, there may very well be people out there who are prejudiced against us. This is not surprising if you consider that people hold stereotypes about many different things. Whatever you look like, wherever you're from, whatever your interests, chances are good that at least some people will approach you with predisposed beliefs about what you're like. Sadly, for many groups of people, these beliefs have negative connotations, leading to discriminatory behavior. Here we will de-

scribe some of the most prevalent targets of discrimination in American society today.

Prejudice Based on Age.   As people are living longer and the birthrate is holding steady, the median age of Americans is rising all the time. Despite this
trend—often referred to as the "graying of America"—prejudice against older
people is all too common. Although U.S. laws (e.g., the Age Discrimination in
Employment Act) have done much to counter employment discrimination
against older workers, prejudices continue to exist. Part of the problem resides
in stereotypes that older workers are too set in their ways to train, and that they
will tend to be sick or accident-prone. As in the case of many attitudes, these
prejudices are not founded on accurate information. In fact, survey findings
paint just the opposite picture: A Yankelovich poll of 400 companies found that
older workers are considered very good or excellent, especially in such critical
areas as punctuality, commitment to quality, and practical knowledge.

It is not just older workers who find themselves victims of prejudice but
younger ones too. For them, part of the problem is that as the average age of
the work force advances (from an average of 29 in 1976 to 39 in 2000), there
develops a gap in expectations between the more experienced older workers
who are in charge, and the younger employees just entering the work force.
Specifically, compared to older workers, who grew up in a different time,
today's under-thirty employees view the world differently. They are more
prone to question the way things are done, to not see the government as an
ally, and to not expect loyalty. They are likely to consider self-development to
be their main interest and are willing to learn whatever skills are necessary to
make them marketable. These differing perspectives may lead older employees, who are likely to be their superiors, to feel uncomfortable with their
younger colleagues. This is especially problematic as the nature of work shifts
so that people with different skills are brought together to work in teams (see
Chapter 7).

One reason why negative attitudes based on age persist despite evidence
to the contrary is that people often have strongly held beliefs about the activities that are most appropriate at different ages. For example, first-line supervisors are implicitly assumed to be in their late twenties or early thirties, department heads should be in their mid-thirties to mid-forties, and vice presidents
should be at least forty. Given such beliefs, individuals who attain a position
sooner than expected may profit from an age-related halo, whereas those who
attain it later than anticipated may be evaluated negatively. To the extent that
people continue to associate certain ages with certain job levels, it should not
be surprising to find that age-related prejudices persist.

Prejudice Based on Physical Condition.   There are currently some 43 million
Americans with disabilities, 14.6 million of whom are of working age, between
16 and 65. However, less than 30 percent of these individuals are working—

and among these, most only work part time or irregularly. Clearly, there exist barriers that are keeping millions of potentially productive people from gainful employment.

Legal remedies have been enacted to help break down these barriers. For example, in the early 1990s, legislation known as the Americans with Disabilities Act (ADA) was enacted in the United States to protect the rights of people with physical and mental disabilities. Its rationale is simple: Just because an employee is limited in some way, it does not mean that accommodations cannot be made to help the individual perform his or her job. Companies that do not comply are subject to legal damages. In fact, the first award under the ADA, $572,000, was presented to an employee fired after missing work while recovering from cancer, and as many as 15,000 discrimination claims were filed in the law's first year alone.

Many companies are finding that it is possible for them to meet the needs of disabled employees quite easily and with little expense. For example, Greiner Engineering in Irving, Texas was able to accommodate its employees in wheelchairs by simply substituting a lighter-weight door on its restrooms and raising a drafting table by putting bricks under its legs. Although not all accommodations are as easily made, experts are confident that the ADA will be an effective way of minimizing discrimination against employees based on their physical condition.

Importantly, the most formidable barriers are not physical ones but attitudinal. Most people who are not physically challenged don't know how to treat and what to expect from those who are. Experts advise that people with disabilities don't want to be pitied but respected for the skills and commitment to work they bring to their jobs. That is, they wish to be recognized as whole people who just happen to have a disabling condition, rather than a special class of "handicapped people."

Prejudice Based on Sexual Orientation.   Unlike people with physical disabilities, who are protected from discrimination by federal law, no such protection exists (yet, at least) for another group whose members are frequently victims of prejudice—gay men and lesbian women. (However, several states and over 100 municipalities have enacted laws to protect the rights of gays and lesbians in the workplace.) Unfortunately, although more people than ever are tolerant of nontraditional sexual orientations, antihomosexual prejudice still exists in the workplace. Indeed, about two-thirds of CEOs from major companies admit their reluctance to put a homosexual on a top-management committee. Not surprisingly, without the law to protect them, and widespread prejudices against them, many gays and lesbians are reluctant to openly make their sexual orientations known.

Fears of being "discovered," exposed as a homosexual, represent a considerable source of stress among such individuals. For example, a gay vice president of a large office-equipment manufacturer admitted in a magazine in-

terview that he'd like to become the company's CEO, but fears that his chances would be ruined if his sexual orientation were to become known. If the pressure of going through working life with a disguised identity is disruptive, imagine the cumulative effect of such efforts on organizations in which several employees are homosexual. Such misdirection of energy can become quite a serious threat to productivity. In the words of consultant Mark Kaplan, "gay and lesbian employees use a lot of time and stress trying to conceal a big part of their identity."[7] To work in an organization with a homophobic culture, to have to endure jokes slurring gays and lesbians, can easily distract even the most highly focused employees.

To help avoid these problems—and out of respect for diverse sexual orientations—many organizations have adopted internal fair employment policies that include sexual orientation. In addition, some companies are actively working to prohibit discrimination on the basis of sexual orientation. Extending this idea, still other companies are now extending fringe benefits, which traditionally have been offered exclusively to opposite-sex partners, to same-sex domestic partners as well. For example, companies such as Ben and Jerry's Homemade (in Waterbury, Vermont), MCA (in Universal City, California), and Beth Israel Medical Center (in New York) extend fringe benefits to their employees' partners regardless of whether they are of the same sex or the opposite sex. Russ Campanello, vice president of human resources for Lotus Development Corp. (the software developer recently purchased by IBM), notes that his organization's reputation for having such a program has been an important key to its success in attracting highly talented technical personnel. Clearly, although some companies are passively discouraging diversity with respect to sexual orientation, others encourage it, much to their own—and their employees'—advantages.

Prejudice Based on Race or National Origin.   The history of the United States is marked by struggles over acceptance of people of various racial and ethnic groups. Although the American workplace is now more diverse than ever, it is clear that prejudice lingers on.

Not only do members of various minority groups believe they are the victims of prejudice and discrimination, they are also taking action. As evidence, the number of complaints of discrimination based on national origin filed at the Equal Employment Opportunity Commission (EEOC) has been increasing steadily in recent years. Moreover, discrimination victims have been winning such cases. For example, in 1993 the Supreme Court of the state of Washington upheld a $389,000 judgment against a Seattle bank brought by a Cambodian-American employee fired because of his accent.

Outside the courtroom, companies that discriminate pay in other ways as well—notably, in lost talent and productivity. According to EEOC Commissioner Joy Cherian, employees who feel victimized "may not take the ini-

tiative to introduce inventions and other innovations," adding, "every day, American employers are losing millions of dollars because these talents are frozen."[8] Some companies are taking concrete steps to help minimize these problems. For example, AT&T Bell Labs in Murray Hill, New Jersey is working with managers to find ways of helping the company's many ethnic minority employees get promoted more rapidly. Similarly, Hughes Aircraft Co. of Los Angeles has been assigning mentors to minority group employees to help teach them about the company's culture and the skills needed to succeed. Although both examples are only modest steps, they represent very encouraging trends intended to help reduce a long-standing problem.

Prejudice Against Women.   There can be no mistaking the widespread—and evergrowing—presence of women in today's work force. In 1991 women composed 46 percent of the American work force, up from 43 percent in 1981. Also, in 1991, 41 percent of managers were women, compared to only 27 percent ten years earlier. Still, female senior executives (individuals reporting directly to the CEO) are relatively rare—only 3 percent are women. Is this likely to change in the next ten years? Eighty-two percent of executives completing a recent *Business Week*/Harris poll indicated that it was not likely that their company would have a female CEO in the next ten years. Thus, it appears that "women populate corporations, but they rarely run them."[9] Equality for women in the workplace is improving, although it is a slow victory, to be sure.

> *Although women typically don't reach the top ranks of management in the world of retailing, this is not the case at* **Nordstrom**. *Two-thirds of store managers and one-quarter of its top officers are women.*

Why is this the case? Although sufficient time may not have passed to allow more women to work their way into the top echelons of organizations, there appear to be more formidable barriers. Most notably, it is clear that powerful *sex role stereotypes* persist, narrow-minded beliefs about the kinds of tasks for which women are most appropriately suited. For example, 8 percent of the respondents to the *Business Week*/Harris poll indicated that females are not aggressive or determined enough to make it to the top. Although this number is small, it provides good evidence of the persistence of a nagging—and highly limiting—stereotype.

It is also possible that many women do not advance as quickly as men because they have lower expectations of career success. For example, female college graduates generally expect to receive lower starting and peak salaries than males. This may be due to several factors, including the tendency for females to specialize in lower-paying areas, and the observation that women are, in general, paid less than men (about one-third less overall), and come to expect less. Whatever the basis, people tend to get what they expect. Thus, the lower expectations held by females may be one factor operating against them.

STRATEGIES FOR OVERCOMING WORKPLACE PREJUDICE: MANAGING A DIVERSE WORK FORCE

It's one thing to identify prejudicial attitudes and quite another to eliminate them. Traditionally, in the United States, **affirmative action programs** have been used to promote the ethical treatment of women and members of minority groups in organizations. Derived from civil rights initiatives of the 1960s, these generally involve efforts to give employment opportunities to groups of individuals who traditionally have been disadvantaged. The rationale is quite reasonable: By encouraging the hiring of women and minority group members into positions in which they traditionally have been underrepresented, more people will be exposed to them, forcing them to see that their negative stereotypes were misguided. Then, as these stereotypes begin to crumble, prejudice will be reduced, along with the discrimination on which it is based. After some 30 years of experience with affirmative action programs, there have been some appreciable gains in the opportunities available to women and minority groups. However, prejudice continues to exist, as does the glass ceiling that limits all employees from enjoying truly equal opportunities in organizations.

In recent years, organizations have become increasingly proactive in their attempts to eliminate prejudice and have taken it upon themselves to go beyond affirmative action requirements. Their approach is not just to hire a broader group of people than usual, but to create an atmosphere in which diverse groups can flourish. They are not merely trying to obey the law or attempting to be socially responsible, but they recognize that diversity is a business issue. As one consultant put it, "A corporation's success will increasingly be determined by its managers' ability to naturally tap the full potential of a diverse work force."[10] It is with this goal in mind that three-quarters of American organizations are adapting **diversity management programs**—efforts to celebrate diversity by creating supportive, not just neutral, work environments for women and minorities. Simply put, the underlying philosophy of diversity management programs is that cracking the glass ceiling requires that women and minorities are not just tolerated, but valued. This sentiment was expressed nicely by Darlene Siedschlaw, the director of diversity for U.S. West (the Denver-based telecommunications firm), when she said, "Tapping all available human resources is the key to our corporate survival."[11]

Diversity management programs consist of various efforts to not only create opportunities for diverse groups of people within organizations, but also to train people to embrace differences between them. For example, Xerox's "Step-Up" program, in existence for some 30 years, has been one of the most thorough and sustained efforts to hire minority group members and train them to succeed. Similarly, Pacific Bell and U.S. West also have made great strides at reaching out to minority group members (e.g., through internship programs), creating jobs for them in positions that have broad opportunities for

advancement. Although they have been highly successful, these efforts have focused more on changing the system so as to give opportunities to a diverse group of individuals than on changing the attitudes of the people involved.

Digital Equipment Corporation (DEC) has extended these initiatives in its "Valuing Differences" program, an approach that focuses on not just accepting people (e.g., giving them opportunities to succeed), but valuing them *because* of their differences. DEC officials rationalize that the broader the spectrum of differences in the workplace, the richer the depth of ideas upon which the organization can draw—hopefully, leading it to be more productive. DEC does several things to capitalize on the differences between its employees. For example, it invests in special training sessions designed to get employees to understand the diversity in their workplace, examining the cultural norms of the different people who work there. DEC also celebrates these differences by sponsoring a calendar of special cultural and educational events designed to provide ways of learning about different people (e.g., "Black History Month," "Gay and Lesbian Pride Week," and "International Women's Month"). As part of this, they help organize support groups for members of various groups who find it beneficial to meet with others of their own race or nationality who can give them needed emotional support and/or career guidance. Finally, DEC supports an informal network of small ongoing discussion groups referred to as *core groups*. These are groups of between seven and nine members who meet monthly to openly discuss their stereotypes and ways of improving relationships with others they regard as different. DEC officials and employees are convinced that its "Valuing Differences" program is a huge success.

■ *Table 4-1 Diversity Management: Some Current Practices*

Many of today's companies are taking proactive measures to celebrate the diverse backgrounds of their employees. Presented here are just a few illustrative practices. (Based on material in Rosen, 1991; see Note 6.)

Company	Program	Description
Gannett	Partners in Progress	Promotes advancement of minorities and women in its broadcasting and advertising operations.
Dow Jones	Quad Squads	Mentoring programs in which senior managers meet with and counsel a white male, a woman, and a member of a minority group.
Du Pont Corp.	Committee to Achieve Cultural Diversity	Focus groups leading to career development programs and fair performance evaluations.
Pace Foods	Bilingual Operations	All staff meetings and company publications are presented in both English and Spanish.
AT&T	Gay and Lesbian Awareness Week	Designates one week in which gay and lesbian issues are discussed and celebrated.

DEC's efforts at managing diversity represent just one of a broad range of approaches that have been used by companies in recent years. Pepsi-Cola, American Express Travel Related Services, and the accounting firm Coopers & Lybrand are just a few of the companies that also have been actively engaged in diversity management efforts. For a summary of some of the many different approaches to diversity management that have been used by organizations, see Table 4-1 on p. 117.

Although most companies have been pleased with the ways their diversity management efforts have promoted harmony between employees, such programs are not automatically successful. For diversity management activities to be successful, experts caution that they must focus on accepting a range

GROUP EXERCISE

Auditing Organizational Biases

Is your organization biased against certain groups of people? Even if you answer "no," chances are good that you may have missed some subtle and unintentional forms of prejudice lurking about. This exercise is designed to help you uncover some of·these.

DIRECTIONS

1. Reproduce the following checklist, making one copy for each member of the class.

2. Guided by this checklist, gather the information indicated for the organization in which you work (or, if you don't work, for any organization to which you have access) and check all items that apply.

3. In answering, either use your existing knowledge of the company, or ask those who might know. (If you do ask others, be sure to tell them that it's for a class project!)

4. Report back to the class after one week.

Does Your Organization . . .

_____ have signs and manuals in English only despite the fact that several employees speak other languages?

_____ ignore important holidays celebrated by people of certain cultures, such as Martin Luther King Day, Yom Kippur, Cinco de Mayo, or Chinese New Year?

of differences between people. That is, they should not treat someone as special because he or she is a member of a certain group, but because of the unique skills, or abilities he or she brings to the job. To the extent that managers are trained to seek, recognize, and develop the talents of their employees without regard to the groups to which they belong, they will help break down the stereotypes on which prejudices are based. This, in turn, will bring down the barriers that made diversity training necessary in the first place. (One of the most difficult steps in eliminating prejudicial attitudes involves recognizing the sometimes subtle ways that these have infiltrated the culture of an organization. The **Group Exercise** below presents one useful way to help identify these negative attitudes.)

_____ limit social events to married people?

_____ restrict training opportunities available to women and people from minority groups?

_____ emphasize male-oriented sporting events, such as football?

_____ limit its recruitment efforts to colleges and universities that have predominately white students?

_____ hire predominately females for secretarial positions?

_____ discourage styles of dress that allow for the expression of varied cultural and ethnic backgrounds?

QUESTIONS FOR DISCUSSION

1. How many of the eight items did you check? How about the members of the class? What was the class average?

2. What items represented the biggest sources of bias? What are the potential consequences of these actions?

3. What steps could be taken to change these practices? Do you think the company would be willing to do so?

4. Going beyond this checklist, what other subtle (or not so subtle) signs of institutional prejudice can you identify in your company?

5. To what extent do you believe that your own awareness of prejudicial practices has been enhanced by this exercise?

SUMMARY:
PUTTING IT TO USE

Job satisfaction refers to people's attitudes toward their jobs. The *two-factor theory of job satisfaction* distinguishes between two separate types of variables: those associated with the job itself (e.g., chances for growth and development), known as *motivators*, and those associated with conditions surrounding the job (e.g., pay, relations with others), known as *hygiene factors*. Motivators promote job satisfaction, and hygiene factors help avoid job dissatisfaction. Drawing on this theory, companies have sought to promote satisfaction by giving people more varied work, and to avoid dissatisfaction by creating pleasant working conditions.

Another approach to job satisfaction, *value theory* claims that satisfaction results when there exist only small gaps between the things people want from their jobs and what they already have. Employee surveys are often used to gather this information. Organizations need to be concerned about avoiding employee dissatisfaction insofar as it has been linked to two problems—*voluntary turnover* and *absenteeism*. Although these links are not exceptionally strong, the problems can be costly. Also weak is the link between job satisfaction and traditional measures of performance (e.g., quantity and quality). However, informal forms of helping one's company and coworkers, known as *organizational citizenship behaviors* (e.g., helping a coworker in need), are strongly linked to job satisfaction. Methods to promote job satisfaction include: paying people fairly, improving the quality of supervision, decentralizing the control of organizational power, and matching people to jobs that are congruent with their interests.

Organizational commitment refers to people's attitudes toward their organizations. Three types include: *continuance commitment,* the desire to remain because of the high costs of quitting (e.g., lack of alternative jobs), *affective commitment,* the desire to remain due to agreement with the company's values, and *normative commitment,* the desire to remain due to social pressures against leaving. Absenteeism and turnover are lower when people are highly committed to their organizations. Moreover, committed employees are likely to make the sacrifices needed for their companies to prosper. Organizational commitment can be enhanced by enriching jobs, aligning the interests of the company with those of the employees, and recruiting and selecting prospective employees whose values closely match those of the organization.

An all too prevalent negative attitude in organizations today is *prejudice*—negative attitudes toward other people. Prejudices are frequently based on erroneous beliefs about people based on characteristics associated with their group membership, known as *stereotypes*. Prejudices predispose people to engage in discrimination—acting in ways that disadvantage others. Everyone is a potential victim of prejudicial attitudes. Historically, victims of prejudice in the workplace have included employees who are particularly young or old, those who have physical or mental handicaps, gays and lesbians, members of racial and ethnic minority groups (e.g., African-Americans, Asian-Americans, and Hispanic-Americans), and women (despite the fact that they comprise almost 50 percent of the work force!). Such individuals frequently face a *glass ceiling,* an invisible barrier of prejudice that holds them back in the workplace.

Affirmative action programs consist of laws designed to promote equal opportunities for members of groups that have been underrepresented in the workplace. Although greater equality now exists because of such initiatives, today's organizations are going a step further by creating atmospheres in which differences between people are celebrated and members of different groups can flourish. These efforts are collectively known as *diversity management programs.* They have included efforts to attract and train people from diverse groups, and to support activities that enable them to celebrate (rather than hide or merely tolerate) their backgrounds.

You Be the Consultant

The president of a small manufacturing firm comes to you with a problem: The company is spending a lot of money training new employees, but 75 percent of them quit after working less than a year. Worse, they are taking jobs at the company's biggest competitor. Answer the following questions relevant to this situation based on the material in this chapter.

1. Drawing on research and theory on job satisfaction, what would you suspect is the cause of the turnover? What advice can you offer about how to eliminate the problem?

2. Drawing on research and theory on organizational commitment, what would you suspect is the cause of the turnover? What advice can you offer about how to eliminate the problem?

3. Suppose you find out that the greatest levels of dissatisfaction exist among employees belonging to minority groups. What would you recommend doing to eliminate the prejudice that may be responsible for the turnover?

CHAPTER 5

Joining Up and Fitting In: Socialization, Culture, and Careers

PREVIEW OF CHAPTER HIGHLIGHTS

Organizational socialization is the process through which people move from outsiders to participating members of their organizations. It involves three stages—anticipatory socialization, the encounter stage, and the metamorphosis stage.

A mentor is someone, usually older and more experienced, who advises, counsels, and enhances the personal development of a new employee, referred to as a **protégé**. Despite potential costs, mentor–protégé relationships generally benefit both parties.

Organizational culture is the set of attitudes, values, behavioral norms, and expectations shared by organization members. Culture is transmitted by several means, such as symbols, stories, jargon, ceremonies, and statements of principle.

Organizational culture changes as the composition of the work force changes, mergers and acquisitions occur, and planned changes in operations are carried out.

Careers are the evolving sequences of work experiences over time. They move through three stages—early career, mid-career, and late career, each of which is associated with its own special issues.

Today's organizations are making adjustments to accommodate the special needs of **dual-career couples** who face **work–family conflicts**. These include flextime, family leaves, child care, personal support, and job sharing.

If there is only one aspect of life at work that all people have in common, it is surely the experience of being new to the job. Indeed, everyone has a first day, and everyone has to learn the ropes. The process of becoming a member of an organization and learning all about it is known as *organizational socialization.* This important process is one of the major topics covered in this chapter.

As you might imagine, becoming socialized involves more than learning where the lunchroom is and what forms to fill out. It also involves coming to know what the organization stands for—that is, the beliefs, expectations, and values shared by other people in the company referred to as *organizational culture.* As we will describe in this chapter, embracing an organization's culture is an important requirement for fitting in with others in the company.

When people do fit in, they are likely to advance their way through a series of positions. Over the course of people's lives the sequences of jobs they hold are referred to as *careers.* Insofar as organizational socialization, organizational culture, and careers are all related aspects of the processes of joining up and fitting in, they will all be discussed in this chapter.

ORGANIZATIONAL SOCIALIZATION: BECOMING PART OF THE COMPANY

It's your first day on the job. After years of training and experience, you have all the skills needed to succeed, but you still have a lot to learn. Some things may be minor, such as finding out where to find the coffee machine or the water fountain. Others may be more critical, such as policies regarding the treatment of customers or informal standards about how hard to work. The process through which people move from outsiders to effective, participating members of their organizations is referred to as **organizational socialization.** In this section of the chapter we will describe this process and the ways organizations go about making the socialization process effective.

THE THREE STAGES OF SOCIALIZATION

As you might imagine, people do not become fully socialized members of their organizations instantly, or even after a few weeks. Rather, organizational socialization is a gradual process. In fact, scientists have characterized it as involving three discrete stages.[1]

The first stage, **anticipatory socialization,** is concerned with "getting in." This involves learning about an organization from the outside, before one may even consider becoming a part of it. If this sounds strange, just ask yourself if there is a specific organization in which you would be interested in working someday. What makes you so attracted to it? If you can answer this question, even tentatively, it's clear that you may know quite a bit about an organization even before you begin working there.

How do such expectations develop? First, as friends or relatives who work in an organization share their experiences with you, you may develop an image of the company. Second, there are also formal sources, such as professional journals, magazine and newspaper articles, and corporate annual reports. These also provide information that may help cultivate an impression of what it would be like to work in a certain organization. Unfortunately, both formal and informal sources of information may be biased. For example, you may only hear your acquaintances talk about their jobs when they have negative things to say. By the same token, press reports about organizations are often reserved for sensationalistic accounts of either extremely positive news (e.g., record-breaking earnings) or negative news (e.g., violations of moral standards). Thus, although we often rely on secondhand information from personal contacts and popular press accounts of organizational activities as bases for our judgments about organizations, it is important to keep in mind that the information they provide may be questionable.

The most direct way of learning about an organization is to get the information "straight from the horse's mouth," so to speak—that is, by listening to corporate recruiters. Sometimes, however, these individuals paint overly rosy pictures of their organizations. In response to intense competition for the best job candidates, they may describe their companies in glowing terms, glossing over internal problems and emphasizing the positive aspects of the organization. The result is that potential employees often receive unrealistically positive impressions of what it would be like to work in those organizations. When new employees actually arrive on the job and find that their expectations are not met, strong feelings of disappointment, confusion, and disillusionment may result—what is referred to as **entry shock.** In fact, research has shown that the less employees' job expectations are met, the less satisfied and committed they are, and the more likely they are to think about quitting, and to actually do so.

With this in mind, the trick for corporate recruiters is not to give job candidates unrealistically positive descriptions, but rather, highly accurate descriptions—both positive and negative—of the jobs they will perform and the organizations they will enter. Such descriptions are called **realistic job previews.**[2] Research has shown that people exposed to realistic job previews later report higher satisfaction and show lower turnover than those who receive glowing but often unrealistic information about the companies in question. By making their expectations more realistic, employees are less likely to resign when they confront negative conditions. For this reason, it makes sense for recruiters to not only inform prospective employees about the many benefits of working for their companies (as they are already prone to do), but to supplement this information with realistic accounts of what life will be like in the organization.

Several companies have been doing just this. For example, recruiters at AT&T have used realistic job previews to recruit operators and customer service representatives, and at NBD Bank they have been used to recruit tellers.

In probably the largest-scale example, realistic job previews are used in the process of recruiting men and women for all branches of the Canadian Armed Forces. Clearly, these organizations have a great deal of confidence in realistic job previews as a tool for avoiding entry shock and avoiding problems associated with turnover.

The second stage in organizational socialization, the **encounter stage,** begins when individuals actually assume their new duties. During this stage, they face several key tasks. First, of course, they must master the skills required by their new jobs. Second, they must become oriented to the practices and procedures of the new organization—that is, the way things are done there. Third, new members of an organization must establish good social relations with others. They must get to know these people and gain their acceptance. Only when they do can they become effectively functioning members of the work team.

It is during the encounter stage that formal **corporate orientation programs** are conducted. These are sessions designed to teach new employees about their organizations. This includes not only the ways they operate but also information about their histories, missions, and traditions. Such programs are considered a vital part of employee training insofar as they help new employees fit in and understand what their organization is all about. Although much of what is covered in such sessions may be picked up informally over time, formal orientation programs are highly efficient ways of indoctrinating new employees and of introducing them to company officials. Of course, such efforts are merely supplements to the informal socialization between coworkers that may be expected to go on continuously. (To get a feel for the variety of corporate orientation programs used by organizations in your community, see the **Group Exercise** on p. 126.)

New employees at **Valasis Communications,** *a printer of cents-off coupons, come to learn about their company in a highly personal way: They are given personalized welcome notes from their fellow employees, including the company president.*

The third stage of organizational socialization, the **metamorphosis stage,** occurs as the individual enters an organization and attains full member status. Just as a caterpillar undergoes a metamorphosis when it becomes a butterfly, so too does a trainee when he or she becomes a full-fledged member of the organization. Sometimes this entry is marked by a formal event, such as a dinner, reception, or graduation ceremony. At this time, we can expect one's title to change from a temporary one, such as trainee or apprentice, to a permanent one, such as associate or partner. In other cases, especially when training has been short or informal, full acceptance into the work group may not be marked by any specific ceremony at all. Instead, it may be acknowledged by informal actions, such as being invited to lunch by one's new coworkers.

Whatever form it takes, the metamorphosis phase of socialization marks important shifts both for individuals and for organizations. Employees now make permanent adjustments to their jobs (e.g., they resolve conflicting de-

Corporate Orientation: What Really Goes On?

To see how seriously organizations take the process of organizational socialization, it is useful to survey companies about the formal practices they use. This exercise is designed to generate an inventory of the corporate orientation programs used by companies in your area.

DIRECTIONS

1. As a class, generate a list of the largest companies in your community. (Larger companies are more likely to have formal programs than smaller ones.) Then assign one student to each company.

2. Each student should call the company to which he or she is assigned and ask to speak to someone in the human resources department. (Because you represent your school, be sure to act extremely professional!)

3. After reaching the appropriate person, politely explain that as part of a class project, you are seeking material describing various companies' corporate orientation programs and that you would like information on theirs.

4. Either arrange to pick up written materials in person, or set up a time when it is mutually convenient to discuss the program over the phone (if so, take careful notes on what is said).

5. Carefully review the materials, or your notes, and come to class prepared to report on the company's orientation activities.

6. In class, each student should take a turn describing the corporate orientation practices he or she found. As each student speaks, the instructor should summarize the information by writing notes on the board.

QUESTIONS FOR DISCUSSION

1. Generally, companies are interested in sharing information about themselves. Did you find that the companies contacted were willing to disclose the requested information, or were they reluctant to do so?

2. What formal practices (e.g., training seminars, policy manuals, and so on) were most commonly used for orientation programs?

3. What aspects of the company were most frequently covered in those programs (e.g., company values, pay policies, and so on)?

4. Were there any aspects of employee socialization that you were surprised to find not covered in the formal programs?

5. What were the most unusual practices found by anyone in the class? Do you think these programs would be effective if used in other companies? Why or why not?

mands between their jobs and their personal lives). And organizations begin treating them as if they will be long-term members of the work team.

MENTORING: INDIVIDUAL SOCIALIZATION

Some of the most effective forms of socialization involve the one-on-one contact between senior and junior people. For example, at Fu Associates Ltd. (a computer consulting firm in Arlington, Virginia) all new employees start out working directly with a mid-level manager who shows them the ropes. After a few months, Ed Fu, the owner and senior systems analyst, selects a few of the more promising new employees to work with him on important projects. This is an example of **mentoring**—the process by which a more experienced employee, known as a **mentor,** advises, counsels, and otherwise enhances the personal development of a new employee, known as a **protégé.** If you've ever had an older, more experienced employee take you under his or her wing and guide you, then you probably already know how valuable mentoring can be. Indeed, research has shown that mentoring is strongly associated with career success: The more mentoring people receive, the more promotions and pay raises they subsequently receive during their careers.[3]

Trade-offs in Mentor–Protégé Relationships. Mentors do many important things for their protégés. For example, they provide much-needed emotional support and confidence. For those who are just starting out and are likely to be insecure about their abilities, this can be a big help. Mentors also help pave the way for their protégés' job success, such as by nominating them for promotions and by providing opportunities for them to demonstrate their competence. They also suggest useful strategies for achieving work objectives—especially ones that protégés might not generate for themselves. In doing all these things, they help bring the protégé to the attention of top management—a necessary first step for advancement. Finally, mentors often protect their protégés from the repercussions of errors and help them avoid situations that may be risky for their careers.

"True mentoring is a process by which you buy into another's dream," according to Ben Borne, a human resources consultant. "It is a dynamic partnering that benefits all the participants."[4] The main benefits to protégés, of course, are the various types of career support just described. But Mr. Borne is correct in implying that mentor–protégé relationships may benefit the mentor as well. Indeed, it would be misleading to depict mentors as totally selfless benefactors who seek nothing in return for their guidance.

Often people become mentors because they are so very appreciative of having received such help earlier in their careers. For example, Mr. Borne recalls how senior managers at Motorola and Kaiser Aluminum helped him get started some 35 years ago. Knowing what it's like to have people pay attention to you, he is pleased to be in the position to offer help to junior colleagues who now need his assistance. In other words, mentors may reap psychological benefits from feeling needed, and a sense of accomplishment in helping the younger generation.

However, gratification is not the only source of benefit for mentors. Often, in exchange for their guidance, mentors expect certain things from their protégés that help them in other ways. First, they expect their protégés to work hard at the tasks assigned to them—a way of getting a highly productive employee. Second, mentors often expect protégés to be loyal supporters within their organization. (After all, they are now members of the mentor's team!) Third, mentors may gain recognition from others in the company for their work in helping nurture young talent, and can vicariously enjoy the successes achieved by their protégés.

This discussion of benefits is not meant to imply that mentor–protégé relationships are totally without costs. Indeed, there are several potential risks. For example, protégés may find that their own success hinges on the success of their mentor. If the mentor should happen to be a falling star in the company and suffers setbacks, the protégé's own career may be in jeopardy. Likewise, because the protégé's behavior reflects on the mentor, any failures on the part of the protégé may harm the mentor's reputation. In addition, there's always the risk that a mentor's advice might not be as good as possible. This can be problematic, regardless of whether the protégé follows the bad advice (and receives a negative outcome), or does not follow it (and risks insulting the mentor). To the extent that the mentor and protégé blame each other for the poor result, their relationship is likely to develop an uncomfortable level of conflict. Finally, there's always the risk that protégés will become so highly dependent on their mentors that they will become slow to develop as self-reliant individuals. By the same token, it's possible for mentors to grow overly reliant on their protégés for help, giving them too many responsibilities that they should be discharging themselves. It is, of course, one thing to help guide someone, and another to have them do too much of your work for you. In conclusion, whereas mentoring offers many rewards, it is wise to keep in mind its potential costs.

Development of the Mentoring Process. As you might expect, mentor–protégé relationships do not develop in a haphazard fashion. Rather, they follow certain regular patterns. Notably, mentors are usually older than their protégés (by about 8 to 15 years). They also tend to be individuals with considerable power and status in their companies. As a result, they can assist rising young stars without themselves feeling threatened. On some occasions, mentor–protégé relationships are initiated by the mentor, who recognizes something impressive about the junior person. However, it is also possible for junior employees to approach prospective mentors about the possibility of entering into a mentoring relationship. Regardless of which party initiates the relationship, for it to succeed, both must enter into it willingly—and, of course, the organization must be supportive of this association.

Some organizations so strongly believe in the benefits of mentoring that they are unwilling to leave the process to chance, and formally encourage or even require mentoring in corporatewide programs. For example, at Colgate-Palmolive, all new white-collar employees are assigned higher-ranking employees who serve as mentors. Other companies make mentoring more of a group process. For example, at NYNEX, "mentoring circles" are formed in which six lower-ranking female employees meet monthly with two higher-ranking female employees to discuss work-related issues. These are only two of a wide variety of different types of mentoring in use today.

Despite their different formats, most mentor–protégé relationships pass through several distinct phases. The first, known as *initiation,* lasts from six months to a year, and represents the period during which the relationship gets started and takes on importance for both parties. The second phase, known as *cultivation,* may last from two to five years. During this time, the bond between mentor and protégé deepens, and the young individual may make rapid career strides because of the skilled assistance he or she is receiving.

The third stage, *separation,* begins when the protégé feels it is time to assert independence and strikes out on his or her own, or when there is some externally produced change in their roles (e.g., the protégé is promoted, or the mentor is transferred). Separation also can occur if the mentor feels unable to continue providing support and guidance to the protégé (e.g., if the mentor becomes ill). As you might imagine, this phase can be quite stressful if the mentor resents the protégé's growing independence, or if he or she feels that the mentor has withdrawn support prematurely.

If this separation is successful, the relationship may enter its final stage, termed *redefinition.* Here both parties perceive their bond primarily as one of friendship. They come to treat one another as equals, and the roles of mentor and protégé fade away completely. However, the mentor may continue to take pride in the accomplishments of his or her former protégé. Likewise, the protégé may continue to feel a debt of gratitude toward the former mentor. Although there is bound to be variation in the way mentor–protégé relationships actually develop, it is safe to say that these phases represent a relatively good picture of the way in which these important relationships generally unfold (see summary in Figure 5-1 on p. 130).

Viking Freight Systems *helps its hourly employees, many of whom belong to ethnic minorities, become managers by providing them with mentors. Half of the company's top executives started out working on the loading dock.*

Mentoring Diverse Groups. When you think of a mentor, the image probably comes to mind of an older male senior executive helping a younger male junior executive work his way up the corporate ladder by introducing him to the "old boy network," the small group of established, power-

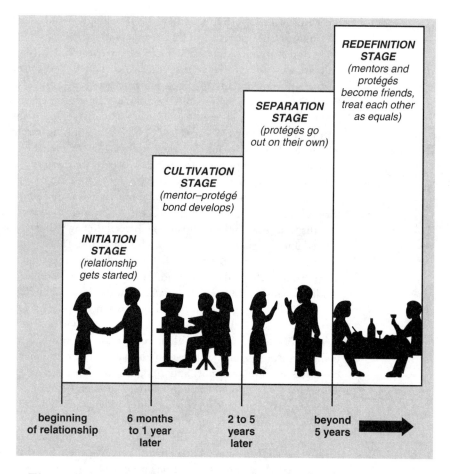

INITIATION
STAGE
(relationship
gets started)

CULTIVATION
STAGE
(mentor–protégé
bond develops)

SEPARATION
STAGE
(protégés go
out on their own)

REDEFINITION
STAGE
(mentors and
protégés
become friends,
treat each other
as equals)

beginning
of relationship

6 months
to 1 year
later

2 to 5
years
later

beyond
5 years

■ *Figure 5-1 Mentoring: A Four-Stage Process*

Relationships between mentors and their protégés tend to develop following the four stages summarized here. (*Source:* Based on suggestions by Kram, 1985; see Note 3.)

ful people who really run an organization. By definition, any old *boy* network is sexist. Indeed, women often seem to have less access to suitable mentors than do men.

There appear to be several reasons for this. First, there are simply fewer female executives available to serve as mentors for young female employees. Of course, the problem is cyclical and self-fulfilling: Fewer mentors attract fewer potential protégés, leading to fewer future mentors, and so on. With this in mind, Chubb & Son has found that its Sponsorship Program has led to the promotion of over half of the company's female protégés within only two years. This one company's efforts, at least, appear to be helping to break the cycle.

A second reason why women may have fewer mentoring opportunities than men is that women are less willing to enter into mentoring relationships because they anticipate greater risks than men in doing so. Specifically, a recent survey found that women expressed more concern than men about the potential for negative exposure that might come from the increased visibility they assume because of their protégés. Moreover, compared to men, women believed that they lacked the necessary qualifications to become a mentor. Interestingly, it was found that women were equally as willing as men to engage in mentoring but perceived that there would be more drawbacks in actually doing so.

Unfortunately, barriers to mentoring exist not only between men and women, but also between members of different racial groups. Insofar as mentors and protégés often get together because they have similar backgrounds and share similar attitudes, it is not surprising to find that people from different races face difficulties in their mentor–protégé relationships—if they form at all. With this in mind, some companies have gone out of their way to bring together mentors and protégés from diverse groups. For example, at Dow Jones, high-level mentors are grouped with three others, including a white male, a woman of any race, and a minority group member of either gender. The intention is twofold: to provide mentoring to those who might not receive it informally, and to encourage exposure to diverse groups who would not be likely to interact with each other (see Chapters 4 and 12). At Du Pont, where a formal mentoring program has been in place since 1985, mentoring has helped minority group members secure positions that otherwise might have been unattainable. Notably, at Du Pont, the proportion of minorities in top management has risen from 10 percent to 30 percent in recent years, even as the overall number of management jobs has dropped. It would appear that mentoring is a vital tool in the arsenal of those attempting to eliminate prejudicial attitudes and discriminatory behaviors toward minority groups (see Chapter 4).

ORGANIZATIONAL CULTURE: THE ESSENCE OF ORGANIZATIONS

As you become socialized to different organizations, you probably come to realize that each is somehow unique—even those in the same business. For example, whereas Wal-Mart employees are taught to focus on service and customer satisfaction, clerks at some other retail chains are encouraged to pressure customers to make unnecessary purchases. What is it that makes organizations so consistent over time and so different from each other? To a great extent, the answer lies in the impact of **organizational culture**—*the set of* *attitudes, values, behavioral norms, and expectations shared by organization members.* As we will describe in this section of the chapter, organizational culture exerts strong influences on organizations and those working in them.

Of all the characteristics that may distinguish organizations, four in particular have been identified as residing at the core of organizational culture.[5] First, organizations differ with respect to their *sensitivity to the needs of customers and employees.* For example, whereas UPS used to be relatively rigid and inflexible with respect to customer needs, its new culture places a high value on customer service and satisfaction.

Second, organizations differ with respect to their *interest in having employees generate new ideas.* Walt Disney Co. employees—or, "cast members," as they are called—undergo lengthy orientation programs to ensure that they know exactly what to say and how to behave toward guests. By contrast, people working at MCI are encouraged to be unique and to bring fresh ideas to their work. (In fact, company founder Bill McGowan is so adamant about this that procedure manuals are nowhere to be found at MCI.)

Third, companies also differ with respect to the *value placed on taking risks.* For example, whereas the Bank of America is very conservative, making only the safest investments, clothing buyers at The Limited are discouraged from making too many "safe" choices, and are rewarded for going out on a limb.

The fourth core value has to do with the *openness of available communication options.* In some companies, such as Du Pont and Tandem Computers, employees are expected to freely make decisions and to communicate with whomever is needed to get the job done. At IBM, however, the tradition has been to work within the proper communication channels and to vest power in the hands of only a few key individuals (although this appears to be changing). As these examples illustrate, different sets of core values are reflected in the cultures of organizations.

CULTURE'S ROLE IN ORGANIZATIONS

The organizational culture at Intel is regarded as so tough that it's like being in the Marine Corps. However, at electronics manufacturer Odetics, events are sponsored to keep the culture friendly and lots of fun. It even has a "Fun Committee" to organize special events.

Culture plays several important roles in organizations. Most obviously, an organization's culture provides a *sense of identity* for its members. The more clearly an organization's shared perceptions and values are defined, the more strongly people can associate themselves with their organization's mission and feel a vital part of it. For example, employees at Southwest Airlines feel special because of their company's emphasis on having fun and joking around on the job (a widespread practice initiated by founder, Herb Kelleher). Southwest's employees feel strongly associated with the company, that they belong there. As a result, they only infrequently resign to take other positions in the airline industry.

This example also illustrates the important role of company founders in creating organizational culture. In general, founders often possess dynamic personalities, strong values, and a clear vision of how the organization should operate. Since they are on the scene first, and play a key role in hiring initial staff, their attitudes and values are readily transmitted to new employees. As a result, these views become the accepted ones in the organization and persist as long as the founders are on the scene. For example, the culture at Microsoft calls for working exceptionally long hours, in large part because that's what cofounder Bill Gates has always done. Sometimes, founders' values can continue to drive an organization's culture even after that individual is no longer with the organization. For example, the late Ray Kroc founded the McDonald's restaurant chain on the values of good food at a good value served in clean, family-oriented surroundings—key cultural values that persist today. Likewise, although he's no longer with us, Walt Disney's wholesome family values are still cherished at the company that bears his name—in large part because employees ask themselves, "What would Walt think?" These individuals' values continue to permeate their entire companies and are central parts of their dominant cultures.

A second important function of culture involves *generating commitment to the organization's mission.* Sometimes it's difficult for people to go beyond thinking of their own interests. However, when there is a strong, overarching culture, people feel that they are part of that larger, well-defined whole and involved in the entire organization's work. Bigger than any one individual's interests, culture reminds people of what their organization is all about.

A third important function of culture is that it serves to *clarify and reinforce standards of behavior.* Although this is essential for newcomers, it is also beneficial for seasoned veterans. In essence, culture guides employees' behavior, making it clear what they should do or say in a given situation. In this sense, it provides stability to behavior, both with respect to what one individual might do at different times, but also what different individuals may do at the same time. By serving these three important roles, it is clear that culture is an important force influencing behavior in organizations.

TRANSMITTING ORGANIZATIONAL CULTURE: HOW IS IT ACCOMPLISHED?

How are cultural values transmitted between people? In other words, how do employees come to learn about their organization's culture? There are several key mechanisms involved, most importantly: *symbols, stories, jargon, ceremonies,* and *statements of principle.*

Symbols: Objects That Say More Than Meets the Eye. First, organizations often rely on **symbols**—material objects that connote meanings that extend beyond their intrinsic content. For example, some companies use impressive buildings to convey the organization's strength and significance, signifying that it is a large, stable place. The famous pyramid-shaped Transamerica building in San Francisco is a good example. Other companies rely on slogans to symbolize their values, such as General Electric's "Progress is our most important product," or Ford's "Quality is job 1." Corporate cars (or even jets!) are also used to convey information about an organization's culture—in particular, to indicate who wields power.

Stories: "Remember the time when . . .".   Organizations also transmit information about culture by virtue of the **stories** that are told in them, both formally and informally. Stories illustrate key aspects of an organization's culture, and telling them can effectively introduce those values to new employees and reaffirm them among existing employees. It is important to note that stories need not involve some great event, such as someone who saved the company with a single wise decision, but may be small tales that become legends because they so effectively communicate a message. For example, employees at the British confectionery firm, Cadbury, are purposely told stories about the company's founding on Quaker traditions to get them to appreciate and accept the basic Quaker value of hard work.

Jargon: The Special Language that Defines a Culture.   Even without telling stories, the everyday language used in companies helps sustain culture. For example, the slang or **jargon** that is used in a company helps employees define their identities as members of an organization (we will describe jargon more fully in Chapter 6). For example, for many years employees at IBM referred to disk drives as "hard files" and circuit boards as "planar boards," nonstandard terms that defined the insulated nature of their culture. Over time, as organizations—or even departments within them—develop unique language to describe their work, their terms, although strange to newcomers, serve as a common factor that brings together individuals belonging to a corporate culture.

Ceremonies: Special Events that Commemorate Corporate Values.   Organizations also do a great deal to sustain their cultures by conducting various types of **ceremonies.** Indeed, ceremonies may be seen as celebrations of an organization's basic values and assumptions. Just as a wedding ceremony symbolizes a couple's mutual commitment and a presidential inauguration ceremony marks the beginning of a new administration, various organizational ceremonies also celebrate some important accomplishment. For example, one accounting firm celebrated its move to much better facilities by throwing a party, a celebration signifying that it "has arrived," or "made it to the big time." Such ceremonies convey meaning to people inside and outside the organization. As one pair of experts on organizational culture put it, "Ceremonies are to the culture what the movie is to the script . . . values that are difficult to express in any other way."[6]

Statements of Principle: Defining Culture in Writing. A fifth way in which culture is transmitted is via direct **statements of principle.** Some organizations have explicitly written their principles for all to see.[7] For example, Forrest Mars, the founder of the candy company M&M Mars, developed his "Five Principles of Mars," which still guide his company today: quality (everyone is responsible for maintaining quality), responsibility (all employees are responsible for their own actions and decisions), mutuality (creating a situation in which everyone can win), efficiency (most of the company's 41 factories operate continuously), and freedom (giving employees opportunities to shape their futures). (For some excerpts from several corporate statements of principle, see Table 5-1.) Some companies have chosen to make explicit the moral aspects of their cultures by publishing **codes of ethics**—specific statements of a company's ethical values. According to Hershey Foods' chief exec-

■ *Table 5-1 Statements of Principle: Some Examples*

Organizations frequently communicate important aspects of their cultures in explicit statements referred to as *statements of principle*. Some brief excerpts from several such statements are reproduced here. (Excerpted from material in Falsey, 1989; see Note 7.)

Company	*Statement*
Kimberly Clark	"Serve the customers well and deal fairly to gain their confidence and good will."
Baxter Travenol	"Provide quality and value in the goods and services we offer our customers."
Lever Brothers	"To . . . make life more enjoyable and rewarding for the people who use our products."
Stanley Works	"Conducting all of our business and community relations with integrity."
Northwestern Mutual	"To rank first in benefits to policyowners rather than first in size."
Winn-Dixie Stores	"To innovate and implement better and more efficient ways of serving our customers."
Gerber Products	"To strive in all things, and with all people, to do the best we can and to make our best better."
Worthington Industries	"We treat our customers, employees, investors and suppliers as we would like to be treated."
Rolm	"To create a great place to work."

utive officer, Richard Zimmerman, this is an effective device:

> *[O]ften, an individual joins a firm without recognizing the type of environment in which he will place himself and his career. The loud and clear enunciation of a company's code of conduct ... [allows] that employee to determine whether or not he fits that particular culture.*[8]

THE IMPACT OF ORGANIZATIONAL CULTURE

Organizational culture exerts many effects on individuals and organizations — some dramatic and others more subtle. Culture generates strong pressures on people to go along, to think and act in ways consistent with the existing culture. An organization's culture can strongly affect everything from the way employees dress (e.g., the white shirts traditionally worn by male employees of IBM) and the amount of time allowed to elapse before meetings begin, to the time it takes to get promoted.

It is also important to consider culture's effects on such vital issues as organizational performance. Is there any one type of organizational climate that is more closely tied to success than others? Although it would certainly make it easy on companies if the answer were yes, it does not appear that any one particular culture carries with it the key to organizational success. Rather, just as people with different personalities achieve success in their own ways, so too do organizations with different cultures. In the case of organizations, there are so many factors responsible for success (such as governmental regulations, the economy, competitors, and so on) that the effects of culture alone may be overridden.

However, it would be misleading to conclude that organizational culture does not influence key organizational variables. In this regard, one key factor appears to be not culture alone, but the extent to which employees hold values and beliefs that match those of their organizations—a factor known as **person–organization fit.** In fact, research has shown that the greater the fit between employees and their organizations on core values, the more both benefit. Specifically, high degrees of person–organization fit have been linked to high degrees of employee satisfaction, commitment, and low rates of turnover (see Chapter 4). With this in mind, it makes a great deal of sense for organizations to work hard to socialize employees so that they accept the organization's values, and to select future employees who already do so.

THE DYNAMIC NATURE OF ORGANIZATIONAL CULTURE

Our discussion of organizational culture seems to imply that it is static and not subject to change. However, insofar as the basic nature of organizations change (see Chapter 11), so too does organizational culture. In fact, several factors contribute to such change.

Composition of the Work Force.   Over time, the people entering an organization may differ in important ways from those already in it, and these differences may impinge on the existing culture of the organization. For example, people from different ethnic or cultural backgrounds may have contrasting views about various aspects of behavior at work. For example, they may hold dissimilar views about style of dress, the importance of being on time (or even what constitutes "on-time" behavior), the level of deference one should show to higher-status people, and even what foods should be served in the company cafeteria. In other words, as people with different backgrounds and values enter the workplace, changes in organizational culture may be expected to follow.

An interesting example of this phenomenon may be seen at Ford Motor Company, where growing numbers of women are now employed in positions, such as auto designer, which traditionally have been held by men. Until recently, the prevailing culture of Ford's design teams was insensitive to the idea that women may have special concerns when picking out a car. Mimi Vandermolen, a designer responsible for the Ford Probe, sought to change the culture of Ford's traditionally male design unit. To do this, not only did she make countless presentations about the needs of women in car design, she even produced a film demonstrating some of them (e.g., the difficulties women have getting in and out of vehicles). The culture of Ford's design team is now more attuned to the concerns of women than ever. As a result, the Probe was redesigned with such features as upholstery that won't snag pantyhose, glove box latches that allow for long fingernails, and pedals that are designed at the proper angle for drivers wearing high heels. These redesigned elements, which make the Probe friendlier to woman, neatly illustrate how the changing demographics in one large organization changed its culture (and the nature of its products!).

Mergers and Acquisitions.   Another and even more dramatic source of cultural change is mergers and acquisitions—events in which one organization purchases or otherwise absorbs another. Although these events are likely to generate careful financial analyses of the acquired organization, little consideration tends to be given to the acquired organization's culture. This is unfortunate, however, insofar as there have been several cases in which the merger of two organizations with incompatible cultures leads to serious problems, commonly referred to as **culture clashes.**

A classic example is provided by the 1988 merger of Nabisco (a producer of cookies and other baked goods famous for such brands as Fig Newtons and Oreos) with RJ Reynolds (a major producer of tobacco products), to become RJR Nabisco. Nabisco was headquartered in New York, and its executives were known to enjoy perks such as corporate jets, penthouse apartments, and lavish parties. Yet, Nabisco employees prided themselves on their company's "American-as-apple-pie" image, and valued the high degree of autonomy permitted in performing their jobs. Several hundred miles away in Winston-Salem, North Carolina, RJ Reynolds had a strikingly different culture. It was characterized by a strong work ethic, much less autonomy for employees, and a deep commitment to its local community and to philanthropic activities.

When the two companies merged, sparks flew. Nabisco executives resented the tighter controls imposed by Tylee Wilson, CEO of Reynolds. As some put it, "You have to raise your hand to go to the bathroom!" The fact that their company was not afforded the level of independence within the new corporation promised before the merger upset many Nabisco employees. As a result, bitter internal feuds soon erupted, resulting in the takeover of the new company by Ross Johnson, CEO of Nabisco. Once in power, he quickly purged the company of virtually all former Reynolds executives and moved the merged company headquarters to a neutral location, Atlanta. Now, years later, the merged organization still suffers from low productivity in some units, high turnover, and strong internal divisions. Clearly, when organizational cultures collide, the changes that follow can be severe and quite long-lasting.

It has been noted that in too many cases of merger the larger, more powerful, acquiring company attempts to dominate the smaller, acquired company, based on the mistaken belief that it knows best. However, insofar as clashes are likely to result in such cases, it has been recommended that mergers be handled by having the companies first work collaboratively on a joint venture and then merge only after it is clear that their organizational cultures can peacefully coexist. For example, the successful partnership between Sony and CBS was preceded by years of experience with each other. In short, just as the marriage of two people requires keen attention to their individual personalities, so too does the marriage of two companies suggest the need to be sensitive to their different organizational cultures. Among organizations, as among individuals, dating prior to marriage would appear to be wise.

Planned Organizational Change.   Even if an organization doesn't change by acquiring another, cultural change still may result from other planned changes, such as conscious decisions to alter the internal structure or the basic operations of an organization (see Chapter 11). A good example of this can be seen in IBM in recent years. In response to staggering losses IBM realized that one of its problems was that it was heavily bureaucratic, making it difficult for lower-level people to make on-the-spot decisions. As a result, IBM changed the nature of its corporate structure from one in which there was a steep hierarchy with many layers of management to a "delayered" one with far fewer managers (see Chapter 10). As you might imagine, the newly "right-sized" IBM developed a new corporate culture. Once known for a highly rigid, autocratic culture in which decision making was centralized in the hands of just a few, the reorganized company is now much more open and democratic in its approach than ever before. (When it comes to the changing nature of organizations, culture isn't only important in large organizations, such as IBM, but small ones too. For a look at the vital role of culture in one small but fast-growing organization, see the **Winning Practices** section on p. 140.)

CAREERS: SEQUENCES OF WORK EXPERIENCES

Over the course of our lives we tend to find ourselves becoming socialized to many different jobs in several different organizations, a journey that exposes us to a variety of organizational cultures. In fact, during the course of his or her working life, the average American holds eight different jobs. In most cases, these positions are interconnected in some systematic way, weaving a path, however twisted and indirect, representing a **career.** Formally, a career can be defined as *the evolving sequence of work experiences over time.* In this section of the chapter we will turn our attention to careers. Specifically, we will focus on the ways careers develop, and the challenges people face as they attempt to balance the demands of their careers with those of their personal lives.

At the risk of oversimplifying the pleasures of living, it's clear that our lives tend to progress in systematic fashion, and with it, different foci: school, then marriage, children, and before you know it, grandchildren. The same can be said with respect to the paths taken by our careers. And, at the risk of oversimplifying these, organizational scientists have distinguished between various issues arising at three stages of careers, simply referred to as *early career, middle career,* and *late career* stages.

EARLY CAREER: GETTING STARTED

The question, "what do you want to be when you grow up?" is surely among the most commonly considered ones throughout childhood (if not later, too!). Before you know it, you have to answer seriously. Indeed, when we are just beginning our careers, usually in our twenties, we are faced with the issue of **career planning**—the process of deciding what jobs and activities we wish to be doing in the future. When making these choices, we tend to rely on our perceptions of our own talents, abilities, needs, motives, attitudes, and values. Then, usually by our mid-thirties, we are strongly guided by these perceptions as we make our career choices. Scientists have referred to these self-perceptions as **career anchors** insofar as they firmly attach people's careers to their underlying abilities, needs, and values. Five major career anchors have been identified.[10] These are as follows:

- **technical or functional**—concentration on jobs focusing on specific content areas (e.g., auto mechanics, graphic arts)

WINNING PRACTICES

Getting Big by Thinking Small: Winning the Organizational Culture Game at Knowledge Adventure

Although the name Knowledge Adventure (KA) may not ring a bell, chances are good that fans of multimedia education and entertainment software are highly familiar with some of its hit products, such as "Dinosaur Adventure," "Isaac Asimov's Science Adventure II," and "3-D Body Adventure." Working out of crowded offices in suburban Los Angeles, company founder Bill Gross is proud of the fact that his company reached sales of $35 million in 1994, only three years after it was founded.[9] But, rather than letting success go to the head of its 100 employees, Gross has worked hard to maintain the small-company feel and the sense of community that he and his employees enjoy so much.

For this reason, there are no trappings of success at KA. Each employee has a desk made by laying a $14 plain wooden door from a local hardware store across two two-drawer steel file cabinets. Gross's rationale is that by maintaining a small-company atmosphere, KA can do a better job of fighting off such rivals as giant Microsoft by beating them to market with the hottest products. For example, in the summer of 1993, when *Jurassic Park* was all the rage, KA's "Dinosaur Adventure" game was the first on the market. When Microsoft introduced its competing product, "Dinosaur," KA employees banded together, working day and night on their "Dinosaur" killer, "3-D Dinosaur Adventure," a highly animated theme park simulation game. By Christmas that year, it was KA's games that were flying off the shelves, outselling Microsoft by 300 percent. The key to success, according to Gross, is the company's ability to respond quickly to the desires of customers in the $1 billion CD-ROM market.

Gross recognizes that a small, private company can do this, whereas a large, publicly traded one cannot. As soon as he has to pay greater attention to shareholders than employees, Gross fears, it will be harder to keep employees feeling part of the family that has made the company so successful, and that has treated them well in return (e.g., he treated the whole company and their spouses to a trip to Yosemite). Gross keeps things highly democratic, allowing employees to participate in such key decisions as where to relocate the new corporate offices. So adamant is Gross about the importance of this corporate culture to the company's success that it caused him to lock horns with a fellow executive who pushed to go public with the company, and to adopt a more autocratic management style. That executive resigned after less than a year. Game over; Gross won! Today, the culture at KA reflects the community spirit that Gross has labored to retain—and the bottom line: KA still remains one of the smallest big companies around.

- **managerial competence**—focus on jobs that allow for analyzing business problems and dealing with people (e.g., executive)

- **security and stability**—attraction to jobs that are likely to continue into the future (e.g., the military)

- **creativity or entrepreneurship**—primary interest in starting new companies from visions of unique products or services, but not necessarily running them (e g., inventor)

- **autonomy and independence**—attraction to jobs that allow for freedom from constraints, and to work at one's own pace (e.g., novelists and creative artists)

Beyond developing their career anchors, people in the early stages of their careers typically confront frequent job changes. As we begin our careers, for example, we may find that a particular job may not be as desirable as expected. Similarly, we may find that it is difficult or impossible to gain entry into some professions. (If you have ever tried to become a professional actor, you probably know only too well what we mean!) The result, in either case, is the same: You pursue a different job. Indeed, people are far more likely to change jobs when they are young than when they grow older. During this early period in their lives, when career expectations are just forming, and life responsibilities make it easier to be mobile, job changes are inevitable.

With this, the question arises as to *how* people make vocational choices. Although the issue is certainly very complicated, we may identify three major factors. The first one was mentioned earlier in this chapter—*person–organization fit.* That is, people tend to choose jobs that match their skills, interests, and values. Second, people also select jobs that match their self-concepts—that is, their images of who they are. In other words, we tend to match ourselves to prototypes of job incumbents, our beliefs about what the typical holder of a job is like. So, for example, if you see yourself as being more like a musician than a banker, you are probably more likely to pursue a job in the world of music. Of course, *which* particular job will depend on your career anchor. This may lead you to play guitar in a rock band, be an artist's agent or manager, a record producer, or the head of a record company.

Finally, a note of realism: People's vocational choices are guided to a great extent by options and opportunities. No matter how much you are attracted to the romantic image of the old village blacksmith, it's unlikely that you will be able to pursue this line of work today. By contrast, however, there are many different careers in which opportunities abound and options are plentiful.[11] And, as people learn about these types of jobs early in their careers, they stand good chances of preparing for them and subsequently succeeding in them. For an overview of some of the hottest careers today, see Table 5-2 on p. 142.

■ *Table 5-2 Today's Hottest Job Prospects*

Some of the most promising career opportunities involve jobs that are growing in popularity. Here are some jobs that may seem unusual, but which offer considerable prospects for growth in the future. (Based on material in "The 25 hottest carrers"; see Note 11.)

Job	Description
50-Plus Marketer	Specialists in advertising to the growing group of affluent baby boomers, who are now turning 50.
Managed-Care Manager	People who help organizations manage relations with insurance companies to help find the most appropriate options for employees and rates for employers.
Diversity Manager	Experts who help highly diverse groups of employees work effectively in organizations; working with employers to attract and retain minority candidates, and training employees to adjust to diversity among their coworkers.
Employee Leasing Agents	Companies are beginning to "lease" employees from agents who make all the arrangements for insurance and taxes, and ensure compliance with legal regulations, releasing employers from these responsibilities.

MIDDLE CAREER: CONFRONTING THE CAREER PLATEAU

If early career issues pertain to people in their twenties and thirties, then middle-career issues apply to the forty-something crowd. This is sometimes a difficult period in which people look down the road and realize that they may never fulfill their career aspirations. The point at which one's career has peaked and is unlikely to develop further is known as a **career plateau.** Today, as companies are reducing the sizes of their staffs and competition for jobs becomes intense, more and more people are reaching their plateaus earlier than expected. Faced with poor chances for promotion and few alternatives for employment, they may feel unmotivated and simply stick out their jobs until they retire from them.

   If you think this picture is depressing, imagine how serious the problem becomes when companies are faced with large cohorts of mid-career employees who are unmotivated because their careers have plateaued. Surely, a work force composed of people who are merely "going through the motions" will be neither very productive nor satisfied. So, to avoid these problems, organizations have been relying on **career development interventions**—systematic efforts to help manage people's careers while simultaneously helping the organizations in which they work. Different companies follow different approaches to career development. For example, at Chevron, employees are counseled to seek outside hobbies during periods in which their jobs offer little gratification. Some are encouraged to make lateral moves within the company in order to keep their work lives stimulating. Not only have Chevron employees done this, but so too have thousands of employees at General Motors, where the white-collar work force has been reduced by half over the last few years. In fact, it has been reported that GM has spent some $10 million per year helping their plateaued employees find appropriate new positions within the company.

Much of what goes on in career development interventions involves helping employees assess the skills and interests they have so that they may be placed into positions for which they are well suited. Some companies, such as Hewlett-Packard and Lawrence Livermore Laboratories, provide *self-assessment exercises* for this purpose. Others, such as Coca-Cola and Disney, rely on *individualized counseling sessions* in which employees meet with trained professionals. Still others, including AT&T, IBM, Ford, Shell Oil, and Kodak, take it a step further, offering *organizational assessment programs* through which employees are systematically tested to discover their profiles of skills and interests. (For an overview of what such tests look like, and a chance to examine your own career aspirations, see the **Self-Assessment Exercise** on pp. 144–145.[12]) At the very least, companies such as CBS, Merck, Aetna, and General Electric all provide *information services,* such as job posting systems and career resource centers through which employees can learn about new career options within their companies. And, when companies find that they must reduce the size of their work forces, terminated employees at Exxon, Mutual of New York, General Electric, and other companies receive the services of *outplacement programs.* These generally include assistance in developing the skills needed to find new jobs (such as networking, interviewing skills, résumé writing, and the like).

A recent trend observed among plateaued mid-career employees is that they completely abandon their traditional jobs and start their own small businesses. In recent years, such "dropouts" have been referred to as *corporate refugees.* Although it is quite difficult to begin new business ventures, corporate refugees are generally not looking for an easy way out. Instead, they seek to regain the challenges left behind in their corporate jobs and to find a more fulfilling existence.

LATE CAREER: FOCUSING ON SUCCESSION AND RETIREMENT

When we speak of late career issues, the image probably comes to mind of the faithful employee retiring after some 40 years of employment with the same company, proudly showing off the gold watch he just received to an audience

---

Finding the Right Career for You

An important part of selecting an appropriate career begins with understanding who you are, and what special personality characteristics you bring with you to your job. This exercise (adapted from Morrison, 1994; see Note 12) is a highly simplified version of one kind of test that is sometimes used in career counseling. Complete it to get a feel for what such tests are like, and to learn something about your own career interests. Such a simple exercise cannot be completely accurate, of course, but considering your answers carefully may give you some interesting self-insights.

DIRECTIONS

For each of the seven following sets of adjectives select the letter corresponding to the one adjective that best describes yourself.

1. (a) forceful   (b) enthusiastic   (c) systematic   (d) patient
2. (a) adventurous (b) outgoing   (c) diplomatic   (d) loyal
3. (a) demanding   (b) emotional   (c) conscientious (d) stable
4. (a) daring   (b) sociable   (c) conventional   (d) team-oriented
5. (a) decisive   (b) generous   (c) analytical   (d) calm
6. (a) self-assured (b) convincing   (c) sensitive   (d) deliberate
7. (a) competitive (b) trusting   (c) accurate   (d) passive

SCORING

1. Add the number of times you selected the adjectives corresponding to each letter.

2. If the majority of your choices were in the "a" category, you are likely to excel at jobs requiring the generation of new ideas, making decisions, solv-

---

of adoring soon-to-be-former coworkers. Indeed, preparation for retirement is an important issue faced during one's fifties and sixties. Psychologically, there is a reorientation from being directed in one's life by work activities to an increased focus on leisure-time activities. Preparing for retirement also involves careful planning to meet the special challenges faced by retired workers, including adjustment to reduced earnings. Fortunately, it has been shown that through careful planning, people can greatly enjoy the new era of their lives

ing problems, and taking charge. Careers in management might be right for you.

3. If the majority of your choices were in the "b" category, you are likely to excel at jobs requiring motivating others and generating enthusiasm in them, interacting with people and lending them assistance. Careers in teaching might be right for you.

4. If the majority of your choices were in the "c" category, you are likely to excel at jobs requiring careful following of orders and performing jobs with great care and precision. Careers in scientific laboratory work might be right for you.

5. If the majority of your choices were in the "d" category, you are likely to excel at jobs requiring patience and understanding of others, loyalty, and being a good listener. Careers in the clergy might be right for you.

QUESTIONS FOR DISCUSSION

1. What would you say are the underlying assumptions of this test? Are these reasonable?

2. Did you find it easy or difficult to describe yourself by using only these adjectives? Was it hard for you to select only one adjective? Why or why not?

3. Do you agree with the conclusions about the career best suited to your characteristics based on the scoring? Why or why not?

4. Did this exercise tell you something about yourself that you didn't know? Or did it merely confirm things you already believed? If so, does this limit the value of the test, or might it still be useful? Explain.

5. What would you consider to be the limitations of tests such as this when it comes to career counseling?

that begins when their working lives end. To help ensure that this occurs, many companies are offering intensive counseling services for their employees to prepare them for retirement. For example, employees of Capital Cities/ABC (the giant broadcasting company) and their spouses are invited to seminars in which their incomes and financial needs are carefully investigated before it's time to retire. As a result, when the day that the gold watch comes, employees will not have to hock it to pay their bills.

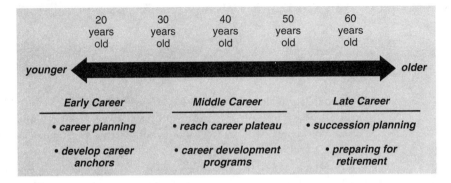

■ *Figure 5-2 The Three Stages of Career Development*

Careers generally develop in three stages, each of which occurs at different ages and is associated with different issues.

Before people retire, especially those at high organizational levels, they frequently help their companies prepare for the void created by their departure. Typically, this involves **succession planning**—the process of identifying who will take over key organizational positions after job incumbents retire. After one spends years building a successful business, it's unlikely that he or she would feel comfortable retiring without taking steps to preserve what has been done and to ensure that it is left in good hands. People generally also want to pass the baton on to another whose goals and values match their own. And, of course, careful planning of this nature is in the best interest of the company as well. One way of identifying successors, particularly for top executives, is by having the retiring individual identify and develop a successor (over a course of years, if possible). Mentoring at this level not only assures the retiring executive that he or she will have a successor qualified to fill the post, but also helps prepare the successor for the job, and eases his or her transition within the organization.

In conclusion, careers progress through three distinct stages (see summary in Figure 5-2). Each stage is associated with a series of unique issues that must be faced. Organizations are growing increasingly sensitive to the special needs of employees at each stage and offer various forms of assistance in helping to meet the challenges confronted.

BALANCING CAREERS AND PERSONAL LIVES: A DIFFICULT CHALLENGE

It's no secret that today's families are quite different from those of just one generation ago. Twenty to thirty years ago, the typical nuclear family consisted of a husband who worked outside the home, a wife working as a homemaker, and two children. Today, however, this configuration exists in less than 4 percent of all American households. In fact, in over half of all American families both spouses work outside the home (these are known as **dual-career couples**). In addition, about twice as many children are currently being raised in single-parent families (mostly by mothers) compared to 1970, and two-thirds of these single parents work outside the home.

As you might imagine, these changing demographics have had considerable impact on the nature of people's careers, and organizational scientists have been highly involved in studying them. When both members of married couples work outside the home, it becomes particularly challenging to be able to balance the demands of one's job (e.g., to work late to meet special projects) with the demands of one's family life (e.g., caring for the children). This has been referred to as a **work–family conflict.** Research has shown that work–family conflicts are major sources of stress that can have profound negative impact on people's satisfaction with both their work lives and their family lives, increasing depression and lowering overall life satisfaction. In addition, because the demands of one's family life can interfere with one's work, job performance can suffer, and lowered income can result.

In view of the changing nature of the workplace and the adjustments that people must make, many companies are making special efforts to resolve some of the problems of work–family conflict, and the logistical problems faced by dual-career couples. Here are some of the main ways they are going about it.

- **Flextime programs**—policies that give employees some discretion over when they can arrive and leave work, thereby making it easier to adapt their work schedules to the demands of their personal lives. Typically, employees must work a common core of hours, such as 9:00 a.m. to 12 noon and 1:00 p.m. to 3:00 p.m. Scheduling of the remaining hours within certain spans (such as 6:00 to 9:00 a.m. and 3:00 to 6:00 p.m.) is then left up to the employees themselves. Companies such as Pacific Bell and Duke Power Company have found that flexible work scheduling has helped their employees meet the demands of juggling their work and family lives.

Houston's **Methodist Hospital** *allows its employees to work flexible hours and to take personal leaves so that they can successfully balance the demands of their work and family lives.*

- **Family leave programs**—policies that give employees time off their jobs (often some portion of which is paid) to devote to starting a new family. After initiating family leave programs, Aetna Life & Casualty found dramatic increases in the number of female employees who returned to their jobs, saving the company the considerable time and money it would have cost to replace them.

- **Child-care facilities**—sites at or near company locations where parents can leave their children while they are working. America West, for example, believes so strongly in providing child care that it provides these services 24 hours a day, and maintained these benefits even while it was going through bankruptcy proceedings in 1991.

- **Personal support policies**—practices that help employees meet the demands of their family lives, freeing them to concentrate on their work. These are often varied in nature. For example, the SAS Institute (Cary, North Carolina) not only offers its employees free, on-site Montessori child care, but also nutritious take-home dinners. The *St. Petersburg Times* advises its employees about ways to help meet the problems of elderly family members. Wilton Connor Packaging (Charlotte, North Carolina) provides even more unusual forms of support, including an on-site laundry, high school equivalency classes, door-to-door transportation, and a children's clothing swap center.

- **Job sharing**—the practice of allowing pairs of employees to assume the responsibilities of a single job, giving them the flexibility of being able to work while having time off for family obligations. At Xerox, for example, several sets of employees share jobs, including two female employees who were sales rivals but who joined forces to share one job when they each faced the need to reduce their working hours so they could devote time to their new families.

By using such *family-responsive policies* companies derive several important benefits. First, they help retain highly valued employees—not only keeping them from competitors, but also saving the costs of having to replace them. In fact, officials at AT&T found that the average cost of letting new parents take up to a year of unpaid parental leave was only 32 percent of an employee's annual salary, compared with a 150 percent cost to replace that person permanently. Second, by alleviating the distractions of having to worry about nonwork issues, employees are freed to concentrate on their jobs and to be their most creative. Commenting on this idea, Ellen Galinsky, copresident of the Families & Work Institute, said, "There's a cost to *not* providing work and family assistance."[13] A third benefit is that such policies help attract the most qualified human resources, giving companies that use them a competitive edge over those that do not. In conclusion, family-responsive policies represent a key element in the arsenal of tools used by today's human resources professionals.

SUMMARY:
PUTTING IT TO USE

Organizational socialization is the process through which people become participating members of their organizations. During the earliest stage, *anticipatory socialization*, people consider what it would be like to become a member of an organization. To help avoid disappointments and subsequent turnover, it helps for corporate recruiters to provide *realistic job previews*—accurate descriptions of both the negative and positive aspects of a job likely to be encountered. Once people enter the organization, the *encounter stage*, they are likely to be exposed to *corporate orientation programs* designed to systematically socialize them with respect to the operations of the organization as well as its history and traditions. Finally, in the *metamorphosis stage*, new employees become full-fledged members of the organization, a passage sometimes marked by formal ceremonies.

Mentoring is a special one-on-one form of socialization. It involves a *mentor*, a generally older, more experienced person, who counsels and advises a younger, less experienced person known as a *protégé*. Relationships between mentors and their protégés offer benefits to both parties, although they have potential costs as well. Such relationships pass through regular stages during which mentors and protégés work closely together and then begin to separate, as the protégé goes off on his or her own. Several of today's companies have been helping women and members of minority groups gain from mentoring experiences.

Among the most important aspects of socialization involves learning the organization's *culture*—that is, the set of attitudes, values, behavioral norms, and expectations shared by organization members. Cultures give organizations a sense of identity, often promoting the image of the company founder. They also generate commitment to the organization's mission and clarify and reinforce standards of behavior. Culture is both transmitted to new employees and reaffirmed among existing employees via several mechanisms, including symbols, stories, jargon, ceremonies, and statements of principle. Organizational culture is dynamic in nature and is subject to change due to such factors as the changing nature of the work force, mergers and acquisitions (which sometimes result in serious *culture clashes* within the newly formed company), and changes in the organization's structure, size, or way of doing business.

Over the course of their working lives, people tend to have evolving sequences of work experiences referred to as *careers*. In the *early career* stage, during their twenties and thirties, people make career choices that are guided by perceptions of their own talents, referred to as *career anchors*. After working at a career for a while, in the *middle-career* stage, many people reach the point where their careers have peaked and are unlikely to develop further, known as *career plateaus*. To help such employees feel better about their work, or to find suitable new work, companies offer *career development interventions*. These generally include some form of vocational counseling. During one's fifties and sixties, the *late career* stage, two major issues arise—planning for *retirement,* and preparing for a replacement, *succession planning.* Today, because *dual-career couples* are typical, it is not unusual for *work–family conflict* to develop. To assist employees, growing numbers of companies are offering such innovative programs as flextime, family leaves, child care, personal support, and job sharing.

You Be the Consultant

Rubbish World is a small trash removal service located in a metropolitan area. For some time, customers have been complaining that their trash hasn't always been picked up on time. After investigating the matter, the dispatcher discovered that quite a few drivers have been taking time off their routes to run personal errands. The offending parties were disciplined, even dismissed, yet the practice persists. Company officials are concerned because they don't want the problem to continue with the new employees they hire, so they come to you for advice. Answer the following questions relevant to this situation, based on the material in this chapter.

1. How might you use realistic job previews to help select new employees who would not be predisposed to goofing off in this fashion?

2. What would you do to socialize prospective employees about the company's values? Do you think a corporate orientation program would help? If so, what should it emphasize? How about mentors? Would they be effective in this case? Why or why not?

3. Do you think that there may be some aspect of the company culture that is to blame for the problem? If so, what could be done to change it? How might statements of principle help in this regard?

4. After interviewing some employees, you learn that work–family conflicts might lie at the root of the problem. In view of this, what steps can the company take to help alleviate such conflicts?

CHAPTER 6

Organizational Communication and Social Influence

PREVIEW OF CHAPTER HIGHLIGHTS

Communication is the process by which a person, group, or organization transmits some type of information to another person, group, or organization. It involves **encoding** a message, transmitting it along communication channels, **decoding** it, and providing **feedback.**

Verbal communication involves the use of both written and oral language, both of which are commonly used in organizations for communicating different types of messages.

Organizational communication can be both **formal,** following from **organizational structure,** and **informal,** not dictated by organizational requirements.

Organizational communication can be improved by encouraging open feedback, using simple language, avoiding overload, matching words and deeds, and being a good listener.

Social influence refers to attempts to affect others. It can be either based on the office one holds **(position power)** or the characteristics of the individuals involved **(personal power).** There are four major forms of each.

Organizational politics refers to acts of influence designed to promote one's own selfish purposes rather than the interests of the organization. Several techniques can be used to effectively limit the effects of politically-motivated behavior.

One of the main characteristics of behavior in organizations is that it involves the interrelationships between individuals. After all, people don't work in a vacuum. Even security guards assigned to remote outposts must eventually have contact with others. When it comes to the world of work, the old adage, "no one is an island," appears to be true.

The dynamics of the ways in which people relate to each other in organizations will be explored throughout this third section of the book, which focuses on group processes. Specifically, in this chapter, we will focus on two key aspects of interpersonal relations on the job—*communication*—the processes through which people send and receive information to others, and *social influence*—the ways in which people both affect and are affected by others.

THE BASIC NATURE OF COMMUNICATION

For an organization to function, individuals and groups must carefully coordinate their efforts and activities. Waiters must take their customers' orders and pass them along to the chef. Store managers must describe special promotions to their sales staffs. Clearly, *communication* is the key to these attempts at coordination. Without it, people would not know what to do, and organizations would not be able to operate effectively—if at all. It should not be surprising, therefore, that communication has been referred to as "the social glue . . . that continues to keep the organization tied together,"[1] and "the essence of organization."[2] Given the importance of communication in organizations, you may not be surprised to learn that supervisors spend as much as 80 percent of their time engaging in some form of communication (e.g., speaking or listening to others, writing or reading reports, and so on). We will begin our discussion of organizational communication by formally describing the communication process and then describing some of the forms it takes. Finally, building on this foundation, we will describe several ways to improve organizational communication.

THE COMMUNICATION PROCESS
AND ITS ROLE IN ORGANIZATIONS

Formally, we define **communication** as the process by which a person, group, or organization (the *sender*) transmits some type of information (the *message*) to another person, group, or organization (the *receiver*). To clarify this definition and to further elaborate on the process, we have summarized it in Figure 6-1.

The communication process begins when one party has an idea that it wishes to transmit to another (either party may be an individual, a group, or an entire organization). It is the sender's mission to transform the idea into a form that can be sent to and understood by the receiver. This is what happens in the process of **encoding**—translating an idea into a form, such as written or

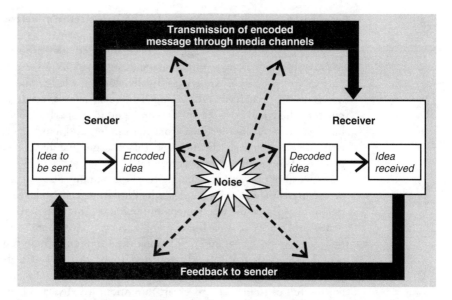

■ *Figure 6-1 The Communication Process*

The process of communication consists of the steps summarized here. It begins when a sender has an idea that he or she wishes to send to a receiver.

spoken language, that can be recognized by a receiver. We encode information when we select the words we use to write a letter or speak to someone in person.

After a message is encoded, it is ready to be transmitted over one or more channels of communication to reach the desired receiver, the pathways along which information travels. Telephone lines, radio and television signals, fiber-optic cables, mail routes, and even the air waves that carry the vibrations of our voices all represent potential channels of communication. Of course, the form of encoding largely determines the way information may be transmitted. Visual information—such as pictures and written words—may be mailed, delivered in person by a courier, shipped by an express delivery service, or sent via modems, fax machines, or satellite dishes. Oral information may be transmitted over the telephone, via radio and television waves, and of course the old-fashioned way, in person. Whatever channel is used, the goal is the same: to send the encoded message accurately to a desired receiver.

Once a message is received, the recipient must begin the process of **decoding**—converting the message back into the sender's original ideas. This can involve many different subprocesses, such as comprehending spoken and written words, interpreting facial expressions, and the like. To the extent that the sender's message is accurately decoded by the receiver, the ideas understood will be the ones intended. Of course, our ability to comprehend and interpret information received from others may be imperfect (e.g., restricted by unclear messages, or by our own language skills).

Finally, once a message has been decoded, the process can continue, with the receiver transmitting a new message back to the original sender. This part of the process is known as **feedback**—knowledge about the impact of messages on receivers. Receiving feedback allows senders to determine whether their messages have been understood properly. Once received, feedback can trigger another idea from the sender, and another cycle of transferring information may begin. For this reason, we have characterized the process of communication as continuous.

Despite its apparent simplicity, the communication process rarely operates as flawlessly as we have described it here. As we will see, there are many potential barriers to effective communication. The name given to factors that distort the clarity of a message is **noise.** As we have characterized it in Figure 6-1, noise can occur at any point along the communication process. For example, messages that are poorly encoded (e.g., written in an unclear way) or poorly decoded (e.g., not comprehended), or channels of communication that are too full of static (e.g., receivers' attentions are diverted from the message), may reduce communication's effectiveness. Such factors may contribute to the distortion of information transmitted from one party to another.

ORAL AND WRITTEN COMMUNICATION: THE POWER OF WORDS

By virtue of the fact that you are reading this book, we are assured you are familiar with **verbal communication**—transmitting and receiving ideas using words. Verbal communication can be either *oral,* using spoken language (e.g., face-to-face talks, telephone conversations), or *written* (e.g., memos, letters, e-mail). Both involve the use of words.

As you know, organizations rely on a wide variety of verbal media. Some forms are considered *rich* because they are highly interactive and rely on a great deal of information. A face-to-face-discussion is a good example. So too are telephone conversations, although these are considered a little less rich because the parties do not have available to them the visual cues that people do while discussing things in person. Other forms of organizational communication are considered *lean* because they are static (one-way) and involve much less information. Flyers and bulletins are a good example insofar as they are broadly aimed and focused on a specific issue. Letters are also a relatively lean form of communication. However, the fact that they are aimed at a specific individual makes them richer than bulletins. All told, communication in organizations relies on a wide variety of different verbal media.

Two types of written media deserve special mention because of the important roles they play in organizations. First, although they are impersonal and aimed at a general audience, **newsletters** serve important functions in organizations. These are regularly published internal documents describing in-

Going beyond newsletters, Nissan *updates the 5,000 employees at its Smyrna, Tennessee plant on company news events by broadcasting on its own closed-circuit television station,* Nissan News Network (NNN). *Programs are transmitted to 120 monitors located around the plant.*

formation of interest to employees regarding an array of business and nonbusiness issues. Approximately one-third of companies rely on newsletters, typically as a way of supplementing other means of communicating important information (e.g., group meetings). A second important internal publication used in organizations is the **employee handbook**—a document describing to employees basic information about the company. It is a general reference regarding the company's background, the nature of its business, and its rules. Specifically, the major purposes of employee handbooks are: (1) to explain key aspects of the company's policies, (2) to clarify the expectations of the company and employees toward each other, and (3) to express the company's philosophy. Handbooks are more popular today than ever before. This is not only because clarifying company policies may help prevent lawsuits, but also because corporate officials are recognizing that explicit statements about what their company stands for is a useful means of effectively socializing new employees and promoting the company's values (see Chapter 5). (For examples of some additional tools for communicating with employees that have proven effective in one large company, see the **Winning Practices** section on p. 156.)

In connection with verbal communication it makes sense to ask: What types—oral or written—are most effective, and when? In this regard, research has shown that communication is most effective when it uses multiple channels—both oral and written messages.[3] Apparently, oral messages are useful in getting others' immediate attention, and the follow-up written portion helps make the message more permanent, something that can be referred to in the future. Oral messages also have the benefit of allowing for immediate two-way communication between parties, whereas written communiqués are frequently only one-way, or take too long for a response. Not surprisingly, two-way communications (e.g., face-to-face discussions, telephone conversations) are more commonly used in organizations than one-way communications (e.g., memos).

Interestingly, it has been found that a medium's effectiveness depends on how appropriate it is for the kind of message being sent. In one study, researchers surveyed a sample of managers about the media they preferred using to communicate messages that differed with respect to their clarity or ambiguity.[4] (For example, "giving a subordinate a set of cost figures" was prejudged to be a very clear message, whereas "getting an explanation about a complicated technical matter" was prejudged to be a very ambiguous message.) They found that the choice of medium was related to the clarity or ambiguity of the messages. Specifically, the more ambiguous the message, the more managers preferred using oral media (such as telephones or face-to-face contact). Furthermore, the clearer the message, the more managers preferred using written media (such as letters or memos). Apparently, many managers were sensitive

At General Motors, Communication Sags No More in Saginaw

For some time, productivity and morale were lower than desired at General Motors' Saginaw Division, and poor communication was believed to be the culprit. When it became clear that GM management and its 20,000 local employees had developed suspicions and distrust about each other, several steps were taken to open up a dialogue between them. A multipronged approach was adopted.

First, top management was presented with detailed information from technical journals and popular magazines that underscored the importance of opening the lines of communication within the company. Without making a clear case that effective communication can boost the bottom line, it was feared that any efforts to improve communication would not be taken seriously.

The content of the company's *Daily Newsletter* was changed so that it paid less attention to general reports about the auto industry, and had more coverage of matters of local interest. Readership soared in all quarters; GM labor and management enjoyed reading about what was happening under its roof.

Several other publications were launched as well. For example, a monthly tabloid, the *Steering Column*, was sent to GM employees at home. It contained more detailed accounts of news events at the division. Other publications were targeted at specific groups. For example, *Report to Supervisors* was published bimonthly. It not only presented advance information about key issues, but also tips on how to present them to the rank and file. A quarterly video magazine, *Perspective*, containing interviews with managers, customers, employees, and suppliers, was quite effective in keeping people informed and getting them to talk to each other.

Just in case people weren't reading or viewing these official materials, a series of face-to-face meetings between labor and management were held. Believing that management and labor were out of touch with each other, such meetings became good opportunities to have frank discussions about issues that previously would have been ignored.

After four years of such intensive communication efforts, things have dramatically improved at GM's Saginaw Division. The level of trust between management and labor, which had been seriously low, jumped considerably—and with it, employees' willingness to work hard for the company. Operating costs dropped, and on-time deliveries improved 100 percent. Company officials are convinced that communications that have brought everyone together on the same side played a large part in the company's turnaround. Today similar efforts at intensive communication are in place in all other GM divisions. Chances are good that GM officials need little further convincing about the importance of communication in their organization.

to the need to use communications media that allowed them to take advantage of the rich avenues for two-way oral communications when necessary, and to use the more efficient one-way, written communications when these were adequate. In fact, the study found that those who followed this pattern were generally considered better managers than those who did not. Such findings suggest that demonstrating sensitivity to communicating in the most appropriate fashion is an important determinant of managerial success.

FORMAL COMMUNICATION: USING ORGANIZATIONAL STRUCTURE TO DIRECT THE FLOW OF MESSAGES

A letter from the president appearing in the employee handbook of **Marquette Electronics,** *a medical equipment manufacturer, explains that the company strives to avoid restricting communication to channels dictated by organizational charts. The door is always open to communicate with any official, no matter how high ranking.*

Organizations are often designed in ways that dictate who may and may not communicate with whom. The formally prescribed pattern of interrelationships existing between the various units of an organization is referred to as **organizational structure.** Although we will discuss this topic more fully in Chapter 10, here we describe the many important ways in which organizational structure influences communication. An organization's structure is commonly described by using an **organizational chart.** Such a diagram provides a graphic representation of an organization's structure, an outline of the planned, formal connections between its various units. An organizational chart showing the structure of part of a fictitious organization, and an overview of the types of communication expected to occur within it, is shown in Figure 6-2 on p. 158.

Note the various boxes in the diagram and the lines connecting them. Each box represents a person performing a specific job. The diagram shows the titles of the individuals performing the various jobs and the formally prescribed pattern of communication between them. The lines connecting the boxes in the organizational chart are lines of authority, showing who must answer to whom. Each person is responsible to (or, answers to) the person at the next higher level to which he or she is connected. At the same time, people are also responsible for (or, give orders to) those who are immediately below them. The pattern of boxes and lines indicates those specific others with whom people have to communicate for the organization to operate.

As you might imagine, the nature of communication varies greatly as a function of people's relative positions within an organization. Even a quick look at an organizational chart reveals that information may flow up (from lower to higher levels), down (from higher to lower levels), or horizontally (between people at the same level). However, different types of information typically travel in different directions within a hierarchy.

To illustrate this, imagine that you are a supervisor. What types of messages do you think would characterize communication between you and your

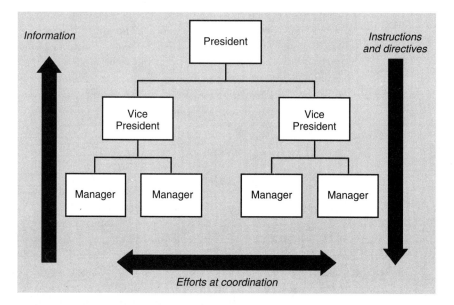

■ *Figure 6-2 The Organizational Chart: A Summary of Formal Communication Paths*

The organizational chart indicates the formal pattern of communication within an organization—that is, which individuals are required to communicate with each other. The types of messages that tend to be communicated across different levels are identified here.

subordinates? Typically, *downward communication* consists of instructions, directions, and orders—messages telling subordinates what they should be doing. We also would expect to find feedback on past performance flowing in a downward direction (such as when managers tell subordinates how well they have been working). A sales manager, for example, might direct members of the sales force to promote a certain product and may then congratulate them for being successful.

Downward communication flows from one level to the next lowest one, slowly trickling down to the bottom. As a message passes through various levels, it often becomes less accurate (especially if the information is spoken). Thus, it is not surprising to find that the most effective downward communication techniques are ones directly aimed at those who are most affected by the messages—namely, small group meetings and organizational publications targeting specific groups. Such methods are being used successfully in several companies (such as General Motors' Saginaw Division described earlier). For example, executives at Tandem Computers hold monthly teleconferences with their employees. Such efforts at improving downward communication have been credited with improving productivity and reducing turnover.

Upward communication flows from lower levels to higher levels within an organization, such as from subordinates to supervisors. Messages flowing in this direction tend to contain the information managers need to do their jobs, such as data required for decision making and the status of various projects. In short, upward communication is designed to keep managers aware of what is going on. Among the various types of information flowing upward are suggestions for improvement, status reports, reactions to work-related issues, and new ideas.

Upward communication is not simply the reverse of downward communication. The difference in status between the communicating parties makes for some important distinctions. For example, it has been established that upward communication occurs much less frequently than downward communication. In fact, one classic study found that 70 percent of assembly-line workers initiated communication with their supervisors less than once a month. Moreover, managers direct less than 15 percent of their total communication to their superiors. And, when people do communicate upward, their conversations tend to be shorter than discussions with peers.

Perhaps more important, upward communication often tends to suffer from serious inaccuracies. For example, subordinates frequently feel they must highlight their accomplishments and downplay their mistakes if they are to be looked upon favorably. Similarly, some individuals fear that they will be rebuked by their supervisors if they anticipate that their remarks will be perceived as threatening. As a result, many people frequently avoid communicating bad news to their supervisors, or simply "pass the buck" for doing so to someone else. This general reluctance to transmit bad news is referred to as the **MUM effect.** As you might imagine, because superiors rely on information when making decisions, keeping silent about important news, even if it's bad, may be one of the worst things a subordinate can do. As one executive put it, "All of us have our share of bonehead ideas. Having someone tell you it's a bonehead idea before you do something about it is really a great blessing."[5]

Finally, we note that *horizontal communication* also occurs within organizations. Messages that flow laterally (at the same organizational level) are characterized by efforts at coordination (attempts to work together). Consider, for example, how a vice president of marketing would have to coordinate efforts to initiate an advertising campaign for a new product with information from the vice president of production about when the first products will be coming off the assembly line. Unlike vertical communication, in which the parties are at different status levels, horizontal communication involves people at the same level and, therefore, tends to be easier and friendlier. Communication between peers also tends to be more casual and occurs more quickly because fewer social barriers exist between the parties. Note, however, that even horizontal communication can be problematic. For example, people in different departments may feel that they are competing against each other for valued organizational resources and may show resentment toward each other, thereby substituting an antagonistic, competitive orientation for the friendlier, cooperative one needed to get things done.

INFORMAL COMMUNICATION: BEYOND THE ORGANIZATIONAL CHART

It should be quite obvious that communication in organizations goes far beyond the formal messages communicated up, down, and across the organizational chart. To get a true picture of organizational communication we also must pay attention to **informal communication**—information shared without any formally imposed obligations or restrictions.

Informal communication is characterized by the fact that it occurs between individuals at different organizational levels. People can tell anyone whatever informal information they wish. For example, jokes and funny stories tended to cross organizational boundaries, and are freely shared by those in both the managerial and nonmanagerial ranks of organizations. In contrast, it would be considered "out of line" for a lower-level employee to communicate something to an upper-level employee about how to do the job. What flows within the pathways of informal communication is "unofficial" information, messages unrelated to individuals' work.

It is easy to imagine how important the flow of informal information may be within organizations. People transmit information to those with whom they come into contact, thereby providing conduits through which messages can travel. Such informal connections may explain a very important organizational phenomenon—turnover. Specifically, in a fast-food restaurant scientists traced the pattern of people who left their jobs for new ones. They found a striking pattern: Voluntary turnover was related to informal communication. Specifically, the people who left their jobs were ones who communicated with others who left earlier. It is easy to imagine how informal conversations with one's workmates about better job opportunities elsewhere may lead to patterns of turnover closely tied to informal contact (hence, access to information).

When anyone can tell something informally to anyone else, it results in a very rapid flow of information along what is commonly referred to as the **grapevine**—the pathways along which unofficial, informal information travels. In contrast to a formal organizational message, which might take several days to reach its desired audience in a large organization, information traveling along the organizational grapevine tends to flow very rapidly, often reaching everyone within hours. This is not only because informal communication can cross formal organizational boundaries, but also because informal information tends to be communicated orally. As we noted earlier, oral messages are communicated faster than written ones, but may become increasingly inaccurate as they flow from person to person. Because of the confusion grapevines may cause, some people have sought to eliminate them, but they are not necessarily bad. Informally socializing with our coworkers can help make work groups more cohesive, and may also provide excellent opportunities for desired human contact, keeping the work environment stimulating. Grapevines must be considered an inevitable fact of life in organizations.

Generally speaking, the information communicated along the grapevine may be accurate in some respects but inaccurate in other key ones. And, as a result, these reports can be dangerous. In extreme cases, information may be transmitted that is almost totally without any basis in fact and usually unverifiable. Such messages are known as **rumors.** Typically, rumors are based on speculation, an overactive imagination, and wishful thinking, rather than on facts. Rumors race like wildfire through organizations because the information they present is so interesting and ambiguous. The ambiguity leaves it open to embellishment as it passes orally from one person to the next. Before you know it, almost everyone in the organization has heard the rumor, and its inaccurate message becomes taken as fact ("It must be true, everyone knows it"). Hence, even if there was, at one point, some truth to a rumor, the message quickly becomes untrue.

If you've ever been the victim of a rumor, you know how difficult rumors can be to quell, and how profound their effects can be. This is especially the case when organizations are the victims of rumors. For example, a rumor about the use of worms in McDonald's hamburgers circulated in the Chicago area in the late 1970s. Although the rumor was completely untrue, sales dropped as much as 30 percent in some restaurants. You may recall that in June 1993 stories appeared in the press stating that people across the United States found syringes in cans of Pepsi-Cola. Although the stories proved to be completely without fact, the hoax cost Pepsi plenty in terms of investigative and advertising expenses.

What can be done to counter the effects of rumors? Although this is a difficult question to answer, evidence suggests that directly refuting a rumor may not always counter its effects. Although Pepsi officials denied the reports about their tainted product, that particular rumor was not only implausible but was also quickly disproven by independent investigators from the Food and Drug Administration. Sometimes, however, rumors are more difficult to disprove and do not die quickly. In such cases, directly refuting the rumors only fuels the fire. When you directly refute a rumor (e.g., "I didn't do it") you actually may help spread it among those who have not already heard about it ("Oh, I didn't know people thought that") and strengthen it among those who have already heard it ("If it weren't true, they wouldn't be protesting so much"). Directing people's attention away from the rumor may help, focusing instead on other things they know about the target of the rumor. In research studying the McDonald's rumor, for example, it was found that reminding people about other things they thought about McDonald's (e.g., that it is a clean, family-oriented place) helped counter the negative effects of the rumor.[6]

If you should ever become the victim of a rumor, try immediately to refute it with indisputable facts if you can. But, if it lingers on, try directing people's attention to other positive things they already believe about you. Although rumors may be impossible to stop, their effects can, with some effort, be effectively managed.

STRATEGIES FOR IMPROVING ORGANIZATIONAL COMMUNICATION

Given how important it is for people in organizations to communicate with each other in a thorough, open, and accurate fashion, it is worthwhile to consider ways of improving organizational communication. We will briefly present several tried-and-true strategies.

Encourage Open Feedback.   In theory, it's simple: If accurate information is the key to effective communication, then organizations should encourage feedback since, after all, feedback is a prime source of information. However, we say "in theory" because many executives fear finding out the truth—or, at least, what others believe it to be. Likewise, subordinates may be apprehensive about baring their souls, for fear of repercussion (recall our earlier discussion of the *MUM effect*). It's important to foster an atmosphere in which executives search for feedback and in which lower-level employees feel that they can speak their minds with impunity. To help in this regard, Harry Rosenbluth, CEO of a travel agency in Philadelphia that bears his name, invites new employees to a social gathering during their first week on the job. During this time he emphasizes the importance of openly sharing information within the agency.

Some companies go far out of their way to solicit employees' opinions of how well the top bosses are doing. Upward evaluation of this type is known as **360-degree feedback**—formal evaluations of superiors and the company by subordinates. A growing number of companies, including Alcoa, BellSouth, General Mills, Hewlett-Packard, Merck, Motorola, *Reader's Digest,* and 3M have been actively soliciting 360-degree feedback. And, even if these companies are not always happy about what they hear, they most certainly find it useful to hear it. For example, at UPS, employees indicated that their managers were not especially useful in helping them develop their skills. And, as a result of having encouraged such feedback, UPS officials have been working hard to improve in this important respect.

Organizations have been doing many things to solicit feedback from employees. One simple but effective tool is a **suggestion system**—a mechanism (e.g., a suggestion box) for employees to submit ideas about what can be done to make things better. Typically, good ideas are implemented, and the employees who thought of them are rewarded. Kodak has been using suggestion systems for several years. In fact, the idea to mount boxes of film onto cards that could be hung from display stands, so common today, originally came from one Kodak employee.

Another mechanism for soliciting feedback is **corporate hotlines**—telephone lines staffed by corporate officials ready to answer questions and listen to comments. This direct form of communication has been used by many companies, and has been particularly useful during times in which they are undergoing change. For example, AT&T used hotlines in the early 1980s during the period of its antitrust divestiture.

Of course, lines of communication may be opened even before a time of uncertainty. With this in mind, **brown bag meetings** are often used to bring together over informal meals people from different organizational levels who might not otherwise talk during the course of their jobs. These various techniques, despite their different forms, are all ways of facilitating feedback and opening lines of communication that might otherwise be blocked.

At the software firm, **Lotus Development,** *quarterly meetings are held in which all employees gather in a large hotel ballroom to ask questions of the company president. To include employees located at distant sites around the world, teleconferencing technology is used.*

Use Simple Language.   No matter what field you're in, chances are good that it has its own special language—its **jargon.** (Recall our discussion of jargon as a tool for communicating organizational culture in Chapter 5.) Although jargon may greatly help communication within specialized groups, it can severely hamper it when dealing with the uninitiated. So it is important to know your audience. If the individuals to whom you are speaking or writing fully understand your jargon, using it can help. If not, avoid it, favoring straightforward language instead. And we do mean straightforward—in fact, outright simple language is generally best. After all, communication is clearest when it involves language that everyone understands. Although there may be times when you seek to impress someone by using big words, by doing so you risk causing confusion or misunderstanding in your audience. With this in mind, communications experts recommend endorsing the **K.I.S.S. principle**—that is, **k**eep **i**t **s**hort and **s**weet. Or, ignoring our own advice, eschew obfuscation.

Avoid Overload.   When people are confronted with more information than they can process at any given time, they face a condition known as **overload.** To the extent that one is overloaded, the flow of information is slowed down through a bottleneck, threatening organizational functioning. As an example, consider how highly inefficiently a manufacturing company would operate if thousands of requisitions for parts were funneled through a single individual who could only process a few per hour.

Fortunately, several things can be done to avoid, or at least minimize, overload. Among them is using **gatekeepers**—people whose jobs require them to control the flow of information to potentially overloaded units. For example, newspaper editors make decisions about which stories are important enough to publish, thereby avoiding overloading readers with too much information. Similarly, administrative assistants control who has access to the time of busy executives so that they are also not overloaded. Overload also can be avoided through **queuing**—that is, lining up incoming information so that it can be managed in an orderly fashion. This is precisely what is done by air traffic controllers when they "stack" incoming planes in a holding pattern, preventing them from tragically "overloading" the runway. Both using gatekeepers and queuing can be quite helpful in avoiding overload.

Match Words and Deeds.   When it comes to good communication, action definitely speaks louder than words. Too often communication is hampered by the practice of saying one thing but meaning another. And if *implicit* messages (e.g., "we may be cutting jobs") contradict *official* messages (e.g., "don't worry, the company is stable"), confusion is sure to result. This is especially problem-

---

GROUP EXERCISE

Sharpening Your Listening Skills

Are you a good listener, a *really* good listener, who understands exactly what others are saying to you? Most of us tend to think that we are much better than we really are when it comes to this important skill. After all, we've been listening to people our whole lives. And, with that much practice, we must certainly be okay. To gain some insight into your own listening skills, try the following group exercise.

Directions

1. Divide the class into pairs of people who do not already know each other. Arrange the chairs so that the people within each pair are facing one another but are separated from the other pairs.

2. Within each pair, one person should be selected as the speaker, and the other as the listener. The speaker should tell the listener about a specific incident on the job in which he or she was somehow harmed (e.g., disappointed by not getting a raise, being embarrassed by another, losing a battle with a coworker, getting fired, and so on), and how he or she felt about it. The total discussion should last about 10 to 15 minutes.

3. Listeners should carefully attempt to follow the suggestions for good listening summarized in Table 6-1 (on p. 166). To help, the instructor should discuss these with the class.

4. After the conversations are over, review the suggestions with your partner. Discuss which ones the listener followed and which ones were ig-

atic when the inconsistency comes from the top. In fact, one of the most effective ways of fostering effective organizational communication is for CEOs to "walk the talk," that is, to behave consistently with what they say. At the risk of being labeled a hypocrite, a boss cannot say, "my door is always open, you can talk to me whenever you want," and then not be available for consultation. Good communication demands consistency. And, for the words to be heard just as loud as the actions, they must be the same.

Be a Good Listener.   Effective communication involves more than just presenting messages clearly. It also involves doing a good job of comprehending others. A key skill in this regard is being a good listener. Most of us are probably not as good at listening as we should be, and as a result, we fully compre-

nored. Try to be as open and honest as possible about assessing your own and the other's strengths and weaknesses. Speakers should consider the extent to which they felt the listeners were really paying attention to them.

5. Repeat steps 2 through 4, but change roles. Speakers now become listeners, and listeners now become speakers.

6. As a class, share your experiences as speakers and listeners.

QUESTIONS FOR DISCUSSION

1. What did this exercise teach you about your own skills as a listener? Are you as good as you thought? Do you think you can improve?

2. Was there general agreement or disagreement about each listener's strengths and weaknesses? Explain.

3. After the discussion about the first listener's effectiveness, you might expect the second listener to do a better job. Was this the case in your own group or throughout the class?

4. Which particular listening skills were easiest and which most difficult to put into practice? Are there certain conditions under which good listening skills may be difficult to implement?

5. Do you think you have learned something from this exercise that will get you to improve your listening skills in other situations? If so, what? If not, why not?

■ *Table 6-1 Tips for Improving Your Listening Skills*

Being a good listener is an important skill that can enhance the effectiveness of communication in organizations. Although it may be difficult to follow the suggestions outlined here, the benefits may make it worthwhile to try to do so. (Based on suggestions by Morrison, 1994; see Note 7.)

Suggestion	Description
Do not talk while being spoken to.	It is difficult, if not impossible, to listen to another while you are speaking to that person.
Make the speaker feel at ease.	Help the speaker feel that he or she is free to talk as desired.
Eliminate distractions.	Don't focus on other things; pay attention only to the speaker.
Show empathy with the speaker.	Try to put yourself in the speaker's position, and try to see his or her point of view.
Be as patient as possible.	Take the time needed to hear everything the speaker has to say.
Hold your arguments.	If you're busy forming your own arguments, you cannot focus on others' points.
Ask questions.	By asking questions, you demonstrate that you are listening, and make it possible to clarify areas of uncertainty.

hend only a small portion of the information directed at us. So, what can we do to improve? Experts have offered several good suggestions, some of which are summarized in Table 6-1.[7] Although it requires some effort, incorporating these suggestions into your own listening habits cannot help but make you a better listener.

Many organizations are actively working to improve their employees' listening skills. For example, Unisys has long used seminars and self-training audiocassettes to train thousands of its employees in effective listening skills. Such systematic efforts at improving listening skills make sense insofar as people tend to overestimate their capacity to listen effectively. And good listening pays off. Indeed, research has clearly shown that the more effective one is as a listener, the more likely he or she is to get promoted and to perform effectively as a manager. (To practice your listening skills, and to help others do the same, see the **Group Exercise** section on pp. 164–165.)

SOCIAL INFLUENCE: HAVING AN IMPACT ON OTHERS

If you were to think about the most effective managers you have known, chances are good that you'd recognize that they were all pretty good at one important thing—getting others to do as they wished. That is, they are successful at **social influence**—attempts to affect another in some desired fashion. Now, if you thought about it further, you'd probably recognize that despite being so highly influential, these managers accomplished what they wanted using very different strategies. For example, one manager may have been very straightforward, explaining why it is best to behave a certain way ("this works best because . . ."). Another may have brought pressure to bear ("do it this way, or else . . ."). This raises an important question that we will consider in this section of the chapter: In what ways do people influence others in organizations?

INFLUENCE THAT COMES WITH THE OFFICE: POSITION POWER

A great deal of the power people have in organizations comes from the posts they hold. In other words, they are able to influence others because of the formal power associated with their jobs. This is known as **position power.** For example, there are certain powers that the president of the United States has simply due to the authority given to the office holder (e.g., signing bills into law, making treaties, and so on). These formal powers remain vested in the position and are available to anyone who holds that position. When the president's term is up, these powers transfer to the new office holder. There are four bases of position power: *legitimate power, reward power, coercive power,* and *information power.*

The power that people have because others recognize and accept their authority is known as **legitimate power.** As an example, students recognize that their instructors have the authority to make class policies and to determine grades, giving them legitimate power over the class. If someone were to challenge the teacher's decision, saying, "who are you to do that?" the answer might be, "I'm the instructor, that's who." This exchange would clarify the legitimacy of the office holder's behavior. However, it is important to note that legitimate power covers a relatively narrow range of influence, and that it may be inappropriate to overstep these bounds. For example, whereas a boss may require her secretary to type and fax a company document using her legitimate power to do so, it would be an abuse of power to ask that secretary to type her son's homework assignment. This is not to say that the secretary might not take on the task as a favor, but doing so would not be the direct result of the boss's formal authority. Legitimate power applies only to the range of behaviors that are recognized and accepted as appropriate by the parties and institutions involved.

Associated with holding certain jobs comes the power to control the rewards others receive—that is, **reward power.** Extending our teacher–student example, instructors have reward power over students insofar as they may reward them with high grades and glowing letters of recommendation. In the case of managers, the rewards available may be either tangible, such as raises and promotions, or intangible, such as praise and recognition. In both cases, access to these desired outcomes gives power to the individuals who control them.

By contrast, power also results from the capacity to control punishments—that is, **coercive power.** Although most managers do not like using the threat of punishments, it is a fact of organizational life that many people rely on coercive power. If any boss has ever directly told you, "do what I say, or else," or even implied it, you are probably all too familiar with coercive power. Often people have power simply because others know that they have the opportunity to punish them, even if the threat of doing so is not made explicit. For example, in the military, when your commanding officer asks you to do something, you must comply since that request can turn into an order with severe consequences for not going along. In private organizations, threats of demotions, suspensions without pay, and assignments to undesirable duties may enhance the coercive power of many managers.

The fourth source of power available to people by virtue of their positions is based on the data and other knowledge at their disposal—known as **information power.** Traditionally, people in top positions have available to them unique sources of information that are not available to others (e.g., knowledge of company performance, market trends, and so on). As they say, "knowledge is power," and such information greatly contributes to the power of people in many jobs. Although information power still exists, it is becoming a less potent source of influence in many of today's organizations. The reason is that technology has made it possible for more information to be available to more people than ever before. As a result, information need no longer be the unique property of a few people holding special positions.

INFLUENCE THAT COMES FROM THE INDIVIDUAL: PERSONAL POWER

Thus far, all the sources of influence we've discussed have been based on an individual's position in an organization. However, this is not the only way people are able to influence others. There's also power derived from an individual's own unique qualities or characteristics. This is known as **personal power.** There are four sources of personal power: *rational persuasion, referent power, expert power,* and *charisma.*

In the early 1990s Apple Computer's chairman John Scully didn't like what he saw when he looked into the future. Apple was doing well, but computer sales threatened to flatten out in the years ahead. The future of the company, he envisioned, involved applying Apple's user-friendly digital technology in new areas. Integrating telephones, computers, televisions, and entertainment systems was the key. So, Scully's first task was to get Apple's Chief Operating Officer, Michael H. Spindler, and the board of directors to share his dream. After drawing on all his knowledge of the computer business and carefully studying what needed to be done to make the dream a reality, Scully thoroughly explained his plan for changing Apple from a single-product company with a straightforward distribution system to a multiproduct, multi-business conglomerate. Spindler and the board were convinced, and Apple's new strategy was launched.

Scully used a very popular technique of social influence known as **ratio-nal persuasion.** This approach relies on logical arguments and factual evidence to convince others that a certain idea is acceptable. Rational persuasion is highly effective when the parties involved are intelligent enough to make their cases strongly and to understand them clearly (there can be no doubt about this among Apple's top brass!). Given that it is based on clear logic, good evidence, and the desire to help the company, rational persuasion is likely to be highly effective. Not surprisingly, it has been found to be among the most popular types of influence used in organizations.

In addition to rational persuasion, it's clear that Scully's ideas were accepted because of the considerable expertise he had in the business. Thus, it can be said that he had **expert power**—that is, power based on superior knowledge of a certain field. Likewise, a coach has power over athletes to the extent that he or she is recognized as knowing what is best. Once experts have proven themselves, their power over others can be considerable. After all, people will respect and want to follow those in the know. However, should a supervisor's expertise be shown to be lacking, any power he or she may have based on that expertise is threatened. Insofar as no one is expected to be an expert on everything, this is not necessarily problematic. The less-than-expert person can simply admit his or her shortcomings and seek guidance from others. Where problems develop, however, is if someone in a position of power has not yet developed a level of expertise that is acknowledged and respected by lower-ranking persons (especially when these individuals believe they are more expert!). Those who have not demonstrated their expertise clearly lack this important source of power. However, people whose expertise is highly regarded are among the most powerful people in organizations.

As you surely know, it is not only expertise, but personal qualities, that form the basis of our admiration for others in organizations. Individuals who are liked and respected by others can get others to alter their actions, a type of influence known as **referent power.** Senior managers who possess desirable qualities and good reputations may find that they have referent power over younger managers who identify with them and wish to emulate them.

Some people are liked so much by others that they are said to have the quality of **charisma**—an engaging and magnetic personality. (We will discuss charisma more fully as a characteristic of effective leadership in Chapter 8.) There's no ignoring the fact that some people become highly influential because of their charismatic ways. What makes such individuals so influential? There appear to be several factors involved. First, highly charismatic people have definite visions of the future of their organizations and how to get there. Mary Kay Ash, the founder of Mary Kay Cosmetics, is widely regarded to be such a visionary. Second, people with charisma tend to be excellent communi-

SELF-ASSESSMENT EXERCISE

To What Forms of Social Influence Are You Subjected?

One of the main ways of learning about social influence in organizations is to use questionnaires in which people are asked to describe the behaviors of their superiors. If a consistent pattern emerges with respect to the way subordinates describe superiors, some very strong clues are provided as to the nature of that superior's influence style. Questionnaires similar to this one are used for this purpose.[8] Complete this questionnaire to gain some indication of the types of social influence favored by your supervisor.

DIRECTIONS

Indicate how strongly you agree or disagree with each of the following statements as it describes your immediate supervisor. Answer by using the following scale: 1 = strongly disagree; 2 = disagree; 3 = neither agree nor disagree; 4 = agree; 5 = strongly agree. For each statement select the number corresponding to the most appropriate response.

My supervisor can:

_____   1. Recommend that I receive a raise.

_____   2. Assign me to jobs I dislike.

_____   3. See that I get the promotion I desire.

_____   4. Make my life at work completely unbearable.

_____   5. Make decisions about how things are done.

_____   6. Provide useful advice on how to do my job better.

_____   7. Comprehend the importance of doing things a certain way.

_____   8. Make me want to look up to him or her.

_____   9. Share with me the benefit of his or her vast job knowledge.

_____   10. Get me to admire what he or she stands for.

_____   11. Find out things that nobody else knows.

_____   12. Explain things so logically that I want to do them.

_____   13. Have access to vital data about the company.

_____   14. Share a clear vision of what the future holds for the company.

_____   15. Come up with the facts needed to make a convincing case about something.

_____   16. Put me in a trance when he or she communicates to me.

SCORING

1. Add the numbers assigned to statements 1 and 3. This is the *reward power* score.

2. Add the numbers assigned to statements 2 and 4. This is the *coercive power* score.

3. Add the numbers assigned to statements 5 and 7. This is the *legitimate power* score.

4. Add the numbers assigned to statements 6 and 9. This is the *expert power* score.

5. Add the numbers assigned to statements 8 and 10. This is the *referent power* score.

6. Add the numbers assigned to statements 11 and 13. This is the *information power* score.

7. Add the numbers assigned to statements 12 and 15. This is the *rational persuasion* score.

8. Add the numbers assigned to statements 14 and 16. This is the *charisma* score.

QUESTIONS FOR DISCUSSION

1. With respect to which dimensions did your supervisor score highest and lowest? Are these consistent with what you would have predicted in advance?

2. Does your supervisor behave in ways consistent with the dimension along which you gave him or her the highest score? In other words, does he or she fit the description given in the text?

3. How do you think your own subordinates would answer the various questions with respect to yourself?

4. Which of the eight forms of social influence do you think are most common and least common, and why?

5. What additional statements, beyond the two given here, could be used to describe each form of social influence?

6. How easy or difficult do you believe it would be to change the forms of influence people tend to use?

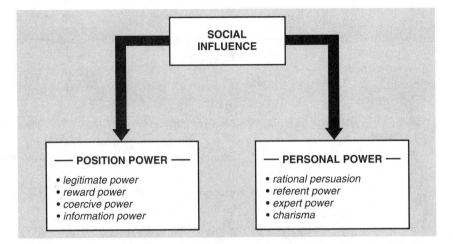

■ *Figure 6-3 Social Influence: Its Basic Forms*

Social influence can be based on the position one holds—*position power,* and an individual's own traits and characteristics—*personal power.* The various forms of each type of power are listed here.

cators. They tend to rely on colorful language and exciting metaphors to excite the crowd. They also supplement their words with emotionally expressive and animated gestures. The president of Coca-Cola has been known to do this. Third, charismatic individuals inspire trust. Their integrity is never challenged, and is a source of their strength. Former U.S. president John F. Kennedy has been so described by many historians. Fourth, people with charisma make others feel good about themselves. They are receptive to others' feelings and acknowledge them readily. "Congratulations on a job well done" is a phrase that may flow freely from a charismatic individual.

To summarize, people may influence others by virtue of both the jobs they have, and their individual characteristics. For a summary of the factors within each category, refer to Figure 6-3. (To see how scientists measure different types of social influence, and to make some preliminary judgments about the types of influence your own supervisor uses, see the **Self-Assessment Exercise** on pp. 170–171.)

ORGANIZATIONAL POLITICS:
SELFISHLY MOTIVATED INFLUENCE

Underlying our discussion of social influence has been the assumption that people attempt to affect others in ways consistent with an organization's goals. Although this is generally true, sometimes, however, people purposely influence others in ways that are not in the best interest of their organizations, but which aid them personally. Such acts are referred to as **organizational poli-**

tics, which we formally define as actions not officially approved by an organization that people take to influence others in ways that advance their own self-interests.

Politically motivated acts are most likely to occur in organizational units in which clear policies are nonexistent or lacking (such as among members of boards of directors), as opposed to those in which there are clearly defined rules and regulations (such as production and accounting departments). Similarly, because of the inherently high levels of ambiguity associated with human resources management tasks (such as personnel selection and performance appraisal), political behavior is likely to occur when these functions are being performed. In general, it may be said that political activity is likely to occur in the face of ambiguity. When there are clear-cut rules about what to do, it is unlikely that people will be able to abuse their power by taking political action. However, when people face highly novel and ambiguous situations, in which the rules guiding them are unclear, the stage is set for political behavior to result.

> *Although organizational politics are not uncommon in the field of journalism, employees at the* **Knight-Ridder** *newspaper chain note that it doesn't exist at their company. The reason? A strong sense of corporate unity discourages employees from taking advantage of others.*

Tactics of Organizational Politics. To understand organizational politics, we must recognize the various forms political behavior can take. Five major techniques of organizational politics are used most often.[9]

- **Restricting access to information.** Although outright lying and falsifying information may be used only rarely in organizations (in part because of the consequences of getting caught), people can control access to information in ways that enhance their organizational position. This includes: (1) withholding information that makes you look bad (e.g., negative sales information), (2) avoiding contact with those who ask for information you prefer not to disclose, (3) being very selective in the information you disclose, and (4) overwhelming others with information that may not be completely relevant.

- **Cultivating a favorable impression.** People interested in being highly influential tend to go out of their way to engage in some degree of **image building**—attempts to enhance the goodness of one's impressions on others. These efforts may take many forms, such as: (1) associating oneself with the successful accomplishments of others (or, in extreme cases, taking credit for others' successes), and (2) drawing attention to one's own successes and positive characteristics, making sure others are aware of them.

- **Developing a base of support.** To successfully influence people, it is often useful to gain the support of others within the organization. With this in mind, managers may: (1) lobby for their ideas before they officially present them at meetings (thereby ensuring that others are committed to them in advance and avoiding the embarrassment of public rejection), and (2) "scatter IOUs" throughout the organization by doing favors for others who may feel obligated to repay them in the form of supporting their ideas. "Calling in" favors is a well-established and widely used mechanism for developing organizational power.

- **Blaming and attacking others.** A commonly used political tactic is finding a *scapegoat,* someone who could take the blame for some failure or wrongdoing. A supervisor, for example, may explain that the failure of a sales plan he or she designed was based on the serious mistakes of a subordinate—even if this is not entirely true. Explaining that "it's someone else's fault," that is, making another "take the fall" for an undesirable event, gets the real culprit "off the hook" for it.

- **Aligning oneself with more powerful others.** One of the most direct ways to gain power is by connecting oneself with more powerful others. There are several ways to accomplish this. These include: (1) finding a very powerful mentor who can protect one's interests (recall our discussion of mentor–protégé relationships in Chapter 5), (2) forming coalitions—relatively powerless groups or individuals that derive strength by banding together to achieve some common goal (e.g., overthrowing a current corporate CEO), (3) aligning oneself with more powerful others by giving them "positive strokes" in the hope of getting more powerful people to like them and help them (a process known as **ingratiation**). Agreeing with someone more powerful may be an effective way of getting that person to consider you an ally—an alliance that may prove indispensable when you are looking for support within an organization.

Coping with Organizational Politics: Some Techniques.   Given how fundamental the need for power appears to be among people, and how differences in power between employees are basic to organizations, it is safe to say that organizational politics is inevitable. This is not good news, however, as many of the effects of organizational politics are quite negative. As such, managers must consider ways to minimize the effects of political behavior. Although it may be possible to abolish organizational politics altogether, managers can do several things to limit its effects.

- **Clarify job expectations.** You will recall that political behavior is nurtured by highly ambiguous conditions. To the extent that managers help reduce uncertainty, they can minimize the likelihood of political behavior. For example, managers should give very clear, well-defined work assignments. They should also clearly explain how work will be evaluated. Employees who know precisely what they are supposed to do and what level of performance is considered acceptable will find it unnecessary to rely on political games to assert their power. Under such conditions, recognition will come from meeting job expectations instead of from less acceptable avenues.

- **Open the communication process.** People have difficulty trying to foster their own goals at the expense of organizational goals when the communication process is open to scrutiny by all. Compare, for example, a department manager who makes budget allocation decisions in a highly open fashion (announced to all) and one who makes the same decisions in secret. When decisions are not openly shared and communicated to all, conditions are ideal for unscrupulous individuals to abuse their power. Decisions that can be monitored by all are unlikely to allow any one individual to gain excessive control over desired resources.

- **Be a good role model.** It is well established that higher-level personnel set the standards by which lower-level employees operate. As a result, any manager who is openly political in the use of power is likely to send the message that it is acceptable for subordinates to behave the same way. Engaging in dirty political tricks teaches subordinates not only that such tactics are appropriate, but also that they are the desired way of operating within the organization. Managers will certainly find it difficult to constrain the political actions of their subordinates unless they set a clear example of honest and reasonable treatment of others in their own behavior.

- **Do not turn a blind eye to game players.** Suppose you see one of your subordinates attempting to gain power over another by taking credit for that individual's work. Immediately confront this individual and do not ignore what he or she did. If the person believes he or she can get away with it, that person will try to do so. What's worse, if he or she suspects that you are aware of what really happened, but didn't do anything about it, you are indirectly reinforcing this unethical political behavior — showing your subordinate that he or she can get away with it.

In conclusion, it is important for practicing managers to realize that because power differences are basic to organizations, attempts to gain power advantages through political maneuvers are to be expected. However, a critical aspect of a manager's job is to redirect these political activities away from any threats to the integrity of the organization. Although expecting to eliminate dirty political tricks would be totally unrealistic, we believe the suggestions offered here provide some useful guidelines for minimizing their impact.

SUMMARY: PUTTING IT TO USE

Communication is the process by which a person, group, or organization transmits some type of information to another person, group, or organization. It involves several steps including: *encoding* a message (putting it into a form that can be understood by another, e.g., language), *transmitting* the message along communication channels, *decoding* the message (converting it back into the original ideas), and *feedback* (providing knowledge about the impact of the message). This process operates imperfectly, as various barriers known as *noise* are involved (e.g., messages may be unclear, or not well understood).

Verbal communication involves the use of words, either *written* or *oral*. In organizations, key tools of verbal communication include *newsletters*—internal documents describing areas of interest to employees, and *employee handbooks*—written guides as to the company's policies, expectations, and philosophy. Oral messages (e.g., telephone discussions or face-to-face meetings) are generally better at getting immediate attention and are particularly good for communicating ambiguous messages. However, written messages (e.g., memos and letters) are useful for communicating information that needs to be referred to in the future.

Formal communication is dictated by an organization's *structure* (as summarized by an *organizational chart*), dictating who is supposed to communicate with whom during the course of their jobs. Typically, different types of formal information flow in different directions within an organizational chart. Specifically, instructions, orders, and directions flow from top to bottom, reports and information flow from bottom to top, and attempts at coordination flow horizontally.

Communication also occurs in the form of information that is of interest to anyone in the organization, regardless of their organizational position. Such *informal communication* may involve jokes, funny stories, or *rumors* that are unofficial in nature. Rumors often contain inaccurate information of a harmful nature to either individuals or organizations. When facts can be presented that directly refute a rumor, this approach is highly effective in combating the rumor's effects. Otherwise, directly denying a rumor may be less effective than simply having people focus on other things about the organization or individual subjected to the rumor.

The effectiveness of communication can be improved in several ways. These include encouraging open feedback, using simple language, avoiding overload, matching one's words and deeds, and being a good listener.

Social influence refers to attempts to affect another in some desired fashion. Influence can be associated with the office one holds and can take several forms including: *legitimate power* (the accepted capacity of people to do certain things by virtue of their positions), *reward power* (the capacity to reward others), *coercive power* (the capacity to punish others), and *information power* (the capacity to control access to information). Influence also can be associated with an individual's unique personal characteristics and can take several forms including: *rational persuasion* (presenting logical evidence in support of a position), *expert power* (superior knowledge of a certain field), *referent power* (the willingness to go along with one who is liked), and *charisma* (the power derived from one's engaging, magnetic personality).

Some influence attempts are selfishly motivated and designed to promote one's own personal interests over those of the organization. Such acts are referred to as *organizational politics*. Political behavior may take the form of restricting access to information, cultivating a favorable impression, developing a base of support, blaming and attacking others, and aligning oneself with more powerful others. Such behaviors may be minimized by clarifying job expectations, opening the communication process, being a good role model, and not allowing people to take credit for others' work.

You Be the Consultant

"Everyone is moving in different directions, no one seems to have any sense of what the company is and where it is going. Making things worse, people around here are as selfish as can be; they're all a bunch of backstabbers." These are the words of an operations director of a large credit card processing center, who asks you to look into these problems on behalf of the company. Answer the following questions relevant to this situation based on the material in this chapter.

1. Casting the problem as one of poor communication between company officials and lower-level employees, what steps could be taken to fill everyone in on the company's plans, goals, and activities?

2. What forms of social influence are likely to contribute to the problem? What forms should be used instead, and why?

3. What evidence of organizational politics would you look for in this company? If you find it, what could be done to reduce political activity to acceptable levels?

CHAPTER 7

Groups and Teams in Organizations

Groups are defined as collections of two or more interacting individuals with a stable pattern of relationships between them who share common goals and who perceive themselves as being a group.

Norms are generally agreed-upon rules that guide behavior. They dictate what people can and cannot do within groups.

When working in the presence of others, people tend to either perform better or worse than they would while working alone, a phenomenon known as **social facilitation.**

When people pool their individual contributions to a group task, they tend to do less work than when performing alone. In fact, the greater the size of the group, the less the individual performance contributions—a phenomenon known as **social loafing.**

A team is a group whose members have complementary skills and are committed to a common purpose or set of performance goals for which they hold themselves mutually responsible.

Work teams are generally very productive in organizations, although making them successful is not easy. Group members must be very well trained and accept the group's mission for them to work effectively. It is also necessary for organizations to compensate contributions to group performance and to work to ensure cooperation between teams.

What do the following situations have in common? A committee meets to prepare the budget for next year. The company bowling team gathers at the lanes for the night's big match. Seven engineers work together to find ways to improve product safety. The answer is that all three involve the coordinated interaction between individuals working together for some specific purpose. In other words, they are *groups*. As you know, a great deal of the work performed in organizations is done by groups. In view of this, it makes sense to understand the types of groups that exist and the variables governing the interrelationships between them and individuals—commonly referred to as *group dynamics*. This will be our focus in the first half of this chapter.

Then, after examining the general nature of groups, we will shift our focus to a specific type of group that is growing in popularity in today's organizations—*teams*. These are groups in which people are strongly committed to achieving their goals and direct themselves toward attaining them. We will clarify the nature of teams, about which there has been some confusion, and then review cases in which teams have been used successfully in organizations. However, insofar as using teams can be tricky, we will also describe some obstacles to team effectiveness and how they may be overcome.

THE NATURE OF GROUPS

To understand the operation of groups in organizations, it is necessary to understand exactly what a group is and the types of formal and informal groups that exist. We will focus on these issues in this section of the chapter.

WHAT IS A GROUP?

Imagine waiting in a line at the bank one day along with five other people. Now compare this collection of individuals to your company's board of directors. Although in our everyday language we may refer to the people waiting in line as a group, they certainly are not a group in the same sense as the members of the board. Obviously, a group is more than simply a collection of people. But what exactly is it that makes a group a group?

Social scientists have formally defined a **group** as *a collection of two or more interacting individuals with a stable pattern of relationships between them who share common goals and who perceive themselves as being a group.* Let's consider the various elements of this definition separately.

First, groups are composed of *two or more people in social interaction*. In other words, the members of a group must have some influence on each other. Whether the interaction between the parties is immediate and occurs face to face, such as in committee meetings, or is delayed, such as might occur when a written draft of a document is circulated for comments, the parties must have some impact on each other to be considered a group.

Second, groups must possess a *stable structure*. Although groups can change, and often do, there must be some stable relationships that keep group members together and functioning as a unit. A collection of individuals that constantly changes (e.g., those waiting on the bank line with you) cannot be thought of as a group.

A third characteristic of groups is that *members share common interests or goals.* For example, members of a company's safety committee all share a common goal in keeping the workplace free of danger.

Fourth and finally, to be a group, the individuals involved must *perceive themselves as a group.* Groups are composed of people who recognize each other as a member of their group and can distinguish these individuals from non-members. Whether it's the members of a corporate board of directors or a company softball team, people know who is in their group and who is not. In contrast, the people waiting with you in line at the bank probably don't think of each other as being members of a group. Although they stand close together and may have passing conversations, they have little in common (except, perhaps, a shared interest in reaching the end of the line) and fail to identify themselves with the others in the line.

As these four characteristics suggest, groups are very special collections of individuals. Despite these specific requirements, there is a wide variety of different types of groups that may be identified within organizations.

FORMAL AND INFORMAL GROUPS

Although a military combat unit, the president's cabinet, and the three-person cockpit crew of a commercial airliner are certainly all very different from each other, they are all groups. So, to clarify our understanding of the nature of groups, it is helpful to describe the different types of groups that exist.

In this regard, it is useful to distinguish between *formal groups* and *informal groups* (see Figure 7-1). **Formal groups** are created by the organization and are intentionally designed to direct members toward some important organizational goal. One type of formal group is referred to as a *command group*—a group determined by the connections between individuals who are a formal part of the organization (i.e., those who can legitimately give orders to others; see Chapter 5). For example, a command group may be formed by the vice president of marketing who gathers together regional marketing directors from around the country to hear their ideas about a new national advertising campaign. Command groups are determined by the organization's rules regarding who reports to whom, and usually consist of a supervisor and his or her subordinates.

A formal organizational group also may be formed around some specific task. Such a group is referred to as a *task group.* Unlike command groups, task groups may be composed of individuals with some special interest or expertise in a specific area regardless of their positions in the organizational hierarchy. For example, a company may have a committee on equal employment oppor-

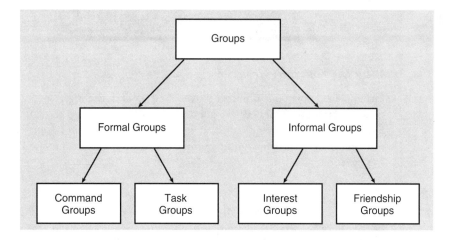

■ *Figure 7-1 Types of Groups*

Within organizations there are likely to be both *formal groups* (such as command groups and task groups) and *informal groups* (such as interest groups and friendship groups).

tunities whose members monitor the fair hiring practices of the organization. It may be composed of personnel specialists, corporate vice presidents, and workers from the shop floor. Whether they are permanent committees, known as *standing committees,* or temporary ones formed for special purposes (such as a committee formed to recommend solutions to a parking problem), known as *ad hoc committees* or *task forces,* task groups are commonly found in organizations.

Not all groups are as formal as those we've identified; many are informal in nature. **Informal groups** develop naturally among an organization's personnel without any direction from the management of the organization within which they operate. One key factor in the formation of informal groups is a common interest shared by its members. For example, a group of employees who band together to seek union representation, or who march together to protest their company's pollution of the environment, may be called an *interest group.* The common goal sought by members of an interest group may unite workers at many different organizational levels. The key factor is that membership in an interest group is voluntary—it is not dictated by the organization but encouraged by an expression of common interests.

Of course, sometimes the interests that bind individuals together are far more diffuse. Groups may develop out of a common interest in participating in sports, or going to the movies, or just getting together to talk. These kinds of informal groups are known as *friendship groups.* Friendship groups extend beyond the workplace because they provide opportunities for satisfying the so-

SELF-ASSESSMENT EXERCISE

Why Do You Join Groups?

Groups are important in people's lives, and we join them for several different reasons. However, chances are good that you haven't given too much thought to the matter of why you may have joined certain groups in the first place. So, to identify these reasons, you may find it enlightening to complete the following questionnaire.

DIRECTIONS

Think of a group you recently joined (e.g., a sports league, a campus club, a fraternity or sorority, a committee in your company). Then indicate the importance of each of the following reasons for joining by using the following scale: 1 = not at all important; 2 = slightly important; 3 = moderately important; 4 = greatly important; 5 = extremely important.

I joined this group because . . .

_____ 1. I had something important in common with the other members.

_____ 2. By joining the group, I had greater clout.

_____ 3. People in the group shared my interests.

_____ 4. The group helped me fell safe and secure.

_____ 5. I enjoy being with other people.

_____ 6. I thought the people in the group would make me feel good about myself.

cial needs of workers that are so important to their well-being (as you may recall from our discussion of Maslow's need hierarchy theory in Chapter 3).

Informal work groups are an important part of life in organizations. Although they develop without direct encouragement from management, friendships often originate out of formal organizational contact. For example, three employees working along side each other on an assembly line may get to talking and discover their mutual interest in basketball, and decide to get together after work to shoot hoops. As we will see, such friendships can bind people together, helping them cooperate with each other, having beneficial effects on organizational functioning. (Our discussion thus far has suggested that people have many different reasons for joining groups. For a look at some of the key reasons—and to see which ones apply to you—see the **Self-Assessment Exercise** above.)

_____   7.   I wanted to feel less lonely.

_____   8.   I expected the group members to recognize my accomplishments.

SCORING

1.   Add your responses to numbers 1 and 3. This score reflects your interest in joining the group *to seek the satisfaction of mutual interests and goals.*

2.   Add your responses to numbers 2 and 4. This score reflects your interest in joining the group *to achieve security.*

3.   Add your responses to numbers 5 and 7. This score reflects your interest in joining the group *to fill social needs.*

4.   Add your responses to numbers 6 and 8. This score reflects your interest in joining the group *to seek the fulfillment of self-esteem (feeling good about yourself) that others can provide.*

QUESTIONS FOR DISCUSSION

1.   What were your strongest (highest score) and weakest (lowest score) reasons for joining this group?

2.   Besides the four reasons identified here, what other reasons did you have for joining this group?

3.   Would your scores be different if you focused on another group you may have joined? Repeat the questionnaire to find out.

GROUP DYNAMICS: PEOPLE WORKING WITH OTHERS

To understand the dynamics of groups it is essential to consider the way groups influence individuals and the way individuals influence groups. We will examine several of the ways in which this occurs in this section of the chapter.

GROUP NORMS: UNSPOKEN RULES OF GROUP BEHAVIOR

From your own experiences in groups you probably already know one important way in which groups influence people—that is, by imposing ways of thinking and acting that are considered acceptable. If anyone has ever told you, "that's not the way we do things around here," then you probably already know how potent these effects can be. What you might not know, however, is that such informal forces constitute a key aspect of group dynamics known as **norms.** Specifically, a norm is a generally agreed-upon set of rules that guides the behavior of group members.[1]

To promote the norm of equal treatment for all, San Francisco's **Morrison & Foerster** *law firm does not have separate dining facilities or sumptuous corner offices for its top partners. All employees are on a first-name basis.*

Norms differ from organizational policies in that they are informal and unwritten. In fact, norms may be so subtle that group members may not even be aware that they are operating. Yet, their effects can be quite profound. For example, group norms may regulate such key behaviors as honesty (e.g., whether or not to steal from the company), manners of dress (e.g., whether or not a coat and tie is required), and the punctuality of meetings and appointments (e.g., whether or not they generally begin on time). In so doing, norms help regulate groups and keep them functioning in an orderly fashion.

It is important to note that norms can be either *prescriptive*, dictating what should be done, or *proscriptive*, dictating the behaviors that should be avoided. For example, groups may develop prescriptive norms to follow their leader, or to help a group member who needs assistance. They also may develop proscriptive norms to avoid absences, or to refrain from blowing the whistle on each other. Sometimes the pressure to conform to norms is subtle, as in the dirty looks given a manager by his or her peers for going to lunch with one of the assembly-line workers. Other times, normative pressures may be quite severe, such as when one production worker sabotages another's work because he or she is performing at too high a level, making other coworkers look bad.

How Do Norms Develop?   Why do norms come about? Several key factors appear to be involved. First, norms develop due to *precedents set over time*. Whatever behaviors emerge at a first group meeting will usually set the standard for how that group is to operate. Initial group patterns of behavior frequently become normative, such as where people sit, and how formal or informal the meeting will be. Such routines help establish a predictable, orderly interaction pattern.

Second, norms develop because of *carryovers from other situations*. Group members usually draw from their previous experiences to guide their behaviors in new situations. The norms governing professional behavior apply here. For example, the norm for a physician to behave ethically and to exercise a pleasant bedside manner is generalizable from one hospital to another. Such *carryover norms*, ones that generalize between different contexts, can assist in making interaction easier in new social situations.

Third, sometimes norms also develop in *response to an explicit statement by a superior or coworker*. As described in Chapter 5, newcomers to groups quickly "learn the ropes" when people describe what is expected of them. Such an ex-

planation is an explicit statement of the group's or organization's norms insofar as it describes what one should do or avoid doing to be accepted by the
group.

Fourth and finally, group norms may develop out of *critical events in the
group's history.* If an employee releases an important organizational secret to a
competitor, causing a loss to the company, a norm to maintain secrecy may develop out of this incident. To the extent that norms guide people away from
making similar mistakes, they may be a helpful way of ensuring that the group
or organization learns from its past experiences.

SOCIAL FACILITATION: PERFORMING IN THE PRESENCE OF OTHERS

Imagine that you have been taking piano lessons for ten years, and you are
now about to go on stage for your first major solo concert performance. You
have been practicing diligently for several months, getting ready for the big
night. But now, you are no longer alone in your own living room, but on stage
in front of hundreds of people. Your name is announced, and silence breaks
the applause as you are seated in front of the concert grand. How will you perform now that you are in front of an audience? Will you freeze, forgetting the
pieces you practiced so intensely on your own? Or will the audience spur you
on to your best performance yet? In other words, what impact will the presence of the audience have on your behavior?

After studying this question for a century, using a wide variety of tasks
and situations, social scientists found that the answer to this question is not
straightforward.[2] Sometimes people were found to perform better in the presence of others than when alone, and sometimes they were found to perform
better alone than in the presence of others. This tendency for the presence of
others to enhance an individual's performance at times and to impair it at
other times is known as **social facilitation.** (Although the word *facilitation* implies improvements in task performance, scientists use the term *social facilitation* to refer to both performance improvements *and* decrements stemming
from the presence of others.) What accounts for these seemingly contradictory
findings?

Scientists have found that the matter boils down to several basic psychological processes.[3] First, it appears that social facilitation is the result of the
heightened emotional arousal (e.g., feelings of tension and excitement) people
experience when in the presence of others. (Wouldn't you feel more tension
playing the piano in front of an audience than alone?) Second, when people
are aroused, they tend to perform the most dominant response—that is, their
most likely behavior in that setting. (Returning the smile of a smiling
coworker may be considered an example of a dominant act; it is a very well-
learned act to smile at another who smiles at you.) If someone is performing a
very well-learned act, the dominant response would be a correct one (such as

playing the right notes on the piano). However, if the behavior in question is relatively novel and newly learned, the dominant response would likely be incorrect (such as playing the wrong notes). Together, these ideas combine to form the **drive theory of social facilitation.** According to this approach (summarized in Figure 7-2), the presence of others increases arousal, which increases the tendency to perform the most dominant responses. If these responses are correct, the resulting performance will he enhanced; if they are incorrect, the performance will be impaired. Based on these processes, performance may either be helped (if the task is well learned) or hindered (if the task is not well learned).

A considerable amount of research has shown support for this theory, finding that people perform better on tasks in the presence of others if that task is very well learned, but poorer if it is not well learned. However, it is still unclear exactly *why* this effect occurs. One possibility is that social facilitation results from **evaluation apprehension** — the fear of being evaluated or judged

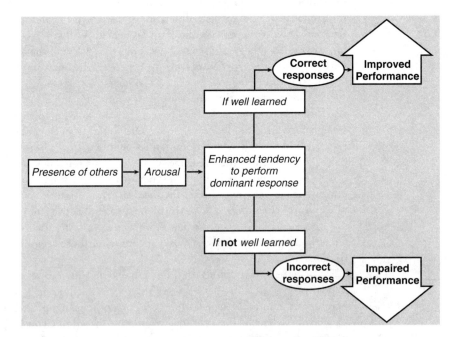

■ *Figure 7-2 The Drive Theory of Social Facilitation*

According to the *drive theory of social facilitation*, the presence of others is arousing, which in turn enhances the tendency to perform dominant responses. If these behaviors are correct (such as when the task is well learned), performance will be improved. If, however, these behaviors are incorrect (such as when the task is novel), performance will be impaired.

by another person. Indeed, people may be aroused by performing a task in the presence of others because of their concern over what those others might think of them. For example, lower-level employees may suffer evaluation apprehension when they are worried about what their supervisor thinks of their work. It is also possible that the presence of others creates a conflict between paying attention to others and paying attention to the task at hand. This conflict leads to increased arousal, which in turn leads to social facilitation. This is known as the **distraction-conflict theory.** If you've ever tried doing a homework assignment while your friends or family watch television nearby, you're probably already aware of the conflict that competing demands for your attention can create.

Regardless of the processes underlying social facilitation, it is clear that the social facilitation effect itself may have a profound influence on organizational behavior. For example, consider the effects it may have on people whose work is monitored, either by others who are physically present or by connections made via computer networks. The rationale behind **performance monitoring** (the practice of supervisors observing subordinates while working) is that it will encourage people to perform at their best. But does it really work this way? According to the drive theory of social facilitation, monitoring should improve task performance if the people monitored know their tasks extremely well. However, if they are relatively new at the task, their performance should suffer.

Research has shown that this happens under controlled laboratory conditions.[4] In one study, the performance of three groups of people performing a clerical task at a computer was measured—those who performed the task alone, those who performed it while someone stood behind them and looked on, and those who performed the task believing that others could monitor their work via a distant computer. How well did the groups do? The findings confirmed the drive theory of social facilitation: Because the task was novel to those performing it, performance was considerably lower among those whose work was monitored (either in person or by computer) than those who worked alone. Clearly, in this case, performance monitoring did not have the intended effects. Indeed, supervisors seeking to raise employees' performance levels by introducing performance monitoring should carefully consider the effects of social facilitation before doing so.

SOCIAL LOAFING: "FREE RIDING" WHEN WORKING WITH OTHERS

Have you ever worked with several others helping a friend move into a new apartment, each carrying and transporting part of the load from the old place to the new one? Or how about sitting around a table with others stuffing political campaign letters into envelopes and addressing them to potential donors? Although these tasks may seem quite different, they actually share an important common characteristic: Performing each requires the efforts of only a single individual, but several people's work can be pooled to yield greater outcomes. Because each person's contributions can be added together with another's, such tasks have been referred to as **additive tasks.**

If you've ever performed additive tasks, such as the ones described here, there's a good chance that you found yourself working not quite as hard as you would have if you did them alone. Does this sound familiar to you? Indeed, a considerable amount of research has found that when several people combine their efforts on additive tasks, each individual contributes less than he or she would when performing the same task alone.[5] As suggested by the old saying "Many hands make light the work," a group of people working together would be expected to be more productive than any one individual working alone. However, when several people combine their efforts on additive tasks, each individual's contribution tends to be less. Five people working together raking leaves will *not* be five times more productive than a single individual working alone; there are always some who go along for a "free ride." In fact, the more individuals who are contributing to an additive task, the less each individual's contribution tends to be—a phenomenon known as **social loafing.**

This effect was first noted many years ago by a German scientist named Max Ringelmann, who compared the amount of force exerted by different size groups of people pulling on a rope. Specifically, he found that one person pulling on a rope alone exerted an average of 63 kilograms of force. However, in groups of three, the per-person force dropped to 53 kilograms, and in groups of eight it was reduced to only 31 kilograms per person—less than half the effort exerted by people working alone! Social loafing effects of this type have been observed in many different studies conducted in recent years. The general form of the social loafing effect is portrayed graphically in Figure 7-3.

The phenomenon of social loafing has been explained by **social impact theory.**[6] According to this theory, the impact of any social force acting on a group is divided equally among its members. The larger the size of the group, the less the impact of the force on any one member. As a result, the more people who might contribute to a group's product, the less pressure each person faces to perform well—that is, the responsibility for doing the job is diffused over more people. Hence, each group member feels less responsible for behaving appropriately, and social loafing occurs.

Tips for Eliminating Social Loafing.   Obviously, the tendency for people to reduce their effort when working with others could be a serious problem in organizations. Fortunately, research has shown that there are several ways in which social loafing can be overcome. One possible antidote to social loafing is to *make each performer identifiable.* Social loafing may occur when people feel they can get away with "taking it easy"—namely, under conditions in which each individual's contributions cannot be determined.

A variety of studies on the practice of "public posting" support this idea.

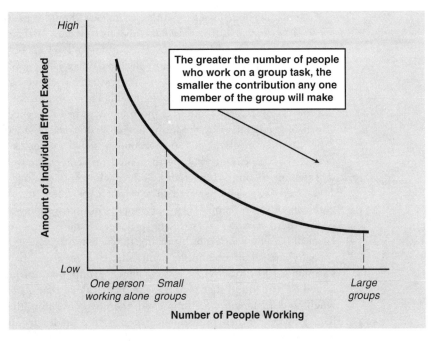

The greater the number of people who work on a group task, the smaller the contribution any one member of the group will make

Figure 7-3 The Social Loafing Effect

When individuals work together on additive tasks, the greater the size of the group, the less effort each individual exerts. This phenomenon is known as *social loafing*.

This research has found that when each individual's contribution to a task is displayed where it can be seen by others (e.g., weekly sales figures posted on a chart), people are less likely to slack off than when only overall group (or companywide) performance is made available. In other words, the more one's individual contribution to a group effort is highlighted, the more pressure each person feels to make a group contribution. Thus, social loafing can be overcome if one's contributions to an additive task are identified: Potential loafers are not likely to loaf if they fear getting caught.

Another way to overcome social loafing is to *make work tasks more important and interesting.* Research has revealed that people are unlikely to go along for a free ride when the task they are performing is believed to be vital to the organization. For example, it has been found that the less meaningful salespeople believed their jobs were, the more they engaged in social loafing—especially when they thought their supervisors knew little about how well they were working. To help in this regard, corporate officials should deliberately attempt to make jobs more intrinsically interesting to employees (perhaps, enriching them as described in Chapter 3). To the extent that jobs are interesting, people may be less likely to loaf.

It also has been suggested that managers should *reward individuals for contributing to their group's performance*—that is, encourage their interest in their group's performance. Doing this (e.g., giving all salespeople in a territory a bonus if they jointly exceed their sales goal) may help employees focus more on collective concerns and less on individualistic concerns, increasing their obligations to their fellow group members. This is important, of course, in that the success of an organization is more likely to be influenced by the collective efforts of groups than by the individual contributions of any one member.

Another mechanism for overcoming social loafing is to *use punishment threats*. To the extent that performance decrements may be controlled by threatening to punish the individuals slacking off, loafing may be reduced. This effect was demonstrated in a recent experiment involving members of high school swim teams.[7] The participants in this study swam either alone or in four-person relay races during practice sessions. In some conditions, the coach threatened the team by telling them that everyone would have to swim "penalty laps" if anyone on the team failed to meet a specified difficult time for swimming 100 yards freestyle. In a control group, no punishment threats were issued. It was found that people swam faster alone than as part of relay teams when no punishment was threatened, thereby confirming the social loafing effect. However, when punishment threats were made, group performance increased, thereby eliminating the social loafing effect. (It's one thing to read about the effects of social loafing, and quite another to see it for yourself. The following **Group Exercise** is designed to help you do just this.)

TEAMS: EMPOWERED WORK GROUPS

In recent years as organizations have been striving to hone their competitive advantage, many have been organizing work around specific types of groups known as *teams*. Because the team movement frequently takes different forms, some confusion has arisen regarding exactly what teams are. In this section we will clarify the basic nature of teams by describing their key characteristics and then identify the various types of teams that exist.

WHAT IS A TEAM? KEY CHARACTERISTICS

At the Miller Brewing Company in Trenton, Ohio groups ranging from six to nineteen employees work together to perform all operations, including brewing (Miller Genuine Draft beer is made at this facility), packaging, and distribution. They schedule their own work assignments and vacations, conduct assessments of their peers' performance, maintain the equipment, and perform other key functions. Each group is responsible for meeting prespecified targets for production, quality, and safety—and to help, data regarding costs and performance are made available. Clearly, these groups are different in key respects from the ones we have been describing thus far, such as a budget com-

Demonstrating the Social Loafing Effect

The social loafing effect is quite strong, and is likely to occur in many different situations in which people make individual contributions to an additive group task. This exercise is designed to demonstrate the effect firsthand in your own class.

DIRECTIONS

1. Divide the class into groups of different sizes. Between five and ten people should work alone. In addition, there should be a group of two, a group of three, a group of four, and so on, until all members of the class have been assigned to a group. If the class is small, assign students to groups of vastly different sizes, such as two, seven, and fifteen. Form the groups by putting together at tables people from the same group.

2. Each person should be given a page or two from a telephone directory and a stack of index cards. Then have the individuals and the members of each group perform the same additive task—copying entries from the telephone directory onto index cards. Allow exactly 10 minutes for the task to be performed, and encourage everyone to work as hard as they can.

3. After the time is up, count the number of entries copied.

4. For each group, and for all the individuals, compute the average per-person performance by dividing the total number of entries copied by the number of people in the group.

5. At the board, the instructor should graph the results. Along the vertical axis show the average number of entries copied per person. Along the horizontal axis show the size of the work groups—one, two, three, four, and so on. The graph should look like the one in Figure 7-3.

QUESTIONS FOR DISCUSSION

1. Was the social loafing effect demonstrated? What is the basis for this conclusion?

2. If the social loafing effect was not found, why do you think this occurred? Do you think it might have been due to the possibility that your familiarity with the effect led you to avoid it? Test this possibility by replicating the exercise using people who do not know about the phenomenon (e.g., another class), then compare the results.

3. Did members of smaller groups feel more responsible for their group's performance than members of larger groups?

4. What could have been done to counteract any "free riding" that may have occurred in this demonstration?

mittee or company ski club. The Miller employees are all members of special kinds of groups known as teams. Formally, we define a **team** as *a group whose members have complementary skills and are committed to a common purpose or set of performance goals for which they hold themselves mutually accountable.* Applying this definition to our description of the way work is done at Miller's Trenton plant, it's clear that teams are in use at this facility. Given the complicated nature of teams, we will highlight some of their key characteristics and distinguish them from the traditional ways in which work is structured (for a summary, see Table 7-1).[8]

First, *teams are organized around work processes rather than functions.* So, for example, instead of having traditional departments (such as engineering, planning, quality control, and so on) each focusing on a specialized function, team members have many different skills and come together to perform key processes, such as designing and launching new products, manufacturing, and distribution (we will describe this approach more fully in Chapter 11 when we discuss the topic of *reengineering*). As an example, Sterling Winthrop (an Australian manufacturer of liquid analgesics) used to have 21 different departments looking into various aspects of the manufacturing process. Today, all facets of production (e.g., scheduling, blending, and so on) are carried out by members of teams who work together on the entire production process.

Second, *teams "own" the product, service, or processes on which they work.* By this we mean that people feel part of something meaningful, and understand how their work fits into the big picture (recall our discussion of the motivating properties of this belief in Chapter 3). For example, employees at Florida's

■ *Table 7-1 Teams versus Traditional Work Structures: Some Key Distinctions*

Teams differ from traditional work structures with respect to the six key distinctions identified here. (Adapted from Wellins, Byham, & Dixon, 1994; see Note 8).

Traditional Structure	*Teams*
Design around functions	Design around work processes
No sense of ownership over the work products	Ownership of products, services, or processes
Workers have single skills	Team members have many skills
Outside leaders govern workers	Team members govern themselves
Support staff and skills are found outside the groups	Support staff and skills are built into teams
Organizational decisions are made by managers	Teams are involved in making organizational decisions for themselves

Cape Coral Hospital work in teams within four mini-hospitals (surgical, general, specialty medical, and outpatient)—not only to boost efficiency, but to help them feel more responsible for their patients. By working in small units, team members have greater contact with patients and are more aware of the effects of their work on patient care. This is in contrast to the traditionally more distant way of organizing hospital work, in which employees tend to feel less connected to the results of their actions.

Third, *members of teams are trained in several different areas and have a variety of different skills.* For example, at Milwaukee Insurance, policies are now processed by team members who rate policies, underwrite them, and then enter them into the system. Before the switch to teams, these three tasks were performed by specialists in three separate departments. In fact, this is typical. Traditionally, people only learned single jobs and performed them over and over again, unless there was some need for retraining.

Fourth, *teams govern themselves.* And, as a result, team leaders may be thought of as *coaches* who help members of the team, rather than bosses who use more authoritarian means of leadership (see Chapter 8). For example, at Texas Instruments' defense electronics plant, teams appoint their own leaders, called "coordinators," who do exactly what the name implies—they work to ensure the smooth interaction between the efforts of team members. At some companies, such as Mine Safety Appliances, "team captains" are self-selected, and handle all the paperwork for a few weeks, until the job is rotated to someone else.

Fifth, *in teams support staff and responsibilities are built in.* Traditionally, such functions as maintenance, engineering, and human resources operate as separate departments that provide support to other groups requiring their services. Insofar as this often causes delays, teams may contain members who have expertise in needed support areas. For example, at K Shoes, a British footwear manufacturing firm, there are no longer any quality inspectors. Instead, all team members are trained in matters of inspection and quality control. Or sometimes organizations hire people with highly advanced or specialized skills who are assigned to work as members of several different teams at once. For example, teams at Texas Instruments have access to specialized engineering services in this way. Regardless of how it's done, the point is that teams do not rely on outside support services to help get their jobs done; they are relatively self-sufficient.

Sixth and finally, *teams are involved in companywide decisions.* This is in contrast to the traditional practice of using managers to make all organizational decisions. For example, team members at Tennessee Eastman, a manufacturer of chemicals, fibers, and plastics, are actively involved on company-level committees that develop policies and procedures affecting everyone. The underlying idea is that the people who are closest to the work performed should be the ones most involved in making the decisions.

TYPES OF TEAMS

According to one expert, most major U.S. companies are now either using some form of teams or are seriously considering using them. Although there has been a great amount of recent interest in teams, they have been around the workplace in one form or another for some time. In fact, many corporations (e.g., Cummins Engine, General Motors, Digital Equipment, and Ford Motor Company) have been using them for quite a few years. Some, such as Procter & Gamble, have used teams for well over three decades.

In view of their widespread popularity, it should not be surprising to learn that there are many different kinds of teams. To help make sense out of these, scientists have categorized these along three major dimensions. The first has to do with their primary *purpose or mission*. In this regard, some teams—known as *work teams*—are primarily concerned with the work done by the organization, such as developing and manufacturing new products, providing services for customers, and so on. Their principle focus is on using the organization's resources to effectively create its results (be they goods or services). The several examples of groups noted thus far are of this type. Other teams—known as *improvement teams*—are primarily oriented toward the mission of increasing the effectiveness of the processes that are used by the organization. For example, Texas Instruments has relied on teams to help improve the quality of operations at its plant in Malaysia.

Some work teams at SC Johnson Wax have chosen nontraditional work schedules. They work 12-hour shifts for four days one week and three days the following week, averaging 44 hours per week.

A second dimension has to do with *time*. Specifically, some teams are only *temporary* and are established for a specific project with a finite life. For example, a team set up to develop a new product would be considered temporary. As soon as its job is done, it disbands. However, other kinds of teams are *permanent* and stay intact as long as the organization is operating. For example, teams focusing on providing effective customer service tend to be permanent parts of many organizations.

The third dimension reflects the team's connection to the organization's overall *authority structure*—that is, the connection between various formal job responsibilities. In some organizations, teams may cross over various functional units (e.g., marketing, finance, human resources, and so on) and are said to be *overlaid* (i.e., their activities are superimposed over the functioning of various organizational units). For example, a quality improvement team may be expected to get involved with the activities of several different organizational units. (The mission of improving quality does not belong to any one unit working alone.) As you might expect, such arrangements are often difficult because of ambiguities regarding authority. By contrast, some organizations use teams that are *intact* with respect to the existing structure of the organization. In fact, some organizations, such as General Motors and Ralston-Purina, are structured such that people work together on certain products all the time and do not apply their specialties to a wide range of products. Within such organizations, teams can operate without the ambiguities created by having to cross functional lines.

It is important to note that the boundaries between all teams must be considered permeable. Indeed, people are frequently members of more than one team—a situation often required for organizations to function effectively. For example, members of an organization's manufacturing team must carefully coordinate their activities with members of its marketing team. To the extent that people are involved in several different kinds of teams, they may gain broader perspectives and make more important contributions to their various teams.

WORK TEAMS: WHAT IS THE PAYOFF?

Now that you have a solid understanding of the basic nature of teams, we are prepared to explore the issue of how successful teams have been in organizations. After reviewing the evidence bearing on this question, we will turn to the very practical matter of identifying the potential obstacles to team success and ways these may be overcome.

TEAMS AT WORK: HOW GOOD IS THEIR TRACK RECORD?

The question of how effective teams are in the workplace is not easy to answer. Not only are there many different kinds of teams doing different kinds of jobs operating in organizations, but their effectiveness is influenced by a wide variety of factors that go well beyond any possible benefits of teams, such as managerial support, the economy, available resources, and the like. As a result, understanding the true effectiveness of teams is a tricky business at best. This difficulty has been fueled in recent years by stories in the top business periodicals touting the success of teams. How much of this is hype stemming from the latest management fad, and how much should be accepted as valid evidence for the effectiveness of teams? Fortunately, several studies have investigated this issue.

Probably the most direct way to learn about companies' experiences with work teams is to survey the officials of organizations that use them. One large-scale study did just this.[9] The sample consisted of several hundred of the 1,000 largest companies in the United States. About 47 percent used some work teams, although these were typically in place at only a few selected sites, and not throughout the entire organizations. Where they were used, however, they were generally highly regarded. Moreover, teams were viewed as becoming increasingly popular over time.

These optimistic results are further supported by in-depth case studies of numerous teams in many different organizations.[10] Research of this type, although difficult to quantify and to compare across organizations, provides some interesting insight into what makes teams successful and why. Consider, for example, the work teams used in General Motors' battery plant in Fitzgerald, Georgia. The 320 employees at this facility operate in various teams, including managers working together in *support teams*, middle-level teams of *coordinators* (similar to foremen and technicians), and *employee teams*, natural work units of three to nineteen members performing specific tasks. Although the teams work closely together, coordinating their activities, they function almost as separate businesses. Because plant employees must perform many different tasks in their teams, they are not paid based on their positions but for their knowledge and competence. In fact, the highest-paid employees are individuals who have demonstrated their competence (usually by highly demanding tests) on all the jobs performed in at least two different teams. This is GM's way of rewarding people for broadening their perspectives, appreciating "the other guy's problems." By many measures, the Fitzgerald plant has been very effective. Its production costs are lower than comparable units in traditionally run plants. Furthermore, employee turnover is also much lower than average. Employee satisfaction surveys also reveal that job satisfaction at this plant is among the highest found at any General Motors facility.

Teams also have been successful in service businesses. For example, consider IDS, the financial services subsidiary of American Express. In response to rapid growth in the mid-1980s, IDS officials realized that their operations were becoming highly inefficient, and created several teams to work on reorganizing the company's operations. Like many companies, the move to teams wasn't readily accepted by all employees. Particularly resistant were individuals who before teams had high-status jobs, with high pay to match. Naturally, they resented becoming coequals with others when teams were formed. Still, these employees—and all others, for that matter—soon benefited from the company's improved operations. Accuracy in the processing of paperwork (e.g., orders to buy or sell stock) rose from 70 percent before teams were created to over 99 percent afterwards. With the help of employee teams, IDS's operations became so efficient that response time improved by 96 percent: from several minutes to only a few seconds. During the stock market crash of October 1987, this quick response capability is credited for saving the day (not to mention lots of money) for IDS's customers.

These cases are two examples of very different companies that used teams in different ways, but with something in common—high levels of success (albeit not without some difficulties). And there are many more.[11] Although there are far too many cases to review here, we think you'll find it fascinating to review the summary of company experiences with teams in Table 7-2.[12]

As Table 7-2 indicates, many companies have reported having successful experiences with teams. Case studies paint a consistent picture of the effectiveness of teams, making the use of teams one of today's most popular manage-

■ *Table 7-2 The Effectiveness of Teams:*
Some Impressive Results

Teams have helped many organizations enjoy dramatic gains in productivity. Here is a sampling of these impressive results. (Based on information in Wellins et al., 1994, see Note 8; and Katzenbach & Smith, 1993, see Note 15.)

Company	Result
Wilson Sporting Goods	Average annual cost savings of $5 million
Kodak Customer Assistance Center	Accuracy of responses increased 100 percent
Corning	Defects dropped from 1,800 ppm to 3 ppm
Sealed Air	Waste reduced by 50 percent
Exxon	$10 million saved in six months
Carrier	Unit turnaround reduced 2 weeks to 2 days
Xerox	Productivity increased by 30 percent
Westinghouse	Product costs down 60 percent
Texas Instruments	Costs reduced by more than 50 percent

ment trends. The problem with such reports, of course, is that they may not be entirely objective. After all, companies may be unwilling to broadcast their failures to the world. This is not to say that case studies cannot be trusted. Indeed, when the information is gathered by outside researchers (such as those reported here), the stories they tell about how teams are used and the results of using them can be quite revealing. Still, there is a need for completely objective, empirical studies of team effectiveness.

Research of this type is now just beginning to be done. In one such investigation comparisons were made between various aspects of work performance and attitudes of two groups of employees at a railroad car repair facility in Australia: those who were assembled into teams that could freely decide how to do their jobs, and those whose work was structured in the more traditional, nonautonomous fashion.[13] After the work teams had been in place for several months, it was found that they had significantly fewer accidents, as well as lower rates of absenteeism and turnover. However, not all empirical studies paint such an optimistic picture of the benefits of work teams. For example, in one study examining work teams in an English manufacturing plant it was found that employees were more satisfied with their jobs in teams compared to those in conventional work arrangements (in which individuals take orders from a supervisor), but they were individually no more productive. However, because the use of teams made it possible for the organization to eliminate several supervisory positions, the company became more profitable.

Taken together, these studies suggest that teams are well received. People generally enjoy working in teams, at least after they have become adjusted to them. However, they are not always responsible for making individuals any more productive. Certainly, teams help create commitment among employees, and as we described in Chapter 4, there are benefits to be derived from this (e.g., reduced absenteeism and turnover). From an organizational perspective, teams appear to be an effective way of eliminating layers of management, getting more work done by fewer people. And for this reason, teams help organizations remain competitive. In fact, it is precisely these types of beneficial out-

---

WINNING PRACTICES

Tips for Building Team Performance: Learning from Companies That Do It Best

Making teams work effectively is no easy task. Success is not automatic. Rather, teams need to be carefully cared for and maintained in order for them to accomplish their missions. As one expert expressed it, "Teams are the Ferraris of work design. They're high performance but high maintenance and expensive."[14] What, then, could be done to help make teams as effective as possible? Based on analyses of successful teams, several keys to success may be identified.[15] Here are five such tips.

First, it is important to *communicate the urgency of the team's task*. The rationale is that team members are prone to rally around challenges that compel them to meet high performance standards. For example, a few years ago, employees at Ampex Corporation (a manufacturer of videotape equipment for the broadcasting industry) worked hard to make their teams successful when they recognized the changes necessitated by the shift from analog to digital technology. Unless the company met these challenges, the plug surely would be pulled. Realizing that the company's future was at stake, work teams fast-forwarded Ampex into a position of prominence in its industry.

Second, it is important to *select team members based on their skills, or potential skills*. Insofar as the success of teams demands that they work together closely on a wide variety of tasks, it is essential for them to have a complementary set of skills. This includes not only job skills but also interpersonal skills (especially since getting along with one's teammates is so very important). With this in mind, at Ampex three-person subsets of teams are used to select their own new members insofar as they have the best ideas about what skills are needed and who would best fit into the teams. It is also frequently important for teams to project future skills that may be needed, and to train team members in these skills. With this in mind, work teams at Colgate-Palmolive Company's liquid

comes that have been reported by the case studies summarized previously. (In view of the growing popularity of teams (as many as half of us will be working in teams by the end of this decade, according to one estimate!), it is important to consider some things teams can do to build performance. Based on the experiences of companies that have been successful with teams, several recommendations can be made for ways of building effective team performance. We have summarized these in the **Winning Practices** section below.)

detergents plant in Cambridge, Ohio initially receive 120 hours of training in such skills as quality management, problem solving, and team interaction, and subsequently receive advanced training in all these areas.

Third, *make the rules of behavior clear.* Effective teams have clear rules about what behaviors are and are not expected. For example, at Texas Instruments' Defense System and Electronics Group, rules about good attendance, giving only constructive criticism, and maintaining confidentiality are carefully followed.

Fourth, *regularly confront teams with new facts.* Fresh approaches are likely to be prompted by fresh information, and introducing new facts may present the kind of challenges that teams need to stay innovative. For example, when information about pending cutbacks in defense spending was introduced to teams at Florida's Harris Corporation (an electronics manufacturer), new technologies were developed that positioned the company to land large contracts in nonmilitary government organizations—including a $1.7 billion contract to upgrade the FAA's air traffic control system.

Fifth, *acknowledge and reward vital contributions to the team.* As indicated in Chapter 2, rewarding desired behavior is a key way of ensuring that the behavior will be repeated in the future. And rewards don't have to be large to work. For example, members of Kodak's Team Zebra, its black-and-white film-manufacturing group, are given dinner certificates when they are singled out for making special contributions.

It is important to caution that although these suggestions are important, they alone do not ensure the success of work teams. Many other factors such as the economy, the existence of competitors, and the company's financial picture are also important determinants of organizational success. Still, the fact that these practices are followed in many highly successful teams certainly makes them worthy of consideration.

OBSTACLES TO TEAM EFFECTIVENESS— AND HOW TO OVERCOME THEM

Although we have reported success stories about teams, we also have alluded to difficulties in implementing them. After all, working in a team demands a great deal, and not everyone may be ready for teams. As a result, teams sometimes fail. There are several key reasons why.[16]

Insufficient Training.   To be effective, team members must have the right blend of skills needed for the team to contribute to the group's mission. Workers having high degrees of freedom and anonymity require a depth of skills and knowledge that surpasses that of people performing narrower, traditional jobs. For this reason, successful teams tend to be ones in which large investments are made in developing the skills of team members and leaders. In the words of one expert, "Good team members are trained, not born."[17]

Illustrating this maxim is Development Dimensions International, a printing and distribution facility for a human resources company, located in Pittsburgh, Pennsylvania. This small company has each of its 70 employees spend some 200 hours in training (in such areas as interaction skills, customer service skills, and various technical areas) during their first year—even more for new leaders. Then, after this initial period, all employees receive a variety of training on an ongoing basis.

One key area in which all team members require training is in how to be a team member. Linda Godwin, a mission specialist at NASA's Johnson Space Center in Houston, likens team success to the kind of interpersonal harmony that must exist within space shuttle crews. "We have to be willing to compromise and to make decisions that benefit everyone as a whole," says Ms. Godwin, who is a veteran of two successful shuttle missions.[18] In this regard, there are several key interpersonal skills in which training is most useful, and these are summarized in Table 7-3.

Compensation Systems.   Because the United States and Canada are highly individualistic cultures, most North American workers are used to highly individualistic compensation systems—ones that recognize individual performance. However, when it comes to teams, it is also very important to recognize group performance. Teams are no places for hot shots who want to make their individual marks—rather, teams require "team players." And the more organizations reward employees for their teams' successes, the more strongly team spirit will be reinforced. Several companies in which teams are widely used—including the Hannaford Brothers retail food distribution company in New York, Board na Mona (a peat-extraction company in Ireland), and Westinghouse's defense and commercial electronics plant in Texas—rely on **gain-sharing plans** to

Team members at **Worthington Industries,** *a steel processing company, receive quarterly checks reflecting the company's profitability. These have been averaging 35 to 55 percent of each employee's base pay.*

■ *Table 7-3 Interpersonal Skills Required by Team Members*

Experts have advocated that team members be trained in the various interpersonal skills summarized here (some of which are described elsewhere in this book). (Based on information in Caudron, 1994, see Note 16.)

Skill	Description
Advocating	Ways of persuading others to accept one's point of view
Inquiring	Listening effectively to others and drawing information out of them (see Chapter 6)
Tension management	Managing the tension that stems from conflict with others
Sharing responsibility	Learning to align personal and team objectives
Leadership	Understanding one's role in guiding the team to success (see Chapter 8)
Valuing diversity	Accepting—and taking advantage of—differences between members (see Chapter 4)
Self-awareness	Willingness to criticize others constructively and to accept constructive criticism from others

reward teams. These plans reward all team members for reaching company-wide performance goals, allowing them to share in the company's profits.

In view of the importance of team members having a variety of different skills, many companies, including Milwaukee Insurance, Colgate-Palmolive, and Sterling Winthrop, have taken to paying employees for their demonstrated skills as opposed to their job performance. Such a system is known as **skill-based pay.** A highly innovative skill-based pay system has been in use at Tennessee Eastman. This company's "pay-for-applied-skills-and knowledge" plan—or PASK, as it is known—requires employees to demonstrate their skills in several key areas, including technical skills and interpersonal skills. The pay scale is carefully linked to the number of skills acquired and the level of proficiency attained. By encouraging the development of vital skills in this manner, the company is ensuring that it has the resources for its teams to function effectively.

Lack of Managerial Support. For teams to survive, let alone thrive, it is essential for them to receive unqualified support from top management. In the absence of such support, the system may falter. Consider, for example, the experience at the Lenexa, Kansas plant of the Puritan-Bennett Corporation, a manufacturer of respiratory equipment. After seven years of working to develop improved software for its respirators, product development teams failed to get the job done (despite an industry average for such tasks of only three years). According to Roger J. Dolida, the company's director of research and development, the problem is that management never made the project a priority, and refused to free up another key person needed to do the job. As he put it, "If top management doesn't buy into the idea ... teams can go nowhere."[19]

Part of the problem is that some managers are unwilling to relinquish control. In general, good supervisors work their way up from the plant floor by giving orders and having them followed. However, team leaders have to build consensus and must allow team members to make decisions together. As you might expect, letting go of control isn't always easy for some to do. This problem emerged at Bausch & Lomb's sunglasses plant in Rochester, New York. In 1989 some 1,400 employees were organized into 38 teams. By 1992 about half the supervisors had not adjusted to the change, despite receiving thorough training in how to work as part of a team. They argued bitterly with team members whenever their ideas were not accepted by the team, and eventually they were reassigned.

An even tougher approach was taken at the Shelby Die Casting Company, a metal-casting firm in Shelby, Mississippi. When its former supervisors refused to cooperate as coequals in their teams, the company eliminated their jobs, and let the workers run their own teams. The result: The company saved $250,000 in annual wages, productivity jumped 50 percent, and company profits almost doubled. The message sent by both companies is clear: Those who cannot adjust to teamwork are unwelcome.

Lack of Employee Support.   In addition to support from managers, it is essential that the basis for the movement to teams be fully understood and accepted by the individuals who are involved. Unless employees can fully understand the importance of cooperating with each other, problems are likely to result. This happened a few years ago at Dow Chemical Company's plastics group in Midland, Michigan, where a team was put into place to create a new plastic resin. Some members (those in the research field) wanted to spend several months developing and testing new options, while others (those on the manufacturing end) wanted to slightly alter existing products and start up production right away. Neither side budged, and the project eventually stalled.

By contrast, when team members share a common vision and are committed to attaining it, they are generally very cooperative with each other, leading to success. For example, members of Hallmark's new-product development team (consisting of artists, designers, printers, and financial experts) work carefully together with each other, contributing to the company's dominance in the greeting cards market. Similarly, by forming teams with highly cooperative members from different fields, Thermos was able to launch its highly successful electric grill.

Cooperation Between Teams.   Team success requires not only cooperation within teams, but between them as well. As one expert put it:

Time and time again teams fall short of their promise because companies don't know how to make them work together with other teams. If you don't get your teams into the right constellations, the whole organization can stall.[20]

This problem occurred in General Electric's medical systems division when it assigned two teams of engineers, one in Waukesha, Wisconsin, and another in Hino, Japan, the task of creating software for two new ultrasound devices. Shortly, teams pushed features that made their products popular only in their own countries, and duplicated each other's efforts. When teams met, language and cultural barriers separated them, further distancing the teams from each other.

Boeing successfully avoided such problems in the development of its new 777 passenger jet — a project involving some 200 teams. As you might imagine, on such a large project, coordination of effort between teams was essential. To help, regular meetings were held between various team leaders who disseminated information to members. And team members could go wherever needed within the organization to get the information needed to succeed. As one Boeing employee, a team leader, put it, "I can go to the chief engineer. Before, it was unusual just to see the chief engineer."[21] Just as importantly, if after getting the information they need, team members found problems, they were empowered to take action without getting management approval. According to Boeing engineer, Henry Shomber: "We have the no-messenger rule. Team members must make decisions on the spot. They can't run back to their functions [department heads] for permission."[22]

To conclude, it is clear that teams can be an effective way for organizations to achieve unheard of levels of performance. However, the path to success is riddled with obstacles; developing effective teams is difficult. It is also time-consuming. According to management expert Peter Drucker, "You can't rush teams . . . It takes five years just to learn to build a team and decide what kind you want."[23] And it may take most organizations over a decade to make a complete transition to teams. Clearly, they are not an overnight phenomenon. But, with patience and careful attention to the obstacles identified here, teams have ushered many companies to extraordinary gains in productivity.

SUMMARY:
PUTTING IT TO USE

Groups are defined as collections of two or more interacting individuals with a stable pattern of relationships between them who share common goals and who perceive themselves as being a group. Within organizations there are both *formal groups* (e.g., command groups and task groups) and *informal groups* (e.g., interest groups and friendship groups).

Norms are generally agreed-upon rules that guide behavior. They can be either *prescriptive*, dictating what should be done, or *proscriptive*, indicating what should not be done. Norms develop due to precedents set over time, carry-overs from other situations, responses to explicit statements by others, and critical events in a group's history.

Social facilitation refers to the tendency for people to perform either better or worse when in the presence of others than when alone. The *drive theory of social facilitation* recognizes that this occurs because of the emotional arousal that people feel when with others. This arousal can come from concerns about what others will think, *evaluation apprehension*. According to the *distraction-conflict theory*, it also can come from conflicts between paying attention to others compared to the task itself. Applying these ideas, the practice of watching over subordinates as they work, *performance monitoring*, can hinder performance among people whose jobs are not well learned.

When people pool their efforts on additive group tasks (ones in which separate individual contributions are combined), each individual's performance tends to be less than when the same task is done alone. In fact, the greater the size of the group, the less the size of the individual contributions to the joint product—a phenomenon known as *social loafing*. This effect may be overcome by making each performer identifiable, making work tasks more important and interesting, rewarding individuals for their individual contributions to group performance, and threatening to use punishment.

A *team* is a group whose members have complementary skills and are committed to a common purpose or set of performance goals for which they hold themselves mutually responsible. Teams are distinguished from ordinary work groups in several ways. Notably: (1) teams are organized around work processes rather than functions, (2) teams "own" the product, service, or processes on which they work, (3) members of teams are trained in several different areas and have a variety of different skills, (4) teams govern themselves, (5) teams have their own support staff and responsibilities built in, and (6) teams are involved in making companywide decisions. *Work teams* are concerned with the organization's work, its products or services, whereas *performance teams* are oriented toward increasing the effectiveness of work. Teams also may be either temporary or permanent, and their work either may cross functional units or remain within them.

Case studies, survey research, and direct experimental comparisons all reveal that teams can bring dramatic improvements in organizational performance. Although this might not stem from improvements in individual productivity, it may be the result of the fact that fewer people are needed to get the jobs done, helping organizations become more efficient. Companies that use teams most effectively take several measures, such as communicating the urgency of the team's task, selecting team members based on their skills, making the rules of behavior clear, regularly confronting teams with new facts, and acknowledging and rewarding vital contributions to the team. Making teams work effectively is not easy. Problems include insufficient training, compensation systems that do not reward contributions to the group, lack of support by all employees, including managers, and a lack of cooperation between teams.

You Be the Consultant

A large manufacturing company has been doing quite well over the years but is now facing dramatic competition from overseas competitors that are undercutting its prices and improving on the quality of its goods. The company president has read a lot about teams in the popular press and has called upon you to help implement a transition to teams for the organization. Answer the following questions relevant to this situation based on the material in this chapter.

1. What would you tell the company president about the overall record of teams in being able to improve organizational performance?

2. The company president notes that the current employees tend to have relatively poor skills and are generally disinterested in acquiring new ones. Will this be a problem when it comes to using teams? Why or why not?

3. What would be the implications of the switch to teams for the company's current compensation system? How would it have to change for the teams to be effective?

4. The company president tells you that several people in the company—including some top executives—are a bit concerned about relinquishing some of their power to teams. Is this likely to be a problem, and if so, what can be done to help alleviate it?

CHAPTER 8

The Quest for Leadership

PREVIEW OF
CHAPTER HIGHLIGHTS

Leadership is the process by which an individual influences others in ways that help attain group or organizational goals.

The **great person theory** stipulates that certain traits (e.g., cognitive ability and flexibility) are key ingredients in leadership effectiveness.

The **behavior approach** focuses on what leaders do. Two types of behavior have been linked to successful leadership—concern for people and concern for production. **Grid training** helps leaders develop both these behavioral skills.

The **leader–member exchange (LMX) model** acknowledges that followers who are favored by leaders (those in the in-group) tend to perform more effectively than those who are not.

Leaders considered **charismatic** generate enthusiasm and loyalty among their followers. Such individuals are good at articulating their vision and getting others to bring it to reality.

Contingency theories of leadership are based on the idea that there is no one best approach. Rather, different styles of leadership are effective under different conditions.

Theories such as **LPC contingency theory, path–goal theory,** and **situational leadership theory** are contingency theories. Each specifies unique conditions under which different styles of leadership are most effective.

If you gathered a group of top executives and asked them to identify the single most important determinant of organizational success, chances are good that the vast majority would reply "effective leadership." Indeed, it is widely believed in the world of business that *leadership* is a key ingredient in the recipe for corporate effectiveness. And this view is by no means restricted to organizations. As you know, leadership is also important when it comes to politics, sports, and many other activities.

Is this view justified? Do leaders really play crucial roles in shaping the fortunes of organizations? A century of research on this topic suggests that they do. Effective leadership, it appears, is indeed a key factor in organizational success. In view of this, we will devote this chapter to describing various approaches to the study of leadership—and their implications for managerial practice. Specifically, we will examine leadership from four major perspectives: the basic traits that make leaders effective, the behaviors in which successful leaders engage, leaders' relationships with their followers, and various contingency approaches to leadership (i.e., theories that consider the most effective leadership under different conditions). Finally, we also will consider the role of leadership in today's "involvement-oriented" organizations. Before launching into this discussion, however, we will begin by defining what we mean by leadership and distinguish it from some other terms with which it is frequently associated.

WHAT IS LEADERSHIP?

When you think of a leader, what image comes to mind? For many, a leader is an individual—often with a title reflecting a high rank in an organization (e.g., president, director, and so on)—who is influential in getting others to behave as required by the organization. Indeed, social scientists think of leaders as individuals who have a great deal of influence over others. Formally, we define **leadership** as *the process by which an individual influences others in ways that help attain group or organizational goals.*

According to this definition, leadership is a type of *social influence*—the process by which a leader changes the behavior or attitudes of others. As we saw in Chapter 6, these techniques may range from highly coercive (e.g., punishing others who do not go along with an order) to extremely open and democratic (e.g., allowing others to freely accept or reject a suggestion to act a certain way). However, in general, leadership refers to the use of relatively noncoercive influence techniques. This characteristic distinguishes a leader from a *dictator*. Whereas dictators get others to do what they want by using threats of physical force, leaders do not. When former Chinese leader Mao Zedong said that "Power grows out of the barrel of a gun," he was referring more to the power of dictators than to the power of leaders. The point is that leadership rests, at least in part, on positive feelings between leaders and their subordinates. In other words, subordinates accept influence from leaders be-cause they respect, like, or admire them—not simply because they hold posi-tions of formal authority.

By emphasizing the role of influence, our definition implies that leader-ship is a two-way process. That is, leaders both influence subordinates in vari-ous ways and are also influenced by them. In fact, it may be said that leader-ship exists only in relation to followers. After all, one cannot lead without followers! Not surprisingly, several of the approaches to leadership described in this chapter focus on the relationships between leaders and followers.

Before closing this section, we have one final point to make—namely, that the everyday practice of using the terms *leader* and *manager* interchange-ably is misleading. The primary function of a *leader* is to create the essential purpose or mission of the organization and the strategy for attaining it. By contrast, the job of the *manager* is to implement that vision. He or she is re-sponsible for achieving that end, taking the steps necessary to make the leader's vision a reality. Essentially, whereas leaders get things started, man-agers keep things running. The confusion between these two terms is under-standable insofar as the distinction between establishing a mission and imple-menting it is often blurred in practice. This is because many leaders, such as top corporate executives, are frequently called upon not only to create a vi-sion, but also to help implement it. Similarly, managers are often required to lead those who are subordinate to them while at the same time carrying out their leader's mission. With this in mind, it has been observed that too many so-called leaders get bogged down in the managerial aspects of their job, creat-ing organizations that are "overmanaged and underled."[1]

THE TRAIT APPROACH: ARE SOME PEOPLE REALLY "BORN LEADERS"?

Common sense leads us to think that some people have more of "the right stuff" than others, and are just naturally better leaders. And, if you look at some of the great leaders throughout history, such as Martin Luther King, Jr., Eleanor Roosevelt, and Abraham Lincoln, to name just a few, it is clear that such individuals are certainly different from ordinary human beings. The question is "how are they different?" That is, what is it that makes great lead-ers so great?

For many years scientists have devoted a great deal of attention to this question, espousing the **great person theory.** According to this approach, great leaders possess key traits that set them apart from most others. Further-more, the theory contends that these traits remain stable over time and across different groups. Thus, it suggests that all great leaders share these character-istics regardless of their role in history. Although these suggestions make a great deal of intuitive sense, they have not always been supported by research, leading some scientists to conclude that leaders do not differ from followers in clear and consistent ways.

Today, however, it is popularly believed that traits *do* matter—namely, that certain traits, together with other factors, contribute to leaders' success in business settings.[2] What are these traits? In Table 8-1 we list and describe some of the key ones. Although you will readily recognize and understand most of these characteristics (drive, honesty and integrity, self-confidence), others require further clarification.

First, consider **leadership motivation.** This refers to a leader's desire to influence others—essentially, to lead. Such motivation, however, can take two distinct forms. On the one hand, it may cause leaders to seek power as an end in itself. Leaders who demonstrate such *personalized power motivation* wish to dominate others, and their desire to do so is often reflected in an excessive concern with status. In contrast, leadership motivation can cause leaders to seek power as a means to achieve desired, shared goals. Leaders who evidence such *socialized power motivation* cooperate with others, develop networks, and generally work with subordinates rather than trying to dominate or control them. Needless to say, this type of leadership motivation is usually far more adaptive for organizations than personalized leadership motivation.

With respect to **cognitive ability,** it appears that effective leaders must be intelligent and capable of integrating and interpreting large amounts of information. However, mental genius does not seem to be necessary and may, in some cases, prove detrimental. Still, leaders must be intelligent enough to do their jobs.

■ *Table 8-1 Characteristics of Successful Leaders*

Research indicates that successful leaders demonstrate the traits listed here.

Trait or Characteristic	*Description*
Drive	Desire for achievement; ambition; high energy; tenacity; initiative
Honesty and integrity	Trustworthy; reliable; open
Leadership motivation	Desire to exercise influence over others to reach shared goals
Self-confidence	Trust in own abilities
Cognitive ability	Intelligence; ability to integrate and interpret large amounts of information
Knowledge of the business	Knowledge of industry, relevant technical matters
Creativity	Originality
Flexibility	Ability to adapt to needs of followers and requirements of situation

A final characteristic, **flexibility,** refers to the ability of leaders to recognize what actions are required in a given situation and then to act accordingly. Evidence suggests that the most effective leaders are not prone to behave in the same ways all the time but are adaptive, matching their style to the needs of followers and the demands of the situations they face.

In short, current research supports the great person theory. Specifically, it has been concluded as follows:

> *Regardless of whether leaders are born or made . . . it is unequivocally clear that* leaders are not like other people. *Leaders do not have to be great men or women by being intellectual geniuses or omniscient prophets to succeed, but they do need to have the "right stuff" and this stuff is not equally present in all people. Leadership is a demanding, unrelenting job with enormous pressures and grave responsibilities. It would be a profound disservice to leaders to suggest that they are ordinary people who happened to be in the right place at the right time. . . . In the realm of leadership (and in every other realm), the individual does matter.*[3]

Given this conclusion, it may be instructive to examine the extent to which certain individuals possess the traits and characteristics associated with great leaders. To do this, complete the **Group Exercise** that follows.

THE BEHAVIOR APPROACH: WHAT DO LEADERS DO?

The great person theory paints a somewhat fatalistic picture, suggesting that some people are, by nature, more prone to being effective leaders than others. After all, some of us have more of "the right stuff" than others. However, other approaches to leadership—particularly, those focusing on what leaders do, rather than who leaders are—paint a more encouraging picture for those of us who aspire to leadership positions. This orientation is known as the **behavior approach.** By emulating the behavior of successful leaders the possibility exists that any one of us may become effective leaders.

TWO CRITICAL LEADERSHIP BEHAVIORS

Precisely what behaviors hold the key to leadership success? Although the answer to this question is quite complex, we can safely point to two very important leadership behaviors. The first is demonstrating a *concern for people,* also known as **consideration.** In describing your boss, would you say that he or she cares about you as a person, is friendly, and listens to you when you want to talk? If so, he or she would show a high amount of consideration.

The second main type of leadership behavior is demonstrating a *concern for getting the job done,* also known as **initiating structure.** In describing your boss, would you say that he or she gives you advice, answers your questions, and lets you know exactly what is expected of you? If so, he or she would show a high amount of initiating structure.

Identifying Great Leaders in All Walks of Life

A useful way to understand the great person theory is to identify those individuals who may be considered great leaders and then to consider what it is that makes them so great. This exercise is designed to guide a class in this activity.

DIRECTIONS

1. Divide the class into four equal-size groups, arranging each in a semicircle.

2. In the open part of the semicircle, one group member—the recorder—should stand at a flip chart, ready to write down the group's responses.

3. The members of each group should identify the ten most effective leaders they can think of—living or dead, real or fictional—in one of the following fields: business, sports, politics/government, humanitarian endeavors. One group should cover each of these domains. If more than ten names come up, the group should vote on the ten best answers. The recorder should write down the names as they are identified.

4. Examining the list, group members should identify the traits and characteristics that the people on the list have in common, but that distinguish them from others who are not on the list. In other words, what is it that makes these people so special? The recorder should write down the answers.

5. One person from each group should present his or her group's responses to members of the class. This should include both the names and the underlying characteristics.

QUESTIONS FOR DISCUSSION

1. How did the traits identified in this exercise compare to the ones described in this chapter as important determinants of leadership? Were they similar or different? Why?

2. To what extent were the traits identified in the various groups different or similar? In other words, were different characteristics associated with success in different walks of life? Or were the ingredients for success more universal?

3. Were there some traits identified that you found surprising, or were they all expected?

4. Is it possible to change the traits identified in this exercise, or are they immutable?

A large body of research, much of it conducted in the 1950s at the University of Michigan and at Ohio State University, suggests that leaders do differ greatly along these dimensions. In these classic investigations subordinates completed questionnaires in which they described their leaders' behavior. Those leaders scoring high on initiating structure were mainly concerned with production and focused primarily on getting the job done. They engaged in actions such as organizing work, inducing subordinates to follow rules, setting goals, and making expectations explicit. In contrast, leaders scoring lower on this dimension showed less tendency to engage in these actions.

Leaders at the high end of the consideration dimension were primarily concerned with establishing good relations with their subordinates and being liked by them. They engaged in actions such as doing favors for subordinates, explaining things to them, and assuring their welfare. People who scored low on this dimension didn't care much about how they got along with subordinates.

At first glance, you might assume that initiating structure and consideration are negatively correlated—that is, that people scoring high on one of these dimensions tend to score low on the other. However, this is *not* the case. These two dimensions are independent. Thus, a leader may score high on both concern for production and concern for people, high on one of these dimensions and low on the other, low on both, moderate on one and high on the other, or any combination.

Is any one of these possible patterns best? Careful study indicates that this is a complex issue; production-oriented and people-oriented leadership behaviors both offer a mixed pattern of pluses and minuses. With respect to showing consideration (high concern with people and human relations), the major benefits are improved group morale. Turnover and absenteeism tend to be low among leaders who show high amounts of consideration. At the same time, because such individuals may be reluctant to act in a directive manner toward subordinates and often shy away from presenting them with negative feedback, productivity sometimes suffers.

With respect to initiating structure (high concern with production), efficiency and performance are indeed sometimes enhanced by this leadership style. However, if leaders focus entirely on production, employees may soon conclude that no one cares about them or their welfare. Their job satisfaction and organizational commitment may suffer as a result.

Having identified these complexities, we should note that there is one specific pattern of behavior in which leaders are likely to be highly successful. This is a pattern in which leaders demonstrate high concern for both people *and* production. Indeed, high amounts of concern for people (showing consideration) and concern for productivity (initiating structure) are not incompatible. Rather, skillful leaders can combine both of these orientations into their overall styles to produce favorable results. Thus, although no one leadership style is best, leaders who combine these two behaviors may have an important edge over leaders who show only one or the other. In the words of U.S. Army Lieutenant General William G. Pagonis:

> *To lead successfully, a person must demonstrate . . . expertise and empathy. In my experience, both of these traits can be deliberately and systematically cultivated; this personal development is the first important building block of leadership.*[4]

DEVELOPING SUCCESSFUL LEADER BEHAVIORS: GRID TRAINING

How can one go about developing these two forms of leadership behavior — demonstrating concern for production and concern for people? A technique known as **grid training** proposes a multistep process designed to cultivate these two important skills.[5]

The initial step consists of a *grid seminar* — a session in which an organization's managers (who have been previously trained in the appropriate theory and skills) help organization members analyze their own management styles. This is done using a specially designed questionnaire that allows managers to determine how they stand with respect to their *concern for production* and their *concern for people*. Each participant's approach on each dimension is scored using a number ranging from 1 (low) to 9 (high).

Managers who score low on both concern for production and concern for people are scored 1,1 — evidence of *impoverished management*. A manager who is highly concerned about production but shows little interest in people, the *task management* style, scores 9,1. In contrast, ones who show the opposite pattern — high concern with people but little concern with production — are described as having a *country club* style of management; they are scored 1,9. Managers scoring moderately on both dimensions, the 5,5 pattern, are said to follow a *middle-of-the-road* management style. Finally, there are individuals who are highly concerned with both production and people, those scoring 9,9. This is the most desirable pattern, representing what is known as *team management*.

These various patterns are represented in a diagram like that shown in Figure 8-1 on the following page, known as the *managerial grid*®.

After a manager's position along the grid is determined, training begins to improve concern over production (planning skills) and concern over people (communication skills) to reach the ideal, *9,9* state. This consists of organizationwide training aimed at helping people interact more effectively with each other. Then training is expanded to reducing conflict between groups that work with each other. Additional training includes efforts to identify the extent to which the organization is meeting its strategic goals and then comparing this performance to an ideal. Next, plans are made to meet these goals, and these

Leaders at Moog, the electrohydraulic valve manufacturer, typically demonstrate both high levels of concern for employees and production. Camaraderie and friendliness run high in this suburban Buffalo company, where leaders concentrate intensely on meeting the precise specifications of its many military contracts.

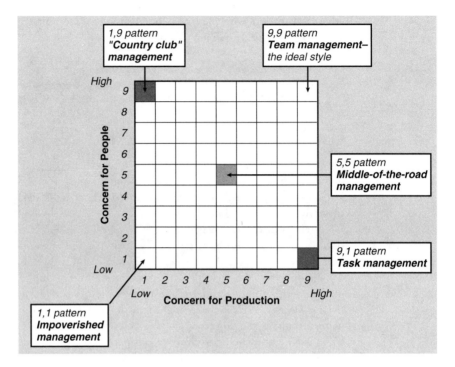

■ *Figure 8-1 The Managerial Grid*®

A manager's standing along two basic dimensions—*concern for production* and *concern for people*—can be illustrated by means of a diagram such as this, known as the *managerial grid*®. To promote effective leadership, people are trained to be high on both dimensions. (*Source:* Based on suggestions by Blake & Mouton, 1969; see Note 5.)

plans are implemented in the organization. Finally, progress toward the goals is continuously assessed, and problem areas are identified.

Grid training is widely considered an effective way of improving the leadership behaviors of people in organizations. Indeed, the grid approach has been used to train hundreds of thousands of people in developing the two key forms of leadership behavior.

LEADERS AND FOLLOWERS

Thus far we have focused on leaders but have ignored followers. However, to understand leadership, we must understand leaders' relations with followers. After all, "Without followers leaders cannot lead. . . . Without followers, even

John Wayne becomes a solitary hero, or, given the right script, a comic figure, posturing on an empty stage."[6] The importance of followers and the complex, reciprocal relationship between leaders and followers are widely recognized by organizational researchers. We will now review two major theories of leadership that take this approach.

THE LEADER–MEMBER EXCHANGE (LMX) MODEL: THE IMPORTANCE OF BEING IN THE "IN-GROUP"

As you know from experience, leaders do not treat all their subordinates in the same manner. This fact is central to an approach known as the **leader–member exchange (LMX) model.**[7]

This theory suggests that for various reasons leaders form different kinds of relationships with various groups of subordinates. One group, referred to as the *in-group,* is favored by the leader. Members of in-groups receive considerably more attention from the leader and larger shares of the resources leaders have to offer (such as time and recognition). By contrast, other subordinates fall into the *out-group.* These individuals are disfavored by leaders. As such, they receive fewer valued resources from their leaders. Leaders distinguish between in-group and out-group members very early in their relationships with them. More often than you'd imagine, this occurs on the basis of surprisingly little information. For example, perceived similarity with respect to personal characteristics such as age, gender, or personality is sufficient to categorize followers into a leader's in-group. Similarly, a particular follower may be granted in-group status if the leader believes that person to be especially competent at performing his or her job.

According to LMX theory, members of in-groups perform their jobs better and hold more positive attitudes toward their jobs than do members of out-groups. Not surprisingly, good relationships with followers can be very valuable, enhancing followers' job satisfaction and organizational commitment (see Chapter 4). How can this be accomplished? The trick is to make all employees feel that they are part of the in-group. Experts note that a key way of keeping subordinates from feeling that they are not in the out-group is by *sharing information equally.* Rather than hoarding power by keeping some people "in the know," while keeping others from it, helping everyone know what's going on in the organization will keep people from feeling that they are left out. It also has been noted that effective leaders can help followers respond to their visions by *supporting teamwork.* To the extent that leaders are willing to share power, and to serve as coaches rather than highly authoritarian bosses (a trend we will discuss later in this chapter), team members are likely to feel that they have equal importance and are not relegated to the secondary status of being in an out-group.

TRANSFORMATIONAL LEADERSHIP: LEADERS WITH CHARISMA

In the 1970s, Chrysler Corporation was being written off as terminal by many analysts of the automobile industry. Lee Iacocca, Chrysler's CEO, however, refused to accept this economic verdict. Instead, he launched a campaign to win government loan guarantees for Chrysler, paving the way for the company's survival. By setting an example of personal sacrifice (by taking only $1 in salary one year) he rallied Chrysler's tens of thousands of employees to unheard of levels of effort and saved the day. Chrysler paid back all its loans ahead of schedule and is now thriving.

World history and the history of organizations are replete with similar examples. Through the ages, some leaders have had extraordinary success in generating profound changes in their followers. Indeed, it is not extreme to suggest that some such people (e.g., Napoleon and John F. Kennedy, to name two) have served as key agents of social change, transforming entire societies through their words and actions. Individuals who accomplish such feats have been referred to as **charismatic** or **transformational leaders.** They transform social, political, or economic reality, possessing the special skills that equip them for this task.

The Nature of Charisma.   At first glance, it is tempting to assume that transformational or charismatic leaders are special by virtue of the traits they possess. In other words, such leadership might be understood as an extension of the great person theory described earlier. Although traits may play a role in transformational leadership, the belief that it makes more sense to view such leadership as involving a special type of relationship between leaders and their followers is growing. Within this framework, charismatic leadership rests more on specific types of reactions by followers than on traits possessed by leaders. Such reactions include:

1. Levels of performance beyond those that would normally be expected.
2. High levels of devotion, loyalty, and reverence toward the leader.
3. Enthusiasm for and excitement about the leader and the leader's ideas.
4. A willingness on the part of subordinates to sacrifice their own personal interests for the sake of a larger collective goal.

In short, transformational or charismatic leadership involves a special kind of leader–follower relationship, in which the leader can, in the words of one author, "make ordinary people do extraordinary things in the face of adversity."[8]

The Behavior of Transformational Leaders.   What, precisely, do transformational or charismatic leaders do to generate this kind of relationship with their subordinates? In general, they gain the capacity to exert profound influence over others through many different tactics. But how?

First, and perhaps most important, transformational leaders *articulate a vision.* They describe, usually in vivid, emotion-provoking terms, an image of what their nation, group, or organization could—and should—become. A dramatic example is provided by the words of Martin Luther King, in his famous "I Have a Dream" speech:

> *So I say to you, my friends, that even though we must face the difficulties of today and tomorrow, I still have a dream. It is a dream deeply rooted in the American dream that one day this nation will rise up and live out the true meaning of its creed—we hold these truths to be self-evident, that all men are created equal.*

But transformational leaders do not simply describe a dream or vision; they *provide a plan for attaining their vision.* In other words, they provide a roadmap for their followers showing how to get from here to there. This too seems crucial, for a vision that appears perpetually out of reach is unlikely to motivate people to try to attain it. (Recall our discussion of goal setting in Chapter 4.)

Third, transformational leaders engage in *framing*—that is, they define the purpose of their movement or organization in ways that give meaning and purpose to whatever actions they are requesting from followers. Perhaps the nature of framing is best illustrated by the well-known tale of two stonecutters working on a cathedral in the Middle Ages. When asked what they were doing, one replied, "Why, cutting this stone, of course." The other replied, "Building the world's most beautiful temple to the glory of God." Which person would be more likely to stimulate others to expend greater effort? The answer is obvious.

In the business world, transformational leaders frame the activities of their organizations in ways that give them added meaning and that tie them closely to the accepted values of society. Consider, for example, the charisma of Mary Kay Ash, the successful founder of the large cosmetics company that bears her name. In describing her company, Mary Kay once said: "My objective was just to help women. It was not to make a tremendous amount of sales. I want women to earn money commensurate with men. I want them to be paid on the basis of what they have between their ears and their brains and not because they are male or female."[9] Imagine if, instead, she had stated: "My objective was to increase our sales by 25 percent annually, so that in five years we'd become the third or fourth largest company in the business. In that way, we'd provide an excellent return to shareholders and build the value of our company's stock." Would you, as a Mary Kay representative, work as hard for these goals and this vision as for the one Ash actually expressed? Probably not. (We will more fully describe the charismatic nature of Mary Kay Ash in the **Winning Practices** section below.)

In addition, transformational leaders often show greater than average *willingness to take risks* and engage in unconventional actions to reach their stated goals. To help thwart the coup that threatened the budding democracy of his nation, Boris Yeltsin rushed to the Russian Parliament, where he stood on top of a tank and pleaded with troops sent there by the new hard-liners to withdraw. By this high-risk behavior, he demonstrated his deep commitment to the forces of reform.

Other qualities shown by transformational leaders include expressing high levels of self-confidence; showing a high degree of concern for their fol-

---

WINNING PRACTICES

Mary Kay Ash: Profile of a Charismatic Leader

There are "rags-to-riches stories," and then there's Mary Kay Ash, the founder of the wildly successful Mary Kay Cosmetics empire.[12] At age 45, in the early 1960s, she became disenchanted with the limited opportunities for women in business, and with only the help of her children she gambled her life savings of $5,000 on a cosmetics business. Some three decades later this investment has grown into a giant corporation with annual sales over $613 million and a sales force some 300,000 strong. Not surprisingly, the woman behind all this has been considered one of the best business leaders in the United States.

Many attribute the company's success in large part to Mary Kay's charismatic ways. By giving her employees, most of whom are women, opportunities to succeed and recognizing their success, she motivates and inspires them. At its annual "Seminar" in Dallas, for example, Mary Kay representatives are awarded such forms of recognition as: pink Cadillacs (some $90 million worth have been given away already), first-class trips abroad, gold bracelets studded in diamonds spelling out "$1,000,000" (for selling that amount of cosmetics), and lapel pins and ribbons denoting other sales milestones. These lavish forms of recognition are matched only by the opulent, Las Vegas-style productions in which they are presented—fetes that take on the noise level and excitement of political conventions.

One of the things Mary Kay executives pride themselves in doing is helping women become financially successful and feel good about themselves. "Give me a hard-working waitress," says national sales director, Shirley Hutton, "and in a year I'll turn her into a director making $35,000." Many do bet-

lowers' needs; demonstrating excellent communication skills, such as the ability to "read" others' reactions quickly and accurately; and a stirring personal style. Finally, transformational leaders are often masters of impression management, engaging in tactics that enhance their attractiveness and appeal to others.

The late Sam Walton used to whip his employees into a frenzy when he visited his Wal-Mart stores by holding store meetings that ran like pep rallies: "Give me a 'W'...."

When you consider these behaviors in conjunction with the captivating and exciting visions of transformational or charismatic leaders, their tremendous impact becomes understandable. Their influence, it appears, does not stem from any magical traits. Rather, it is the result of a complex set of behaviors and techniques. In the final analysis, however, the essence of transformational leadership does appear to rest on the ability of such people to in-

ter—much better. Indeed, 74 sales consultants have earned commissions of over $1 million during their careers. (Hutton earned approximately that amount in 1993 alone!)

Mary Kay is recognized for her sincerity and concern for her employees' well-being. According to Gloria Hilliard Mayfield, a relatively new sales consultant, she is surprisingly approachable. "You wouldn't just walk over to, say, John Akers [CEO of IBM]," she explains. "But Mary Kay calls you her daughter and looks you dead in the eye. She makes you feel you can do anything. She's sincerely concerned about your welfare." When Hutton's daughter was ill, for example, Mary Kay called her several times to cheer her up. Such expressions of personal interest are contagious: many sales consultants treat their customers the same way—sending them birthday cards and showing they're interested in them. *This*, they are convinced, sells makeup!

Recognition from Mary Kay is considered the ultimate form of recognition. At each year's Seminar, she personally crowns four "Queens of Seminar" in recognition of their sales accomplishments. She kisses them, gives them roses, and pats their hands. This personal touch is so important that one year when she was ill, she made an appearance from her sickbed via a closed-circuit television hook-up—just to make her presence felt.

What will happen to Mary Kay, the company, after Mary Kay Ash, the woman, is gone? "There will be a flood of tears unlike anything you've ever seen," says the husband of a sales consultant. "I'd love to have the tissue concession." But no one doubts that the company will continue without its charismatic leader—her legacy is too strong to not be felt.

spire others, through their words, their vision, and their actions. As one expert put it, "If you as a leader can make an appealing dream seem like tomorrow's reality, your subordinates will freely choose to follow you."[10]

The Effects of Charismatic Leadership. As you might imagine, charismatic leaders can have dramatic effects on the behavior of their followers. Indeed, charismatic leadership is positively correlated with job performance and satisfaction. It is easy to imagine how charismatic leaders may inspire their followers to achieve high levels of performance. And, because these leaders are perceived as being so heroic, followers tend to be very pleased with them. Generally, people enjoy working for charismatic leaders. Moreover, they tend to do well under their guidance. In fact, one study has found that U.S. presidents believed to be highly charismatic (as suggested by biographical accounts of their personalities and their reactions to world crises) received higher ratings by historians of their effectiveness as president.[11] In short, evidence suggests that charismatic leadership can have very positive effects.

CONTINGENCY THEORIES
OF LEADER EFFECTIVENESS

It should be clear by now that leadership is a complex process. It involves intricate social relationships and is affected by a wide range of variables. In general, it may be said that leadership is influenced by two main factors—the characteristics of the individuals involved, and the nature of the situations they face. This basic point lies at the heart of several approaches to leadership known as **contingency theories** of leader effectiveness. According to this approach, there is no one best style of leadership. Instead, they suggest that certain leadership styles may prove most effective under certain conditions. Contingency theories seek to identify the conditions and factors that determine whether, and to what degree, leaders will enhance the performance and satisfaction of their subordinates. We will describe three such approaches.

LPC CONTINGENCY THEORY:
MATCHING LEADERS AND TASKS

Earlier we explained that the behaviors associated with effective leadership fall into two major groups—concern for people, and concern for production. Various behaviors in each category contribute to leaders' success. However, a more refined look at this issue leads us to ask exactly when each type of behavior works best. That is, under what conditions are leaders more successful when they demonstrate a concern for people compared to a concern for production?

The Basics of the Theory.   This question is addressed by a widely studied approach to leadership known as **LPC contingency theory** developed by Fred Fiedler. The contingency aspect of the theory is reflected by the assumption that a leader's contribution to successful performance by his or her group is determined both by the leader's traits and by various features of the situation. Different levels of leader effectiveness occur under different combinations of conditions. To fully understand leader effectiveness, both types of factors must be considered.

Fiedler identifies *esteem (liking) for least preferred coworker* (**LPC** for short) as the most important personal characteristic. This refers to a leader's tendency to evaluate in a favorable or unfavorable manner the person with whom she or he has found it most difficult to work. Leaders who perceive this person in negative terms (low LPC leaders) are primarily concerned with attaining successful task performance. In contrast, those who perceive their least preferred coworker in a positive light (high LPC leaders) are mainly concerned with establishing good relations with subordinates. A questionnaire is used to measure one's LPC score. It is important to note that Fiedler considers LPC to be fixed—an aspect of an individual's leadership style that cannot be changed. As we will explain, this has important implications for applying the theory to the task of improving a leader's effectiveness.

Which type of leader—one low in LPC or one high in LPC—is more effective? Fiedler's answer is: It depends. And what it depends on is the degree to which the situation is favorable to the leaders—that is, how much it allows the leaders to have control over their subordinates. This, in turn, is determined largely by three factors:

1. The nature of the leader's relations with group members (the extent to which he or she enjoys their support and loyalty).

2. The degree of structure in the task being performed (the extent to which task goals and subordinates' roles are clearly defined).

3. The leader's position power (his or her ability to enforce compliance by subordinates).

Combining these three factors, the leader's situational control can range from very high (positive relations with group members, a highly structured task, high position power) to very low (negative relations, an unstructured task, low position power).

What types of leaders are most effective under these various conditions? According to the theory, low LPC leaders (ones who are task-oriented) are superior to high LPC leaders (ones who are relations- or people-oriented) when situational control is either very low or very high. In contrast, high LPC leaders have an edge when situational control falls within the moderate range. (Refer to Figure 8-2 on p. 222.)

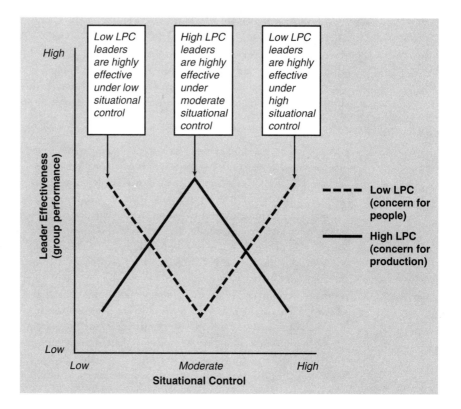

■ *Figure 8-2 LPC Contingency Theory*

LPC contingency theory predicts that low LPC leaders (ones who are primarily task-oriented) will be more effective than high LPC leaders (ones who are primarily people-oriented) when situational control is either very low or very high. The opposite is true when situational control is moderate.

The rationale for these predictions is quite reasonable. Under conditions of low situational control, groups need considerable guidance to accomplish their tasks. Without such direction, nothing would get done. For example, imagine a military combat group led by an unpopular platoon leader. Any chance of effectiveness this person has would result from paying careful attention to the task at hand, rather than hoping to establish better relations with the group. (In fact, in the army, it is often said that a leader in an emergency is better off giving wrong orders than no orders whatsoever.) Since low LPC leaders are more likely to provide structure than high LPC leaders, they usually will be superior in such cases.

Similarly, low LPC leaders are also superior under conditions that offer the leader a high degree of situational control. Indeed, when leaders are liked, their power is not challenged, and when the demands of the task make it clear what a leader should be doing, it is perfectly acceptable for them to focus on the task at hand. Subordinates expect their leaders to exercise control under such conditions and accept it when they do so. This leads to task success. For example, an airline pilot leading a cockpit crew is expected to take charge and to not seek the consensus of others as he or she guides the plane onto the runway for a landing. Surely, the pilot would be less effective if he or she didn't take charge but asked the copilot what should be done.

Things are different, however, when situations offer leaders moderate situational control. Consider, for example, a situation in which a leader's relations with subordinates are good, but the task is unstructured, and the leader's power is somewhat restricted. This may be the case within a research and development team attempting to find creative new uses for a company's products. Here it would be clearly inappropriate for a low LPC leader to impose directives. Rather, a highly nurturant leader who is considerate of the feelings of others would likely be most effective—that is, a high LPC leader.

Applying LPC Contingency Theory.   Practitioners have found LPC contingency theory to be quite useful when it comes to suggesting ways of enhancing leader effectiveness. Because the theory assumes that certain kinds of leaders are most effective under certain kinds of situations, and that leadership style is fixed, the best way to enhance effectiveness is to fit the right kind of leaders to the situations they face.

This involves completing questionnaires that can be used to assess both the LPC score of the leader and the amount of control he or she faces in the situation. Then, using these indexes, a match can be made such that leaders are put into the situations that best suit their leadership styles—a technique known as **leader match.** This approach also focuses on ways of changing the situational control variables—leader–member relations, task structure, and leader position power—when it is impractical to change leaders. For example, a high LPC leader either should be moved to a job in which situational control is either extremely high or extremely low, or alternatively, the situation should be changed (such as by altering relations between leaders and group members, or raising or lowering the leader's position power) so as to increase or decrease the amount of situational control encountered.

Several companies, including Sears, have used the leader match approach with some success. In fact, several studies have found that the technique does a good job of improving group effectiveness.

PATH–GOAL THEORY: LEADERS AS GUIDES TO VALUED GOALS

In defining leadership, we indicated that leaders help their groups or organizations reach their goals. This basic idea plays a central role in **path–goal theory** of leadership.[13] In general terms, the theory contends that subordinates will react favorably to leaders who are perceived as helping them make progress toward various goals by clarifying the paths to such rewards. Specifically, the theory contends that the things a leader does to help clarify the nature of tasks and reduce or eliminate obstacles will increase subordinates' perceptions that working hard will lead to good performance and that good performance, in turn, will be recognized and rewarded. And, under such conditions (as you may recall from our discussion of expectancy theory in Chapter 3), motivation will be enhanced (which may help enhance performance).

How, precisely, can leaders best accomplish these tasks? The answer, as in other contingency theories, is: "It depends." (In fact, this answer is your best clue to identifying any contingency theory.) And what it depends on is a complex interaction between key aspects of *leader behavior* and certain *contingency* factors. Specifically, with respect to leader behavior, path–goal theory suggests that leaders can adopt four basic styles:

- **Instrumental:** an approach focused on providing specific guidance, establishing work schedules and rules.
- **Supportive:** a style focused on establishing good relations with subordinates and satisfying their needs.
- **Participative:** a pattern in which the leader consults with subordinates, permitting them to participate in decisions.
- **Achievement-oriented:** an approach in which the leader sets challenging goals and seeks improvements in performance.

According to the theory, these styles are not mutually exclusive; in fact, the same leader can adopt them at different times and in different situations. (Indeed, as noted earlier in this chapter, showing such flexibility is one important aspect of being an effective leader.)

Which of these styles is best for maximizing subordinates' satisfaction and motivation? The answer depends on several characteristics of subordinates. For example, if followers are high in ability, an instrumental style of leadership may be unnecessary; instead, a less structured, supportive approach may be preferable. On the other hand, if subordinates are low in ability, they may need considerable guidance to help them attain their goals. Similarly, people high in need for affiliation (that is, those desiring close, friendly ties with others) may strongly prefer a supportive or participative style of leadership. Those high in the need for achievement may strongly prefer an achievement-oriented leader, one who can guide them to unprecedented levels of success.

The theory suggests that the most effective leadership style also depends on several aspects of the work environment. Specifically, path–goal theory predicts that when tasks are unstructured and nonroutine, an instrumental approach by the leader may be best; much clarification and guidance are needed. However, when tasks are structured and highly routine, such leadership may actually get in the way of good performance, and may be resented by subordi-

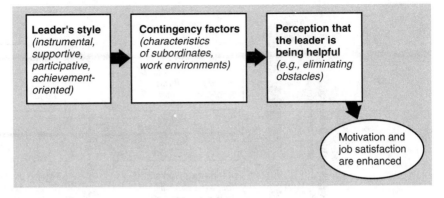

■ *Figure 8-3 Path–Goal Theory*

According to *path–goal theory,* perceptions among employees that leaders are helping them attain valued goals enhance employees' motivation and job satisfaction. Such perceptions are encouraged when a leader's style is consistent with the needs and characteristics of subordinates and various aspects of the work environment. (*Source:* Based on suggestions by House & Baetz, 1979; see Note 13.)

nates who think the leader is engaging in unnecessary meddling. (See Figure 8-3 for an overview of all these aspects of path–goal theory.)

SITUATIONAL LEADERSHIP THEORY: ADJUSTING LEADERSHIP STYLE TO THE SITUATION

Another theory of leadership, **situational leadership theory,** is considered a contingency theory because it focuses on the best leadership style for a given situation. This approach concentrates on a somewhat different concept, the *maturity* of followers—that is, their readiness to take responsibility for their own behavior. This includes both their job knowledge and skills, as well as their willingness to work without taking direction from others. Effective leaders are, according to this theory, able to adjust their styles to accommodate their followers' need for guidance and direction—*task behavior*—as well as their need for emotional support—*relationship behavior.* As shown in Figure 8-4 on p. 226, these two dimensions are independent.

By combining high and low levels of each dimension, four different types of situations are identified, each of which is associated with a leadership style that is most effective.

First, starting in the lower left corner of Figure 8-4 are situations in which followers need very little in the way of emotional hand-holding and guidance with respect to how to do their jobs. In this situation, *delegating* is the best way to treat followers—that is, turning over to followers the responsibility for making and implementing decisions.

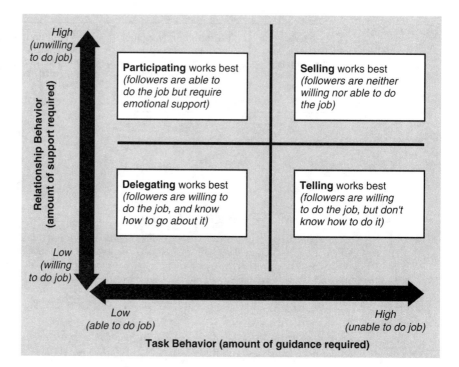

■ *Figure 8-4 Situational Leadership Theory*

According to *situational leadership theory*, the most appropriate leadership style depends on two dimensions: followers' need for guidance and direction *(task behavior)* and their need for emotional support *(relationship behavior)*. The most effective styles under high and low conditions of each of these variables are summarized here.

Second, in the upper left corner of the diagram is a situation in which followers are able but unwilling to do their jobs, requiring high amounts of supportive behavior to motivate them. A *participating* style of leadership works well in this situation because it allows followers to share their ideas, enhancing their desire to perform.

In the third situation, followers are unable and unwilling to do their jobs, requiring both task direction and emotional support. The style known as *selling* is most appropriate here. This involves explaining decisions and providing opportunities for clarification.

Finally, in the lower right corner are situations in which followers are unable but willing to take responsibility for their actions. They are motivated but lack the appropriate skills. The practice of *telling* followers what to do is most useful in such situations—that is, giving them specific instructions and closely supervising their work.

According to this conceptualization leaders must be able to: (1) diagnose the situations they face, (2) identify the appropriate behavioral style, and then (3) implement that response. Because the situations leaders face may change all the time, leaders must constantly reassess them, paying special attention to their followers' needs for guidance and emotional support. To the extent that they do so, they are likely to be effective. Specialized training in these skills has been found to be quite useful. In fact, the approach has been widely used to train leaders in such corporate giants as Xerox, Mobil Oil, and Caterpillar, as well as the U.S. military services. (Which style of leadership are you most prone to follow in your treatment of others? To give you some insight into this question, complete the **Self-Assessment Exercise** on pp. 228–229.)

LEADERSHIP IN TODAY'S "INVOLVEMENT-ORIENTED" ORGANIZATIONS

Traditionally, leaders in the corporate world exercised power in ways that can best be described as "command and control." They were "bosses" who pushed people around. They told people what to do and when to do it. But then something—more accurately, several things—happened. Global competition threatened once stable industries. Technology gave employees at all levels access to unprecedented amounts of information. Highly innovative upstart companies left corporate giants in their dust. Middle layers of organizations were eliminated as organizations were downsized. With these changes came a shift in the nature of work. Less of it was being done by individuals whose loyalty was ensured by the promise of working one's way up the corporate ladder, and more of it was being done by multiskilled people working together in teams (see Chapter 7). As teams developed, the nature of leadership followed suit. In the words of leadership expert Warren Bennis, "whips and chains are no longer an alternative. Leaders must learn to change the nature of power and how it's employed."[14]

By their actions, leaders reflect and reinforce a team's values. When an official at a **Corning Glass** *plant purposely shattered thousands of dollars worth of glass tubing because it failed to meet its customer's specifications, he sent a strong message that product quality mattered greatly.*

But, how? The answer lies in the process of *sharing leadership*, **empowering** workers to make decisions for themselves. When this occurs, leaders act more like teachers and coaches who help employees by providing necessary resources, and guiding them toward the answers they seek. As we described teams in Chapter 7, involvement-oriented organizations give employees both the information and the power to make decisions about their work. They must have the skills and commitment to make good decisions, and leaders must be willing to share their power. Instead of calling the shots, the new breed of leaders focus on developing subordinates by encouraging them to get involved.

Determining Your Leadership Style

To be able to identify and enact the most appropriate style of leadership in any given situation, it is first useful to understand the style to which you are already predisposed. This exercise will help you gain such insight into your own leadership style.

DIRECTIONS

Following are eight hypothetical situations in which you have to make a decision affecting you and members of your work group. For each, indicate which of the following actions you are most likely to take by writing the letter corresponding to that action in the space provided.

A.   Let the members of the group decide themselves what to do.

B.   Ask the members of the group what to do, but make the final decision yourself.

C.   Make the decision yourself, but explain your reasons.

D.   Make the decision yourself, telling the group exactly what to do.

_____   1.   In the face of financial pressures, you are forced to make budget cuts for your unit. Where do you cut?

_____   2.   To meet an impending deadline, someone in your secretarial pool will have to work late one evening to finish typing an important report. Who will it be?

_____   3.   As coach of a company softball team, you are required to trim your squad to 25 players from 30 currently on the roster. Who goes?

_____   4.   Employees in your department have to schedule their summer vacations so as to keep the office appropriately staffed. Who decides first?

_____   5.   As chair of the social committee, you are responsible for determining the theme for the company ball. How do you do so?

Consider, for example, the way leaders operate at the Levi Strauss plant in Blue Ridge, Georgia. Instead of the old "check your brain at the door and sew pockets" mentality that used to reign, today's employees are trained to do three dozen different tasks crossing a wide range of former organizational

_____   6. You have an opportunity to buy or rent an important piece of equipment for your company. After gathering all the facts, how do you make the choice?

_____   7. The office is being redecorated. How do you decide on the color scheme?

_____   8. Along with your associates you are taking a visiting dignitary to dinner. How do you decide what restaurant to go to?

SCORING

1. Count the number of situations to which you responded by marking A. This is your *delegating* score.

2. Count the number of situations to which you responded by marking B. This is your *participating* score.

3. Count the number of situations to which you responded by marking C. This is your *selling* score.

4. Count the number of situations to which you responded by marking D. This is your *telling* score.

QUESTIONS FOR DISCUSSION

1. Based on this questionnaire, what was your most predominant leadership style? Is this consistent with what you would have predicted in advance?

2. According to situational leadership theory, in what kinds of situations would this style be most appropriate? Have you ever found yourself in such a situation, and if so, how well did you do?

3. Do you think that it would be possible for you to change this style if needed?

4. To what extent were your responses to this questionnaire affected by the nature of the situations described? In other words, would you have opted for different decisions in different situations?

boundaries. Workers run plant operations themselves, organizing supplies, setting production goals, and making personnel policies. Although employees receive direction from above, most directives come from their peers. In fact, some 650 pages have been trimmed off the Levi policy manual.

Not surprisingly, Levi's leaders have found it challenging to relinquish some of their power. In the words of Tommye Joe Daves, a grandmother and long-time Levi Strauss employee, "Sometimes it's real hard for me not to push back and say, 'You do this, you do that, and you do this.' Now I have to say, 'How do you want to do this?' I have to realize that their ideas may not be the way to go, but I have to let them learn that for themselves."[15] This is the embodiment of what has been called today's **postheroic leader.** Clearly, this approach has been working: The plant is churning out more products in less time, and at higher quality than ever before. The key, according to Levi Strauss' CEO, Robert Hass, is "syndicating leadership throughout the organization." This is not to downplay the importance of drive, self-confidence, cognitive ability, and flexibility, or any of the key traits that we earlier identified as distinguishing great persons. Rather, in today's work teams these qualities are expected of everyone.

None of this is meant to imply that today's leaders have less responsibility than before. Indeed, empowering others does not require leaders to give up their level of responsibility, but rather, to execute it differently. To borrow an analogy, traditional leaders operated like a game of football, where coaches called in plays from the sidelines and had them executed by individuals with specific roles. However, today's postheroic, involvement-oriented leaders operate more like the game of basketball, where players have to make decisions on the spot, relying on their own expertise.[16] This frees up leaders to spend more time on obtaining the resources teams need to succeed, finding problem areas and looking for solutions, and improving the work environment for employees. These are all tasks that may have been ignored had leaders been spending their time checking up on employees—tasks that help ensure the organization's survival.

If the practices we've been describing here don't square with your own experiences, we're not too surprised. In most organizations, employees are still not highly empowered, and leadership remains rather traditional. But experts say that the change is coming—and fast. If they are correct, by the twenty-first century, leaders relying on the traditional command and control approach will be a thing of the past.

SUMMARY:
PUTTING IT TO USE

Leadership is defined as the process by which an individual influences others in ways that help attain group or organizational goals. Although the terms *leader* and *manager* are frequently used interchangeably, they are different. Whereas leaders are responsible for determining the purpose of an organization and the strategy for attaining it, managers are primarily responsible for implementing those strategies.

The idea that certain traits and characteristics distinguish successful leaders from ordinary ones is basic to the *great person theory* of leadership. Although evidence for the great person theory has been inconsistent, today's theorists believe that successful leaders have the following characteristics: drive, honesty and integrity, self-confidence, leadership motivation (the desire to lead others), cognitive ability, and flexibility.

The *behavior approach* to leadership focuses not on who leaders are, but rather, what leaders do. Research has consistently found that successful leaders demonstrate two distinct types of behaviors—*consideration*, showing concern for people, and *initiating structure*, showing concern for getting the job done. The best leaders demonstrate high amounts of both behaviors. A special technique known as *grid training* focuses on developing both these behavioral skills. It consists of organizationwide efforts at training people to recognize their deficiencies in these areas, and helping them improve their planning and communication skills.

Other approaches to leadership focus on the interrelationships between leaders and followers. For example, the *leader–member exchange (LMX) model* recognizes that leaders tend to favor certain individuals—referred to as the leader's in-group—giving them more attention and direction, and paying less attention to others—the out-group. By sharing information equally within groups and by supporting teamwork, leaders may avoid problems associated with relegating people to out-groups.

Some leaders—such as Mary Kay Ash, the founder of the large cosmetics empire that bears her name—are considered *charismatic* or *transformational leaders*. Such individuals generate enthusiasm, high levels of loyalty, a willingness to make sacrifices, and top performance. Charismatic leaders articulate a vision, provide a plan for attaining that vision, are willing to take risks, and engage in *framing*—that is, defining their purpose in a way that is inspiring.

Contingency theories of leadership are based on the idea that there is no one best style of leadership. Rather, the most effective style depends on the combination of behaviors and situations encountered. One such approach is *LPC contingency theory.* This approach acknowledges that leaders' effectiveness depends on the extent to which they are predisposed to demonstrate concern for people versus concern for production in conjunction with the favorableness of the situation for the leader (i.e., the extent to which the leader has control over the situation). Specifically, it notes that leaders who are primarily production-oriented are more effective than ones who are primarily people-oriented when situational control is either very low or very high. However, leaders who are more production-oriented have an edge when situational control is moderate. The technique known as *leader match* advocates not changing the leaders themselves, but either matching them to those situations that best suit their style, or changing the characteristics of the situation.

Path–goal theory is another contingency theory. It contends that subordinates will react favorably to leaders who are perceived as helping them make progress toward various goals by clarifying the paths to such rewards. It specifies that certain leadership styles are more effective than others in certain situations. For example, a highly directive, instrumental style best helps achieve goals when people have limited ability, or when the tasks are so unstructured that a great deal of guidance is needed.

Situational leadership theory is a third contingency theory. It suggests that depending on the followers' need for guidance and their need for emotional support, one of four different styles of leadership—delegating, participating, selling, and telling—would be most effective. For example, delegating works best when individuals need little guidance and emotional support, whereas telling works best when individuals need great amounts of both.

In keeping with the popularity of work teams in today's organizations, experts note that the role of leadership is changing. Instead of commanding and controlling, today's leaders are empowering others, giving them the skills needed to lead themselves. This frees leaders to spend more time on important tasks essential to the organization's survival—such as obtaining resources teams need to succeed—that otherwise may have been ignored. Although all leaders might not be operating this way yet, experts predict that they will be doing so very shortly.

You Be the Consultant

You are talking to Arthur A. Tarian, the president and founder of a small tool and die casting firm, who tells you as follows: "Nobody around here has any respect for me. They don't like me and they think I don't know what I'm doing. The only reason they listen to me is because this is my company." After talking to the employees, you realize that Mr. Tarian is widely regarded as a highly controlling individual who doesn't let anyone do anything for themselves. Answer the following questions relevant to this situation based on the material in this chapter.

1. What behaviors should Mr. Tarian attempt to emulate so as to improve his leadership style? How may he go about doing so?

2. Under what conditions would you expect Mr. Tarian's leadership style to be most effective? Do you think that these conditions might exist in his company?

3. What would you tell Mr. Tarian as to how he might have to shift his leadership style in the years ahead? What conditions would have to exist in his company before such a change would be necessary?

CHAPTER 9

Making Decisions in Organizations

PREVIEW OF CHAPTER HIGHLIGHTS

Decision making is an eight-step process that focuses on both formulating and implementing solutions to problems.

Organizational decisions can be distinguished with respect to how structured or unstructured the situation is, and how much risk or certainty is involved.

The **rational-economic model** describes how decision makers ideally should behave, whereas the **administrative model** describes how decision makers actually behave.

Imperfect decisions are made due to both individual biases (**framing, heuristics,** and the **escalation of commitment** phenomenon), as well as various organizational limitations.

There are conditions under which groups make better decisions than individuals (e.g., on simple tasks) and conditions under which individuals make better decisions than groups (e.g., when working on creative tasks).

High levels of group cohesiveness can lead to **groupthink,** which has led to several well-known decision fiascoes.

Group decisions can be improved by using the **Delphi technique** and the **nominal group technique.**

Decision making is widely considered one of the most important — if not *the* most important — of all managerial activities. Management theorists and researchers agree that decision making represents one of the most common and most crucial of all work activities. In fact, organizational scientist Herbert Simon, who won a Nobel prize for his work on decision making, has described decision making as synonymous with managing. Every day, people in organizations make decisions about a wide variety of things ranging from the mundane to the monumental. Understanding how these decisions are made and how they can be improved is a major goal of the field of organizational behavior.

This chapter will examine theories, research, and practical managerial techniques concerned with organizational decision making. We will review the basic characteristics of individual decisions and group decisions. For each, we will identify factors that may adversely affect the quality of decisions and techniques for improving decision quality. Then we will compare the quality of individual and group decisions on a variety of tasks and note the conditions under which individuals or groups are better suited for making decisions. Finally, we will describe various techniques that can be used to improve the quality of decisions made by groups. But first, we will begin by taking a closer look at the general process of decision making and the varieties of decisions made in organizations.

THE BASIC NATURE OF
ORGANIZATIONAL DECISION MAKING

Given the central importance of decision making in organizations, we will begin our discussion by highlighting some of the basic steps in the decision-making process and noting the characteristics of organizational decisions.

A GENERAL MODEL OF DECISION MAKING

Traditionally, scientists have found it useful to conceptualize the process of decision making as a series of steps that groups or individuals take to solve problems.[1] A general model of the decision-making process can help us understand the complex nature of organizational decision making (see Figure 9-1). This model highlights two important aspects of the decision-making process: *formulation*, the process of understanding a problem and making a decision about it, and *implementation*, the process of carrying out the decision made. As we present this model, keep in mind that all decisions might not fully conform to the neat, eight-step pattern described (e.g., steps may be skipped and/or combined). However, for the purpose of pointing out the general way the decision-making process operates, the model is quite useful.

The first step in decision making is *identifying the problem*. To decide how to solve a problem, we must first recognize and identify it. For example, an executive may identify as a problem the fact that the company cannot meet its

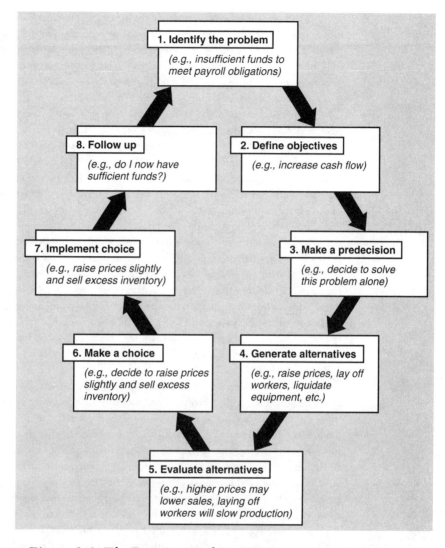

■ *Figure 9-1 The Decision-Making Process*

The process of decision making tends to follow the eight steps outlined here. An example of how a problem, insufficient funds to meet payroll obligations, can be applied to each step is given. (*Source:* Based on suggestions by Wedley & Field, 1983; see Note 1.)

payroll obligations. This step isn't always as easy as it sounds. People frequently distort, omit, ignore, and/or discount information that might provide important cues regarding the existence of problems. This, of course, is problematic. After all, a problem cannot be solved if it is never recognized.

After a problem is identified, the next step is to *define the objectives* to be met in solving it. It is important to conceive of problems in such a way that possible solutions can be identified. The problem identified in our example may be defined as "inadequate cash flow." By looking at it in this way, the objective is clear: Increase available cash reserves. Any possible solution to the problem should be evaluated relative to this objective.

The third step in the decision-making process is *making a predecision*. A **predecision** is a decision about how to make a decision. By assessing the type of problem in question and other aspects of the situation, managers may opt to make a decision themselves, delegate the decision to another, or have a group make the decision. Predecisions should be based on research that tells us about the effectiveness of decisions made under different circumstances, many of which we will review later in this chapter.

For many years, managers have been relying on their own intuition or empirically based information about organizational behavior (contained in books like this) for the guidance needed to make predecisions. Recently, however, computer programs have been developed summarizing much of this information in a form that gives managers ready access to a wealth of social science information that may help them decide how to make decisions.[2] Such **decision support systems (DSS),** as they are called, can only be as good as the information that goes into developing them. Research has shown that DSS techniques are generally quite effective in helping people make decisions about solving problems.

The fourth step in the process is *generating alternatives,* the stage in which possible solutions to the problem are identified. Whenever possible in attempting to come up with solutions, people tend to rely on previously used approaches that may provide ready-made answers. In our example, some possible ways of solving the revenue shortage problem include reducing the work force, liquidating unnecessary equipment, or increasing sales.

Because all these possibilities may not be equally feasible, the fifth step calls for *evaluating alternative solutions.* Which solution is best? What would be the most effective way of raising the revenue needed to meet the payroll? The various alternatives need to be identified. Some may be more effective than others, and some may be more difficult to implement than others. For example, although increasing sales would certainly help, that is much easier said than done. It is a solution, but not an immediately practical one.

Next, is the sixth step, *making a choice.* After several alternatives are evaluated, one that is considered acceptable is chosen. As we will describe shortly, different approaches to decision making offer different views of how thoroughly people consider alternatives and how optimal their chosen alternatives are. Choosing which course of action to take is the step that most often comes to mind when we think about the decision-making process.

The seventh step calls for *implementing the chosen alternative.* That is, the chosen alternative is carried out. The eighth and final step is *following up.* Monitoring the effectiveness of the decisions put into action is important to the success of organizations. Does the problem still exist? Have any new problems been caused by implementing the solution? In other words, it is important to seek feedback about the effectiveness of any attempted solution. For this reason, the decision-making process is presented as circular in Figure 9-1 (see p. 235). If the solution works, the problem may be considered solved. If not, a new solution will have to be attempted.

VARIETIES OF ORGANIZATIONAL DECISIONS

Consider, for a moment, the variety of decisions likely to be made in organizations. Some decisions have far-reaching consequences and others are more mundane. People sometimes make decisions in situations in which the likely outcomes are well known (e.g., the decision to underwrite life insurance on the basis of actuarial data), whereas at other times the outcomes are much more uncertain (e.g., the decision to invade a hostile nation for purposes of freeing hostages). These examples are reflective of the two major characteristics of organizational decisions: how structured or unstructured the situation is, and how much certainty or risk is involved in the decision.

Programmed Versus Nonprogrammed Decisions.   Think of a decision that is made repeatedly and follows a preestablished set of alternatives. For example, a word processing operator may decide to make a backup diskette of the day's work, or a manager of a fast-food restaurant may decide to order hamburger buns as the supply starts to get low. Decisions such as these are known as **programmed decisions**—routine decisions, made by lower-level personnel, that rely on predetermined courses of action.

By contrast, we may identify **nonprogrammed decisions**—ones for which there are no ready-made solutions. The decision maker confronts a unique situation in which the solutions are novel. The research scientist attempting to find a cure for a rare disease faces a problem that is poorly structured. Unlike the order clerk whose course of action is clear when the supply of paper clips runs low, the scientist in this example must rely on creativity rather than preexisting answers to solve the problem at hand.

Certain types of nonprogrammed decisions are known as **strategic decisions.** These decisions are typically made by coalitions of high-level executives and have important long-term implications for the organization. Strategic decisions reflect a consistent pattern for directing the organization in some specified fashion—that is, according to an underlying organizational philosophy or mission. For example, an organization may make a strategic decision to grow at a specified yearly rate, or to be guided by a certain code of corporate ethics. Both of these decisions are likely to be considered strategic because they guide the future direction of the organization.

Table 9-1 summarizes the differences between programmed and nonprogrammed decisions with respect to three important questions. First, what type

■ *Table 9-1 Programmed versus Nonprogrammed Decisions*

Programmed and nonprogrammed decisions differ with respect to the types of tasks on which they are made, the degree to which solutions may be found in existing organizational policies, and the typical decision-making unit.

	Type of Decision	
Variable	*Programmed Decisions*	*Nonprogrammed Decisions*
Type of task	Simple, routine	Complex, creative
Reliance on organizational policies	Considerable guidance from past decisions	No guidance from past decisions
Typical decision maker	Lower-level workers (usually alone)	Upper-level supervisors (usually in groups)

of tasks are involved? Programmed decisions are made on tasks that are common and routine, whereas nonprogrammed decisions are made on unique and novel tasks. Second, how much reliance is there on organizational policies? In making programmed decisions, the decision maker can count on guidance from statements of organizational policy and procedure. However, nonprogrammed decisions require the use of creative solutions that are implemented for the first time; past solutions may provide little guidance. Finally, who makes the decisions? Not surprisingly, nonprogrammed decisions typically are made by upper-level organizational personnel, whereas the more routine, well-structured decisions are usually relegated to lower-level personnel.

Certain Versus Uncertain Decisions. Just think of how easy it would be to make decisions if we knew exactly what the future held in store. Making the best investments in the stock market would simply be a matter of looking up the changes in tomorrow's newspaper. Although we never know for sure what the future holds, but we can be more certain at some times than others. Certainty about the factors on which decisions are made is highly desired in organizational decision making.

The willingness to take risks is cited as a key cause of a financial turnaround at Lyondell Petrochemical—a company that went from the brink of bankruptcy in the oil refinery business to one of the most flexible and innovative companies in its field.

Degrees of certainty and uncertainty are expressed as statements of *risk*. All organizational decisions involve some degree of risk—ranging from complete certainty (no risk) to complete uncertainty, "a stab in the dark" (high risk). To make the best possible decisions in organizations, people seek to "manage" the risks they take—that is, to minimize the riskiness of a decision by gaining access to information relevant to the decision.

What makes an outcome risky or not is the probability of obtaining the desired outcome. Decision makers attempt to obtain information about the probabilities, or odds, of certain events occurring given that other events have occurred. For example, a financial analyst may report that a certain stock has risen 80 percent of the time that the prime rate has dropped, or a meteorologist may report that the precipitation probability is 50 percent (i.e., in the past it rained or snowed half the time certain atmospheric conditions existed). These data may be considered reports of *objective probabilities* because they are based on concrete, verifiable data. Many decisions are also based on subjective probabilities—personal beliefs or hunches about what will happen. For example, a gambler who bets on a horse because it has a name similar to one of his children's, or a person who suspects it's going to rain because he just washed his car is basing these judgments on *subjective probabilities*.

Obviously, uncertainty is an undesirable characteristic in decision-making situations. We may view much of what decision makers do in organizations as attempting to reduce uncertainty so they can make better decisions. In general, what reduces uncertainty in decision-making situations? The answer is information. Knowledge about the past and the present can be used to help make projections about the future. A modern executive's access to data needed to make important decisions may be as close as the nearest computer. A variety of on-line information services are designed to provide organizational decision makers with the latest information relevant to the decisions they are making.

Of course, not all information needed to make decisions comes from computers. Many managerial decisions are also based on the decision maker's past experiences and intuition. This is not to say that top managers rely on subjective information in making decisions (although they might), but that their history of past decisions—both successes and failures—is often given great weight in the decision-making process. In other words, when it comes to making decisions, people often rely on what has worked for them in the past.

Part of the reason this strategy is often successful is because experienced decision makers tend to make better use of information relevant to the decisions they are making. Individuals who have expertise in certain subjects know what information is most relevant and also how to interpret it to make the best decisions. It is therefore not surprising that people seek experienced professionals, such as doctors and lawyers who are seasoned veterans in their fields, when it comes to making important decisions. With high levels of expertise comes information relevant to assessing the riskiness of decision alternatives, and how to reduce it. (When businesses undertake completely new ventures not only do they have to make decisions in which they receive no guidance from the past, but they also confront a great deal of risk. For a look at one venture whose decisions were quite risky—but paid off big—see the **Winning Practices** section on pp. 240–241.)

WINNING PRACTICES

Nonprogrammed Decisions About Programming: The Birth of MTV That Almost Didn't Happen

Whether they're watching *Beavis and Butt-head*, *Unplugged*, or just hours of music videos, hundreds of millions of people in nearly 100 nations tune in to MTV each day. But it wasn't too long ago that MTV was nothing more than a dream launched on a bed of difficult decisions.[3]

In 1979 the cable television business was still in its infancy. There were few viewers wired into the service, and few channels to watch. It was then that Warner Communications decided to find new markets for its entertainment products by developing the cable medium. Partnered with American Express, it launched Warner Cable and began developing new channels. These were mostly commercial-free stations, such as The Movie Channel (TMC), supported by revenue from subscribers' fees. Robert Pittman, who launched TMC, was charged with the responsibility for coming up with the company's first advertiser-sponsored channel, as had been the practice in broadcast television for some three decades. But what kind of channel would generate enough viewers to attract sponsors?

To answer this question, Pittman put together a group of experts. Researching the matter, they decided that the new network should be aimed at teenagers—a well-defined group with disposable income that was hard to reach on broadcast television. Attracting teenagers required focusing on the one interest they had in common—rock music. This decision behind them, challenges still remained—including how to get cooperation from record companies and unions, and the important technical details of how to broadcast in stereo.

After a year of working on such details, Pittman's group presented the idea to Warner Cable's board of directors. They rejected the idea of a music

APPROACHES TO DECISION MAKING IN ORGANIZATIONS

We all like to think that we are rational people who make the best possible decisions. What does it mean to make a rational decision? Organizational scientists view **rational decisions** as ones that maximize the attainment of goals, whether they are the goals of a person, a group, or an entire organization. In this section, we will present two models of decision making that derive from

channel, fearing that it wouldn't make money. But, after working hard on the idea, Pittman remained confident that it was viable. He arranged one final meeting with only the heads of the two parent companies—Steve Ross from Warner Communications, and Jim Robinson from American Express. Pittman showed the two men videos, presented audience research, programming plans, and earnings estimates. Although skeptical, both Ross and Robinson were supportive, and MTV was born.

Then Pittman's real work was ahead of him—finding videos to air. Record companies had to be convinced that investing in videos was an effective way to promote their products. Some had their doubts, but most gave it a try (although MCA and PolyGram refused, at first). The hook: MTV would do something the record companies couldn't get the radio stations to do—identify the songs by title, artist, and label, both at the beginning and end. When MTV first went on the air, August 1, 1981 (its debut video: "Video Killed the Radio Star," by Buggles), it had a small and inconsistent library of only 250 videos to its name—thirty by Rod Stewart alone!

MTV took a few years to catch on, generating losses of $50 million at first. Only a few years later, a brilliant promotional scheme got people screaming to their cable operators, "I want my MTV!" And, they got it—big time. Less than three and a half years after debuting, the company went into the black for the first time. In fact, MTV became so profitable that in 1986, the large conglomerate Viacom (which, by the way, owns the company that publishes this book) bought it for $511 million.

Nonprogrammed decisions? Yes. Risky decisions? You bet! But with good information—not to mention tens of millions of dollars—at one's disposal, good decisions *can* be made. And, although MTV has its critics, to be sure, none of them are questioning its bottom line.

different assumptions about the rationality of individual decision makers: the rational-economic model, and the administrative model.

THE RATIONAL-ECONOMIC MODEL: IN SEARCH OF THE IDEAL DECISION

What would be the most rational way for an individual to go about making a decision? Economists interested in predicting market conditions and prices have relied on a rational-economic model of decision making, which assumes that decisions are perfect and rational in every way. An economically rational decision maker will attempt to maximize his or her profits by systematically searching for the optimum solution to a problem. For this to occur, the decision maker must have complete and perfect information and be able to process all this information in an accurate and unbiased fashion.

In many respects, rational-economic decisions follow the same steps outlined in our general model of decision making (see Figure 9-1). However, what makes the rational-economic approach special is that it calls for the decision maker to recognize all alternative courses of action (step 4), and to accurately and completely evaluate each one (step 5). It views decision makers as attempting to make optimal decisions.

Of course, the rational-economic approach to decision making does not fully appreciate the fallibility of the human decision maker. Based on the assumption that people have access to complete and perfect information and use it to make perfect decisions, the model can be considered a *normative* (also called *prescriptive*) approach—one that describes how decision makers *ideally ought to behave* so as to make the best possible decisions. It does not describe how decision makers actually behave in most circumstances. This task is undertaken by the next major approach to individual decision making, the *administrative model*. (For a comparison between these two approaches, see Table 9-2.)

THE ADMINISTRATIVE MODEL: EXPLORING THE LIMITS OF HUMAN RATIONALITY

As you know from experience, people generally do not act in a completely rational-economic manner. To illustrate this point, consider how a personnel department might select a new receptionist. After several applicants are inter-

■ *Table 9-2 The Administrative Model versus the Rational-Economic Model*

The *rational-economic model* and the *administrative model* of individual decision making are based on a variety of different assumptions about how people make decisions.

Assumption	*Rational-Economic Model*	*Administrative Model*
Rationality of decision maker	Perfect rationality	Bounded rationality
Information available	Complete access	Limited access
Selection of alternatives	Optimal choice	Satisficing choice
Type of model	Normative (prescriptive)	Descriptive (proscriptive)

viewed, the personnel manager might choose the best candidate seen so far and stop interviewing. Had the person been following a rational-economic model, he or she would have had to interview all possible candidates before deciding on the best one. However, by ending the search after finding a candidate who was just good enough, the manager is using a much simpler approach.

The process used in this example characterizes an approach to decision making known as the **administrative model.** This conceptualization recognizes that decision makers may have a limited view of the problems confronting them. The number of solutions that can be recognized or implemented is restricted by the capabilities of the decision maker and the available resources of the organization. Also, because decision makers do not have perfect information about the consequences of their decisions, they cannot tell which one is best.

How are decisions made according to the administrative model? Instead of considering all possible solutions, as suggested by the rational-economic model, the administrative model recognizes that decision makers consider solutions as they become available. Then they decide on the first alternative that meets their criteria for acceptability. Thus, the decision maker selects a solution that may be just good enough, although not optimal. Such decisions are referred to as **satisficing decisions.** Of course, a satisficing decision is much easier to make than an optimal decision. In most decision-making situations satisficing decisions are acceptable and are more likely to be made than optimal ones. The following analogy has been used to compare the two types of decisions: *Making an optimal decision is like searching a haystack for the sharpest needle, but making a satisficing decision is like searching a haystack for a needle just sharp enough with which to sew.* Keeping this distinction in mind should help you keep the two approaches straight.

As we have noted, it is often impractical for people to make completely optimal, rational decisions. The administrative model recognizes the limits under which most organizational decision makers must operate, what is known as **bounded rationality.** The idea is that people lack the cognitive skills required to formulate and solve highly complex business problems in a completely objective, rational way. It should not be surprising to hear that the administrative model does a better job than the rational-economic model of describing how decision makers actually behave. Indeed, it is designed to do just this and is, therefore, said to be *descriptive* (also called *proscriptive*) in nature. This interest in examining the actual, imperfect behavior of decision makers rather than specifying the ideal, economically rational behaviors that decision makers ought to engage in lies at the heart of the distinction between the administrative and rational-economic models. Our point is not that decision makers do not want to behave rationally, but that restrictions posed by the innate capabilities of decision makers themselves and the social environments in which decisions are often made preclude "perfect" decisions. With this idea in mind, we will now explore some of the factors limiting optimal decisions. What factors make decisions so imperfect?

IMPEDIMENTS TO OPTIMAL INDIVIDUAL DECISIONS

The picture of an imperfect decision maker operating in a complex world is supported by many studies that point to the seemingly irrational decisions people make. These imperfections take many forms, several of which we will review here.

COGNITIVE BIASES IN DECISION MAKING: FRAMING AND HEURISTICS

Probably the most obvious limitation on people's ability to make the best possible decisions is imposed by their restricted capacity to process information accurately and thoroughly, like a computer. For example, people often focus on irrelevant information in making decisions. They also fail to use all the information made available to them. Obviously, limitations in people's abilities to process complex information adversely influence their decisions. Beyond these general limitations in human information processing capacity, we may note the existence of several systematic biases in the way people make decisions.

Framing.   One well-established decision-making bias has to do with the tendency for people to make different decisions based on how the problem is presented to them—that is, the **framing** of a problem. Scientists have found that problems framed in a manner that emphasizes the positive gains to be received tend to encourage conservative decisions (i.e., decision makers are said to be *risk averse*), whereas problems framed in a manner that emphasizes the potential losses to be suffered lead to *risk-seeking* decisions. Consider the following example:

> *The government is preparing to combat a rare disease expected to take 600 lives. Two alternative programs to combat the disease have been proposed, each of which, scientists believe, will have certain consequences.* Program A *will save 200 people, if adopted.* Program B *has a one-third chance of saving all 600 people, but a two-thirds chance of saving no one. Which program do you prefer?*

When such a problem was presented to a group of people, 72 percent expressed a preference for *Program A*, and 28 percent for *Program B*. In other

SELF-ASSESSMENT EXERCISE

Are You Risk Seeking or Risk Averse?

It's one thing to read about the effects of framing on riskiness but quite another to experience it firsthand. This exercise will help you demonstrate the effects of framing for yourself.

DIRECTIONS

Read each of the following descriptions of hypothetical situations. Then, for each, answer the following question: *Which project will you select: Alpha or Beta?*

> *Situation 1. You are an executive whose policies have resulted in a $1 million loss for your company. Now you are considering two new projects. One of them, Alpha, will provide a definite return of $500,000. The other, Beta, will provide a fifty-fifty chance of obtaining either a $1 million return or a $0 return.*

> *Situation 2. You are considering one of two new projects to conduct in your company. One of them, Alpha, will provide a definite return of $500,000. The other, Beta, will provide a fifty-fifty chance of obtaining a either $1 million return or a $0 return.*

QUESTIONS FOR DISCUSSION

1. What choice did you make in Situation 1? Most people would select Beta in such a situation because it gives them a fifty-fifty chance of undoing the loss completely. Such a risk-seeking decision is likely in a situation in which people are focusing on undoing loss.

2. What choice did you make in Situation 2? Most people would select Alpha in such a situation because it gives them a sure thing, a "bird in the hand." Such a risk-averse decision is likely in a situation in which people are focusing on gains received.

3. Given that both situations are mathematically identical, why should people prefer one over the other?

4. Can you think of some key failures in history that may be seen as the result of taking high levels of risk?

words, they preferred the "sure thing" of saving 200 people over the one-third possibility of saving them all. However, a curious thing happened when the description of the programs was framed in negative terms. Specifically:

Program C *was described as allowing 400 people to die, if adopted.* Program D *was described as allowing a one-third probability that no one would die, and a two-thirds probability that all 600 would die. Now which program would you prefer?*

Compare these four programs. *Program C* is just another way of stating the outcomes of *Program A,* and *Program D* is just another way of stating the outcomes of *Program B.* However, *Programs* C and D are framed in negative terms, which led to opposite preferences: 22 percent favored *Program C* and 78 percent favored *Program D.* In other words, people tended to avoid risk when the problem was framed in terms of "lives saved" (i.e., in positive terms), but to seek risk when the problem was framed in terms of "lives lost" (i.e., in negative terms).

Scientists believe that such effects are due to the tendency for people to perceive equivalent situations framed differently as not really equivalent. In other words, focusing on the glass as "half full" leads people to think about it differently than when it is presented as being "half empty," although they might recognize intellectually that the two are really the same. Such findings illustrate our point that people are not completely rational decision makers but are systematically biased by the cognitive distortions created by simple differences in the way situations are framed. (To demonstrate framing effects for yourself, see the **Self-Assessment Exercise** on p. 245.)

Heuristics.   Framing effects are not the only cognitive biases to which decision makers are subjected. It also has been established that people often attempt to simplify the complex decisions they face by using **heuristics** — simple rules of thumb that guide them through a complex array of decision alternatives. Although heuristics are potentially useful to decision makers, they represent potential impediments to decision making. Two very common types of heuristics may be identified.

First, the **availability heuristic** refers to the tendency for people to base their judgments on information that is readily available to them — even though it might not be accurate. Suppose, for example, that an executive needs to know the percentage of entering college freshmen who go on to graduate. There is not enough time to gather the appropriate statistics, so she bases her judgments on her own recollections of when she was a college student. If the percentage she recalls graduating, based on her own experiences, is higher or lower than the usual number, her estimate will be off accordingly. In other words, basing judgments solely on information that is conveniently available increases the possibility of making inaccurate decisions. Yet, the availability heuristic is often used when making decisions.

Second, the **representativeness heuristic** refers to the tendency to perceive others in stereotypical ways if they appear to be typical representatives of the category to which they belong. For example, suppose you believe that accountants are bright, mild-mannered individuals, whereas salespeople are less intelligent but much more extroverted. Furthermore, imagine that there are twice as many salespeople as accountants at a party. You meet someone at the party who is bright and mild-mannered. Although mathematically the odds are 2 to 1 that this person is a salesperson rather than an accountant, chances are you will guess that the individual is an accountant because he or she possesses the traits you associate with accountants. In other words, you believe this person to be representative of accountants in general—so much so that you would knowingly go against the mathematical odds in making your judgment. Research has consistently found that people tend to make this type of error in judgment, thereby providing good support for the existence of the representativeness heuristic.

It is important to note that heuristics do not always deteriorate the quality of decisions made. In fact, they can be quite helpful. People often use rules of thumb to help simplify the complex decisions they face. For example, management scientists employ many useful heuristics to aid decisions regarding such matters as where to locate warehouses or how to compose an investment portfolio. We also use heuristics in our everyday lives, such as when we play chess ("control the center of the board") or blackjack ("hit on 16, stick on 17"). However, the representativeness heuristic and the availability heuristic may be recognized as impediments to superior decisions insofar as they discourage people from collecting and processing as much information as they should. Making judgments on the basis of only readily available information, or on stereotypical beliefs, although making things simple for the decision maker, does so at a potentially high cost—poor decisions. Thus, these systematic biases represent potentially serious impediments to individual decision making.

ESCALATION OF COMMITMENT:
THROWING GOOD MONEY AFTER BAD

It is inevitable that some organizational decisions will be unsuccessful. What would you say is the rational thing to do when a poor decision has been made? Intuitively, it makes sense for the ineffective action to be stopped or reversed, to "cut your losses and run." However, people don't always respond this way. In fact, it is not unusual to find that ineffective decisions are sometimes followed up with still further ineffective decisions.

Imagine, for example, that you have invested money in a company, but the company appears to be failing. Rather than lose your initial investment, you may invest still more money in the hope of salvaging your first investment. The more you invest, the more you may be tempted to save those earlier investments by making later investments. That is to say, people sometimes may be found "throwing good money after bad" because they have "too much invested to quit." This phenomenon is known as **escalation of commitment**—the tendency for people to continue to support previously unsuccessful courses

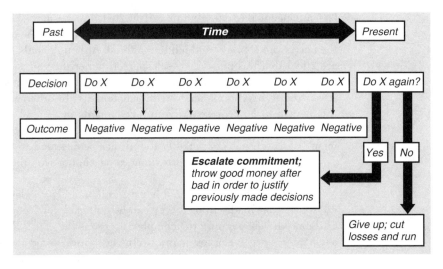

■ *Figure 9-2 Escalation of Commitment*

According to the *escalation of commitment* phenomenon, people who have repeatedly made poor decisions will continue to support those failing courses of action in the future so that they may justify their original decisions.

of action because they have sunk costs invested in them. For a summary of the escalation of commitment phenomenon, see Figure 9-2.

Although this might not seem like a rational thing to do, this strategy is frequently followed. Consider, for example, how large banks and governments may invest money in foreign governments in the hope of turning them around even though such a result becomes increasingly unlikely. Similarly, the organizers of Expo '86 in Vancouver, British Columbia continued pouring money into the fair long after it became apparent that it would be a big money-loser.[4]

Why do people do this? If you think about it, you may realize that the failure to back your own previous courses of action in an organization would be taken as an admission of failure—a politically difficult act to face in an organization. In other words, people may be very concerned about "saving face"—looking good in the eyes of others. Scientists believe that this tendency for self-justification is primarily responsible for people's inclination to protect their beliefs about themselves as rational, competent decision makers by convincing themselves and others that they made the right decision all along and are willing to back it up.

As you might imagine, there are times when people will refrain from escalating their commitment to a failing course of action. In particular, people will stop making failing investments when the available funds for making further investments are limited and the threat of failure is overwhelmingly obvious. For example, when the Long Island Lighting Company decided in 1989 to abandon plans to operate a nuclear power plant in Shoreham, New York, it was in the face of 23 years' worth of intense political and financial pressure (specifically, a strong antinuclear movement and billions of dollars of cost overruns).[5]

It also has been found that people will refrain from escalating commitment when they can diffuse their responsibility for the earlier failing actions. That is, the more people feel they are just one of several people responsible for a failing course of action, the less they are motivated to justify their earlier decisions, and the less likely they are to commit to further failing actions. To conclude, the escalation of commitment phenomenon represents a type of irrational decision making that may occur, but only under certain circumstances.

ORGANIZATIONAL BARRIERS
TO EFFECTIVE DECISIONS

Thus far we have emphasized the human cognitive shortcomings and biases that limit effective decision making. However, we must not ignore several important organizational factors that also interfere with rational decisions. Indeed, the situations faced by many organizational decision makers cannot help but interfere with their capacity to make decisions.

One obvious factor is *time constraints*. Many important organizational decisions are made under severe time pressure. Under such circumstances, it is often impossible for exhaustive decision making to occur. This is particularly the case when organizations face crisis situations requiring immediate decisions. Under such conditions, when decision makers feel "rushed into" taking action, they frequently restrict their search for information and by failing to consider alternatives that may otherwise help them make effective decisions.

The quality of many organizational decisions also may be limited by *political "face-saving" pressure*. In other words, people may make decisions that help them look good to others, although the resulting decisions might not be in the best interest of their organizations. Decisions are frequently made with an eye toward cultivating a good impression, although they may not always be the best ones for the organizations.

In summary, not only are imperfect decisions the result of limitations in the cognitive capacity of human decision makers, but also limitations imposed by organizations themselves. With these problems in mind, important decisions are frequently made not by individuals acting alone, but by groups of people working together.

GROUP DECISIONS: DO TOO MANY COOKS
SPOIL THE BROTH?

Decision-making groups are a well-established fact of modern organizational life. Groups such as committees, study teams, task forces, or review panels are often charged with the responsibility for making important business decisions.

They are so common, in fact, that it has been said that some administrators spend as much as 80 percent of their time in committee meetings. Given this, it is important to consider the strengths and weaknesses of using groups to make organizational decisions.

There is little doubt that much can be gained by using decision-making groups. Several potential advantages of this approach may be identified. First, bringing people together may increase the amount of knowledge and information available for making good decisions. In other words, there may be a *pooling of resources*. A related benefit is that in decision-making groups there can be a *specialization of labor*. With enough people around to share the work load, individuals can perform only those tasks for which they are best suited, thereby potentially improving the quality of the group's efforts. Another benefit is that group decisions are likely to enjoy *greater acceptance* than individual decisions. People involved in making decisions may be expected to understand those decisions better and be more committed to carrying them out than decisions made by someone else.

> *At* **Lincoln Electric,** *a manufacturer of arc welding products, employees participate in decision making by offering suggestions — on average, 200–300 per month, of which 50 tend to be implemented.*

Of course, there are also some problems associated with using decision-making groups. One obvious drawback is that groups are likely to *waste time*. The time spent socializing before getting down to business may be a drain on the group and be very costly to organizations. Another possible problem is that potential disagreement over important matters may breed ill will and *group conflict*. Although constructive disagreement actually can lead to better group outcomes, highly disruptive conflict may interfere with group decisions. Finally, we may expect groups to be ineffective sometimes because of members' *intimidation by group leaders*. A group composed of several "yes" men or women trying to please a dominant leader tends to discourage the open and honest discussion of solutions.

Given the several pros and cons of using groups to make decisions, we must conclude that *neither groups nor individuals are always superior*. Obviously, there are important trade-offs involved in using either one to make decisions.

COMPARING GROUP AND INDIVIDUAL DECISIONS: WHEN ARE TWO (OR MORE) HEADS BETTER THAN ONE?

Since there are advantages associated with both group and individual decision makers, a question arises as to when each should be used. That is, under what conditions might individuals or groups be expected to make superior decisions?

When Are Groups Superior to Individuals?   Imagine a situation in which an important decision has to be made about a complex problem — such as whether one company should merge with another. This is not the kind of problem about which any one individual working alone would be able to make a good decision. Its highly complex nature may overwhelm even an expert, thereby setting the stage for a group to do a better job.

Whether a group actually will do better than an individual depends on several important considerations. For one, we must consider who is in the group. Successful groups tend to be composed of heterogeneous group members with complementary skills. So, for example, a group composed of lawyers, accountants, real estate agents, and other experts may make much better decisions on the merger problem than would a group composed of specialists in only one field. Indeed, the diversity of opinions offered by group members is one of the major advantages of using groups to make decisions.

As you might imagine, it is not enough simply to have skills. For a group to be successful, its members also must be able to freely communicate their ideas to each other in an open, nonhostile manner. Conditions under which one individual (or group) intimidates another from contributing expertise can easily negate any potential gain associated with composing groups of heterogeneous experts. After all, having expertise and being able to make a contribution by using that expertise are two different things. Only when the contributions of the most qualified group members are given the greatest weight does the group derive any benefit from that member's presence. Thus, for groups to be superior to individuals, they must be composed of a heterogeneous collection of experts with complementary skills who can freely and openly contribute to their group's product.

In contrast to complex decision tasks, think of a situation in which a judgment is required on a simple problem with a readily verifiable answer. For example, imagine that you are asked to translate a phrase from a relatively obscure language into English. Groups might do better than individuals on such a task, but probably because the odds are increased that someone in the group knows the language and can perform the translation for the group. However, there is no reason to expect that even a large group will be able to perform such a task better than a single individual who has the required expertise. In fact, an expert working alone may do even better than a group. This is because an expert individual performing a simple task may be distracted by others and suffer from having to convince them of the correctness of his or her solution. For this reason, exceptional individuals tend to outperform entire committees on simple tasks. In such cases, for groups to benefit from a pooling of resources, there must be some resources to pool. The pooling of ignorance does not help. In other words, the question "Are two heads better than one?" can be answered this way: *On simple tasks, two heads may be better than one if at least one of those heads has enough of what it takes to succeed.*

In summary, whether groups perform better than individuals depends on the nature of the task performed and the expertise of the people involved. We have summarized some of these key considerations in Figure 9-3.

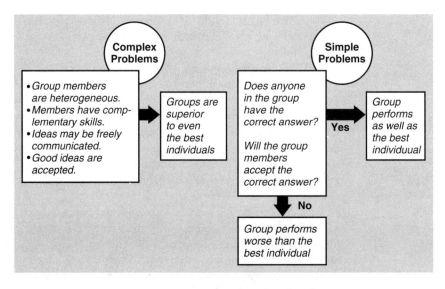

■ *Figure 9-3 Comparing Group and Individual Decisions*

As summarized here, group decisions are superior to those made by individuals under specific conditions.

When Are Individuals Superior to Groups?   Most of the problems faced by organizations require a great deal of creative thinking. For example, a company deciding how to use a newly developed adhesive in its consumer products is facing decisions on a poorly structured task. Although you would expect that the complexity of such creative problems would give groups a natural advantage, this is not the case. In fact, research has shown that on poorly structured, creative tasks, individuals generally perform better than groups.[6]

An approach to solving creative problems commonly used by groups is **brainstorming.** This technique was developed by advertising executive Alex Osborn as a tool for coming up with creative, new ideas.[7] The members of brainstorming groups are encouraged to present their ideas in an uncritical way and to discuss freely and openly all ideas on the floor. Specifically, members of brainstorming groups are required to follow four main rules: (1) avoid criticizing others' ideas, (2) share even far-out suggestions, (3) offer as many comments as possible, and (4) build on others' ideas to create your own.

Does brainstorming improve the quality of creative decisions? To answer this question, researchers conducted a study comparing the effectiveness of individuals and brainstorming groups working on creative problems.[8] Specifically, participants were given 35 minutes to consider the consequences of situations such as "What if

Trying creative new ideas, no matter how crazy, is strongly encouraged at 3M, where many successful products (e.g., Post-it Notes™) have been launched.

everybody went blind?" or "What if everybody grew an extra thumb on each hand?" Clearly, the novel nature of such problems requires a great deal of creativity. Comparisons were made of the number of solutions generated by groups of four or seven people and a like number of individuals working on the same problems alone. The results were clear: Individuals were significantly more productive than groups.

In summary, *groups perform worse than individuals when working on creative tasks.* A great part of the problem is that some individuals feel inhibited by the presence of others although one rule of brainstorming is that even far-out ideas may be shared. To the extent that people wish to avoid feeling foolish as a result of saying silly things, their creativity may be inhibited when in groups. Similarly, groups may inhibit creativity by slowing down the process of bringing ideas to fruition.

GROUPTHINK: TOO MUCH COHESIVENESS CAN BE A DANGEROUS THING

One reason groups may fare so poorly on complex tasks lies in the dynamics of group interaction. As we noted in Chapter 7, when members of a group develop a very strong group spirit—a high level of *cohesiveness*—they sometimes become so concerned about not disrupting the like-mindedness of the group that they may be reluctant to challenge the group's decisions. When this happens, group members tend to isolate themselves from outside information, and the process of critical thinking deteriorates. This phenomenon is referred to as **groupthink.**

The concept of groupthink was proposed initially as an attempt to explain ineffective decisions made by U.S. government officials that led to fiascoes such as the Bay of Pigs invasion in Cuba and the Vietnam War.[9] Analyses of each of these cases have revealed that the president's advisers actually discouraged more effective decision making. An examination of the conditions under which the decision was made to launch the ill-fated space shuttle *Challenger* in January 1986 revealed that it too resulted from groupthink.[10] Post hoc analyses of conversations between key personnel suggested that the team that made the decision to launch the shuttle under freezing conditions did so while insulating itself from the engineers who knew how the equipment should function. Given that NASA had such a successful history, the decision makers operated with a sense of invulnerability. They also worked so closely together and were under such intense pressure to launch the shuttle without further delay that they all collectively went along with the launch decision, creating the illusion of unanimous agreement. For a more precise description of groupthink (and a practical guide to recognizing its symptoms), see Table 9-3 on p. 254.

Groupthink doesn't occur only in governmental decision making, of course, but also in the private sector (although the failures may be less well publicized). For example, analyses of the business policies of large corpora-

■ *Table 9-3 The Warning Signals of Groupthink*

Sometimes the members of highly cohesive groups become more concerned about maintaining positive group spirit than about making the most realistic decisions—a phenomenon known as *groupthink*. The major symptoms of groupthink are listed and described here. (Adapted from Janis, 1982; see Note 9.)

Symptom	*Description*
Illusion of invulnerability	Ignoring obvious danger signals, being overoptimistic, and taking extreme risks
Collective rationalization	Discrediting or ignoring warning signals that run contrary to group thinking
Unquestioned morality	Believing that the group's position is ethical and moral and that all others are inherently evil
Excessive negative stereotyping	Viewing the opposing side as being too negative to warrant serious consideration
Strong conformity pressure	Discouraging the expression of dissenting opinions under the threat of expulsion for disloyalty
Self-censorship of dissenting ideas	Withholding dissenting ideas and counterarguments, keeping them to oneself
Illusion of unanimity	Sharing the false belief that everyone in the group agrees with its judgments
Self-appointed mind guards	Protecting the group from negative, threatening information

tions such as Lockheed and Chrysler have suggested that it was the failure of top-management teams to respond to changing market conditions that at one time led them to the brink of disaster. The problem is that members of very cohesive groups may have considerable confidence in their group's decisions, making them unlikely to raise doubts about these actions (i.e., "the group seems to know what it's doing"). As a result, they may suspend their own critical thinking in favor of conforming to the group. When group members become fiercely loyal to each other, they may ignore potentially useful information from other sources that challenges the group's decisions. The result of this process is that the group's decisions may be completely uninformed, irrational, or immoral.

Fortunately, there are several strategies that can be used to effectively combat groupthink. Here are a few proven techniques.

- **Promote open inquiry.** Remember: Groupthink arises in response to group members' reluctance to "rock the boat." Group leaders should encourage members to be skeptical of all solutions and to avoid reaching premature agreements. It sometimes helps to play the role of *devil's advocate,* that is, to intentionally find fault with a proposed solution. Many executives have found that raising a nonthreatening question to force both sides of an issue can be very helpful in improving the quality of decisions.

- **Use subgroups.** Because the decisions made by any one group may be the result of groupthink, basing decisions on the recommendations of two groups is a useful check. If the two groups disagree, a discussion of their differences is likely to raise important issues. However, if the two groups agree, you can be relatively confident that their conclusions are not both the result of groupthink.

- **Admit shortcomings.** When groupthink occurs, group members feel very confident that they are doing the right thing. Such feelings discourage people from considering opposing information. However, if group members acknowledge some of the flaws and limitations of their decisions, they may be more open to corrective influences. And this may help avoid the illusion of perfection that contributes to groupthink.

- **Hold second-chance meetings.** Before implementing a decision, it is a good idea to hold a second-chance meeting during which group members are asked to express any doubts and propose any new ideas they may have. Alfred P. Sloan, former head of General Motors, is known to have postponed acting on important matters until any group disagreement was resolved. As people get tired of working on problems, they may hastily reach agreement on a solution. Second-chance meetings can be useful devices for seeing if a solution still seems good even after "sleeping on it."

Given the extremely adverse effects groupthink can have on organizations, practicing managers would be wise to press these simple suggestions into action.

GUIDELINES FOR IMPROVING GROUP DECISIONS

As explained in this chapter, certain advantages can be gained from sometimes using individuals and sometimes using groups to make decisions. A decision-making technique that combines the best features of groups and individuals, while minimizing the disadvantages, would be ideal. Several techniques designed to realize the "best of both worlds" have been widely used in organizations.

THE DELPHI TECHNIQUE

According to Greek mythology, people interested in seeing what fate the future held for them could seek the counsel of the Delphic oracle. Today's organizational decision makers sometimes consult experts to help them make the best decisions as well. A technique developed by the Rand Corporation, known as the **Delphi technique,** represents a systematic way of collecting and organizing the opinions of several experts into a single decision.[11] The steps in this process are summarized in Figure 9-4.

The Delphi process starts by enlisting the cooperation of experts and presenting the problem to them, usually in a letter. Each expert then proposes what he or she believes is the most appropriate solution. The group leader compiles all of these individual responses and reproduces them so they can be shared with all the other experts in a second mailing. At this point, each expert comments on the others' ideas and proposes another solution. These individual solutions are returned to the leader, who compiles them and looks for a consensus of opinions. If a consensus is reached, the decision is made. If not, the process of sharing reactions with others is repeated until a consensus is eventually obtained.

The obvious advantage of using the Delphi technique to make decisions is that it allows the collection of expert judgments without the great costs and

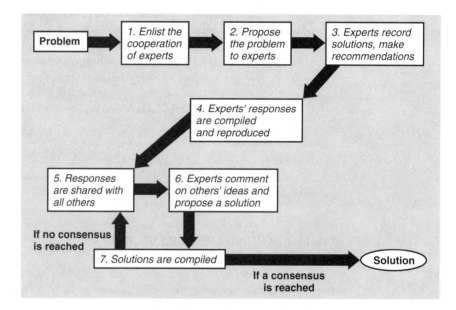

■ *Figure 9-4 Steps in the Delphi Technique*

The *Delphi technique* allows decisions to be made by several experts without encountering many of the disadvantages of face-to-face group interaction.

logistical difficulties of bringing many experts together for a face-to-face meeting. However, the Delphi process can be very time-consuming. Sending out letters, waiting for everyone to respond, transcribing and disseminating the responses, and repeating the process until a consensus is reached can take quite a long time—often several months. Given this limitation, the Delphi approach would not be appropriate for making decisions in crisis situations, or whenever else time is of the essence. However, the approach has been successfully employed to make decisions such as what items to put on a conference agenda and what the potential impact of implementing various new policies would be.

THE NOMINAL GROUP TECHNIQUE

When there are only a few hours available to make a decision, group discussion sessions can be held in which members interact with each other in an orderly, focused fashion aimed at solving problems. The **nominal group technique (NGT)** brings together a small number of individuals (usually about seven to ten) who systematically offer their individual solutions to a problem and share their personal reactions to others' solutions. The technique is referred to as nominal because the individuals involved form a group in name only. Participants do not attempt to agree as a group on any solution, but rather, vote on all the solutions proposed. For an outline of the steps in the process, see Figure 9-5 on p. 259.

As shown in Figure 9-5, the nominal group process begins by gathering the group members together around a table and identifying the problem at hand. Members then write down their solutions. Next, one at a time, each member presents his or her solutions to the group and the leader writes these down on a chart. This process continues until all the ideas have been expressed. Following this, each solution is discussed, clarified, and evaluated by the group members. Each member is given a chance to voice his or her reactions to each idea. After all the ideas have been evaluated, the group members privately rank-order their preferred solutions. The idea given the highest rank is taken as the group's decision.

Although nominal groups traditionally meet in face-to-face settings, advances in modern technology enable nominal groups to meet even when its members are far away from each other. Specifically, a technique known as **automated decision conferencing** has been used, in which individuals in different locations participate in nominal group conferences by means of telephone lines or direct satellite transmissions. The messages may be sent either via characters on a computer monitor or images viewed during a teleconference. Despite their high-tech look, automated decision conferences are really just nominal groups meeting in a manner that approximates face-to-face contact.

The NGT has several advantages and disadvantages. We have already noted that this approach can be used to arrive at group decisions in only a few hours. Another benefit is that it discourages any pressure to conform to the

Running a Nominal Group: Try It Yourself

A great deal can be learned about nominal groups by running one—or, at least, participating in one—yourself. Doing so will not only help illustrate the procedure, but demonstrate how effectively it works.

DIRECTIONS

1. Select a topic suitable for discussion in a nominal group composed of students in your class. It should be a topic that is narrowly defined and one on which people have many different opinions (these work best in nominal groups). Some possible examples include:

   - What should your school's student leaders be doing for you?
   - What can be done to improve the quality of instruction in your institution?
   - What can be done to improve the quality of jobs your school's students receive when graduating?

2. Divide the class into groups of approximately ten. Arrange each group in a circle, or around a table, if possible. In each group, select one person to serve as the group facilitator.

3. Following the steps outlined in Figure 9-5, facilitators should guide their groups in discussions regarding the focal question identified in step 1. Allow approximately 45 minutes to 1 hour to complete this process.

4. If time allows, select a different focal question and a different group leader, and repeat the procedure.

QUESTIONS FOR DISCUSSION

1. Collectively, how did the group answer the question? Do you believe that this answer accurately reflected the feelings of the group?

2. How did the various groups' answers compare? Were they similar or different? Why?

3. What were the major problems, if any, associated with the nominal group experience? For example, were there any group members who were reluctant to wait their turns before speaking up?

4. If you conducted more than one nominal group discussion, with different leaders, was the process smoother the second time around, as everyone learned how it works?

5. How do you think your group experiences would have differed had you used a totally unstructured, traditional face-to-face group instead of a nominal group?

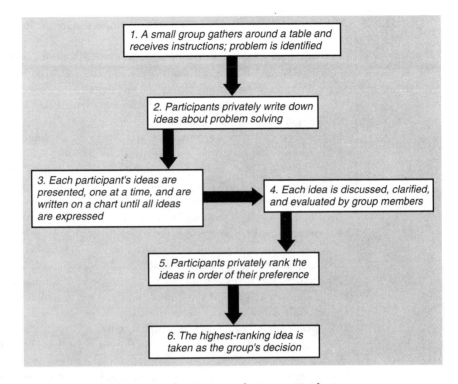

1. A small group gathers around a table and receives instructions; problem is identified

2. Participants privately write down ideas about problem solving

3. Each participant's ideas are presented, one at a time, and are written on a chart until all ideas are expressed

4. Each idea is discussed, clarified, and evaluated by group members

5. Participants privately rank the ideas in order of their preference

6. The highest-ranking idea is taken as the group's decision

■ *Figure 9-5 Steps in the Nominal Group Technique*

The *nominal group technique* structures face-to-face meetings in a way that allows for the open expression and evaluation of ideas.

wishes of a high-status group member because all ideas are evaluated and the preferences are expressed in private balloting. The technique must be considered limited, however, in that it requires the use of a trained group leader. In addition, using NGT successfully requires that only one narrowly defined problem be considered at a time. So, for very complex problems, many NGT sessions would have to be run—and only if the problem under consideration can be broken down into smaller parts.

SUMMARY:
PUTTING IT TO USE

■ *Decision making* is a multistep process. It involves: (1) identifying a problem, (2) defining solution objectives, (3) making a *predecision* (a decision about how to make a decision), (4) generating alternatives, (5) evaluating alternatives,

(6) choosing an alternative, (7) implementing the chosen alternative, and then (8) following up.

The decisions made in organizations can be characterized as being either *programmed*, routine decisions made according to preexisting guidelines, or *nonprogrammed*, decisions requiring novel and creative solutions. Decisions also differ with respect to the amount of risk involved, ranging from those in which the decision outcomes are relatively *certain* to those in which the outcomes are highly *uncertain*. Uncertain situations are expressed as statements of probability based on either objective or subjective information.

Two major approaches to individual decision making have been identified. The *rational-economic model* characterizes decision makers as thoroughly searching through perfect information to make an optimal decision. This is a *normative* approach in that it describes how decision makers ideally ought to behave to make the best possible decisions. In contrast, the *administrative model* is a *descriptive* approach, which describes how decision makers actually behave. It recognizes the inherent imperfections of decision makers and the social and organizational systems within which they operate. Limitations imposed by people's ability to process the information needed to make complex decisions *(bounded rationality)* restrict decision makers to making *satisficing decisions* —solutions that are not optimal, but good enough.

People make imperfect decisions due to cognitive bias. One such bias, *framing*, refers to the tendency of people to make different decisions based on how a problem is presented. For example, when a problem is presented in a way that emphasizes positive gains to be received, people tend to make conservative, risk-averse decisions, whereas when the same problem is presented in a way that emphasizes potential losses to be suffered, people tend to make riskier decisions. Simple rules of thumb, known as *heuristics*, also may bias decisions. For example, according to the *availability heuristic*, people base their judgments on information readily available to them, and according to the *representativeness heuristic*, people are perceived in stereotypical ways if they appear to be representatives of the categories to which they belong.

According to the *escalation of commitment phenomenon*, people continue to support previously unsuccessful courses of action because they have sunk costs invested in them. This occurs in large part because people need to justify their previous actions and wish to avoid having to admit that their initial decision was a mistake. Individual decisions are also limited by organizational factors, such as time constraints, and political "face-saving" pressure.

Studies comparing the decisions made by groups and individuals reveal a complex pattern. Groups have proven superior to individual members when they are composed of a heterogeneous mix of experts who possess complementary skills. However, groups may not be any better than the best member of the group when performing a task that has a simple, verifiable answer. Compared with individuals, face-to-face *brainstorming* groups tend to make inferior decisions on creative problems.

Groupthink is a major obstacle to effective group decisions. It refers to the tendency for strong conformity pressures within groups to lead to the breakdown of critical thinking and to encourage premature acceptance of potentially questionable solutions. Groupthink appears to have been responsible for major decision fiascoes, such as the U.S. invasion of the Bay of Pigs in Cuba, and the decision to launch the ill-fated space shuttle *Challenger*.

The quality of group decisions can be enhanced in several different ways. Using the *Delphi technique*, the judgments of experts are systematically gathered and used to form a single joint decision. The *nominal group technique* is a method of structuring group meetings so as to elicit and evaluate the opinions of all members.

You Be the Consultant

A business associate refers you to the president of a growing environmental management firm. The fact that the company is new and operates in a changing business environment makes all of its decisions especially crucial. As such, you are hired to assist in guiding the president in helping the company make decisions in the most effective way possible. Answer the following questions relevant to this situation based on the material in this chapter.

1. The president has been making decisions about how to deal with governmental regulations all by himself. Should he consider delegating this task to a group instead? Why or why not?

2. What individual biases would be expected to interfere with the quality of the decisions made by individuals in this company?

3. In what ways might the group interaction limit the quality of decisions made? What steps can be taken to overcome these problems?

4. Decision-making groups have found it difficult to reach consensus when they meet. How could group decision meetings be structured so as to avoid this problem?

CHAPTER 10

Designing Effective Organizations

PREVIEW OF CHAPTER HIGHLIGHTS

The formal configuration between individuals and groups with respect to the allocation of tasks, responsibilities, and authority within an organization is known as **organizational structure.** The five basic elements of structure include: **hierarchy of authority, division of labor, span of control, line versus staff positions,** and **decentralization.**

Organizations can be **departmentalized** in several ways, such as by task **(functional)**, by output **(product)**, both task and output **(matrix)**, and process **(horizontal)**.

Classical organizational theories and **neoclassical organizational theories** propose that there is a single most effective way to design organizations.

The modern **contingency approach** to organizational design recognizes that organizations are subject to change, and that different designs are effective under different conditions. For example, **mechanistic organizations** are effective under stable conditions, but **organic organizations** are effective under unstable conditions.

Mintzberg's theory identifies five different organizational designs: **simple structure, machine bureaucracy, professional bureaucracy, divisional structure,** and **adhocracy.**

Organizational designs such as **conglomerates** and **strategic alliances** involve more than one organization.

How should companies organize themselves into separate units so as to be most effective? This question is a venerable one in the field of business—and, as we shall explain in this chapter, a very important one as well. OB researchers and theorists have provided considerable insight into the matter by studying what is called *organizational structure*—the way individuals and groups are arranged with respect to the tasks they perform—and *organizational design*—the process of coordinating these structural elements in the most effective manner. As you may suspect, finding the best way to structure and design organizations is no simple matter. However, because understanding the structure and design of organizations is key to fully appreciating their functioning, organizational scientists have devoted considerable energy to this topic.

We will describe these efforts in this chapter. To begin, we will identify the basic building blocks of organizations, which can be identified by the *organizational chart*, a useful pictorial way of depicting key features of organizational structure. Following this, we will examine how these structural elements can be most effectively combined into productive organizational designs.

STRUCTURAL DIMENSIONS OF ORGANIZATIONS

Think about how a simple house is constructed. It is composed of a wooden frame positioned atop a concrete slab covered by a roof and siding materials. Within this basic structure are separate systems operating to provide electricity, water, and telephone services. Similarly, the structure of the human body is composed of a skeleton surrounded by various systems of organs, muscles, and tissue serving bodily functions such as respiration, digestion, and the like. Although you may not have thought about it much, we can also identify the structure of an organization in a similar fashion.

Let's use as an example an organization with which you are doubtlessly familiar—your college or university. It is probably composed of various departments working together to serve special functions. Individuals and groups are dedicated to tasks such as teaching, providing financial services, maintaining the physical facilities, and so on. Of course, within each group, even more distinctions can be made between the jobs people perform. For example, it's unlikely that the instructor for your OB course is also teaching seventeenth-century French literature. This example illustrates our main point: An organization is not a haphazard collection of people, but a meaningful combination of groups and individuals working together purposefully to meet organizational goals. The term **organizational structure** refers to *the formal configuration between individuals and groups with respect to the allocation of tasks, responsibilities, and authority within organizations.*

Strictly speaking, one cannot see the structure of an organization; it is an abstract concept. However, the connections between various clusters of

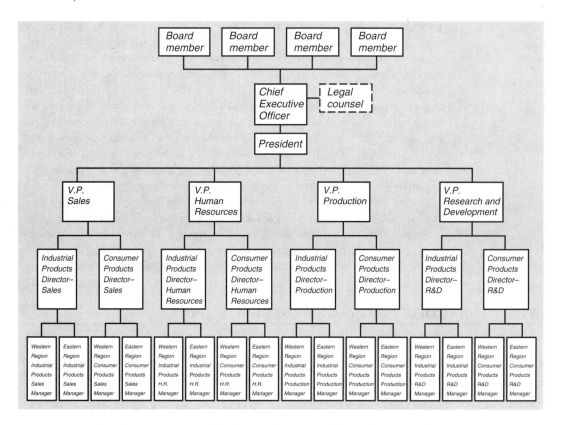

■ *Figure 10-1 Organizational Chart of a Hypothetical*
Manufacturing Firm

An *organizational chart*, such as this one, identifies pictorially the various functions performed within an organization and the lines of authority between people performing those functions.

functions of which an organization is composed can be represented in the form of a diagram known as an **organizational chart.** In other words, an organizational chart can be considered a representation of an organization's internal structure. Organizational charts are useful tools for specifying how various tasks or functions are interrelated within organizations. For example, look at the chart depicting part of a hypothetical manufacturing organization shown in Figure 10-1. Each box represents a specific job, and the lines connecting them reflect the formally prescribed lines of communication between the individuals performing those jobs (see Chapter 6). To specialists in organizational structure, however, such diagrams reveal a great deal more.

HIERARCHY OF AUTHORITY

Organizational charts provide information about who reports to whom—what is known as **hierarchy of authority.** The diagram reveals which particular lower-level employees are required to report to which particular individuals immediately above them in the organizational hierarchy. In our hypothetical example in Figure 10-1, the various regional salespeople (at the bottom of the diagram) report to their respective regional sales directors, who report to the vice president of sales, who reports to the president, who reports to the chief executive officer, who reports to the members of the board of directors. As we trace these reporting relationships, we work our way up the organization's hierarchy. In this case, the organization has six levels. Organizations may have many levels, in which case their structure is considered *tall,* or only a few, in which case their structure is considered *flat.*

In recent years, a great deal has appeared in the news about organizations restructuring their work forces by flattening them out. Although it has not been uncommon for large companies to lay off people in low-level jobs, these days middle managers and executives, long believed to be secure in their positions, find themselves unemployed as companies "downsize," "rightsize," "delayer," or "retrench" by eliminating entire layers of organizational structure (see Chapter 11). In fact, it has been estimated that during the 1980s, one-quarter of all middle-management jobs were eliminated in American companies. In 1990 alone, nearly 1 million managers of American companies with annual salaries over $40,000 lost their jobs due to the flattening of organizational hierarchies.

Whereas **Ford** *has 17 layers of management between its* **CEO** *and its employees on the factory floor, and* **GM** *has as many as 22, the more profitable* **Toyota** *has only seven.*

The underlying assumption behind all these changes is that fewer layers of hierarchy reduce waste and enable people to make better decisions (by moving them closer to the problems at hand), thereby leading to greater profitability. Management experts claim that although some layers of hierarchy are necessary, too many can be needlessly expensive. Moreover, as we will explain in Chapter 12, as technology advances, fewer people are needed to carry out management roles.

DIVISION OF LABOR

The standard organizational chart reflects the fact that the many tasks to be performed within an organization are divided into specialized jobs, a process known as the **division of labor.** The more that tasks are divided into separate jobs, the more those jobs are *specialized* and the narrower the range of activities that job incumbents are required to perform.

In theory, the fewer tasks a person performs, the better he or she may be expected to do them, freeing others to perform the tasks that they do best. (We say "in theory" because if specialization is too great, people may lose their motivation to work at a high level and performance may suffer; see Chapter 3.) Taken together, an entire organization is composed of people performing a collection of specialized jobs. This is probably the most obvious feature of an organization that can be observed from the organizational chart.

As you might imagine, the degree to which employees perform specialized jobs is likely to depend on the size of the organization. The larger the organization, the more the opportunities for specialization are likely to exist. For example, an individual working in a large advertising agency may get to specialize in a highly narrow field, such as writing jingles for radio and television spots for automobiles. By contrast, someone working at a much smaller agency may be required to do all writing of print and broadcast ads in addition to helping out with the artwork and meeting with the clients. Obviously, the larger company might be expected to reap the benefits of efficiently using the talents of employees (a natural result of an extensive division of labor). When companies downsize, many managerial jobs become less specialized. For example, at General Electric, quite a few middle-management positions have been eliminated in recent years. As a consequence, the remaining managers must perform a wider variety of jobs, making their own jobs less specialized.

SPAN OF CONTROL

Over how many individuals should a manager have responsibility? The earliest management theorists and practitioners alike (dating back to the Roman legions) addressed this question. When you look at an organizational chart, the number of people formally required to report to each individual manager is immediately clear. This number constitutes what is known as a manager's **span of control.** Those responsible for many individuals are said to have a *wide* span of control, whereas those responsible for fewer are said to have a *narrow* span of control. In the organizational chart in Figure 10-1, the CEO is responsible for only the actions of the president, giving this individual a narrower span of control than the president himself or herself, who has a span of control of five individuals.

Sometimes, when organization leaders are concerned that they do not have enough control over lower-level employees, they restructure their organizations so that managers have responsibility over smaller numbers of subordinates. This is the case at Canada's largest bank, Royal Bank, where a team of top managers recently recommended that area managers reduce the number of branches under their control to between seven and twelve.

When a manager's span of control is wide, the organization itself has a flat hierarchy. In contrast, when a manager's span of control is narrow, the organization itself has a tall hierarchy. This is demonstrated in Figure 10-2. The diagram at the top shows a *tall* organization—one in which there are many layers in the hierarchy, and the span of control is relatively narrow (i.e., the number of people supervised is low). By contrast, the diagram at the bottom of

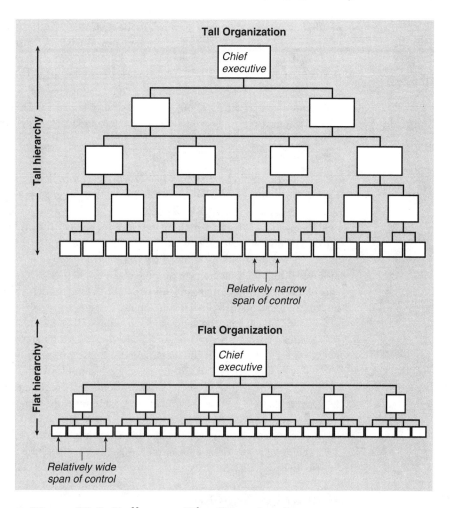

■ *Figure 10-2 Tall versus Flat Organizations*

In *tall organizations*, the hierarchy has many layers, and managers have a *narrow span of control*. However, in *flat organizations*, the hierarchy has few layers and managers have a *wide span of control*.

Figure 10-2 shows a *flat* organization—one in which there are only a few levels in the hierarchy, and the span of control is relatively wide. Although both organizations depicted here have 31 positions, these are arranged differently.

It is not readily possible to specify the "ideal" span of control that should be sought. Instead, it makes better sense to consider what form of organization is best suited to various purposes. For example, because supervisors in a military unit must have tight control over subordinates and get them to respond quickly and precisely, a narrow span of control is likely to be effective. As a result, military organizations tend to be extremely tall. In contrast, people working in a research and development lab must have an open exchange of ideas and typically require little managerial guidance to be successful. Units of this type tend to have very flat structures. (As you might imagine, there may be widespread differences with respect to spans of control in different types of organizations. To learn about this possibility—and the spans of control of some companies in your area, complete the following **Group Exercise.)**

LINE VERSUS STAFF POSITIONS

The organizational chart shown in Figure 10-1 on p. 264 reveals an additional distinction that deserves to be highlighted—that between *line positions* and *staff positions.* People occupying **line positions** (e.g., the various vice presidents and managers) have decision-making power. However, the individual shown in the dotted box—the legal counsel—cannot make decisions but provides advice and recommendations to be used by the line managers. For example, such an individual may help corporate officials decide whether a certain product name can be used without infringing on copyright restrictions. This individual may be said to hold a **staff position.** In many of today's organizations, human resources managers may be seen as occupying staff positions because they may provide specialized services regarding testing and interviewing procedures as well as information about the latest laws on personnel administration.

Differences between line and staff personnel are not unusual. Specifically, staff managers tend to be younger, better educated, and more committed to their fields than to their organizations. Line managers might feel more committed to their organizations not only because of the greater opportunities they have to exercise decisions, but also because they are more likely to perceive themselves as part of a company rather than as an independent specialist whose identity lies primarily within his or her specialty area.

DECENTRALIZATION

During the first half of the twentieth century, as companies grew larger and larger, they shifted power and authority into the hands of a few upper-echelon administrators—executives whose decisions influenced the many people below them in the organizational hierarchy. In fact, it was during the 1920s that Alfred P. Sloan, Jr., then the president of General Motors, introduced the notion of a "central office," the place where a few individuals made policy decisions for the entire company. Another part of Sloan's plan involved pushing lower and lower down the organizational hierarchy decisions regarding the day-to-day operation of the company, thereby allowing those individuals who were most affected to make the decisions. This process of delegating power from higher to lower levels within organizations is known as **decentralization.** It is the opposite of *centralization,* the tendency for just a few powerful individuals or groups to hold most of the decision-making power.

GROUP EXERCISE

Comparing Span of Control in Organizational Charts

One of the easiest things to determine about a company by looking at its organizational chart is its span of control. This exercise will allow you to learn about and compare span of control within companies in your area.

DIRECTIONS

1. Divide the class into four equal-size groups.

2. Assign one of the following industry types to each group: (a) manufacturing companies, (b) financial institutions, (c) public utilities, and (d) charities.

3. Within the industry assigned to each group, identify one company per student. Try to keep these companies within your local area, if possible. Also consider larger organizations inasmuch as these are more likely to have formal organizational charts. For example, if there are five students in the "financial institutions" group, name five different banks or savings and loan institutions.

4. Each student should call or write for a copy of the organizational chart for the company assigned to him or her in step 3. Remember: *You are representing your institution, so present yourself in a polite and professional manner!*

5. Meet as a group to discuss the spans of control of the organizations in your sample.

6. Gather as a class to compare the findings of the various groups.

QUESTIONS FOR DISCUSSION

1. Were you successful in being able to collect the organizational charts, or were the organizations reluctant to share them?

2. Did you find that there were differences with respect to span of control?

3. Were spans of control different at different organizational levels? If so, how? And were these differences the same for all industry groups?

4. In what ways did spans of control differ for the various industry groups? Were the spans broader for some industries and narrower in others? How do you explain these differences? Do these differences make sense to you?

*At **Johnson & Johnson** decentralization is the rule: Both large and small decisions are made locally, rather than at the corporate level. In fact, the corporate headquarters for this giant conglomerate is remarkably small.*

Recent years have seen a marked trend toward increasingly greater decentralization. As a result, organizational charts might show fewer staff positions, as decision-making authority is pushed farther down the hierarchy. Many organizations have moved toward decentralization to promote managerial efficiency and to improve employee satisfaction (the result of giving people greater opportunities to take responsibility for their own actions). For example, in recent years, thousands of staff jobs have been eliminated at companies such as 3M, Eastman Kodak, AT&T, and GE as these companies have decentralized. In particular, people working in research and development positions are likely to enjoy the autonomy to make decisions that decentralization allows. With this in mind, many companies heavily involved in research and development—including parts of Hewlett-Packard, Intel Corporation, Philips Electronics, and AT&T's Bell Laboratories—have shifted to more decentralized designs.

By contrast, people working on production jobs are likely to be less interested in taking responsibility for decisions and may enjoy not having to take such responsibility. In this case, highly centralized authority makes the most sense. For example, at Delta Airlines, CEO Ronald W. Allen must personally approve every expenditure over $5,000 (except jet fuel). By so doing, he can very carefully monitor the company's expenses and keep it afloat during difficult times. Despite the possible benefits likely to result from relieving Allen of these chores, he believes that it is necessary to tightly enforce the decisions made at times when the margin for error is small. To conclude, although the potential exists to derive considerable benefits from decentralization, the process should be avoided under certain conditions. (See the summary in Table 10-1.)

■ *Table 10-1 Decentralization: Benefits When Low and When High*

Various benefits are associated with low decentralization (high centralization) and high decentralization (low centralization) within organizations.

Low Decentralization (High Centralization)	*High Decentralization (Low Centralization)*
Eliminates the additional responsibility not desired by people performing routine jobs	Can eliminate levels of management, making a leaner organization
Permits crucial decisions to be made by individuals who have the "big picture"	Promotes greater opportunities for decisions to be made by people closest to problems

DEPARTMENTALIZATION: WAYS OF STRUCTURING ORGANIZATIONS

Thus far, we have been talking about "the" organizational chart of an organization. Typically, such charts, like the one shown in Figure 10-1 on p. 264, divide the organization according to the various functions performed. However, this is only one option. Organizations can be divided up not only by function but also by product or market, or by a combination of both. We will now take a closer look at these various ways of breaking up organizations into coherent units—that is, the process of **departmentalization.**

FUNCTIONAL ORGANIZATIONS: DEPARTMENTALIZATION BY TASK

Because it is the form organizations usually take when they are first created, and because it is how we usually think of organizations, the **functional organization** can be considered the most basic approach to departmentalization. Essentially, functional organizations departmentalize individuals according to the functions they perform, with people who perform similar functions assigned to the same department. For example, a manufacturing company might consist of separate departments devoted to basic functions such as production, sales, research and development, and human resources (recall Figure 10-1 on p. 264).

Naturally, as organizations grow and become more complex, additional departments are added or deleted as the need arises. Consider, for example, something that is beginning to happen at Johnson & Johnson (J&J). Although this company has long been highly decentralized, certain functions are now beginning to become centralized (e.g., the legal and human resources operations). This makes it possible for resources to be saved by avoiding duplication of effort, resulting in a higher level of efficiency. Not only does this form of organizational structure take advantage of economies of scale (by allowing employees performing the same jobs to share facilities and not duplicating functions), but it also allows people to specialize, thereby performing only those tasks at which they are most expert. The result is a highly skilled work force—a direct benefit to the organization.

Partly offsetting these advantages, however, are several potential limitations. The most important of these stems from the fact that functional organizational structures encourage separate units to develop their own narrow perspectives and to lose sight of overall organizational goals. For example, in a manufacturing company, an engineer might see the company's problems in terms of the reliability of its products, and lose sight of other key considerations, such as market trends, overseas competition, and so on. Such narrow-mindedness is the inevitable result of functional specialization—the downside of people seeing the company's operations through a narrow lens.

PRODUCT ORGANIZATIONS: DEPARTMENTALIZATION BY TYPE OF OUTPUT

Organizations—at least successful ones—do not stand still; they constantly change in size and scope. As they develop new products and seek new customers, they might find that a functional structure doesn't work as well as it once did. Manufacturing a wide range of products using a variety of different methods, for example, might put a strain on the manufacturing division of a functional organization. Similarly, keeping track of the varied tax requirements for different types of business (e.g., restaurants, farms, real estate, manufacturing) might pose quite a challenge for a single financial division of a company. In response to such strains, a **product organization** might be created. This type of departmentalization creates self-contained divisions, each of which is responsible for everything to do with a certain product or group of products. For a look at the structure of a hypothetical product organization, see Figure 10-3.

When organizations are departmentalized by products, separate divisions are established, each of which is devoted to a certain product or group of products. Each unit contains all the resources needed to develop, manufacture, and sell its products. The organization is composed of separate divisions, operating independently, the heads of which report to top management. Although some functions might be centralized within the parent company (e.g., human resources management or legal staff), on a day-to-day basis each division oper-

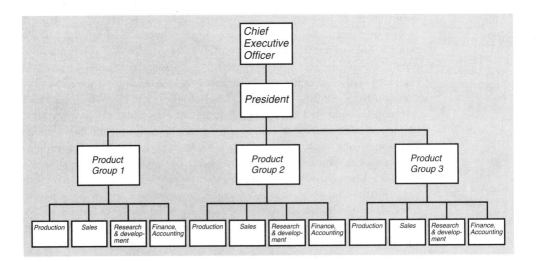

■ *Figure 10-3 A Product Organization*

In a *product organization,* separate units are established to handle different product lines. Each of these divisions contains all the departments necessary for it to operate as an independent unit.

ates autonomously as a separate company or, as accountants call them, "cost centers" of their own.

Consider, for example, how separate divisions of General Motors are devoted to manufacturing cars, trucks, locomotives, refrigerators, auto parts, and the like. The managers of each division can devote their energies to one particular business. Product organizations may be effective from a marketing perspective as well. Consider, for example, Honda's 1987 introduction of its line of luxury cars, Acura. By creating a separate division, manufactured in separate plants and sold by a separate network of dealers, the company made its higher-priced cars look special, and avoided making its less expensive cars look less appealing by putting them together with superior products on the same showroom floors. Given Honda's success with this configuration, it is not surprising that Toyota and Nissan followed suit when they introduced their own luxury lines, Lexus and Infiniti, in 1989.

Product organizations also have several drawbacks. The most obvious of these is the loss of economies of scale stemming from the duplication of various departments within operating units. For example, if each unit carries out its own research and development functions, the need for costly equipment, facilities, and personnel may be multiplied. Another problem associated with product designs involves the organization's ability to attract and retain talented employees. Since each department within operating units is necessarily smaller than a single combined one would be, opportunities for advancement and career development may suffer. This, in turn, may pose a serious problem with respect to the long-term retention of talented employees. Finally, problems of coordination across product lines may arise. In fact, in extreme cases, actions taken by one operating division may have adverse effects on the outcomes of one or more others.

A clear example of such problems was provided by Hewlett-Packard, a major manufacturer of computers, printers, and scientific test equipment. During most of its history, Hewlett-Packard adopted a product design. It consisted of scores of small, largely autonomous divisions, each concerned with producing and selling certain products. As it grew, the company found itself in an increasingly untenable situation in which sales representatives from different divisions sometimes attempted to sell different lines of equipment, often to be used for the same basic purposes, to the same customers! To deal with such problems, top management at Hewlett-Packard decided to restructure the company into sectors based largely on the markets they served (such as business customers, and scientific and manufacturing customers). In short, Hewlett-Packard switched from a fairly traditional product organization to an internal structure driven by market considerations.

The Hewlett-Packard case points out a particular variation on the basic theme of market departmentalization. Self-contained operating units also can be established on the basis of specific geographic regions or territories, and even customers. So, for example, a large retail chain might develop separate divisions for different regions of the country (e.g., Macy's-New York; and Macy's-California), or for different customer bases (e.g., Bloomingdales by Mail and Bloomingdales Retail). Similarly, a large record company (itself likely a division of a larger entertainment company) may establish independent divisions (each with its own labels) to sign, develop, produce, and promote recordings of interest to people in different markets (e.g., children, classical, Latin, pop). By departmentalizing in this fashion, like having separate companies within a large company, a company can give artists the attention they would expect from a smaller company, and the specialization and economies of scale they would expect from a large company.

Regardless of the exact basis for departmentalizing—be it product, region, market, or customer group—the basic rationale remains the same: Divide the organization's operations in a way that enhances efficiency.

MATRIX ORGANIZATIONS: DEPARTMENTALIZATION BY BOTH FUNCTION AND PRODUCT

When the aerospace industry was first developing, the U.S. government demanded that a single manager in each company be assigned to each of its projects so that it was immediately clear who was responsible for the progress of each project. In response to this requirement, TRW established a "project leader" for each project, someone who shared authority with the leaders of the existing functional departments. This temporary arrangement later evolved into what is called a matrix organization, the type of organization in which an employee is required to report to both a functional (or division) manager and the manager of a specific project (or product). In essence, they developed a complex type of organizational structure that combines both the function and product forms of departmentalization. To better understand matrix organizations, let's take a closer look at the organizational chart shown in Figure 10-4.

Employees in matrix organizations have two bosses (or, more technically, they are under *dual authority*). One line of authority, shown by the vertical axes on Figure 10-4, is *functional*, managed by vice presidents in charge of various functional areas. The other, shown by the horizontal axes, is *product* (or it may be a specific project or temporary business), managed by specific individuals in charge of certain products (or projects).

In matrix designs, there are three major roles. First, there is the *top leader*—the individual who has authority over both lines (the one based on function and the one based on product or project). It is this individual's task to enhance coordination between functional and product managers and to maintain an appropriate balance of power between them. Second, there are the *matrix bosses*—people who head functional departments or specific projects. Since neither functional managers nor project managers have complete authority over subordinates, they must work together to assure that their efforts mesh rather than conflict. In addition, they must agree on issues such as promotions

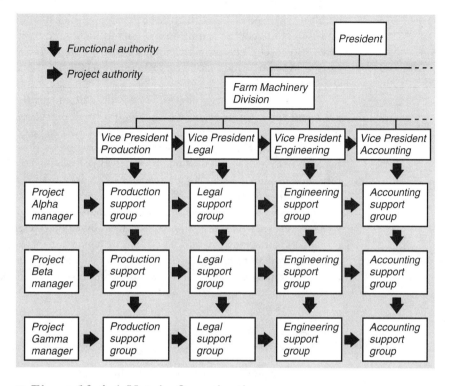

■ *Figure 10-4 A Matrix Organization*

In a *matrix organization,* a product structure is superimposed on a functional structure. This results in a dual system of authority in which some managers report to two bosses—a project (or product) manager and a functional (department) manager.

and raises for specific people working under their joint authority. Finally, there are *two-boss managers*—people who must report to both product and functional managers, and attempt to balance the demands of each. Because people working in this fashion have two bosses, they must have sufficient freedom to attain their objectives. As you might imagine, a fair amount of coordination, flexibility, openness, and trust is essential for such a design to work, suggesting that not everyone adapts well to such a system.

Organizations are most likely to adopt matrix designs when they confront certain conditions. These include a complex and uncertain environment (one with frequent changes), and the need for economies of scale in the use of internal resources. Specifically, a matrix approach is often adopted by medium-size organizations

Dow Corning *has had a matrix organization in effect for over 25 years. Employees report to the leaders of their own functional departments (e.g., accounting, research and development), while also contributing to the design and operation of the particular product line for which they are responsible.*

with several product lines that do not possess sufficient resources to establish fully self-contained operating units. Under such conditions, a matrix design provides a useful compromise. Some companies that have adopted this structure, at least on a trial basis, are TRW Systems Group, Liberty Mutual Insurance, and Citibank.

We have noted several advantages offered by matrix designs. First, they permit flexible use of an organization's human resources. Individuals within functional departments can be assigned to specific products or projects as the need arises and then return to their regular duties when this task is completed. Second, matrix designs offer medium-size organizations an efficient means of responding quickly to a changing, unstable environment. Third, such designs often enhance communication among managers; indeed, they literally force matrix bosses to discuss and agree on many matters. Unfortunately, matrix designs can create frustration and stress caused by having to report to two different supervisors. However, in situations in which organizations must stretch their financial and human resources to meet challenges from the external environment or take advantage of new opportunities, matrix designs can play a useful role.

THE HORIZONTAL ORGANIZATION: STRUCTURING BY PROCESS

If the experts are right, we are in store for a new way of structuring work in tomorrow's organizations—one that means more than just tinkering with the boxes on an organizational chart. We are referring to what has been called the **horizontal organization**—an approach advocated by many organizational experts and touted by consultants from the firm McKinsey & Co. as "the first real, fundamentally different, robust alternative" to the functional organization.[1]

The essence of the idea is simple. Instead of organizing jobs in the traditional, vertical fashion by having a long chain of groups or individuals perform parts of a task (e.g., one group that sells the advertising job, another that plans the ad campaign, and yet another that produces the ads), horizontal organizations have greatly flattened hierarchies. That is, they arrange autonomous work teams (see Chapter 7) in parallel, each performing many different steps in the process (e.g., members of an advertising team may bring different skills and expertise to a single team responsible for all aspects of advertising). Essentially, organizations are structured around *processes* instead of tasks. Performance objectives are based on customers' needs, such as lowered cost or improved service. Once the core processes that meet these needs (e.g., order generation, new-product development) have been identified, they become the company's major components—instead of the traditional departments such as sales or manufacturing (for a summary, see Figure 10-5).

According to consultant Michael Hammer, "In the future, executive positions will not be defined in terms of collections of people, like head of the

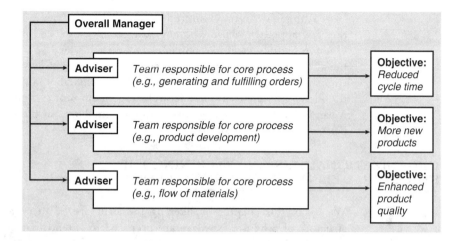

■ *Figure 10-5 A Horizontal Organization*

In a *horizontal organization*, teams of employees with diverse skills are created to meet objectives relating to various core processes that must be performed.

sales department, but in terms of processes, like senior-VP-of-getting-stuff-to-customers, which is sales, shipping, billing. You'll no longer have a box on an organization chart. You'll own part of a process map."[2] Envision it as a whole company lying on its side and organized by process. An ardent believer in this approach, Lawrence Bossidy, CEO of Allied-Signal, says, "Every business has maybe six basic processes. We'll organize around them. The people who run them will be the leaders of the business."[3] In an industrial company, for example, these processes might include things like new-product development, flow of materials, and the order-delivery-billing cycle. Individuals will constantly move into and out of various teams as needed, drawing from a directory of broadly skilled in-house corporate experts available to lend their expertise.

The horizontal organization is already a reality in at least parts of several of today's organizations—including AT&T (network systems division), Eastman Chemical (a division of Kodak), Hallmark Cards, and Xerox. Consider, for example, General Electric's factory in Bayamón, Puerto Rico. The 172 hourly workers, 15 salaried "advisers," plus a single manager manufacture arresters (surge protectors that guard power stations from lightning). That's the entire work force; there are no support staff and no supervisors—only about half as many people as you'd find in a conventional factory. Bayamón employees are formed into separate teams of approximately ten widely skilled members who "own" such parts of the work as shipping and receiving, assembly, and so on. The teams do whatever is needed to get the job done; the advisers get involved only when needed.

Although carefully controlled studies have yet to assess the impact of this new approach, those who have used it are convinced of its effectiveness. One top consultant, for example, claims that this new approach to organizational design can help companies cut their costs by at least one-third. Some companies have done even better. Will the horizontal organization replace the traditional pyramid of the hierarchical organization? Only time will tell. Meanwhile, those who have turned to horizontal organizational structures appear to be glad they did.

ORGANIZATIONAL DESIGN: COMBINING THE STRUCTURAL ELEMENTS OF ORGANIZATIONS

We began this chapter by likening the structure of an organization to the structure of a house. Now we are prepared to extend that analogy for purposes of introducing the concept of *organizational design*. Just as a house is designed in a particular fashion by combining its structural elements in various ways, so too can an organization be designed by combining its basic elements in certain ways. Accordingly, **organizational design** refers to *the process of coordinating the structural elements of organizations in the most appropriate manner.*

CLASSICAL AND NEOCLASSICAL APPROACHES: THE QUEST FOR THE ONE BEST DESIGN

It is not difficult to realize that for organizations to function effectively, their designs must not be static, but dynamic—changing in response to various conditions (e.g., governmental regulations, competition, and so on.). As obvious as this may be to us today, the earliest theorists interested in organizational design paid little attention to the need for organizations to be flexible. Instead, they approached the task of designing organizations as a search for "the one best way," seeking to establish the ideal form for all organizations under all conditions—the universal design.

In Chapter 1, we described the efforts of organizational scholars such as Max Weber, Frederick Taylor, and Henri Fayol. These theorists believed that effective organizations were ones that had a formal hierarchy, a clear set of rules, specialization of labor, highly routine tasks, and a highly impersonal working environment. You may recall that Weber referred to this organizational form as a *bureaucracy*. This **classical organizational theory** has fallen into disfavor because it is insensitive to human needs and is not suited to a changing environment. Unfortunately, the "ideal" form of an organization, according to Weber, did not take into account the realities of the world within which it operates. Apparently, what is ideal is not necessarily what is realistic.

In response to these conditions, and with inspiration from the Hawthorne studies, the classical approach to the bureaucratic model gave way to more of a human relations orientation (see Chapter 1). Organizational scholars such as McGregor, Argyris, and Likert attempted to improve upon the classical model—which is why their approach is labeled **neoclassical organizational theory**—by arguing that economic effectiveness is not the only goal of an industrial organization, but also employee satisfaction. The key, they argued, was not rigidly controlling people's actions, but actively promoting their feelings of self-worth and their importance to the organization. The neoclassical approaches called for organizations to be designed with flat hierarchical structures (minimizing managerial control over subordinates) and a high degree of decentralization (encouraging employees to make their own decisions). Indeed, such design features may well serve the underlying neoclassical philosophy.

Like the classical approach, the neoclassical approach also may be faulted on the grounds that it promoted a single best approach to organizational design. Although the benefits of flat, decentralized designs may be many, to claim that this represents the universal or ideal form for all organizations would be naive. In response to this criticism, more contemporary approaches to organizational design have given up on finding the one best way to design organizations in favor of finding different designs that are appropriate for the different circumstances and contexts within which organizations operate.

THE CONTEMPORARY APPROACH: DESIGN CONTINGENT ON ENVIRONMENTAL CONDITIONS

Today it is widely believed that the best design for an organization depends on the nature of the environment (e.g., the economy, geography, labor markets) in which the organization is operating. This is known as the **contingency approach** to organizational design. Although many features of the environment may be taken into account when considering how an organization should be designed, a key determinant appears to be how stable (unchanging) or unstable (turbulent) the environment is.

Designs for Stable Versus Turbulent Conditions.   If you've ever worked at a McDonald's restaurant, you probably know how highly standardized each step of the most basic operations must be. Boxes of fries are to be stored 2 inches from the wall in stacks 1 inch apart. Making those fries is another matter—one that requires 19 distinct steps, each of which is clearly laid out in a training film shown to new employees. The process is the same, whether it's done in Moscow, Idaho, or Moscow, Russia. This is an example of a highly mechanistic task. Organizations can be highly mechanistic when conditions don't change. Although the fast-food industry has changed a great deal in recent years (e.g., with the introduction of healthier menu items and competitive pricing), making fries at McDonald's has not changed. In fact, the key to mechanization is lack of change. If the environment doesn't change, a highly **mechanistic form** of organization can be very efficient.

An environment is considered stable whenever there is little or no unexpected change in product, market demands, technology, and the like. Have you ever seen an old-fashioned-looking bottle of E. E. Dickinson's witch hazel (a topical astringent used to cleanse the skin in the area of a wound)? Since the company has been making the product following the same distillation process since 1866, it is certainly operating in a relatively stable manufacturing environment. Without change, people can easily specialize. When change is inevitable, specialization is impractical.

Mechanistic organizations can be characterized in several additional ways (for a summary, see Table 10-2). Not only do mechanistic organizations allow for a high degree of specialization, but they also impose many rules. Authority is vested in a few people located at the top of a hierarchy who give direct orders to their subordinates. *Mechanistic organizational designs tend to be most effective under conditions in which the external environment is stable and unchanging.*

Now think about high-technology industries, such as those dedicated to computers, aerospace products, and biotechnology. Their environmental conditions are likely to be changing all the time. These industries are so prone to change that as soon as a new way of operating could be introduced into one of them, it would have to be altered.

It isn't only technology, however, that makes an environment turbulent. Turbulence also can be high in industries in which adherence to rapidly changing regulations is essential. For example, times were turbulent in the hospital industry when new Medicaid legislation was passed, and times were turbulent in the nuclear power industry when governmental regulations dictated the introduction of many new standards that had to be followed. With the dominance of foreign automobiles in the United States, the once stable American auto industry has faced turbulent times. Unfortunately, in this case, the design of the auto companies could not rapidly accommodate the changes needed for more organic forms (since the American auto industry was traditionally highly mechanistic).

■ *Table 10-2 Mechanistic versus Organic Designs*

Mechanistic designs and organic designs differ along several key dimensions identified here. These represent extremes; many organizations fall in between.

| | Structure | |
Dimension	*Mechanistic*	*Organic*
Stability	Change unlikely	Change likely
Specialization	Many specialists	Many generalists
Formal rules	Rigid rules	Considerable flexibility
Authority	Centralized in a few top people	Decentralized, diffused throughout the organization

The pure **organic form** of organization may be characterized in several different ways (see Table 10-2). The degree of job specialization possible is very low; instead, a broad knowledge of many different jobs is required. Very little authority is exercised from the top. Rather, self-control is expected, and an emphasis is placed on coordination between peers. As a result, decisions tend to be made in a highly democratic, participative manner. Be aware that the mechanistic and organic types of organizational structures described here are ideal forms. The mechanistic-organic distinction should be thought of as opposite poles along a continuum rather than as completely distinct options for organization. Certainly, organizations can be relatively organic or relatively mechanistic compared with others, but may not be located at either extreme.

Testing the Contingency Approach.   Research supports the idea that organizational effectiveness is related to the degree to which an organization's structure (mechanistic or organic) is matched to its environment (stable or turbulent). In a classic study, Morse and Lorsch evaluated four departments in a large company—two of which manufactured containers (a relatively stable environment) and two of which dealt with communications research (a highly unstable environment).[4] One department in each pair was evaluated as being more effective than the other.

It was found that for the container manufacturing departments, the more effective unit was the one structured in a highly mechanistic form (roles and duties were clearly defined). In contrast, the more effective communications research department was structured in a highly organic fashion (roles and duties were vague). Additionally, the other, less effective departments were structured in the opposite manner (i.e., the less effective manufacturing department was organically structured, and the less effective research department was mechanistically structured). Taken together, these results made it clear that departments were most effective when their organizational structures fit their environments. This notion of "Which design is best under which conditions?" lies at the heart of the modern orientation—the contingency approach—to organizational structure. Rather than specifying *which* structure is best, the contingency approach specifies *when* each type of organizational design is most effective. (Although it has not yet been tested, it is an intriguing idea that the effectiveness of each form is also related to people's feelings about that type of organization. The **Self-Assessment Exercise** that follows will give you some insight into your individual preferences for mechanistic and organic organizations.)

MINTZBERG'S FRAMEWORK: FIVE ORGANIZATIONAL FORMS

Although the distinction between mechanistic and organic designs is important, it is not terribly specific with respect to exactly how organizations should be designed. Filling this void, however, is the work of contemporary organiza-

SELF-ASSESSMENT EXERCISE

Which Do You Prefer—Mechanistic or Organic Organizations?

Because mechanistic and organic organizations are so different, it is reasonable to expect that people will tend to prefer one of these organizational forms over the other. This questionnaire is designed to help you identify your own preferences (and, in so doing, to help you learn about the different forms themselves).

DIRECTIONS

Each of the following questions deals with your preferences for various conditions that may exist where you work. Answer each one by checking the one alternative that best describes your feelings.

1. When I have a job-related decision to make, I usually prefer to:

    _____ a. make the decision myself.

    _____ b. have my boss make it for me.

2. I usually find myself more interested in performing:

    _____ a. a highly narrow, specialized task.

    _____ b. many different types of tasks.

3. I prefer to work in places in which working conditions:

    _____ a. change a great deal.

    _____ b. generally remain the same.

4. When a lot of rules are imposed on me, I generally feel:

tional theorist, Henry Mintzberg.[5] Specifically, Mintzberg claims that organizations are composed of five basic elements, or groups of individuals, any of which may predominate in an organization. The one that does will determine the most effective design in that situation. The five basic elements are:

- **The operating core:** employees who perform the basic work related to the organization's product or service. Examples include teachers in schools and chefs and waiters in restaurants.

- **The strategic apex:** top-level executives responsible for running the entire organization. Examples include the entrepreneur

_____ a. very comfortable.

_____ b. very uncomfortable.

5. I believe that governmental regulation of industry is:

_____ a. usually best for all.

_____ b. rarely good for anyone.

SCORING

1. Give yourself 1 point each time you answered as follows: 1 = b; 2 = a; 3 = b; 4 = a; 5 = a. This score is your preference for *mechanistic organizations.*

2. Subtract this score from 5. The resulting score reflects your preference for *organic organizations.*

3. Interpret your scores as follows: Higher scores (closer to 5) reflect stronger preferences, and lower scores (closer to 0) reflect weaker preferences.

QUESTIONS FOR DISCUSSION

1. How did you score? That is, which organizational form did you prefer?

2. Think back over the jobs you've had. Have these been in organizations that were mechanistic or organic?

3. Do you think you performed better in organizations whose designs matched your preferences than those in which there was a mismatch?

4. Do you think you were more committed to organizations whose designs matched your preferences than those in which there was a mismatch?

who runs his or her own small business, and the general manager of an automobile dealership.

- **The middle line:** managers who transfer information between the strategic apex and the operating core. Examples include middle managers, such as regional sales managers (who connect top executives with the sales force) and the chair of an academic department in a college or university (an intermediary between the dean and the faculty).

- **The technostructure:** those specialists responsible for standardizing various aspects of the organization's activities. Examples include accountants and auditors, and computer systems analysts.

- **The support staff:** individuals who provide indirect support services to the organization. Examples include consultants on technical matters, and corporate attorneys.

What organizational designs best fit under conditions in which each of these five groups dominate? To answer this question, Mintzberg has identified five specific designs: *simple structure, machine bureaucracy, professional bureaucracy,* the *divisionalized structure,* and the *adhocracy.*

Simple Structure.   Imagine that you open up an antique shop and hire a few people to help you out around the store. You have a small, informal organization in which there is a single individual with the ultimate power. There is little in the way of specialization or formalization, and the overall structure is organic in nature. The hierarchy is quite flat, and all decision-making power is vested in a single individual—you. An organization so described, simple in nature, with the power residing at the strategic apex, is referred to by Mintzberg as having a **simple structure.** As you might imagine, organizations with simple structure can respond quickly to the environment and be very flexible. For example, the chef-owner of a small, independent restaurant can change the menu to suit the changing tastes of customers whenever needed, without first consulting anyone else. The downside of this, however, is that the success or failure of the entire enterprise is dependent on the wisdom and health of the one individual in charge. Not surprisingly, organizations with simple structure are risky ventures.

Machine Bureaucracy.   If you've ever worked for your state's department of motor vehicles, you probably found it to be a very large place, with numerous rules and procedures for employees to follow. The work is highly specialized (e.g., one person gives the vision tests, and another completes the registration forms), and decision making is concentrated at the top (e.g., you need to get permission from your supervisor to do anything other than exactly what's expected). This type of work environment is highly stable and does not have to change. An organization so characterized, where power resides with the technostructure, is referred to as a **machine bureaucracy.** Although machine bureaucracies can be highly efficient at performing standardized tasks, they tend to be dehumanizing and very boring for the employees (see Chapter 1).

Professional Bureaucracy.   Suppose you are a doctor working at a large city hospital. You are a highly trained specialist with considerable expertise in your field. You don't need to check with anyone else before authorizing a certain medical test or treatment for your patient; you make the decisions as they are needed, when they are needed. At the same time, the environment is highly formal (e.g., there are lots of rules and regulations for you to follow). Of course, you do not work alone; you also require the services of other highly qualified professionals such as nurses and laboratory technicians.

Organizations of this type (e.g., universities, libraries, consulting firms, and hospitals) maintain power with the operating core, and are called **professional bureaucracies.** Such organizations can be highly effective because they allow employees to practice those skills for which they are best qualified. However, sometimes specialists become so overly narrow that they fail to see the "big picture," leading to errors and potential conflict between employees.

Divisional Structure. When you think of large organizations, such as General Motors, Du Pont, Xerox, and IBM, the image that comes to mind is probably closest to what Mintzberg describes as **divisional structure.** Such organizations consist of a set of autonomous units coordinated by a central headquarters (i.e., they rely on departmental structure based on products, as described on pages 272–274). In such organizations, because the divisions are autonomous (e.g., a General Motors employee at Buick does not have to consult with another at Chevrolet to do his or her job), division managers (the *middle line* part of Mintzberg's basic elements) have considerable control.

Divisional designs preclude the need for top-level executives to think about the day-to-day operations of their companies, freeing them to concentrate on larger-scale, strategic decisions. At the same time, companies organized into separate divisions frequently tend to have high duplication of effort (e.g., separate order processing units for each division). Having operated as separate divisions for the past 70 years, General Motors is considered the classic example of divisional structure. Although the company has undergone many changes during this time—including the addition of the Saturn Corporation—it has maintained its divisional structure. IBM is another company that has had a divisional structure that has changed many times.[6] For a look at its most recent divisional structuring, see Figure 10-6.

Adhocracy. After graduating from college, where you spent years learning how to program computers, you take a job at a small software company. Compared to your friends who found positions at large accounting firms, your professional life is much less formal. You work as a member of a team developing a new time-management software product. There are no rules, and schedules are made to be broken. You all work together, and although there is someone who is "officially" in charge, you'd never know it. Using Mintzberg's framework, you work for an **adhocracy**—an organization in which power resides with the support staff.

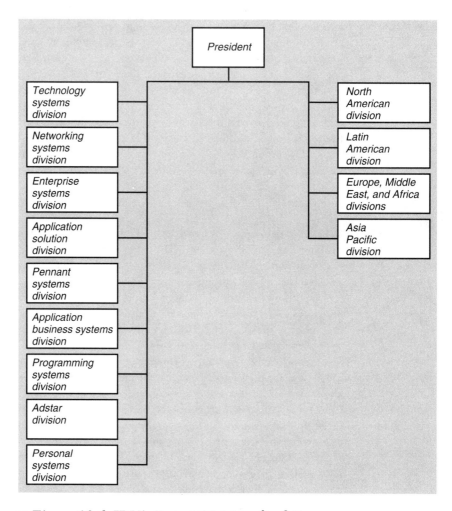

■ *Figure 10-6 IBM's Latest Divisionalized Structure*

In 1992 IBM reorganized into thirteen major divisions—nine of which are based on product lines (left side), and four of which are based on geographic region (right side). (*Source:* Based on suggestions by Kirkpartick, 1992, see Note 6.)

Essentially, this is the epitome of the organic structure identified earlier. Specialists coordinate with each other not because of their shared functions (e.g., accounting, manufacturing), but as members of teams working on specific projects. The primary benefit of the adhocracy is that it fosters innovation. Some large companies, such as Johnson & Johnson, nest within their formal divisional structure units that operate as adhocracies. In the case of

J&J, it's the New Products Division, a unit that has been churning out an average of 40 products per year during recent years.

As in the case of all other designs there are disadvantages to adhocracies. In this case, the most serious limitations are their high levels of inefficiency (they are the opposite of machine bureaucracies in this regard), with the greatest potential for disruptive conflict.

INTERORGANIZATIONAL DESIGNS: GOING BEYOND THE SINGLE ORGANIZATION

All the organizational designs we have examined thus far have concentrated on the arrangement of units within an organization—what may be termed *intraorganizational designs*. However, sometimes at least some parts of different organizations must operate jointly. To coordinate their efforts on such projects, organizations must create *interorganizational designs*, plans by which two or more organizations come together. Two such designs are commonly found: *conglomerates* and *strategic alliances*.

CONGLOMERATES: DIVERSIFIED "MEGACORPORATIONS"

When an organization diversifies by adding an entirely unrelated business or product to its organizational design, it may be said to have formed a **conglomerate.** Some of the world's largest conglomerates may be found in the Orient. For example, in Korea, companies such as Samsung and Hyundai produce home electronics, automobiles, textiles, and chemicals in large, unified conglomerates known as *chaebols*.[7] These are all separate companies overseen by the same parent company leadership. In Japan, the same type of arrangement is known as a *keiretsu*.[8] A good example of a keiretsu is the Matsushita Group. This enormous conglomerate consists of a bank (Asahi Bank) and a consumer electronics company (Panasonic), and has close ties to several insurance companies (e.g., Sumitomo Life, Nippon Life). These examples are not meant to suggest that conglomerates are unique to the Orient. Indeed, many large U.S.-based corporations, such as IBM and Tenneco, are also conglomerates, as is Johnson & Johnson.

Companies form conglomerates for several reasons. First, as an independent business, the parent company can enjoy the benefits of diversification. Thus, as one industry languishes, another may excel, allowing for a stable economic outlook for the parent company. In addition, conglomerates may provide built-in markets and access to supplies, since companies typically support other organizations within the conglomerate. For example, General Motors cars and trucks are fitted with Delco radios, and Ford cars and trucks have engines with Autolite spark plugs, separate companies that are owned by their respective parent companies. In this manner conglomerates can benefit by providing a network of organizations that are dependent on each other for products and services, thereby creating considerable advantages.

In recent years, however, many large conglomerates have been selling off parts of themselves in a move to concentrate on their core business. For example, the giant Korean chaebol, Hyundai (which accounts for 10 percent of Korea's gross national product) has recently dismantled parts of its sprawling corporate structure, selling controlling interests in its heavy manufacturing and shipping companies, and severing all ties with its hotel, insurance, and department store companies. Compared to the 1960s, which was a period of growth for many conglomerates, the 1990s appears to be a period of decline.

STRATEGIC ALLIANCES

A **strategic alliance** is a type of organizational design in which two or more separate firms join their competitive capabilities to operate a specific business. The goal of a strategic alliance is to provide benefits to each individual organization that could not be attained if they operated separately. They are low-risk ways of diversifying (adding new business operations) and entering new markets. Some companies have strategic alliances with many others. For example by 1986, General Electric had formed over 100 alliances, and Ford formed over 40 in 1987 alone.

Companies often form strategic alliances with foreign firms to gain entry into that country's market. For example, Korea's **Daewoo** *receives technical information and is paid to manufacture automobiles for companies with which it has entered into strategic alliances, including* **General Motors, Opel, Isuzu,** *and* **Nissan.**

There are direct managerial benefits to be derived from extending one company's organizational chart into another's. These primarily come from improved technology and greater economies of scale (e.g., sharing functional operations across organizations). For these benefits to be realized, a high degree of coordination and fit must exist between the parties, each delivering on its promise to the other. Finally, it is noteworthy that strategic alliances with companies in nations with transforming economies (such as China and Eastern Europe) provide good opportunities for those nations' economies to develop. Given the rapid move toward globalization of the economy, we may expect to see many companies seeking strategic alliances in the future as a means for gaining or maintaining a competitive advantage.

As you might imagine, not all strategic alliances are successful. For example, AT&T and Olivetti tried unsuccessfully to work together on manufacturing personal computers. Strong differences in management styles and organizational culture (see Chapter 5) were cited as causes. Similarly, a planned alliance between Raytheon and Lexitron, a small word processing company, failed because of the clashes between the rigid culture of the much larger Raytheon, and the more entrepreneurial style of the smaller Lexitron. Clearly,

The Successful Strategic Alliance Between Universal Card and TSYS: Lessons Learned

If you have a credit card, chances are pretty good that it's an AT&T Universal Card. After all, there are over 19 million such card holders, making it second only to Citicorp in the number of cards issued.[9] What makes this particularly impressive is that the Universal Card has only been in existence since 1990, and also that AT&T is not in the banking business!

AT&T officials thought that entering the credit card business would not only be another good source of income, but also a useful way to extend its traditional calling card business. To help, it entered into a strategic alliance with Total System Services (TSYS), a firm with a successful track record with respect to credit cards and large-volume data processing. Combined with AT&T's brand name, superiority as a long-distance carrier, and access to a gigantic mailing list, the prospect of combining forces on the Universal Card seemed promising. And history proved them right. The Universal Card was carried by over 1 million people within the first 72 days of the company's existence, and over 10 million within the first two years.

This alliance worked well for several reasons. First, the alliance was based on the strengths of each partner. AT&T's outstanding reputation paired with TSYS's leadership in the technology of data processing allowed each to do what it does best. Second, both parties have benefited financially. AT&T found the card to be profitable after only three years, and the added volume helped TSYS reduce its per-unit costs of processing accounts. Third, the cultures of both companies meshed nicely. Executives of both companies have a very conservative, businesslike style common among telephone companies and banks. Fourth, the companies complement each other's strategic interests. Both companies are driven by the desire to give the best possible customer service. The alliance between them helped each achieve this objective.

Beyond simply helping both companies achieve their strategic goals, the alliance between AT&T and TSYS helped each improve what it already does well—and, in several ways. First, the alliance has raised both companies' quality standards, making them higher than ever before. For example, in the area of customer service, representatives are now available around the clock to answer questions, as is an automated voice response system that allows customers to access information about their accounts at any time. Second, the alliance has helped each company develop state-of-the-art facilities in which to operate. Finally, and very importantly, the alliance has benefited both companies such that their core businesses are enhanced. AT&T's calling card revenues have increased (40 percent in the card's first year, alone), as has TSYS's capacity to develop more effective hardware and software for processing credit cards. The fact that the parent companies have added value to each other's operations keeps the strategic alliance alive and well.

for strategic alliances to work, the companies must not only be able to offer each other something important, but they also must be able to work together to make it happen. (For a description of a highly successful strategic alliance, see the **Winning Practices** section on p. 289.)

SUMMARY:
PUTTING IT TO USE

The formal configuration between individuals and groups with respect to the allocation of tasks, responsibilities, and authority within organizations is known as *organizational structure,* an abstract concept that can be represented by an *organizational chart.* Such diagrams represent five different elemental building blocks of organizational structure: *hierarchy of authority* (a summary of reporting relationships), *division of labor* (the degree to which jobs are specialized), *span of control* (the number of individuals over which a manager has responsibility), *line* versus *staff positions* (jobs permitting direct decision-making power versus jobs in which advice is given), and *decentralization* (the degree to which decisions can be made by lower-ranking employees as opposed to a few higher-ranking individuals).

Within organizations, groups of people can be combined into departments in various ways. The most popular approach is the *functional organization,* organizations created by combining people in terms of the common functions they perform (e.g., sales, manufacturing). An alternative approach is to departmentalize people by virtue of the specific products for which they are responsible, known as the *product organization.* Another form of departmentalization combines both of these approaches into a single form known as the *matrix organization.* In such organizations, people have at least two bosses; they are responsible to a superior in charge of the various functions and a superior in charge of the specific product. Employees also may have to answer to high-ranking people responsible for the entire organization, the top leader. There is an emerging trend toward the *horizontal organization.* This involves flattening organizational hierarchies and using autonomous teams working together on basic processes, rather than separate tasks.

The process of coordinating the structural elements of organizations in the most appropriate manner is known as *organizational design. Classical organizational theorists* believed that a universally best way to design organizations exists, an approach based on high efficiency. *Neoclassical organizational theorists* also believe that there is one best way to design organizations, although their approach emphasized the need to pay attention to basic human needs to succeed and express oneself.

In contrast, the contemporary *contingency approach* to organizational design is predicated on the belief that the most appropriate way to design organizations depends on the external environments within which they operate. Specifically, a key factor has to do with the degree to which the organization is subject to change: A stable environment is one in which business conditions do not change, whereas a turbulent environment is one in which conditions change rapidly. Research has shown that when conditions are stable, a *mechanistic organization* is effective. A mechanistic organization is one in which people perform specialized jobs, many rigid rules are imposed, and authority is vested in a few top-ranking officials. When conditions are turbulent, an *organic organization* is effective. These are organizations in which jobs tend to be very general, there are few rules, and decisions can be made by low-level employees. The mechanistic and organic forms are pure types, and organizations can be located in between these two extremes.

Five specific organizational forms have been identified by Mintzberg. Organizations with *simple structure* are small and informal, and have a single powerful individual, often the founding entrepreneur, who is in charge of everything (e.g., a small retail store owned by a sole proprietor). In a *machine bureaucracy* work is highly specialized, decision making is concentrated at the top, and the work environment is not prone to change (e.g., a government office). In *professional bureaucracies,* such as hospitals and universities, there are lots of rules to follow, but employees are highly skilled and free to make decisions on their own. *Divisional structure* characterizes many large organizations (such as General Motors) in which separate autonomous units are created to deal with entire product lines, freeing top management to focus on larger-scale, strategic decisions. Finally, the *adhocracy* is a highly informal, organic organization in which specialists work in teams, coordinating with each other on various projects (e.g., many software development companies).

Other organizational designs represent ways of combining more than one organization. Such interorganizational designs include *conglomerates* (large corporations that diversify by getting involved in unrelated businesses), and *strategic alliances* (organizations combining forces to operate a specific business).

You Be the Consultant

The president of a small but rapidly growing software company asks you to consult with him about an important matter. As the company expands, several options for designing the company's operations are being considered, and your job is to help him make a decision about which route to take. Answer the following questions relevant to this situation based on the material in this chapter.

1. What would you recommend with respect to the following structural variables: hierarchy of authority (tall or flat), division of labor (specialized or general), span of control (wide or narrow), and degree of centralization (highly centralized or highly decentralized)? Explain the reasons behind your recommendations.

2. How do you think the company should be departmentalized—by task (functional), by output (product), both task and output (matrix), or process (horizontal)? What are your reasons for these conclusions?

3. Given the company's highly organic characteristics, what organizational design should work best? On what basis do you make this claim?

4. If the company were thinking about entering into a strategic alliance with another, what factors would have to be considered? What kind of company would be an effective partner in an alliance with this software firm?

Managing Change in Organizations

PREVIEW OF CHAPTER HIGHLIGHTS

Organizations undergo changes that are both planned and unplanned. **Organizational changes** focus on structure, technology, and people.

Employees accept organizational change whenever the benefits associated with changing are believed to outweigh the costs.

People resist change due to both individual factors (e.g., economic insecurity) and organizational factors (e.g., threats to the existing balance of power).

Resistance to change may be overcome by educating the work force about the effects of change and including employees in the change process.

Systematic techniques for adapting to change are known as **organizational development (OD) interventions.** Such techniques include: **survey feedback, quality of work life** programs, **management by objectives (MBO), sensitivity training,** and **team building.**

Although difficult to assess objectively, OD interventions are generally more successful at improving organizational functioning than at improving individual satisfaction.

Some claim that OD interventions are highly manipulative and therefore unethical, whereas others counter that it is a tool that can be used to promote the welfare of all.

Think of some of the changes you may have seen in recent years in the way businesses operate.

- The prices of many fast-food items have dropped
- Some auto dealerships have adopted no-haggle pricing policies
- Accommodations for people with handicaps have appeared in the workplace
- Just about everything you can imagine has become computerized

Signs of the impact of **organizational change** can be found everywhere. However, most people have difficulty accepting that they may have to alter their work methods. After all, if you're used to working a certain way, a sudden change can be very unsettling.

Fortunately, social scientists have developed various methods, known collectively as **organizational development** techniques, that are designed to implement needed organizational change in a manner that both is acceptable to employees and enhances the effectiveness of the organizations involved.

We will examine these techniques and their effectiveness in this chapter. Before doing so, however, we will take a closer look at the organizational change process by chronicling different forces for change that are known to affect organizations. Then we will explore some major issues involved in the organizational change process, such as what is changed, when change will occur, why people are resistant to change, and how this resistance can be overcome.

FORCES FOR ORGANIZATIONAL CHANGE

A century ago, advances in machine technology made farming so highly efficient that fewer hands were needed to plant and reap the harvest. The displaced laborers fled to nearby cities, seeking jobs in newly opened factories, opportunities created by some of the same technologies that sent them from the farm. The economy shifted from agrarian to manufacturing, and the *industrial revolution* was under way. With it came drastic shifts in where people lived, how they worked, how they spent their leisure time, how much money they made, and how they spent it. Today's business analysts claim that we are currently experiencing *another* industrial revolution—one driven by a new wave of economic and technological forces. As one observer put it, "This workplace revolution . . . may be remembered as a historic event, the Western equivalent of the collapse of communism."[1]

In recent years, just about all companies, large and small, have made adjustments in the ways they operate, some more pronounced than others. Citing just a few examples, General Electric, Allied Signal, Ameritech, and Tenneco all have radically altered the way they operate: their culture, the technology they use, their structure, and the nature of their relations with employees. With so many companies making such drastic changes, the message is clear: *Either adapt to changing conditions or shut your doors.*

Unfortunately, many companies fail to change when required and find themselves out of business as a result. In fact, fully 62 percent of new ventures fail to last as long as five years, and only 2 percent make it for as long as 50 years. Amazingly, however, some American companies have beaten the odds—so soundly, in fact, that they have remained in business for well over 200 years. As you might imagine, these "corporate Methuselahs" have undergone *many* changes during their years of existence. For example, the oldest U.S. company, J. E. Rhoads & Sons, now makes conveyer belts, although it originally started out in 1702 making buggy whips. Another company, Dexter, in Windsor Locks, Connecticut began in 1767 as a grist mill. As you might imagine, it no longer does that; now it makes adhesives and coatings for aircraft. Earlier it manufactured specialty papers for stationery and for tea bags. Obviously, this company is not adverse to change. According to Dexter spokesperson Ellen Cook, "We have no traditions, whatsoever. None."[2]

Obviously, ever-changing conditions pose a formidable challenge to organizations, which must adapt to them. However, not all organizational changes are the result of unplanned factors. Some organizational changes are planned and quite intentional.

PLANNED CHANGE

A great deal of organizational change comes from the strategic decision to alter the way an organization does business or the very nature of the business itself.

Changes in Products or Services.   Imagine that you and a friend begin a small janitorial business. The two of you divide the duties, each doing some cleaning, buying supplies, and performing some administrative work. Before long, the business grows and you expand, adding new employees, and really begin "cleaning up." Many of your commercial clients express interest in window cleaning, and so you and your partner think it over and decide to expand into the window-cleaning business as well. This decision to take on a new direction to the business, to add a new, specialized service, will require a fair amount of organizational change. Not only will new equipment and supplies be needed, but also new personnel will have to be hired and trained, new insurance will have to be purchased, and new accounts will have to be secured. In short, the planned decision to change the company's line of services necessitates organizational change.

This is exactly the kind of change that Federal Express (now FedEx) encountered in 1989 when it sought to expand its package delivery service, formerly limited exclusively to North America, to international markets, or that Citicorp, a longtime leader in consumer banking, encountered when it attempted to become an international leader in corporate banking. As you are undoubtedly aware, the rash of new products and services offered to consumers each year is staggering. Unfortunately, many of these are unsuccessful; only about one out of every eight ever becomes profitable. In fact, both Federal Express and Citicorp have experienced difficult financial battles in their attempts to expand their service markets beyond their traditional boundaries.

Changes in Administrative Systems.   Although an organization may be forced to change its policies, it is not unusual for changes in administrative systems to be strategically planned in advance. Such changes may stem from such forces as the desire to improve efficiency or to change the company's image. As an example of this, let's consider the decision by PepsiCo to structurally reorganize. For many years, PepsiCo had a separate international food service division, which included the operation of 62 foreign locations of the company's Pizza Hut and Taco Bell restaurants. Because of the great profit potential of these foreign restaurants, PepsiCo officials decided to reorganize, putting these operations directly under the control of the same executives responsible for the successful national operations of Pizza Hut and Taco Bell. This type of departmentalization allows the foreign restaurants to be managed under the same careful guidance as the national operations (see Chapter 10).

Changes in Organizational Size and Structure.   Just as organizations change their products, services, or administrative systems to stay competitive, so too do they alter the size and basic configurations of their organizational charts—that is, they *restructure*. In many cases, this has meant reducing the number of employees needed to operate effectively—a process known as **downsizing.** Typically, this involves more than just laying off people in a move to save money. It is directed at adjusting the number of employees needed to work in newly designed organizations and is, therefore, also known as **rightsizing.** Whatever you call it, the bottom line is painfully clear: Many organizations need fewer people to operate today than in the past—sometimes far fewer.[3] For some sobering statistics on this form of organizational change, see Table 11-1. (How well prepared are you for the eventuality of becoming a victim of downsizing?[4] Completing the **Self-Assessment Exercise** on p. 298 will help you find out.)

Another way organizations are restructuring is by completely eliminating parts of themselves that focus on noncore sectors of the business, and hiring outside firms to perform these functions instead—a practice known as **outsourcing.** For example, companies like ServiceMaster, which provides janitorial services, and ADP, which provides payroll processing services, make it possible for organizations to concentrate on the business functions most cen-

■ *Table 11-1 Where Are the Layoffs Occurring?*

During the first seven months of 1993 millions of jobs were eliminated. The greatest numbers of layoffs were announced in the industries shown here. As noted, the job axe cut particularly deep in some industries. (*Source:* Based on information reported in Richman, 1993; see Note 3.)

Industry	Total Number of Layoffs Announced (January–July 1993)	Companies Most Affected
Aerospace	89,890	28,000 jobs lost at Boeing
Computers	86,257	60,000 jobs lost at IBM
Retailing	62,090	50,000 jobs lost at Sears
Food processing, consumer goods	23,504	13,000 jobs lost at Procter & Gamble
Transportation	12,073	Jobs eliminated by most airlines
Communications	10,329	6,200 jobs lost at GTE, 1,400 jobs lost at AT&T

tral to their missions, thereby freeing them from these peripheral support functions.

In some cases, the only way people can tell that their part of the organization no longer exists is that they receive paychecks from someone else. For example, Xerox has taken over all the internal service functions of Bankers Trust (e.g., mailroom, print shop, employee record-keeping, payroll, telephone switchboard), employing in many cases the same individuals who used to perform these functions while working for Bankers Trust. Ironically, some businesses providing outsourcing services, such as EDS, a data processing firm with $8.2 billion in annual sales, have become so large that they may outsource some services themselves while providing outsourcing services to their clients.

> *When* **Apple Computer** *introduced its first notebook computer, the Macintosh Powerbook 100, it subcontracted its manufacturing to* **Sony,** *enabling it to speed entry into the market.*

Some critics fear that outsourcing represents a "hollowing out" of companies—a reduction of functions that weakens organizations by making them more dependent on others. Others counter that outsourcing makes sense when the work that is outsourced is not highly critical to competitive success (e.g., janitorial services), or when it is so highly critical that the only way to succeed requires outside assistance. If you think that outsourcing is an unusual occurrence, guess again. One industry analyst has estimated that 30 percent of the largest American industrial firms outsource over half their manufacturing. (If your organization is downsized, will you be caught off guard?

Are You Prepared for Downsizing?

As difficult as it may be to confront, downsizing is a way of life in today's re-structuring organizations. It is the wise employee who is prepared for this eventuality. If you lose your job to downsizing in your organization, are you ready to move on to another position with only minimal disruption? This exercise will help you answer this question. (*Source:* Based on information in Half, 1986; see Note 4.)

DIRECTIONS

Check each of the following statements that applies to you.

_____   1.   I keep a record of all my work accomplishments.
_____   2.   I keep my résumé ready to go at all times.
_____   3.   My communication skills are finely tuned.
_____   4.   I keep a notebook full of business and social contacts who
             would be useful leads in finding a new job.
_____   5.   I do whatever I can to be indispensable to my company.
_____   6.   I constantly work to further my professional education and training.
_____   7.   I try hard to always be pleasant and courteous.
_____   8.   I stay abreast of the latest job openings in my field.
_____   9.   I regularly read the trade papers in my profession.

QUESTIONS FOR DISCUSSION

1.   How many items did you check? The more you checked, the better prepared you are for finding a new job, should you need to do so.

2.   In addition to the items on this checklist, what further steps can you take to prepare for the possibility of having to take a new job?

3.   Are you concerned that being highly prepared to step into a new position may lower your commitment to your present job (possibly making your need for a new job self-fulfilling)?

Introduction of New Technologies.   As you know (and as we will describe in Chapter 12), advances in technology have produced changes in the way organizations operate. Senior scientists and engineers, for example, can probably tell you how their work was drastically altered in the mid-1970s, when their ubiquitous plastic slide rules gave way to powerful pocket calculators. Things changed again only a decade later, when calculators were supplanted by powerful desktop microcomputers, which have revolutionized the way documents are prepared, transmitted, and filed in an office. Manufacturing plants also have seen a great deal of growth recently in the use of computer-automated technology and robotics. Each of these examples represents an instance in which technology has altered the way people do their jobs.

Advances in Information Processing and Communication. Although we now take for granted everyday innovations such as fax machines and e-mail, these things were merely exotic dreams not too many years ago. If you've ever seen an old western film in which the Pony Express rider struggled through uncharted territories to deliver messages to people in distant western cities, you are well aware of the difficulties that people faced communicating over long distances. Of course, with today's sophisticated satellite transmission systems, fiber-optic cables crisscrossing the planet, cellular phones, teleconferencing facilities and the like, it is easier than ever for businesses to communicate with each other and with their clients. The key point is that as such communication systems improve, opportunities for organizational growth and improvement follow.

UNPLANNED CHANGE

Not all forces for change are the result of strategic planning. Indeed, organizations must often be responsive to changes that are unplanned—especially those derived from factors internal to the organization. Two such forces are changes in the demographic composition of the work force and performance gaps.

Changing Employee Demographics. It is easy to see how, even within your own lifetime, the composition of the work force has changed. As we will detail in Chapter 12, the American work force is now more highly diverse than ever. To people concerned with the long-term operation of organizations, these are not simply curious sociological trends, but shifting conditions that will force organizations to change. For example, questions regarding how many people will be working, what skills they will bring to their jobs, and what new influences they will bring to the workplace are of key interest to human resources managers. In the words of Frank Doyle, corporate vice president for external and industrial relations at General Electric, the impending changes in work force demographics "will turn the professional human-resources world upside down."[5] Indeed, some companies such as American Express have already responded to these changes by educating their supervisors on how to manage a changing, increasingly diversified work force.

Performance Gaps. If you've ever heard the phrase "If it's not broken, don't fix it," you already have a good feel for one of the most potent sources of unplanned internal changes in organizations—*performance gaps*. A product line that isn't moving, a vanishing profit margin, a level of sales that isn't up to corporate expectations—these are examples of gaps between real and expected levels of organizational performance. Few things force change more than sudden and unexpected information about poor performance. Organizations usually stay with a winning course of action and change in response to failure. In other words, they follow a *win-stay/lose-change rule*. Indeed, a performance gap is one of the key factors providing an impetus for organizational innovation. Those organizations that are best prepared to mobilize change in response to unexpected downturns are expected to be the ones that succeed.

Government Regulation.   One of the most commonly witnessed unplanned organizational changes results from government regulations. In the late 1980s, restaurant owners in the United States had to alter the way they report the income of waiters and waitresses to the federal government for purposes of collecting income taxes. In recent years, the U.S. federal government has been involved in both imposing and eliminating regulations in industries such as commercial airlines (e.g., mandating inspection schedules, but no longer controlling fares) and banking (e.g., restricting the amount of time checks can be held before clearing, but no longer regulating interest rates). Such activities have greatly influenced the way business is conducted in these industries.

An excellent example of how government activities drive organizational change is provided by the 1984 divestiture of AT&T. A settlement of antitrust proceedings dramatically rearranged the activities of almost 1 million employees of the Bell System. Among other things, the agreement led to the creation of seven new independent companies. At Southwestern Bell, CEO Zane Barnes remarked that the divestiture forced them to "rethink the functions of some 90,000 employees," a process likened to "taking apart and reassembling a jumbo jet while in flight."[6] Not surprisingly, the company relied on its expertise in satellite and communications technology to provide information about the change process to its employees in 57 locations.

> *In response to growing competition, **Procter & Gamble** was forced to streamline its highly bureaucratic organizational structure. Its decision-making process used to be so centralized that many decisions that could have been made at lower levels were being made by top corporate personnel—such as the color of the cap on cans of decaffeinated instant Folgers coffee.*

Economic Competition in the Global Arena.   It happens every day: Someone builds a better mousetrap—or at least a cheaper one. As a result, companies often must fight to maintain their shares of the market, advertise more effectively, and produce goods less expensively. This kind of economic competition not only forces organizations to change but also demands that they change effectively if they are to survive.

Although competition has always been crucial to organizational success, today competition comes from all over the world. As it has become increasingly less expensive to transport materials around the world, the industrialized nations have found themselves competing with each other for shares of the global marketplace. This extensive globalization of the economy presents a strong need to change and be innovative. For example, consider how the large American automobile manufacturers suffered by being unprepared to meet the world's growing demand for small, high-quality cars—products their Japanese competitors were only too glad to supply to an eager marketplace. With this rapidly changing growth in globalization, one thing is certain: Only the most adaptive organizations can survive.

As we have been describing in this part of the chapter, organizations change in many ways and for many reasons. For a summary of these sources of organizational change, see Figure 11-1.

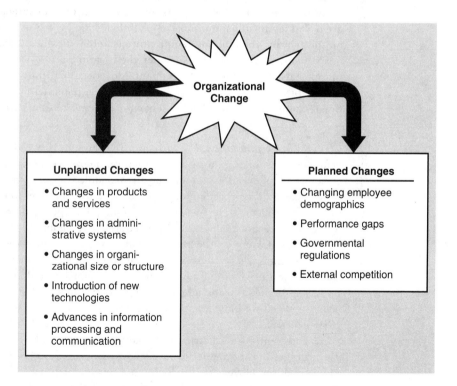

■ *Figure 11-1 Planned and Unplanned Organizational Changes*

Organizational changes may be considered either planned or unplanned. Some examples of each are listed here.

THE PROCESS OF ORGANIZATIONAL CHANGE: FOUR BASIC QUESTIONS

When it comes to organizational change, several basic questions warrant consideration. First, *what* are the targets of organizational change efforts? Second, *when* will organizational change occur? Third, *why* is organizational change resisted? Fourth, *how* can resistance to change be overcome? We will now address these questions.

TARGETS: WHAT IS CHANGED?

Imagine that you are an engineer responsible for overseeing the maintenance of a large office building. The property manager has noted a dramatic increase in the use of heat in the building, causing operating costs to skyrocket. In other words, a need for change exists—specifically, a reduction in the building's heat usage. You cannot get the power company to lower its rates, so you realize you must bring about changes in the use of heat. But how? One possibility is to rearrange job responsibilities so that only maintenance personnel are permitted to adjust thermostats. Another option is to put timers on all thermostats so that the building temperature is automatically lowered during periods of nonuse. Finally, you consider the idea of putting stickers next to the thermostats, requesting that occupants do not adjust them. These three options represent excellent examples of the three potential targets of organizational change we will consider—changes in *organizational structure, technology, and people* (see Figure 11-2).

Changes in Organizational Structure.   In Chapter 10 we described the key characteristics of organizational structure. Here we note that altering the structure of an organization may be a reasonable way of responding to a need for change. In the preceding example, a structural solution to the heat regulation problem came in the form of reassigning job responsibilities. Indeed, modifying rules, responsibilities, and procedures may be an effective way to manage change. Changing the responsibility for temperature regulation from a highly decentralized system (whereby anyone can make adjustments) to a centralized one (in which only maintenance personnel may do so) is one way of implementing organizational change in response to a problem. This particular solution called for changing the power structure (i.e., who was in charge of a particular task).

Different types of structural changes may take other forms. For example, changes can be made in an organization's span of control, altering the number of employees for which supervisors are responsible. Structural changes also may take the form of revising the basis for creating departments—such as from product-based departments to functional departments. Other structural changes may be much simpler, such as clarifying someone's job description or the written policies and procedures followed.

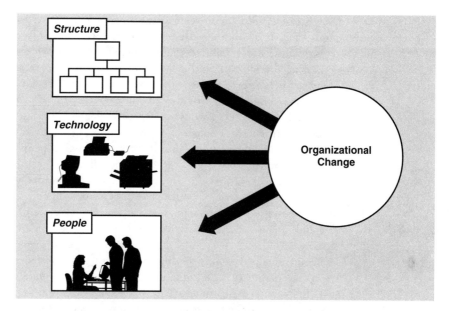

■ *Figure 11-2 Structure, Technology, and People as Targets of Organizational Change*

To create change in organizations, one can rely on altering organizational structure, technology, and/or people. Changes in any one of these areas may necessitate changes in the others.

Changes in Technology. In our thermostat example, we noted that one possible solution would be to use thermostats that automatically reduce the building's temperature while it is not in use. This is an example of a technological approach to the need to conserve heat in the building. Placement of regulating devices on the thermostats that would thwart attempts to raise the temperature also would be possible. The thermostats also could be encased in a locked box, or simply removed altogether. A new, modern, energy-efficient furnace could be installed in the building. All of these suggestions represent technological approaches to the need for change.

The underlying idea is that technological improvements can lead to more efficient work. Indeed, if you've ever prepared a term paper on a typewriter (remember those?), you know how much more efficient it is to do the same job using a computer with word processing software. Technological changes may involve a variety of alterations, such as changing the equipment used to do jobs (e.g., robots) or substituting microprocessors for less reliable mechanical components (e.g., on airline equipment). Each of these changes may be used to bring about improvements in organizational functioning.

Changes in People.   You've probably seen stickers next to light switches in hotels and office buildings asking the occupants to turn off the lights when not in use. These are similar to the suggestion in our opening example to affix signs near thermostats asking occupants to refrain from adjusting the thermostats. Such efforts represent attempts to respond to the needed organizational change by altering the way people behave. The basic assumption is that the effectiveness of organizations is greatly dependent on the behavior of the people working within them.

As you might imagine, the process of changing people is not easy—indeed, it lies at the core of most of the topics discussed in this book. However, theorists have identified three basic steps that summarize what's involved in the process of changing people. The first step is known as *unfreezing*. This refers to the process of recognizing that the current state of affairs is undesirable and in need of change. Realizing that change is needed may be the result of some serious organizational crisis or threat (e.g., a serious financial loss, a strike, or a major lawsuit), or simply becoming aware that current conditions are unacceptable (e.g., antiquated equipment, inadequately trained employees). In recent years, some executives have gotten employees to accept the need to change while things are still good by creating a sense of urgency. They introduce the idea that there is an impending crisis although conditions are, in fact, currently acceptable—an approach referred to as **doomsday management.** This process effectively unfreezes people, stimulating change before it's too late to do any good.

After unfreezing, *changing* may occur. This step occurs when some planned attempt is made to create a more desirable state for the organization and its members. Change attempts may be quite ambitious (e.g., an organizationwide restructuring) or only minor (e.g., a change in a training program). (A thorough discussion of such planned change techniques will be presented in the next major part of this chapter.) Finally, *refreezing* occurs when the changes made are incorporated into the employees' thinking and the organization's operations (e.g., mechanisms for rewarding behaviors that maintain the changes are put in place). Hence, the new attitudes and behaviors become a new, enduring aspect of the organizational system.

READINESS FOR CHANGE: WHEN WILL ORGANIZATIONAL CHANGE OCCUR?

As you might imagine, there are times when organizations are likely to change, and times during which change is less likely. Even if the need for change is high and resistance to change is low (two important factors), organizational change does not automatically occur.

In general, change is likely to occur when the people involved believe that the benefits associated with making a change outweigh the costs involved. The factors contributing to the benefits of making a change are as follows.

- The amount of dissatisfaction with current conditions.
- The availability of a desirable alternative.
- The existence of a plan for achieving that alternative.

Theorists have claimed that these three factors combine multiplicatively to determine the benefits of making a change. Thus, if any one of these factors is zero, the benefits of making a change, and the likelihood of change itself, are zero. If you think about it, this makes sense. After all, people are unlikely to initiate change if they are not at all dissatisfied, or if they don't have any desirable alternative in mind (or any way of attaining that alternative, if they do have one in mind).

Of course, for change to occur, the expected benefits must outweigh the likely costs involved (e.g., disruption, uncertainties). Professionals in the field of organizational development pay careful attention to these factors before they attempt to initiate any formal, ambitious organizational change programs. Only when the readiness for change is high will organizational change efforts be successful.

WHY IS ORGANIZATIONAL CHANGE RESISTED?

Although people may be unhappy with the current state of affairs confronting them in organizations, they may be afraid that any changes will be potentially disruptive and will only make things worse. Indeed, fear of new conditions is quite real and it creates unwillingness to accept change. Organizational scientists have recognized that **resistance to change** stems from both individual and organizational variables.

Individual Barriers to Change. Researchers have noted several key factors that are known to make people resistant to change in organizations.[7]

1. ECONOMIC INSECURITY. Because any changes on the job have the potential to threaten one's livelihood—by either loss of job or reduced pay—some resistance to change is inevitable.

2. FEAR OF THE UNKNOWN. Employees derive a sense of security from doing things the same way, knowing who their coworkers will be, and whom they're supposed to answer to from day to day. Disrupting these well-established, comfortable patterns creates unfamiliar conditions, a state of affairs that is often rejected.

3. THREATS TO SOCIAL RELATIONSHIPS. As people continue to work within organizations, they form strong bonds with their coworkers. Many organizational changes (e.g., the reassignment of job responsibilities) threaten the integrity of friendship groups that provide valuable social rewards.

4.   HABIT. Jobs that are well learned and become habitual are easy to perform. The prospect of changing the way jobs are done challenges people to develop new job skills. Doing this is clearly more difficult than continuing to perform the job as it was originally learned.

5.   FAILURE TO RECOGNIZE NEED FOR CHANGE. Unless employees can recognize and fully appreciate the need for changes in organizations, any vested interests they may have in keeping things the same may overpower their willingness to accept change.

Organizational Barriers to Change.   Resistance to organizational change also results from conditions associated with organizations themselves.[8] Several such factors may be identified.

1.   STRUCTURAL INERTIA. Organizations are designed to promote stability. To the extent that employees are carefully selected and trained to perform certain jobs, and rewarded for doing them well, the forces acting on individuals to perform in certain ways are very powerfully determined — that is, jobs have *structural inertia.*

2.   WORK GROUP INERTIA. Inertia to continue performing jobs in a specified way comes not only from the jobs themselves but also from the social groups within which people work — *work group inertia.* Because of the development of strong social norms within groups (see Chapter 8), potent pressures exist to perform jobs in certain ways. Introducing change disrupts these established normative expectations, leading to formidable resistance.

3.   THREATS TO EXISTING BALANCE OF POWER. If changes are made with respect to who's in charge, a shift in the balance of power between individuals and organizational subunits is likely to occur. Those units that now control the resources, have the expertise, and wield the power may fear losing their advantageous positions resulting from any organizational change.

4.   PREVIOUSLY UNSUCCESSFUL CHANGE EFFORTS. Anyone who has lived through a past disaster understandably may be reluctant to endure another attempt at the same thing. Similarly, groups or entire organizations that have been unsuccessful in introducing change in the past may be cautious about accepting further attempts at introducing change into the system.

Over the past decade, General Electric (GE) has been undergoing a series of widespread changes in its basic strategy, organizational structure, and relationship with employees. In this process, it experienced several of the barriers just identified. For example, GE managers had mastered a set of bureaucratic traditions that kept their habits strong and their inertia moving straight ahead. The prospect of doing things differently was scary for those who were so strongly entrenched in doing things the "GE way." In particular, the company's interest in globalizing triggered many fears of the unknown. Resistance to change at GM was also strong because it threatened to strip power from those units that traditionally possessed most of it (e.g., the Power Systems and Lighting division). Changes also were highly disruptive to GE's "social architecture"; friendship groups were broken up and scattered throughout the company. In all, GE has been a living example of many different barriers to change all rolled into a single company.

HOW CAN RESISTANCE TO ORGANIZATIONAL CHANGE BE OVERCOME?

Because organizational change is inevitable, managers should be sensitive to the barriers to change so that resistance can be overcome. This, of course, is easier said than done. However, several useful approaches have been suggested, and the key ones are summarized here.[9]

1. **SHAPE POLITICAL DYNAMICS.** In Chapter 6 we described the important role of organizational politics in achieving desired goals. Politics is also involved in getting organizational changes accepted. Politically, resistance to change can be overcome by winning the support of the most powerful and influential individuals. Doing so builds a critical internal mass of support for change. Demonstrating clearly that key organizational leaders endorse the change is an effective way to get others to go along with it—either because they share the leader's vision or because they fear the leader's retaliation. Either way, the political support will facilitate acceptance of change.

2. **EDUCATE THE WORK FORCE.** Sometimes people are reluctant to change because they are uncertain about what the future has in store for them. Fears about economic security, for example, may be put to rest by a few reassuring words from powerholders. As part of educating employees about what organizational changes may mean for them, top management must show a considerable amount of emotional sensitivity. Doing so makes it possible for the people affected by change to become instrumental in making it work. Some companies have found that simply answering the question, "what's in it for me?" can help allay a lot of fears.

> *Sales reps at* **Sandoz Pharmaceuticals** *balked at first when required to use laptop computers for compiling and transmitting sales reports. After it was explained how this technology would free them from the cumbersome job of writing weekly sales reports, the computers were not only accepted, but embraced.*

3. **INVOLVE EMPLOYEES IN THE CHANGE EFFORTS.** It is well established that people who participate in making a decision tend to be more committed to the outcomes of the decision than are those who are not involved. Accordingly, employees who are involved in responding to

GROUP EXERCISE

Recognizing Impediments to Change — And How to Overcome Them

To confront the reality of organizational change, one of the most fundamental steps involves recognizing the barriers to change. Then, once these impediments have been identified, consideration can be given to ways of overcoming them. This exercise is designed to help you practice thinking along these lines while working in groups.

DIRECTIONS

1. Divide the class into groups of approximately six and gather each group around a circle.

2. Each group should consider each of the following situations.

    Situation A: *A highly sophisticated e-mail system is being introduced at a large university. It will replace the practice of transmitting memos on paper.*

    Situation B: *A very popular employee who has been with the company for many years is retiring. He will be replaced by a completely new employee from the outside.*

3. For each situation, discuss three major impediments to change.

4. Identify a way of overcoming each of these impediments.

5. Someone from the group should record the answers and present them to the class for a discussion session.

QUESTIONS FOR DISCUSSION

1. For each of the situations, were the impediments to change similar or different?

2. Were the ways of overcoming the impediments similar or different?

3. How might the nature of the situation confronted dictate the types of change barriers confronted and the ease with which these may be overcome?

unplanned change, or who are made part of the team charged with planning a needed organizational change, may be expected to have very little resistance to change. Organizational changes that are "sprung" on the work force with little or no warning might be expected to encounter resistance simply as a knee-jerk reaction until employees are able to assess how the changes will affect them. In contrast, employees who are involved in the change process are better able to understand the need for change, and are therefore less likely to resist it.

Says Duane Hartley, general manager of Hewlett-Packard's microwave instruments division, "I don't think people really enjoy change, but if they can participate in it and understand it, it can become a positive [experience] for them."[10] It is precisely these kinds of efforts at participative management that are credited with the ready acceptance of changes in Southwestern Bell after the breakup of AT&T.

4. **REWARD CONSTRUCTIVE BEHAVIORS.** One rather obvious and quite successful mechanism for facilitating organizational change is rewarding people for behaving in the desired fashion. Changing organizational operations may necessitate changing the kinds of behaviors that need to be rewarded by the organization. This is especially critical when an organization is in the transition period of introducing the change. For example, employees who are required to learn to use new equipment should be praised for their successful efforts. Feedback on how well they are doing not only provides a great deal of useful assurance to uncertain employees but also helps shape the desired behavior.

Although these four suggestions may be easier to state than to implement, efforts at following them will be well rewarded. Given the many forces that make employees resistant to change, managers should keep these guidelines in mind. (For a chance to think more about resistance to organizational change and ways to overcome it, see the preceding **Group Exercise.**)

ORGANIZATIONAL DEVELOPMENT INTERVENTIONS: IMPLEMENTING PLANNED CHANGE

Now that we have examined the basic issues surrounding organizational change, we are ready to look at planned ways of implementing it—collectively known as techniques of **organizational development (OD).** Formally, we may define organizational development as *a set of social science techniques designed to plan and implement change in work settings for purposes of enhancing the personal development of individuals and improving the effectiveness of organizational functioning.* By planning organizationwide changes involving people, OD seeks to enhance organizational performance by improving the quality of the work environment and the attitudes and well-being of employees.

Over the years, many different strategies for implementing planned organizational change (referred to as *OD interventions*) have been used by specialists attempting to improve organizational functioning (referred to as *OD practitioners*). All the major methods of organizational development attempt to produce some kind of change in individual employees, work groups, and/or entire organizations. This is the goal of the five OD interventions we will review here.

SURVEY FEEDBACK

For effective organizational change to occur, employees must understand the organization's current strengths and weaknesses. That's the underlying rationale behind the **survey feedback** method. This technique follows the three steps summarized in Figure 11-3. First, data are collected that provide information about matters of general concern to employees, such as organizational climate, leadership style, and job satisfaction. This may take the form of intensive interviews or structured questionnaires, or both. Because it is important that this information be as unbiased as possible, employees providing feedback should be assured that their responses will be kept confidential. For this reason, this process is usually conducted by outside consultants.

The second step calls for reporting the information obtained back to the employees during small group meetings. Typically, this consists of summarizing the average scores on the attitudes assessed in the survey. Profiles are created of feelings about the organization, its leadership, the work done, and related topics. Discussions also focus on why the scores are as they are, and what problems are revealed by the feedback. The final step involves analyzing problems dealing with communication, decision making, and other organizational processes to make plans for dealing with them. Such discussions are usually most effective when they are carefully documented and a specific plan of implementation is made, with someone put in charge of carrying it out.

Survey feedback is a widely used organizational development technique. This is not surprising in view of the advantages it offers. It is efficient, allowing a great deal of information to be collected relatively quickly. Also it is very flexible and can be tailored to the needs of different organizations facing a variety of problems. However, the technique can be no better than the quality of the questionnaire used—it must measure the things that really matter to employees. Of course, to derive the maximum benefit from survey feedback, it must have the support of top management. The plans developed by the small

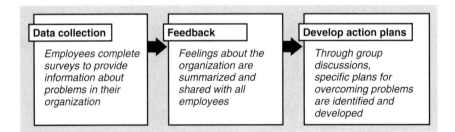

■ *Figure 11-3 Survey Feedback*

The *survey feedback* method of OD follows the three steps outlined here: collecting data, giving feedback, and developing action plans.

discussion groups must be capable of being implemented with the full approval of the organization. When these conditions are met, survey feedback can be a very effective OD technique.

QUALITY OF WORK LIFE PROGRAMS

When you think of work, do you think of drudgery? Although many people believe these two terms go together naturally, it has grown increasingly popular to systematically improve the quality of life experienced on the job. As more people demand satisfying and personally fulfilling places to work, OD practitioners have attempted systematically to create work situations that enhance employees' motivation, satisfaction, and commitment—factors that may contribute to high levels of organizational performance. Such efforts are known collectively as **quality of work life (QWL)** programs. Specifically, such programs are ways of increasing organizational output and improving quality by involving employees in the decisions that affect them on their jobs. Typically, QWL programs support the highly democratic treatment of employees at all levels and encourage their participation in decision making. Although many approaches to improving the quality of work life exist, they all share a common goal: humanizing the workplace.

One popular approach to improving the quality of work life involves **work restructuring**—the process of changing the way jobs are done to make them more interesting to workers. We already discussed several such approaches to redesigning jobs—including *job enlargement, job enrichment,* and the *job characteristics model*—in our discussion of motivation in Chapter 3. These techniques are also considered effective ways of improving the quality of work life for employees.

Another approach to improving the quality of work life is **quality circles (QCs).** These are small groups of volunteers (usually around ten) who meet regularly (usually weekly) to identify and solve problems related to the quality of the work they perform and the conditions under which people do their jobs. An organization may have several QCs operating at once, each dealing with a particular work area about which it has the most expertise. To help them work effectively, the members of the circle usually receive some form of training in problem solving. Large companies such as Westinghouse, Hewlett-Packard, and Eastman Kodak, to name only a few, have included QCs as part of their QWL efforts. Groups have dealt with issues such as how to reduce vandalism, how to create safer and more comfortable working environments, and how to improve product quality. Research has shown that although quality circles are very effective at bringing about short-term improvements in quality of work life (i.e., those lasting up to 18 months), they are less effective at creating more permanent changes.

As you might imagine, a variety of benefits (even if short-term ones) might result from QWL programs. These fall into three major categories. The most direct benefit is usually improvements in work-related attitudes and the benefits associated with them (see Chapter 4)—that is, increased job satisfaction, organizational commitment, and reduced turnover. A second benefit is increased productivity. Related to these first two benefits is a third—namely, increased organizational effectiveness (e.g., profitability, goal attainment). Many companies, such as Ford, General Electric, and AT&T, have active QWL programs and are reportedly quite pleased with their results.

Achieving these benefits is not automatic, however. Two major potential pitfalls must be avoided for QWL programs to be successfully implemented. First, both *management and labor must cooperate in designing the program.* Should any one side believe that the program is really just a method of gaining an advantage over the other, it is doomed to fail. Second, the *plans agreed to by all concerned parties must be fully implemented.* It is too easy for action plans developed in QWL groups to be forgotten amid the hectic pace of daily activities. It is the responsibility of employees at all levels—from the highest-ranking executive to the lowest-level laborer—to follow through on their parts of the plan.

MANAGEMENT BY OBJECTIVES

In Chapter 3 we discussed the motivational benefits of setting specific goals. As you might imagine, not only individuals but entire organizations stand to benefit from setting specific goals. For example, an organization may strive to "raise production" and "improve the quality" of its manufactured goods. These goals, well-intentioned though they may be, may not be as useful to an organization as more specific ones, such as "increase production of widgets by 15 percent" or "lower the failure rate of widgets by 25 percent." After all, as the old saying goes, "It's usually easier to get somewhere if you know where you're going." Management expert Peter Drucker, consulting for General Electric during the early 1950s, was well aware of this idea and is credited with promoting the benefits of specifying clear organizational goals—a technique known as **management by objectives (MBO).**

The MBO process, summarized in Figure 11-4, consists of three basic steps. First, goals are selected that employees will try to attain to best serve the needs of the organization. The goals should be selected by managers and their subordinates together and not simply imposed. Furthermore, these goals should be directly measurable and have some time frame attached to them. Goals that cannot be measured (e.g., "make the company better") or that have no time limits are useless. It is also crucial that managers and their subordinates work together to plan ways of attaining the goals they have selected—developing what is known as an *action plan.*

Once goals are set and action plans have been developed, the second step calls for *implementation*—carrying out the plan and regularly assessing its progress. Is the plan working? Are the goals being approximated? Are there any problems being encountered in attempting to meet the goals? Such ques-

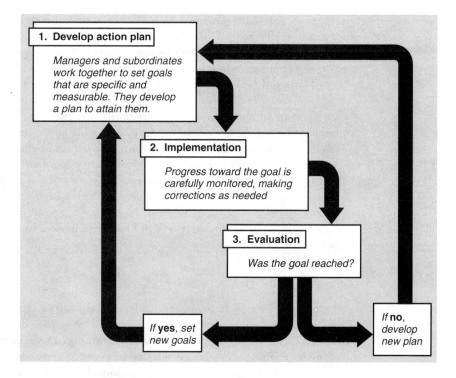

1. Develop action plan

Managers and subordinates work together to set goals that are specific and measurable. They develop a plan to attain them.

2. Implementation

Progress toward the goal is carefully monitored, making corrections as needed

3. Evaluation

Was the goal reached?

If **yes***, set new goals*

If **no***, develop new plan*

■ *Figure 11-4 Management by Objectives*

The OD technique of *management by objectives (MBO)* requires managers and their subordinates to work together on setting and trying to achieve important organizational goals. The basic steps of the process are outlined here.

tions need to be considered while implementing an action plan. If the plan is failing, a midcourse correction may be in order—changing the plan, the way it's carried out, or even the goal itself. Finally, after monitoring progress toward the goal, the third step may be instituted: *evaluation*—assessing goal attainment. Were the organization's goals reached? If so, what new goals should be set to improve things still further? If not, what new plans can be initiated to help meet the goals? Because the ultimate assessment of the extent to which goals are met helps determine the selection of new goals, MBO is a continuous process.

MBO represents a potentially effective source of planning and implementing strategic change for organizations. Individual efforts designed to meet organizational goals get the individual employee and the organization itself working together toward common ends. Hence, systemwide change results. Of course, for MBO to work, everyone involved has to buy into it. Because MBO programs typically require a great deal of participation by lower-level

employees, top managers must be willing to accept and support the cooperation and involvement of all. Making MBO work also requires a great deal of
time—anywhere from three to five years. Hence, MBO may be inappropriate
in organizations that do not have the time to commit to making it work.

Despite these considerations, MBO has become one of the most widely
used techniques for affecting organizational change in recent years. It not only
is used on an ad hoc basis by many organizations, but it also constitutes an in-
grained element of the organizational culture in some companies, such as
Hewlett-Packard and IBM. An MBO program was used effectively by Northwest Airlines in 1989 to help improve various areas of performance in its At-
lanta-based crew. The program was reportedly effective in meeting such vital
goals as reducing injuries by 50 percent and raising on-time departures to 95
percent, thereby helping to improve Northwest's overall safety and performance record. Given the success MBO has experienced, its widespread use is
not surprising.

SENSITIVITY TRAINING

The method by which small, face-to-face group interaction experiences are
used to give people insight into themselves (e.g., who they are, the way others
respond to them) is known as **sensitivity training.** Developed in the 1940s,
sensitivity training groups (also referred to as *encounter groups, laboratory groups,*
or *T-groups*) were among the first organizational development techniques used
in organizations (such as Standard Oil and Union Carbide). The rationale behind sensitivity training is that people are usually not completely open and
honest with each other, a condition that thwarts insights into oneself and others. However, when people are placed in special situations within which open,
honest communication is allowed and encouraged, personal insights may be
gained. To do this, small groups (usually about eight to fifteen) are created
and meet away from the pressures of the job site for several days. An expert
trainer (referred to as the *facilitator*) guides the group at all times, helping assure that the proper atmosphere is maintained.

The sessions themselves are completely open with respect to what is discussed. Often, to get the ball rolling, the facilitator will frustrate the group
members by not getting involved at all, appearing to be passively goofing off.
As members sit around and engage in meaningless chit-chat, they begin to feel
angry at the facilitator for wasting their time. Once these expressions of anger
begin to emerge, the facilitator has created the important first step needed to
make the session work—he or she has given the group a chance to focus on a
current event. At this point, the discussion may be guided into how each of the
group members expresses his or her anger toward the others. They are encouraged to continue discussing these themes openly and honestly, and not to
hide their true feelings as they would often do on the job. So, for example, if
you think someone is relying too much on you, this is the time to say so. Par-

ticipants are encouraged to respond by giving each other *immediate feedback* to what was said. By doing this, it is reasoned, people will learn more about how they interrelate with others, and will become more skilled at interpersonal relations. These are among the major goals of sensitivity groups.

It probably comes as no surprise to you that the effectiveness of sensitivity training is difficult to assess. After all, measuring insight into one's own personality is clearly elusive. Even if interpersonal skills seem to be improved, people will not always be able to successfully transfer their newly learned skills when they leave the artificial training atmosphere and return to their jobs. As a result, sensitivity training tends not to be used extensively by itself for OD purposes. Rather, as we will see, it is often used in conjunction with, or as part of, other OD techniques.

TEAM BUILDING

The technique of **team building** applies the techniques and rationale of sensitivity training to work groups. The approach attempts to get members of a work group to diagnose how they work together, and to plan how this may be improved. Given the importance of group efforts in effective organizational functioning, attempts to improve the effectiveness of work groups are likely to have profound effects on organizations. If one assumes that work groups are the basic building blocks of organizations, it follows that organizational change should emphasize changing groups instead of individuals.

Team building begins when members of a group admit that they have a problem and gather data to provide insight into it. The problems that are identified may come from sensitivity training sessions or more objective sources, such as production figures or attitude surveys. These data are then shared, in a *diagnostic session*, to develop a consensus regarding the group's current strengths and weaknesses. From this, a list of desired changes is created, along with some plans for implementing these changes. In other words, an *action plan* is developed—some task-oriented approach to solving the group's problems as diagnosed. Following this step, the plan is carried out, and its progress is evaluated to determine whether the originally identified problems remain. If the problems are solved, the process is completed and the team may stop meeting. If not, the process should be restarted. (See Figure 11-5 on p. 316 for a summary of these steps.)

Work teams have been used effectively to combat a variety of important organizational problems. For these efforts to be successful, however, all group members must participate in the gathering and evaluating of information as well as the planning and implementing of action plans. Input from group members is also especially crucial in evaluating the effectiveness of the team-building program.[11] Keep in mind that because the team-building approach is highly task-oriented, interpersonal problems between group members may be disruptive and need to be neutralized by an outside party. With interpersonal

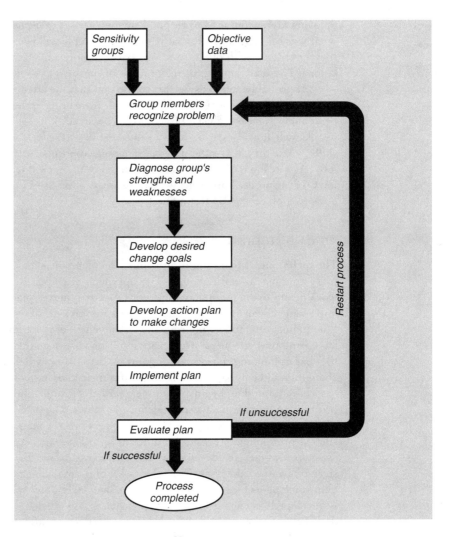

■ *Figure 11-5 Team Building*

Team building, a popular OD technique, follows the steps outlined here.

strain out of the way, the stage is set for groups to learn to effectively solve their own problems. However, this does not happen overnight. To be effective, team building should *not* be approached as a one-time exercise undertaken during a few days away from the job. Rather, it should be thought of as an on-going process that takes several months (or even years) to develop. Given the great impact effective teams can have on organizational functioning (see Chapter 8), efforts to build effective work teams seem quite worthwhile.

Some techniques used in team-building exercises for attaining high levels of interpersonal trust are highly unorthodox. For example, as part of many team-building exercises, group members are put into highly challenging real-life situations that are metaphors for how they have to pull together to meet challenges on the job. The idea is that by facing these difficult off-the-job challenges successfully, they will develop the skills needed for working together effectively on the job. (For a look at the growing business of helping businesses conduct such adventures, see the following **Winning Practices** section.)

CRITICAL ISSUES IN ORGANIZATIONAL DEVELOPMENT

No discussion of organizational development would be complete without addressing two very important questions—do the techniques work, and are they ethical?

THE EFFECTIVENESS OF ORGANIZATIONAL DEVELOPMENT: DOES IT REALLY WORK?

Thus far, we have described some of the major techniques used by OD practitioners to improve organizational functioning. As is probably clear, carrying out these techniques requires a considerable amount of time, money, and effort. Accordingly, it is appropriate to ask if this investment is worthwhile. In other words, does OD really work? Given the popularity of OD in organizations, this question is very important.

Research has revealed that the answer is a qualified "yes." In other words, although many studies have revealed beneficial effects associated with OD programs, the findings are far from unanimous. Consider, for example, research on quality circles. Although many researchers have found that QCs help reduce organizational costs and improve employees' attitudes, other studies reported no such beneficial effects.[15] Mixed results also have been obtained in many studies assessing the effectiveness of sensitivity training programs. For example, whereas such programs often lead to temporary differences in the way people interact with others, the results tend to be short-lived on the job and are not related to permanent changes in the way people behave. Thus, whereas OD may have many positive effects, not all desired outcomes may be realized.

Recently, scientists compared the results of 49 OD studies published between 1975 and 1986.[16] Among the different types of OD interventions studied were those we described: MBO, QWL, survey feedback, sensitivity groups, and team building. The investigators categorized the research with respect to whether they found the effects of the interventions to be beneficial,

Successful Adventures Hold the Key to Successful Ventures

What do the following have in common: rafting down the rapids, guiding a dog sled through the frozen tundra, and finding your way out of a wilderness preserve? The answer, believe it or not, is that they are all techniques designed to build strong bonds between employees of companies who work together in teams.

To build team skills, executives at the French conglomerate Groupe Bull have gone on a white-water rafting expedition. Forsaking the comfort and safety of their conference table, they braved the swirling waters of the river Spey in the mountains of Scotland in a small raft. In theory, learning to work together on navigating a raft down a treacherous river can help team members recognize how they interact with each other while navigating the rough waters of business.

But white-water rafting is not the only metaphor that has been called on to help develop work teams. Another challenging activity that takes executives outdoors to learn to work together has become popular lately—sled dog trips into the northern wilderness, known as *mushing*. In response to growing corporate interest in these experiences, several companies have gone into the business of outfitting and organizing such excursions. According to Ted Young, manager of northern Minnesota's Boundary Country Trekking, "It's a real team-building experience. You can't do a dog sled trip without helping each other."[12] In the words of the editor of *Mushing* magazine, "Mushing seems to be the up and coming executive thing."[13]

The analogies between mushing dogs and managing people back on the job are fascinating. To begin the expedition, for example, five to seven dogs have to be harnessed into sleds. While completing this hour-long process, executives can see how the dogs react differently based on how they are paired. Each is an individual, and they need to be put together so that they can work effectively—just like people. The ultimate lesson has been nicely articulated by Walter Kissling, the CEO of the Minneapolis-based chemical company, H.B. Fuller: "Five rather small dogs [35 to 55 pounds] can be very powerful. If you can get a team pulling in one direction, you can get enormous power out of them. If you can do that in management, think of what the results are."[14]

Sure, these adventures are fun and interesting, but the key question is: Do they work? Ultimately, the effectiveness of such an approach depends on the extent to which participants come away from the experience with the type of insight desired and the ability to translate these new-found ideas into meaningful work-related activities. By itself, some rafting or trekking expeditions are not likely to make executives become a cohesive team. However, such adventures can be very valuable when they are part of an ongoing program of regular team development.

harmful, or nonexistent. The outcomes studied were both individual (e.g., job satisfaction) and organizational (e.g., profit, productivity) in nature. A sizable percentage of the studies found the effects of the various interventions to be beneficial—mostly in the area of improving organizational functioning.

We hasten to add that any conclusions about the effectiveness of OD should be qualified in several important ways. First, OD interventions tend to be more effective among blue-collar employees than among white-collar employees. Second, the beneficial effects of OD can be enhanced by using a combination of several techniques (e.g., four or more together) instead of any single one. Finally, the effectiveness of OD techniques depends on the degree of support they receive from top management: The more programs are supported from the top, the more successful they tend to be.

Despite the importance of attempting to evaluate the effectiveness of OD interventions, a great many of them go unevaluated. Although there are undoubtedly many reasons for this, one key factor is the difficulty of assessing change. Because many factors can cause people to behave differently in organizations, and because such behaviors may be difficult to measure, many OD practitioners avoid the problem of measuring change altogether. In a related vein, political pressures to justify OD programs may discourage some OD professionals from honestly and accurately assessing their effectiveness. After all, in doing so, one runs the risk of scientifically demonstrating that one has wasted time and money.

We may conclude that despite some limitations, organizational development is an approach that shows considerable promise in its ability to benefit organizations and the individuals working within them.

IS ORGANIZATIONAL DEVELOPMENT INHERENTLY UNETHICAL? A DEBATE

By its very nature, OD applies powerful social science techniques in an attempt to change attitudes and behavior. From the perspective of a manager attempting to accomplish various goals, such tools are immediately recognized as very useful. However, if you think about it from the perspective of the individual being affected, several ethical issues arise.

For example, it has been argued that OD techniques impose the values of the organization on the individual without taking the individual's own attitudes into account. OD is a very one-sided approach, reflecting the imposition of the more powerful organization on the less powerful individual. A related issue is that the OD process does not provide any free choice on the part of the employees. As a result, it may be seen as *coercive* and *manipulative*. When faced with a "do it, or else" situation, employees tend to have little free choice and are forced to allow themselves to be manipulated, a potentially degrading prospect.

Another issue is that the unequal power relationship between the organization and its employees makes it possible for the true intent of OD techniques to be misrepresented. As an example, imagine that an MBO technique is presented to employees as a means of allowing greater organizational participation, whereas in reality it is used as a means for holding individuals responsible for their poor performance and punishing them as a result. Although such an event might not happen, the potential for abuse of this type does exist, and the potential to misuse the technique—even if not originally intended— might later prove to be too great a temptation.

Despite these considerations, many professionals do not agree that OD is inherently unethical. Such a claim, it has been countered, is to say that the practice of management is itself unethical. After all, the very act of going to work for an organization requires one to submit to the organization's values and the overall values of society at large. One cannot help but face life situations in which others' values are imposed. This is not to say that organizations have the right to impose patently unethical values on people for the purpose of making a profit (e.g., stealing from customers). Indeed, because they have the potential to abuse their power (such as in the preceding MBO example), organizations have a special obligation to refrain from doing so.

Although abuses of organizational power are all too common, OD itself is not necessarily the culprit. Indeed, like any other tool (even a gun!), OD is not inherently good or evil. Instead, *whether the tool is used for good or evil will depend on the individual using it.* With this in mind, the ethical use of OD interventions will require that they be supervised by professionals in an organization that places a high value on ethics. To the extent that top-management officials embrace ethical values and behave ethically themselves, norms for behaving ethically are likely to develop in organizations. When an organization has a strong ethical culture, it is unlikely that OD practitioners would even think of misusing their power to harm individuals. The need to develop such a culture has been recognized as a way for organizations to take not only moral leadership in their communities, but financial leadership as well.

SUMMARY:
PUTTING IT TO USE

Changes in organizations may be either planned or unplanned. Planned changes may include changes in products or services, changes in administrative systems, or changes in organizational size and structure. Decisions to engage in *downsizing* (reorganizing the structure of an organization in a manner that reduces the need for as many employees) and *outsourcing* (eliminating peripheral organizational functions and purchasing them from outside the organization) fall into this category. Planned changes also include the introduction of new technologies and advances in information processing and communication. Unplanned changes include shifts in the demographic characteristics of the work force, responses to performance gaps, governmental regulation, and economic competition.

Organizations may change with respect to their organizational structure (responsibilities and procedures used), the technology used on the job, and the people who perform the work. Change is likely to occur whenever the benefits associated with making a change (i.e., dissatisfaction with current conditions, the availability of desirable alternatives, and the existence of a plan for achieving that alternative) outweigh the costs involved. In general, people are resistant to change because of individual factors (e.g., economic insecurity, fear of the unknown) and organizational factors (e.g., the stability of work groups, threats to the existing balance of power). However, resistance to change can be overcome in several ways, including educating the work force about the effects of the changes and involving employees in the change process.

Techniques for planning organizational change in order to enhance personal and organizational outcomes are collectively known as **organizational development (OD)** practices. For example, **survey feedback** uses questionnaires and/or interviews as the basis for identifying organizational problems, which are then addressed in planning sessions. **Quality of work life** programs attempt to humanize the workplace by involving employees in the decisions affecting them (e.g., through quality circle meetings) and by restructuring the jobs themselves. **Management by objectives (MBO)** focuses on attempts by managers and their subordinates to work together at setting important organizational goals and developing a plan to help meet them. **Sensitivity training** is a technique in which group discussions are used to enhance interpersonal awareness and reduce interpersonal friction. Finally **team building** involves using work groups to diagnose and develop specific plans for solving problems with respect to their functioning as a work unit. The rationale underlying all six of these techniques is that they may enhance organizational functioning by involving employees in identifying and solving organizational problems.

The effectiveness of most organizational development programs has not been systematically assessed in practice, and the few studies that have attempted to measure the success of such programs have not been carefully conducted. However, those studies that have systematically evaluated organizational development programs generally find them to be successful in improving organizational functioning and, to a lesser degree, individual satisfaction. Some have argued that OD is unethical for several reasons, most notably because it has the potential to be used for illegitimate purposes. However, others counter that OD is just a tool and that it is people who are at fault for using it inappropriately.

You Be the Consultant

Things have been rough for the former employees at Small Town S&L ever since their institution was bought up by Big City Trust. Big City's culture and operating procedures are much more formal and nowhere as casual as those formerly found at Small Town. The CEO of Big City is concerned about the employees' adjustment to the change and calls you in to help. Answer the following questions relevant to this situation based on the material in this chapter.

1. Besides new operating procedures, what other planned and un-planned changes would you suspect as being responsible for the em-ployees' negative responses?

2. What are the barriers to change encountered in this situation, and what steps would you propose to overcome them?

3. Do you think that an OD intervention would help in this case? If so, which one do you propose, and why?

CHAPTER 12

Confronting Challenges in Today's Organizations

PREVIEW OF CHAPTER HIGHLIGHTS

Stress is a pattern of emotional states and physiological reactions occurring in response to demands (known as **stressors**) from outside or inside an organization. Prolonged exposure to stress can result in **burnout,** in which exhaustion is coupled with feelings of inadequacy.

Because stress reactions can be very severe (adversely affecting both health and job performance), many measures can be taken to alleviate its effects.

The high levels of **diversity** found in today's American work force sometimes cause disruptive intergroup conflict. Fortunately, steps can be taken to minimize this problem.

Technology has been used in ways that both eliminate jobs and make it possible for many people to do their work away from the office (i.e., **telecommute**).

The rise of **the global economy** has given birth to **multinational corporations,** in which communication problems must be confronted.

Today's organizations are concerned with promoting quality and rely on **total quality management** and **reengineering** as approaches to delivering better goods and services.

Although **unethical business practices** still occur, people have grown intolerant of them. Several steps can be taken to promote ethical behavior on the part of individual employees.

As we have detailed throughout this book, there is not much about the behavior of people in organizations that can be considered simple and straightforward. In fact, it is subject to influence by a wide variety of different factors, thereby making it extremely complex to understand and difficult to predict with certainty. All of this makes the task of managing behavior in organizations especially challenging.

Elevating this challenge are certain trends and forces acting on today's organizations that conspire to make the manager's job more formidable than ever. Insofar as they promise to complete our understanding of behavior in organizations, we will highlight some of these challenges in this final chapter. Some of these challenges reside in the nature of the work force. These include working under extremely stressful conditions and confronting conflicts found in organizations whose employees come from highly diverse backgrounds. Additional challenges are created by the high-tech nature of today's organizations. For example, technology appears to be responsible for reductions in the number of permanent jobs available and the growing tendency for people to do their work from remote locations, often without ever leaving their homes. Finally, today's organizations face challenges associated with society at large. Among these are the need to adapt to a global economy, a growing focus on producing high quality goods and services, and heightened interest in doing things that are socially responsible and ethical. We will consider all of these challenges in this chapter.

CHALLENGES ASSOCIATED WITH THE WORK FORCE

Various aspects of today's work force make it particularly difficult to manage people at work. Two such forces are particularly noteworthy and will be considered in this section of the chapter: the high levels of stress and burnout occurring among many of today's employees, and conflicts arising from the coming together of people from highly diverse racial and ethnic groups.

ALL STRESSED OUT AND NO PLACE TO GO: BURNOUT IN THE 1990s

A recent survey by the Northwestern National Life Insurance Company found that in recent years one American in three had seriously considered quitting his or her job due to work-related stress. Those who stick it out are likely to face the consequences—accidents, poor job performance, and illnesses as serious as cancer, colitis, and heart disease. In fact, in less than a decade, the incidence of stress-induced disabilities has more than doubled. And the victims of stress are not only individual workers but their organizations as well, which have been estimated to bear an average cost of $73,270 per employee due to stress-induced absenteeism and turnover. There can be little doubt that this phenomenon represents a daunting challenge to organizations.

Basic Definitions. Whether it's a holiday gathering, a change in working conditions, the birth of a new baby, or the loss of your favorite suit by the dry cleaner, life is full of events that put demands on us. Such stimuli are known as **stressors,** defined as *any demands, either physical or psychological in nature, encountered during the course of living.* The way we respond to these demands is known as **stress**—*the pattern of emotional states and physiological reactions occurring in response to demands from inside or outside organizations (i.e., stressors).*

Contrary to popular belief, reactions to stress are not always negative. For example, an intense game of racquetball can be quite stressful but interpreted very positively. In order for reactions to stressors to be negative, people must cognitively appraise the situation they confront as both threatening and beyond their control. So, for example, a person facing job loss or transfer to a new facility may find these situations very stressful. Both impose threats and conditions that are difficult to do anything about. Sometimes physiological and psychological stress reactions are so great that they take their toll on the body and mind, resulting in such maladies as insomnia, cardiovascular disease, and depression. Such reactions are referred to as **strain,** defined as *deviations from normal states of human functioning resulting from stressful events.*

Although most people manage to keep their stress under control, others are not as fortunate. Over time they are worn down by stress and suffer from a condition commonly known as **burnout.** Formally, burnout is *a syndrome in which exhaustion is coupled with feelings of personal inadequacy as a result of prolonged exposure to intense stress.* Specifically, burnout is characterized by four key symptoms:

- **Physical exhaustion**—fatigue, lack of energy, insomnia, headaches
- **Emotional exhaustion**—depression, feelings of hopelessness
- **Attitudinal exhaustion**—cynicism, negative views of others and oneself
- **Feelings of low personal accomplishment**—recognizing one's lack of success

For a summary of the relationships between stressors, stress, strain, and burnout, see Figure 12-1 on p. 326.

Causes of Stress and Burnout. Unfortunately, the workplace is a virtual minefield of factors resulting in stress and burnout. Here are a few key determinants.[1]

- **Occupational demands.** As you might imagine, some jobs (e.g., police officer, emergency room doctor) are potentially more stressful than others (e.g., librarian, janitor). In general, the

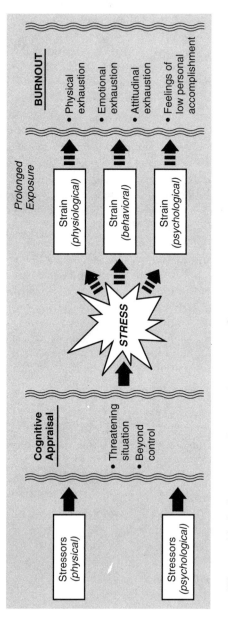

■ *Figure 12-1 Stressors, Stress, Strain, and Burnout*

Stimuli known as stressors lead to stress reactions when they are cognitively appraised as threatening and beyond one's control. The deviations from normal states resulting from stress are known as strain. Prolonged stressful experiences lead to burnout.

stressful jobs tend to involve unstructured tasks, unpleasant working conditions, and the making of important decisions.

- **Conflict between work and nonwork life.** It is very common today for people to face conflicts between the demands imposed by their jobs and their families. Being a good spouse or parent requires spending time with the family, time that may be required to perform one's job. The resulting conflict is an all-too-prevalent source of stress.

- **Uncertainty.** Quite often, people find that a fair amount of ambiguity surrounds their jobs. They don't know exactly what is expected of them, or how to divide their time between various tasks. Such uncertainty is generally disliked and is a common source of stress.

- **Overload and underload.** As organizations downsize (see Chapter 11), the remaining employees often experience *overload*, and are expected to do more work than ever before. This may be very stress-inducing. Likewise, stress results when people are not being used to their full capacity. Such *underload* results in boredom and can be just as stressful as overload.

- **Sexual harassment.** As many as 30 percent of women report that they have been the victims of *sexual harassment*—that is, unwanted contact or communication of a sexual nature. Direct affronts to the victim's personal dignity and the harasser's interference with the victim's ability to perform the job make sexual harassment a serious source of stress.

Effects of Stress and Burnout. Unfortunately, the problems associated with prolonged exposure to stressful conditions read like a list of everything negative you can imagine—both for individuals and the organizations in which they work. Here are a few of the major problems.

- **Poor job performance.** Although some people do better than others under stressful conditions, research makes it clear that in general, even relatively low levels of stress take their toll on job performance. Not only does performance suffer on physical tasks, but also cognitive ones—such as decision making.

- **Medical ailments.** Prolonged exposure to stressful conditions has been linked to such degenerative diseases as lung disease, cancer, diabetes, heart disease, and stroke, and also infectious diseases, such as colds and flu.[2]

- **Behavioral problems.** People respond to stress by exhibiting such problematic behaviors as abusing alcohol and drugs, and smoking. Stress also has been linked to accident proneness and to acts of violence (such as those in recent years by some U.S. Postal Service employees).

- **Psychological problems.** Stress has been found to cause such problems as sexual dysfunction, depression, family conflict, and sleep disturbances (e.g., insomnia).

Following from all these problems is another—chronic absenteeism. It makes sense that people with such serious problems as those noted here will often be absent from their jobs. In view of these adverse effects, it should not be surprising to learn that many of today's organizations are taking steps to re-

---

SELF-ASSESSMENT EXERCISE

Training Yourself to Relax

One of the most effective things we can do to control our own stress levels is to relax. Relaxation helps reduce physiological strain on the body, minimizing the long-term damage that may be caused by exposure to stressors. Although you already know how to relax, we're talking here about a deeper kind of relaxation than normal. Give it a try—but carefully read the following directions and hints before beginning.

DIRECTIONS

As in other things, preparation is critical. Find a quiet, comfortable place where you can be free from distractions for approximately 20 minutes. Then follow each of these steps (adapted from Quick & Quick, 1984; see Note 1).

1. Sit quietly in a comfortable position.

2. Close your eyes.

3. Starting at your feet and working your way up toward your head, deeply relax each of your muscles. (This will take some concentration and practice.)

4. Breathe easily and naturally through your nose, concentrating on each individual breath. Each time you exhale, repeat the word "one" (or any similar simple sound) silently to yourself. (This is your *mantra.*)

5. Continue this process for about 10 to 20 minutes. (It's okay to open your eyes occasionally to check the clock, but *do not use an alarm!*) After you're finished, do not jump up; remain quietly seated for a few minutes longer and then slowly rise.

duce, avoid, or eliminate the problems of stress. We will now describe some of these measures.

Stress Management: Some Effective Techniques.   Stress stems from so many different sources that it is virtually impossible to eliminate. However, several effective steps can be taken to help people *cope* with stress—that is, to reduce its intensity and minimize its harmful effects.

At the organizational level, reduced levels of stress have been found to occur under several conditions. For example, employees tend to suffer less stress when their organizations are highly decentralized, therefore allowing

HINTS

1. Don't obsess about reaching a deep level of concentration. You probably won't be able to do so at first. But with practice, you will be able to achieve relaxation very quickly.

2. When distracting thoughts enter your mind, simply ignore them and return to repeating your mantra.

3. Practice this technique once or twice daily, but never within two hours after eating a meal (the process of digestion interferes with the ability to relax). It might take several weeks, or even months, to get to the point where you can relax without mental interference, so be patient.

QUESTIONS FOR DISCUSSION

1. Were you skeptical about this process at first? How did trying this technique change the way you feel? Did you become a greater believer in the benefits of relaxation?

2. At first, how long did it take you to achieve deep relaxation? With practice, were you successful at reducing this time?

3. Did you find that the more you practiced this technique, the less you became distracted by outside thoughts entering your mind?

4. Did this technique work for you? In other words, has it helped relieve stress in your life? If so, what particular sources of stress were most effectively alleviated?

them to have a fair amount of control over the decisions regarding their work (see Chapter 10). Similarly, stress is likely to be abated among people performing jobs that are enlarged—that is, when the scope of job activities is broadened so as to reduce boredom (see Chapter 3).

As you might imagine, it is often impractical for companies to change the way they structure their organization as a whole or the jobs that employees do. This does not mean, however, that the harmful effects of stress cannot be managed. Fortunately, stress can be controlled at the individual level in several ways. These include the following:

- **Lifestyle management.** A healthy diet, especially one low in saturated fats and salt and high in fiber and vitamins, helps the body cope with the physiological effects of stress. So too does physical fitness: People who exercise regularly are less likely to suffer the medical problems linked to stress. For this reason, many companies provide "wellness programs" and exercise facilities for their employees. The Adolph Coors Co., for example, has a separate building housing an elaborate gym and nutritional counseling services for its employees.

- **Behavior management.** There are several behaviors that people can learn to help them reduce the effects of stress. For example, when faced with a stressor, people may take a *time out,* interrupting the cycle of tension that accompanies stress by taking a short break. It also helps to build pleasurable events into one's life, such as by engaging in leisure pursuits or hobbies.

- **Relaxation training.** When we relax, our bodies dissipate tension, making it possible for us to not only stay healthy, but also to concentrate more carefully on what we're doing. For these reasons, companies such as Marriott and Polaroid teach their employees to relax—not to goof off, mind you, but to systematically train their muscles to relax whenever they feel themselves becoming tense. (For a demonstration of one way this may be done, see the **Self-Assessment Exercise** on pp. 328–329.)

INTERGROUP CONFLICT IN A DIVERSE WORK FORCE

Only a few years ago the American work force was composed predominantly of white males. But now things are changing. White males represent less than half of the current American work force, and this figure is expected to drop to under 40 percent by 2005. One key reason why this proportion is changing so rapidly is that growing numbers of African-Americans, Hispanic-Americans, Asian-Americans, and foreign nationals are entering the American work force, making it more ethnically diverse than ever. Additionally, the work force is fast approaching gender parity. In fact, by 2000, it is estimated that nearly half the work force will be composed of women and that over 60 percent of all American adult women will be working outside the home.

These demographic trends bring along with them several challenges. For the white male, it is clear that the era of dominance in the workplace is over. Indeed, research has shown that white men, so used to being the majority, are highly threatened by the prospect of losing this status.[3] For females and members of ethnic minority groups, old barriers to success still must be broken, and acceptance by others (not to mention one's own self-image!) must be gained as old stereotypes and prejudicial attitudes fade only slowly (see Chapters 2 and 4). Despite corporate America's best efforts to celebrate diversity (see Chapter 4), it is clear that society is in a state of transition that makes it difficult for all people to perceive each other as equals.

Although parity with respect to numeric representation in the workplace is approaching, it is also clear that prejudice is still with us. Combining these trends, diversity expert Taylor Cox notes, conditions are ripe for intergroup conflict to occur.[4] We are referring to opposing interests between the majority group and the various minority groups as well as among different minority groups themselves. To the extent that diversity is a fact of life in today's workplaces, and that organizations benefit from having a diverse work force, the challenge lies in effectively managing the intergroup conflict that may result. There are several ways to go about doing this.

First, intergroup conflict may fade as people *focus on superordinate goals* — that is, the overarching mission of the organization. Employees have something in common: the organization in which they work. And, to the extent that they focus on this common situation, they are likely to concentrate on the similarities between themselves rather than the differences. This is likely to occur when all employees must pitch in together on some mutual organizational problem, such as introducing a new product on time, or meeting a new sales objective. Just as a common enemy may unite citizens in their battles against outside invaders, superordinate organizational goals may likewise get employees to focus more on their similarities than their differences.

A second suggestion for avoiding intergroup conflict is to try to *get the members of different cultural groups speaking to one another*. Sometimes problems arise simply because people belonging to different groups have difficulty communicating. In such cases, not only do intergroup relations suffer, but also the organization itself suffers, as any attempts at coordinating efforts by working together cooperatively evaporate. With this in mind, such companies as Espirit de Corp., Economy Color Card, and Pace Foods have taken a big but simple step: They teach English to their non-English-speaking employees, and teach the other language commonly spoken in these companies (Spanish, in these cases) to the English-speaking employees. "Official" company documents, such as the policy manual, are bilingual. This small step goes a long way toward minimizing conflict between these groups. After all, it's hard to get along if you can't "speak the same language."

A third way of minimizing intergroup conflict is by *changing the power structure of the organization.* This may occur by promoting minority group representation within powerful organizational positions. U.S. West and Equitable Life Insurance do this by creating diverse groups of advisers who give direct input to senior management. Other companies, such as Xerox—as part of its "Balanced Workforce Plan"—go a step further, putting members of underrepresented groups in top positions. Although some white male employees at Xerox were at first threatened by this practice, efforts to explain how diverse representation benefits the company as a whole have since facilitated its acceptance.

In conclusion, diversity in the American workplace is a reality, but the intergroup conflict that comes with it need not be. The several techniques outlined here can be quite effective in helping organizations reap the benefits of a diverse workplace while minimizing the intergroup conflict that might occur. Until such time as people become more accepting of each other and prejudicial attitudes disappear (a difficult task, as we noted in Chapter 4), such practices may be considered very useful.

CHALLENGES ASSOCIATED WITH THE HIGH-TECH NATURE OF WORK

Today's organizations don't only confront challenges related to the nature of the work force, but also the rapidly changing nature of the work people do—changes stemming largely from sophisticated computer technology. In this regard, we will discuss two key developments—the elimination of permanent jobs, and the demise of the permanent office—both due to the effects of information technology.

THE RAPIDLY DISAPPEARING JOB: "INFORMATING" THE WORKPLACE GIVES RISE TO THE "CONTINGENCY WORK FORCE"

Figures from the Bureau of Labor Statistics tell us that when people lose their jobs today, they are likely to have a hard time finding another. A key reason lies in the fact that jobs are becoming increasingly scarce due to the "informating" of the work force. Harvard Professor Shoshana Zuboff coined the term **informate** to refer to *the process by which workers manipulate products by "inserting data" between themselves and those objects.*[5]

When jobs are informated, modern information technology is used to change a formerly physical task into one that involves manipulating a sequence of digital commands. So, for example, a modern factory worker can move around large sheets of steel by pressing a few buttons on a keypad. Likewise, with the right programming, an order entered into a salesperson's laptop computer can trigger a chain of events involving everything associated with the job: placing an order for supplies, manufacturing the product to exact specifications, delivering the final product, sending out the bill, and even crediting the proper commission to the salesperson's payroll check.

The result of this process is that jobs that used to take many people to complete now require only a few. For example, whereas Ford employs some 400 people in its accounts payable department, Mazda's informated system does the same work with only five people! Although Mazda is considerably smaller, this difference is striking and nicely illustrates our main point: Informated work systems eliminate jobs.

People have been replaced by robots—even in jobs where the work is not particularly dirty or unsafe. For example, Boston television station **WHDH** *has replaced live camera operators with six robotic studio cameras all operated by a technician in front of a PC in the control room.*

A popular fear in the 1960s, when computers first came into widespread use in business, was that they eventually would replace people in many jobs. Although this concern has become a reality, it never quite took the form envisioned: a bunch of robots moving papers from place to place. Instead, today's offices are rapidly becoming paperless, allowing for improvements in service that were unimaginable in the past.

Consider, for example, some of the banking services that are now widely available around the clock, including ATMs that disburse cash and automated systems that provide access to account information via telephones. In France and Japan they already have "smart cards" embedded with a computer chip that contains information on your bank accounts. A quick scan through a terminal at the merchant's location is all it takes to record a transaction, debit your account, credit the merchant's account, and update your balance on the chip— all instantaneously. There are no monthly statements to be sent out and no checks to write. It all happens electronically—and with fewer employees.

In addition to services, product manufacturing also has been informated. At GE's Faunc Automation plant in Charlottesville, Virginia, for example, circuitboards are manufactured by half as many employees as required before informating the facility. But it is not only blue-collar, manual labor jobs that are eliminated. White-collar, mental labor jobs have been eliminated as well. In many places, middle managers are no longer needed to make decisions that can now be made by computers. It's little wonder that middle managers, while only 10 percent of the work force, comprise 20 percent of recent layoffs (see Chapter 11).

When jobs are lost, what happens to the individuals who used to perform them? Surely, some are retrained, and go to work for companies that make the machines that put them out of work ("if you can't beat 'em, join 'em"). Many others either go into business for themselves or take a succession of temporary jobs. Indeed, the largest U.S. employer, with some 600,000 people on its payroll, is the temporary-employee firm, Manpower. Analysts predict that by the year 2000 half of all working Americans—some 60 million people—will be working on a part-time or freelance basis. Although some believe such claims are far-fetched, organizational consultant Charles Handy has described tomorrow's organizations as being more like an apartment than a home for life, "an association of temporary residents gathered together for mutual convenience."[6]

People hired to perform temporary work caused by unexpected or short-lived organizational changes are referred to as the **contingency work force.** And contrary to the stereotypical image of a clerical "temp," today's temporary employees work at all organizational levels. For example, at Silicon Graphics Corp., they do sophisticated electrical engineering work; at Parker Hannifin's aerospace group, temps do systems engineering; and at Charles Schwab Corp., they work as senior benefits analysts. Imcor, a temporary-employment firm based in Stamford, Connecticut, specializes in providing companies with still higher-ranking personnel—senior executives.

If you think this is far-fetched, consider that some organizations have done away with permanent employees entirely, and now "lease" all their employees. For example, Home Corp., the Alabama company that owns and manages apartment complexes in ten states, leases 500 employees ranging from groundskeepers to resident managers—its whole property-management staff. The company benefits by not having to worry about the administrative headaches of payroll preparation and taxes, as well as by having great flexibility—adding or subtracting workers as needed.

Still, many corporate officials strongly believe that quality performance depends on the kind of skill and commitment to the organization that temporaries cannot offer. Says Georgia-Pacific's CEO, Pete Correll, "Our manufacturing facilities need operators who are well trained and who understand the quality requirements of the job. You can't just drop someone into that. We want workers who will buy into our dream."[7] Thus, although there may be a growing number of contingency employees, permanent employees are not yet extinct—although they are clearly on the "endangered species" list.

TELECOMMUTING: THE REALITY OF THE "VIRTUAL OFFICE"

Question: What current organizational activity simultaneously helps alleviate child-care problems, reduces traffic jams, and cuts air pollution and fuel consumption, while also saving millions of dollars on office space? The answer is **telecommuting**—*the practice of using communications technology so as to enable work to be performed from remote locations, such as the home.*

Advanced technology and enlightened attitudes toward work have made it possible for today's employees to no longer be confined to traditional offices. They can work from their homes, cars, or the decks of their yachts—virtually anywhere you can plug in a computer and phone line. In fact, as wireless communications become more advanced, workers can be completely untethered and hide away with their laptops on a desert island, if they so desire. Statistics indicate that telecommuting is in full swing today.[8]

- There are currently 7.6 million telecommuters—a figure expected to jump to 25 million by the year 2000.

- Among employees of *Fortune* 500 firms, 78 percent perform significant amounts of work off site.

- Telecommuting is most prevalent among smaller firms: 77 percent of telecommuters work for organizations employing fewer than 100 people.

Not surprisingly, the computer giant, IBM has been one of the first to apply its technology to telecommuting. Although IBM's Midwest division is headquartered in Chicago, few of its 4,000 employees (including salespeople and customer service technicians) show up more than once or twice a week. Instead, they have "gone mobile," using the company's ThinkPad computers, fax-modems, e-mail, and cellular phones to do their work from remote locations. In just a few years, the company has reduced real estate space by 55 percent, reduced the number of fixed computer terminals required, and does a better job of satisfying its customers' needs. And, at the same time, telecommuting has done well for IBM employees themselves: 83 percent report not wanting to return to a traditional office environment. Reports from companies such as Great Plains Software, The Traveler's Insurance Co., U.S. West Communications, and the NPD Group have all reported similar benefits with respect to savings in office expenses, gains in productivity, and satisfaction among employees.

As you might imagine, telecommuting is not for everyone; it also has its limitations.[9] Notably, when employees do not come into contact with each other, it is difficult to build the team spirit that is needed to establish quality goods and services in some organizations (see Chapters 7 and 11). Additionally, telecommuting does not lend itself to all jobs. It works best for jobs that involve information handling, significant amounts of automation, and relatively little face-to-face contact. Sales representatives, computer programmers, word processing technicians, insurance agents, and securities traders are all good candidates for telecommuting.

This is not to say that all such individuals performing these jobs should be issued a laptop and sent packing. Good candidates for telecommuting must have the emotional maturity and self-discipline to work without direct supervision. To assist those who have difficulty adjusting to telecommuting, IBM carefully monitors the work of its telecommuters and offers counseling to those who appear to be having trouble.

To function effectively, workers who telecommute must be thoroughly trained in the use of the technologies that are required for them to do their

WINNING PRACTICES

Need an Office Away from the Office?
Check into a "Telecommuting Center"

Some telecommuters prefer working in a "real office" environment, but don't relish the long commutes to their corporate headquarters. At the same time, companies are discovering that maintaining conventional offices is prohibitively expensive. What's needed is a convenient office away from the main office that can be used (and paid for!) only when needed. Ready to fill this need comes the latest advance in working environments—**telecommuting centers.** These are state-of-the-art office spaces rented on an as-needed basis, complete with conference rooms, and all the facilities you could want—from furniture to fax machines.[10] Think of them as hotels, but with spaces specially designed for working instead of sleeping.

In suburban Valencia, California, 35 miles from Los Angeles, the Newhall Land and Farming Company has created one of the nation's first telecommuting centers in a 30,000 square foot space that used to be a warehouse. Spaces are in such great demand—leasing to such customers as CareAmerica, Cigna, and Great Western Savings—that the facility enjoyed a 100 percent occupancy rate before it was open even a year. This center's great appeal lies in its convenience (good access to major freeways), great flexibility (offices are available unfurnished, or as completely furnished as desired), and its great high-tech beauty and first-rate facilities (the spaces were carefully designed by experts to provide the look and equipment desired today). According to a Newhall Land and Farming official:

> *The center provides a place for telecommuters and others to work in their own community. People find they no longer have to spend hours on the freeway getting to and from the office. It has improved their productivity and the quality of their lives.*[11]

On the heels of Newhall's great success, other similar facilities may be opening soon throughout the country. At least one consultant predicts that they will be springing up at airport locations, a true convenience for the harried business traveler. In the words of this expert, "By fashioning the concept for the '90s and providing cutting-edge capabilities, non-traditional workers have far more options available. Ultimately, that benefits them and the company."[12]

work off site, as well as the proper conditions for working safely (e.g., avoiding physical problems resulting from staring into video terminals for hours on end, and from overusing wrist muscles). They also must be trained in ways to function independently, such as how to manage their time effectively, and how to avoid interference from their families while working.

Companies also face the issue of establishing fair wages for telecommuters. For workers who are paid by the amount of work produced, such as the number of insurance claims processed, this is not a problem. Clear criteria for measuring performance (e.g., specific quantity and quality goals) are enormously helpful when paying telecommuters. However, for salaried employees doing jobs for which clear performance criteria are difficult to come by, policies need to be established regarding what telecommuters should do, say, when they complete their work in less than the allotted time. At the office, they would pitch in and help others, but away from the office, they may be tempted to goof off. The key task is to resolve all potentially thorny policy issues regarding pay and performance expectations *before* employees begin telecommuting—and ensuring that they are clearly understood and accepted.

> *Telecommuting is quite common in the telecommunications industry. Companies such as **Pacific Bell** and **Atlantic Bell** have invested heavily in equipment that allows operators and directory assistance agents to work directly from their homes while connected to the company's main computer.*

Finally, telecommuting works best among those who have access to sites that provide a hospitable atmosphere for working, one without distraction. (Although some people can work just fine from their homes, boats, or campsites, others require more traditional, structured environments. As described in the **Winning Practices** section on p. 336, this need has spawned a new kind of business.)

CHALLENGES ASSOCIATED WITH SOCIETY AT LARGE

In this final section of the chapter we will describe several organizational challenges imposed by the changing nature of society at large. Three forces are particularly noteworthy: the global nature of the economy, increasing demands for quality, and sensitivity to ethical business practices.

ADAPTING TO THE GLOBAL ECONOMY: EXPANDING THE CORPORATE BACKYARD

Not too many years ago, companies made products at home and sold them at home. Only a few of the largest firms, like Coca-Cola and Ford, extended their manufacturing and markets overseas. Today, however, things have changed. Business has become global, and the view of what constitutes "home" has broadened to the point of disappearing entirely; the so-called *global village* has emerged. Many companies today, even small ones, find it necessary to rely on facilities in other countries to provide raw materials and to assemble their goods, as well as to provide skilled labor, and markets that eagerly await their finished products. This state of affairs has several important implications worth mentioning for the field of organizational behavior.

Communication Problems in Multinational Corporations.   As we discussed in Chapter 6, the process of communication is quite complex and fraught with opportunities for failure. With this in mind, imagine how much more problematic communication becomes when organizations are very large, spread out throughout the world, and staffed by people speaking many different languages. This description characterizes **multinational corporations (MNCs)**—organizations that have operations in several different countries.

Companies such as the Dutch firm, N. V. Phillips (see Figure 12-2), Japan's Matsushita Electric (known to most Americans for their Panasonic line), and the American company, Procter & Gamble, are large multi-nationals.[13] In fact, so too are most of the companies on the *Fortune* 500 list. Among the best-known multinational projects is Ford's Escort, touted as "the world car" because it is assembled and sold in different nations (in different versions) from parts manufactured in countries throughout the world.

As you might imagine, the communication challenges imposed by such ventures are formidable, indeed. What makes them possible is the widespread use of technology, including vast e-mail networks, fax machines, closed-circuit television linkages via satellite, and other whiz-bang devices that for all practical purpose eliminate geographic barriers.

But, as you might imagine, while technology makes international communication possible, it is people that make it work. And, for MNCs to survive, communication must work very well. With this in mind, executives find it necessary to be thoroughly trained in not only the language but the social customs of the countries in which they do business. Imposing the values and traditions of one's own culture only creates communication barriers. However, learning and accepting the ways of other people are critical for doing business abroad. And, given the global nature of today's economy, failing to do so is a luxury that no organization can afford.

Understanding—and Accepting—the Free Enterprise System in Russian Organizations.   Without doubt, one of the biggest organizational challenges is faced by companies operating in Russia and the other states of the former Soviet Union. Traditionally, Soviet companies were huge (averaging 800 employees compared to only 80 in Western nations), highly centralized (controlled by a single head, known as a *rukovoditei*), very inefficient monopolies that produced poor-quality goods. And, as this book has made clear, this is *not* the formula for organizational success in today's world.

When Marxist-Leninist doctrine was overthrown in the late 1980s, Russian organizations needed intensive indoctrination in the free enterprise

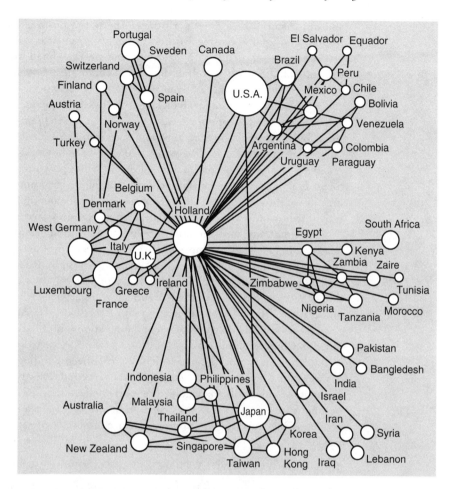

■ *Figure 12-2 N.V. Philips: A Multinational Corporation*

The linkages between units in various countries are highly complex in this major multinational corporation. Circle sizes are drawn in proportion to the relative number of communications sent and received. (*Source:* From Ghoshal & Bartlett, 1990; see Note 13. Reproduced by permission of the *Academy of Management Review* and the authors.)

system—not only techniques of manufacturing and finance, but also ways of managing people. After all, OB concepts such as motivation, career development, and teamwork have little meaning in a dehumanizing system, such as Soviet communism, in which people are assigned to jobs, treated like machines, and are given no autonomy to make decisions.

To characterize the difficulties faced by Russian organizations, consider this description of the typical Soviet worker. "He is lazy, doesn't want responsibility, and doesn't want to even be at work. There is no incentive to work and no reason to be a good performer. There is widespread alienation, disaffection, and apathy among workers. Managers have very few solutions that can overcome years of apathy, disgust, and undisciplined practices."[14] Given this state of affairs, the result of decades of communist rule, it certainly will be difficult to turn around the Soviet system.

Probably the greatest challenge is the need for people to be given—and for them to accept—opportunities to make decisions themselves, to take responsibility for their own actions, and to question authority figures if necessary. It will take time for Russian citizens to become comfortable with these practices, which are second nature to people who grew up in democratic cultures. For those who never felt accountable for their actions or the quality of their work, however, the shift to a private market economy, in which success is dictated by individual performance, is most certainly jarring.

Adaptability and initiative are relatively unimportant among Russian workers. In fact, they are more likely to blame poor product quality on inferior equipment than on their own actions. Not surprisingly, Russia's working people feel powerless to affect change and are reluctant to work together to make things better. Compared to their American counterparts, who frequently coordinate their efforts by communicating with others at their same levels, Russian employees typically do *not* initiate communication with their coworkers. As we noted in Chapter 6, this makes coordination of effort very difficult.

Believe it or not, the bleak picture we've been painting of life in Russian organizations represents an *improvement* over conditions that existed under Communist rule. Still, management experts believe that until Soviet managers become better equipped to get people to be productive in a free society, it will be impossible for Russian companies to compete successfully in the world market.

THE QUALITY REVOLUTION

For many years, people complained, but could do little when the goods they purchased fell apart, or the service they received was second-rate. After all, if everything in the market is shoddy, there are few alternatives. Then Japanese companies such as Toyota and Nissan entered the American auto market. Their cars were more reliable, less expensive, and better designed than the offerings from Ford, General Motors, and Chrysler, companies that became complacent about offering value to their customers. When Japanese automakers began capturing the American auto market in record numbers, American companies were forced to rethink their strategies—and to change their ways.

Today's companies operate quite differently than the American auto companies of decades past. For them, the watchword is not "getting by," but "making things better," what has been referred to as *the quality revolution.* The best organizations are ones that strive to deliver better goods and services at lower prices than ever before. Those that do so flourish, and those that do not tend to fade away. Two approaches to improving quality have been popularly used in recent years—*total quality management* and *reengineering.*

Total Quality Management: A Commitment to Customers. One of the most popular approaches to establishing quality is known as **total quality management (TQM)**—*an organizational strategy of commitment to improving customer satisfaction by developing techniques to carefully manage output quality.* TQM is not so much a special technique as a well-ingrained aspect of corporate culture—a way of life demonstrating a strong commitment to improving quality in everything that is done.

> **FedEx** *has been so very successful in its efforts to achieve quality service for its customers that it was awarded the Malcolm Baldridge Quality Award in 1990. Other winners in this category have included* **AT&T Universal Card Services** *and* **The Ritz-Carlton Hotel Co.** *(both in 1992).*

According to W. Edwards Deming, the best-known advocate of TQM, successful TQM requires that everyone in the organization—from the lowest-level employee to the CEO—must be fully committed to making whatever innovations are necessary to improve quality. This involves both carefully measuring quality (through elaborate statistical procedures) and taking whatever steps are necessary to improve it. Typically, this requires continuously improving the manufacturing process in ways that make it possible for higher quality to result.

For example, in developing its Lexus LS 400, Toyota purchased competing cars from Mercedes and BMW, disassembled them, examined the parts, and developed ways of building an even better car. (This process of comparing one's own products or services with the best from others is known as *benchmarking.*) Spending some $500 million in this process, Toyota was clearly dedicated to creating a superior product. And, given the recognition that Lexus has received among customers for its high quality, it appears as if Toyota's TQM efforts have paid off.

Another key ingredient of TQM is incorporating concern for quality into all aspects of organizational culture (see Chapter 5). At Rubbermaid, for example, concern for quality is not only emphasized in the company's manufacturing process, but also its concern for cost, service, speed, and innovation. Realizing that it is often difficult to create a quality-focused culture, Deming has offered several suggestions; the key ones are summarized in Table 12-1.[15] As you review this list, keep in mind that the basic idea is to keep everyone focused on creating and maintaining sustained levels of extremely high quality.

To assure that they are meeting quality standards, many companies conduct *quality control audits*—careful examinations of how well they are meeting their standards. For example, companies such as PepsiCo and FedEx regularly interview their clients to find out what problems they may be having. These responses are then taken very seriously in making whatever improvements are necessary to avoid them in the future.

■ *Table 12-1 Deming's Suggestions for Improving Quality*

W. Edwards Deming, one of the pioneers of *total quality management*, made the following recommendations for incorporating quality into organizational culture. (Adapted from Walton, 1990; see Note 15.)

Suggestion	Explanation
● Create a constancy of purpose for improving goods and services.	Instead of focusing on making money, focus on constantly improving and innovating. When this is done, the money will follow.
● Change your tolerance for poor quality.	Too many people are tolerant of poor workmanship and service. Mistakes should be considered unacceptable.
● Stop relying on mass inspection.	Instead of relying on one person to make products and another to inspect them, organize the process so that people making products also inspect them and are responsible for the results.
● Don't award business only on the basis of the lowest bid.	Buyers should seek the best possible quality instead of the lowest possible price.
● Make improvements constantly.	Rather than thinking of improvement as a one-time effort, continually look for ways to raise quality.
● Provide training.	Quality work can only result when people know exactly how to do their jobs. Formal training can be very helpful.
● Institute leadership.	Supervisors shouldn't only manage, but also lead employees—sharing their visions for success and showing them ways to do a better job.
● Eliminate fear from the workplace.	Too many employees are afraid to ask questions. Unless people are encouraged to ask questions (and are not ridiculed for doing so), they will continue to make mistakes.
● Break down barriers between staff functions.	Departments must be made to cooperate with each other as a single team rather than compete with each other.
● Eliminate numerical quotas.	Focusing on numerical quotas only encourages people to meet the numbers, often at the expense of quality.
● Eliminate barriers to quality workmanship.	Faulty equipment and materials interfere with people's interest in doing a good job. These barriers should be removed.
● Educate the entire work force.	Everyone must be thoroughly educated in the techniques essential to create high-quality goods and services.
● Take action to make the transformation.	It is essential for top managers to develop an action plan for carrying out the mission of developing sustained high quality.

Reengineering: Starting All Over. Recent articles in the popular business press have referred to *reengineering* as "the hottest trend in management,"[16] noting that "if this radical idea . . . hasn't landed at your company, it's probably on its way."[17] Pioneered by consultants Michael Hammer and James Champy, **reengineering** is defined as *the fundamental rethinking and radical redesign of business processes to achieve drastic improvements in performance.*

Reengineering does not involve fixing anything—rather, as the term implies, starting over from scratch about the fundamental way things are done. Organizations that use reengineering forget all about how work was performed in the past and start anew with a clean sheet of paper, thinking about how things can be done best right now—hence, the term *radical* in the definition.

The main focus of reengineering is the customer. Everything that is done starts with the idea of adding value for the customer: improving service, raising quality, lowering costs. Practices are eradicated simply because they are traditional or convenient for the company if they don't otherwise help the customer. Doing this involves organizing around process rather than function (see Chapter 10). That is, work is arranged according to the processes needed to get the job done most effectively (for this reason, reengineering is also known as *process innovation*). For example, in many companies the simple process of order fulfillment is frequently chopped up into single tasks performed by people in many different departments, although customers may be better served by assigning it to a single unit responsible for the entire process.

As an example of reengineering in action, consider changes made at IBM Credit Corp., a subsidiary responsible for financing IBM's hardware and software. Before reengineering, the task of processing a credit application was cumbersome and very slow—so slow, in fact, that it frequently cost the company sales. A credit request would come in by phone and would be logged on a piece of paper. Then the paper went on a long journey from credit checkers, to "pricers" (who determined what interest rate to charge), to many others who also performed single, specialized functions. Often applications were bounced back and forth between departments before they were properly completed. Total processing time ranged from six days to two weeks.

Out of curiosity, some IBM senior managers decided one day to walk a financing request through the process, taking it from department to department asking personnel in each office to put aside whatever they were doing and process this request in the normal fashion, only without the delay. What they found was quite an eye-opener: The actual process took only *90 minutes;* the remaining time was consumed by handing the form off between departments. Enlightened by this demonstration, IBM Credit reengineered its operations by replacing a series of specialists with generalists. Now one person processes an entire application from beginning to end without handing it off to others.

Did it work? In the newly reengineered jobs credit approval takes only about 4 hours. Furthermore, the number of applications processed has increased a hundredfold—and, using *fewer* employees than before. Other companies, such as Ford, Kodak, Hallmark, Taco Bell, and Bell Atlantic also have used reengineering successfully. Union Carbide claims to have reduced its fixed costs by $400 million in just three years by using reengineering. Don't let all these big names mislead you; small companies also have been using reengineering to achieve success.

Although it is too early to predict the long-term benefits of reengineering, there is good reason to suspect that it will continue to be quite effective — and popular. Because it combines effective principles of job design and enrichment (Chapter 3) and organizational design (Chapter 10), we are optimistic that this burgeoning approach will not soon become tomorrow's outdated fad.

CORPORATE SOCIAL RESPONSIBILITY: THE QUEST FOR ETHICS

The history of American business is riddled with sordid tales of magnates who would go to any lengths in their quest for success, destroying in the process not only the country's natural resources and the public's trust, but also the hopes and dreams of millions of people. For example, Jim Fisk and Jay Gould relied on thugs in "goon squads" to remove anyone who got in the way of their development of railroads. Similarly, tales abound of how John D. Rockefeller, founder of Standard Oil, regularly bribed politicians and stepped all over people in his quest to monopolize the oil industry.

By relating these tales we do not mean to imply that unsavory business practices are only a relic of the past. Indeed, they are all too common today. For example, in recent years, incidents of insider trading have brought down one of the world's most powerful brokerage firms, Drexel Burnham Lambert. And accusations of fraudulent practices in its auto-repair business have tarnished the reputation of the venerable retailing giant, Sears. Clearly, human greed has not faded from the business scene. However, something *has* changed — namely, the public's acceptance of unethical behavior on the part of organizations. Consider this statement by a leading expert on business ethics.

Ethical standards, whether formal or informal, have changed tremendously in the last century. Boldly stated, no one can make the case that ethical standards have fallen in the latter decades of the twentieth century. The reverse is true. Standards are considerably higher. Business-people themselves, as well as the public, expect more sensitive behavior in the conduct of economic enterprise. The issue is not just having the standards, however. It is living up to them.[18]

To the extent that people are increasingly intolerant of unethical business activity, it makes sense for the field of OB to examine the factors that encourage unethical practices. Even more importantly, we need to develop strategies for promoting ethical conduct. We will now turn our attention to these matters.

Why Does Unethical Organizational Behavior Occur?   As noted previously, unethical organizational practices are embarrassingly commonplace. It is easy to define practices such as dumping chemical wastes into rivers, insider trading on Wall Street, and overcharging the government for Medicaid services as morally wrong. Yet these and many other unethical practices go on almost routinely in many organizations. Why is this so? In other words, what accounts for the unethical actions of people within organizations?

One answer to this question is based on the idea that *organizations often reward behaviors that violate ethical standards.* Consider, for example, how many business executives are expected to deal in bribes and payoffs, and how good corporate citizens blowing the whistle on organizational wrongdoings may fear being punished for their actions. Organizations tend to develop *counternorms*—accepted organizational practices that are contrary to prevailing ethical standards.[19] Some of these are summarized in Figure 12-3.

The top of Figure 12-3 identifies "being open and honest" as a prevailing ethical norm. Indeed, governmental regulations requiring full disclosure and freedom of information reinforce society's values toward openness and honesty. Within organizations, however, it is often considered not only acceptable, but desirable, to be much more secretive and deceitful. The practice of *stonewalling*—willingly hiding relevant information—is quite common. One reason is that organizations may actually punish those who are too open and

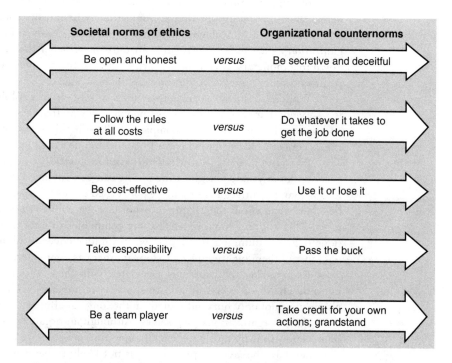

Societal norms of ethics   **Organizational counternorms**

Be open and honest	*versus*	Be secretive and deceitful
Follow the rules at all costs	*versus*	Do whatever it takes to get the job done
Be cost-effective	*versus*	Use it or lose it
Take responsibility	*versus*	Pass the buck
Be a team player	*versus*	Take credit for your own actions; grandstand

■ *Figure 12-3 Societal Norms versus Ethical Counternorms*

Although societal standards of morality dictate the appropriateness of certain actions, counternorms that encourage and support opposite practices often develop within organizations. (*Source:* Based on suggestions by Jansen & Von Glinow, 1985; see Note 19.)

honest. Consider, for example, the disclosure that B. F. Goodrich rewarded employees who falsified and withheld data on the quality of aircraft brakes to win certification. Similarly, it has been reported that executives at Metropolitan Edison encouraged employees to withhold information from the press about the Three Mile Island nuclear accident. In both incidents, the counternorms of secrecy and deceitfulness were accepted and supported by the organization.

As you can see from Figure 12-3, many other organizational counternorms promote ethically questionable practices. That these practices are commonly rewarded and accepted suggests that organizations may be operating within a world that dictates its own set of accepted rules. This reasoning leads to a second explanation as to why organizations act unethically—namely, because *managerial values exist that undermine integrity.* In an analysis of executive integrity, Professor Donald M. Wolfe explains that managers have developed some ways of thinking (of which they may be quite unaware) that foster unethical behavior.[20]

One culprit is referred to as the **bottom line mentality.** This line of thinking supports financial success as the only value to be considered. It promotes short-term solutions that are immediately financially sound, despite the fact that they cause problems for others within the organization or for the organization as a whole. It promotes an unrealistic belief that everything boils down to a monetary game. As such, rules of morality are merely obstacles, impediments along the way to bottom line financial success.

Wolfe also notes that managers tend to rely on an **exploitative mentality**—a view that encourages "using" people in a way that promotes stereotypes and undermines empathy and compassion. This highly selfish perspective sacrifices concern for others in favor of benefits to one's own immediate interests.

In addition, there is a **Madison Avenue mentality**—a perspective suggesting that anything is right if the public can be convinced that it's right. The idea is that executives may be more concerned about their actions *appearing* to be ethical than about their legitimate morality—a public relations-guided mentality. This kind of thinking leads some companies to hide their unethical actions (e.g., by dumping their toxic wastes under cover of night) or to otherwise justify them by attempting to explain them as completely acceptable.

Recognizing the problems associated with these various orientations is not difficult. Their overemphasis on short-term monetary gain may lead to decisions that not only hurt individuals in the long run, but also threaten the very existence of organizations themselves. Although an organization may make an immediate profit by cutting corners, exploiting people, and convincing others that they have behaved appropriately is not likely to be in the long-term best interest of organizations. Just as people are learning that they cannot continue to exploit their natural environments forever without paying a cost, the same may apply to business environments as well. Indeed, society appears to be increasingly intolerant of organizations that continue to violate moral standards in the name of short-term profit.

It has even been argued that when organizations continue to behave unethically, they may actually find that doing so is unprofitable in the long run. Consumers who find the well-publicized unethical actions of various companies objectionable may cast their votes for greater social responsibility by not patronizing those organizations. In contrast, a growing number of organizations—such as the Body Shop and Tom's of Maine, to name only two—have long engaged in highly ethical practices with respect to the treatment of living beings and the environment, and have prospered in great part because of consumers' appreciation of these policies.

What Can Be Done to Promote Ethical Behavior? As you might imagine, getting people to behave ethically isn't a simple matter. Yet, to the extent that "good ethics is good business," as they say, it is worth considering tactics for discouraging unethical behavior.

The first thing that should be done is to *test the ethics of any decision you are contemplating.* In this regard, there are four main questions you should ask yourself.[21]

- **Is it right?** Although it is not always easy to judge whether a certain action is right, there are certain universally accepted principles of right and wrong that should not be violated. For example, it is widely considered wrong to steal.

- **Is it fair?** Fairness demands treating likes as likes. So, for example, two equally qualified people should be paid the same wages for doing the same job.

- **Is it purely selfish?** If the results of your actions benefit only yourself, then they may be unethical. Morally acceptable behaviors are ones that benefit the greatest number and harm the fewest.

- **How would you feel if others found out?** If you think you might be embarrassed by having your actions described on the front page of your local newspaper, then those actions may be ethically dubious.

A second step that can be taken to promote ethical behavior (and one that many organizations have been using) is to *develop a code of ethics.* These are documents describing what the organization stands for, and the general rules of conduct expected of employees (e.g., to avoid conflicts of interest, to be honest, and so on). Some codes are highly specific, stating, for example, the maximum size gifts that can be accepted, and exactly how people will be punished for violating the rules. Research has shown that codes of ethics are especially effective when they are used in conjunction with training programs that reinforce the company's values. In the absence of such training, too many codes are seen as "window dressing," and are ignored—if they are even read at all.

Third, *conduct an ethics audit*. Just as companies regularly audit their books to check on irregularities in their finances, it is advised that they regularly assess the morality of their employees' behavior so as to identify irregularities in this realm as well. Specifically, an ethics audit involves actively investigating and documenting incidents of dubious ethical value. Then these unethical practices should be discussed in an open and honest fashion, and a concrete plan should be developed to avoid such actions in the future.

GROUP EXERCISE

Are You More Ethical Than the Average Manager? Don't Be So Sure!

"The world is full of unethical people," you say—adding, "but I'm not one of them." If we all believe we're ethical, we will be predisposed to trust our own judgments but to question others. This perceptual bias can have major implications for the way we act and how we respond to others. This exercise is designed to demonstrate this phenomenon.

DIRECTIONS
1. Prepare two versions of the following questionnaire, in one using the phrases "you; your job" and in the other, "most managers; their jobs" in the spaces indicated. To tell them apart, print each version on a different color paper.
2. Divide a group of people (e.g., another class) into two groups, and ask them to complete the questionnaire following the directions.

INSTRUMENT
For each of the following statements indicate, by using the following scale, how willing _____ would be to perform the action indicated if it were necessary to protect _____.

0 = Always, 1 = Usually, 2 = Sometimes, 3 = Rarely, 4 = Never

Our fourth recommendation involves something you can do as an individual: *Challenge your rationalizations about ethical behavior.* We all tend to rationalize the things we do so that we can convince ourselves that they are right, although they really may be wrong. Some of the most common rationalizations are as follows:

- **Convincing yourself that something is morally acceptable just because it is legally acceptable**—Think of the law as the minimum standard of acceptable behavior, and strive for higher moral standards.

- **Convincing yourself that something is right just because it benefits you**—It may be easy to talk yourself into accepting a bribe because you feel underpaid. Regardless, it is still wrong.

_____ 1. Keep negative information from a superior.
_____ 2. Lie about facts in a performance report.
_____ 3. Distort information in a financial statement.
_____ 4. Blame a subordinate for one's own mistake.
_____ 5. Break union rules so as to cut costs.
_____ 6. Authorize the use of deceptive marketing techniques.
_____ 7. Exaggerate figures on an expense report.
_____ 8. Pay off an inspector to avoid making costly repairs to already safe equipment.

Scoring

Compute the average scores for each of the two groups. The higher the score, the more it is believed that the focal person ("you" or "most managers") will be ethical.

Questions for Discussion

1. We would expect that the "you" group would have higher scores than the "most managers" group. Is this what you found?

2. Were there some people in the group who consistently responded more extremely than others? If so, ask them to explain what they were thinking.

3. What are the implications of this exercise? What did you learn, and how can you put it to use?

- **Convincing yourself that something is right because you will never get caught** — What's wrong is wrong, even if you don't stand a chance of getting caught!

- **Convincing yourself that something is right because it helps the company** — Don't expect the company to condone your immoral actions, even if doing so gives it an edge. The best companies want to succeed because they have taken the moral high road, not because of the unacceptable practices of their employees.

As you might imagine, it isn't always easy to avoid these rationalizations. Still, you may wish to do your best to catch yourself in the act of rationalizing your actions. To the extent that you are rationalizing, you may be covering up unethical behavior. (One reason why we have such a hard time making ethically appropriate decisions is that we tend to think of ourselves as more ethical than the next guy. And, to the extent that this occurs, we find it easy to justify our actions. To gain insight into this phenomenon, complete the **Group Exercise** on pp. 348–349.)

SUMMARY: PUTTING IT TO USE

Stress is defined as the pattern of emotional states and physiological reactions occurring in response to demands from outside or inside the organization. Such demands are known as *stressors*. The resulting abnormal states (e.g., diseases) that result from stress are known as *strain*. Over time, people are worn down by stress reactions and suffer *burnout* — a syndrome in which exhaustion is coupled with feelings of personal inadequacy as a result of prolonged exposure to intense stress.

Stress is caused by several factors (e.g., occupational demands, conflict between work and nonwork lives) and has damaging effects (e.g., poor job performance, medical ailments, and behavioral and psychological problems). Fortunately, stress may be managed — either at the organizational level (e.g., by giving people more control over their work), or the individual level (e.g., lifestyle management, behavior management, and relaxation training).

Diversity in the American workplace has become a reality. However, with it come potential conflicts between different groups. These conflicts may be eliminated by: focusing on superordinate goals, getting members of different cultural groups speaking to each other, and changing the power structure of the organization, such that more minority group members hold powerful positions.

Much work today has been *informated*—done in such a way that people manipulate materials electronically rather than physically. The result is that fewer people are required to perform many jobs, creating a general reduction in the number of available jobs. In view of this, many people have taken to joining the *contingency work force*—those who perform a succession of temporary jobs for organizations who hire them on an as-needed basis.

Technology also has been responsible for a boom in *telecommuting*—the practice of using communications technology so as to enable work to be performed from remote locations, such as the home. Although many companies have used telecommuting successfully, it is best suited for jobs that involve information handling, significant amounts of automation, and relatively little face-to-face contact (e.g., sales representatives). For telecommuting to be beneficial (such as by avoiding long commutes and reducing the need for office space), workers must be thoroughly trained, fair wage policies must be established, and people must have appropriate sites for working.

In recent years, the economy has become global in scale. As a result, there are many *multinational corporations (MNCs)* in existence today—that is, organizations that have operations in several different countries. Communication problems must be squarely confronted if MNCs are to survive.

Another key global issue today is the indoctrination of Russia into the free enterprise system. Former Soviet workers are not used to working in teams to produce high-quality goods and services, nor are they familiar with taking responsibility for their own work. Until these conditions change, Russian organizations are unlikely to be a major force in the global economy.

Today's organizations are highly focused on delivering quality products and services, those that offer good value to customers. *Total quality management (TQM)* is an organizational strategy of commitment to improving customer satisfaction by developing techniques to carefully manage output quality. It involves not only *benchmarking* (comparing one's own work to the best of others), but also incorporating a concern for quality into all aspects of an organization's culture.

Another approach to quality popular today is *reengineering*—the fundamental rethinking and radical redesign of business processes to achieve drastic improvements in performance. It involves starting over from scratch in developing the way things are done. For example, IBM Credit Corp. redesigned its customer financing process such that the same individuals worked on entire cases instead of small parts of many cases. The result was that a process that used to take several weeks to complete is now done in only four hours. The company is now more productive with fewer employees.

People today have grown increasingly intolerant of unethical business practices. Such behavior often occurs because organizations sometimes develop counternorms (e.g., stonewalling) that reward behaviors that run counter to prevailing moral standards (e.g., being open and honest). Although many companies tend to focus on short-term monetary gain, a growing number of others are highly focused on being socially responsible (and these tend to have loyal followings because of this philosophy). Although it is difficult to get people to behave ethically, this process can be facilitated by testing the ethics of decisions that are being contemplated (e.g., asking if an act is right, fair, and selfish), developing a corporate code of ethics, conducting an ethics audit, and challenging rationalizations about ethical behavior.

You Be the Consultant

You have been asked to help the board of directors of a large food processing company by suggesting directions in which it should guide its short-term training and long-term organizational planning efforts. Answer the following questions relevant to this situation based on the material in this chapter.

1. With respect to the work force itself, what can be done to help alleviate problems caused by employee stress and intergroup conflict between diverse groups?

2. If the company were willing to invest in high-tech devices to gain a competitive advantage, what specific directions would you recommend, and why?

3. The company has been contemplating taking steps that would both introduce its products overseas and improve the quality of its customer service. What specific concerns would you voice, and what directions would you recommend?

4. Plagued by a kickback scandal several years ago, the board is duly concerned about the company's reputation for morality. What can be done to ensure that all company employees live up to the highest ethical standards?

Notes

CHAPTER 1

[1]ROSEN, R. H. (1991). *The healthy company*. New York: Jeremy P. Tarcher/ Perigee (quote, p. 20).

[2]KATZ, D., & KAHN, R. (1978). *The social psychology of organizations*. New York: Wiley.

[3]TAYLOR, F. W. (1947). *Scientific management*. New York: Harper & Row.

[4]DRUCKER, P. F. (1974). *Management: Tasks, responsibilities, practices*. New York: Harper & Row.

[5]See Note 1.

CHAPTER 2

[1]MARTINKO, M. J. (1995). *Attribution theory: An organizational perspective*. Delray Beach, FL: St. Lucie Press.

[2]KELLEY, H. H. (1972). Attribution in social interaction. In E. E. Jones, D. E. Kanous, H. H. Kelley, R. E. Nisbett, S. Valins, & B. Weiner (eds.), *Attribution: Perceiving the causes of behavior* (pp. 1–26). Morristown, NJ: General Learning Press.

[3]SKINNER, B. F. (1969). *Contingencies of reinforcement*. New York: Appleton-Century-Crofts.

[4]HENKOFF, R. (1993, May 15). Companies that train best. *Fortune*, pp. 62–64, 68, 73–75 (quote, p. 64).

[5]See Note 4 (quote, p. 68).

[6]See Note 4 (quote, p. 74).

[7]FREDERIKSEN, L. W. (1982). *Handbook of organizational behavior management*. New York: Wiley.

[8]BARRICK, M. R., & MOUNT, M. K. (1991). The big five personality dimensions and job performance: A meta-analysis. *Personnel Psychology, 44,* 1–26.

[9]ROSENBERG, M. (1965). *Society and the adolescent self-image*. Princeton, NJ: Princeton University Press.

CHAPTER 3

[1]WATERMAN, R. H., JR. (1994). *What America does right: Learning from companies that put people first*. New York: W. W. Norton.

[2]MASLOW, A. H. (1970). *Motivation and personality,* (2nd ed.). New York: Harper & Row.

[3]SHEPHERD, M. D. (1993, February). Staff motivation. *U.S. Pharmacist*, pp. 82, 85, 89–93 (quote, p. 91).

[4]NELSON, B. (1994). *1001 ways to reward employees*. New York: Workman (quote, p, 85).

[5]See Note 4 (quote, p. 86).

[6]ROSS, I. (1985, April 29). Employers win big on the move to two-tier contracts. *Fortune*, pp. 82–92 (quote, p. 87).

[7]ADAMS, J. S. (1965). Inequity in social exchange. In L. Berkowitz (ed.), *Advances in experimental social psychology* (Vol. 2, pp. 267–299). New York: Academic Press.

[8]HARDER, J. W. (1992). Play for pay: Effects of inequity in a pay-for-performance context. *Administrative Science Quarterly, 37*, 321–335.

[9]GREENBERG, J. (1993). Stealing in the name of justice: Informational and interpersonal moderators of theft reactions to underpayment inequity. *Organizational Behavior and Human Decision Processes, 54*, 81–103.

[10]PORTER, L. W., & LAWLER, E. E., III. (1968). *Managerial attitudes and performance.* Homewood, IL: Irwin.

[11]LOCKE, E. A., & LATHAM, G. P. (1990). *A theory of goal setting and task performance.* Englewood Cliffs, NJ: Prentice-Hall.

[12]LATHAM, G., & BALDES, J. (1975). The practical significance of Locke's theory of goal setting. *Journal of Applied Psychology, 60*, 122–124.

[13]TULLY, S. (1994, November 14). Why go for stretch targets. *Fortune*, pp. 145–146, 148, 150, 154, 158 (quote, p. 150).

[14]See Note 10 (quote, p. 145).

[15]LATHAM, G. P., EREZ, M., & LOCKE, E. A. (1988). Resolving scientific disputes by the joint design of crucial experiments by the antagonists: Application to the Erez-Latham dispute regarding participation in goal setting. *Journal of Applied Psychology, 73*, 753–772.

[16]See Note 10 (quote, p. 148).

[17]PRITCHARD, R. D., JONES, S. D., ROTH, P. L., STUEBING, K. K., & EKBERG, S. E. (1988). Effects of group feedback, goal setting, and incentives on organizational productivity. *Journal of Applied Psychology, 73*, 337–358.

[18]CAMPION, M. A., & MCCLELLAND, C. L. (1991). Interdisciplinary examination of the costs and benefits of enlarged jobs: A job design quasi-experiment. *Journal of Applied Psychology, 76*, 186–198.

[19]CAMPION, M. A., & MCCLELLAND, C. L. (1993). Follow-up and extension of the interdisciplinary costs and benefits of enlarged jobs. *Journal of Applied Psychology, 78*, 339–351.

[20]WINPISINGER, W. (1973, February). Job satisfaction: A union response. *AFL-CIO American Federationist*, pp. 8–10 (quote, p. 9).

[21]HACKMAN, J. R., & OLDHAM, G. R. (1980). *Work redesign.* Reading, MA: Addison-Wesley.

[22]ORPEN, C. (1979). The effects of job enrichment on employee satisfaction, motivation, involvement, and performance: A field experiment. *Human Relations, 32*, 189–217.

[23]FINEGAN, J. (1993, July). People power. *Inc.*, pp. 62–63 (quote, p. 63).

CHAPTER 4

[1]HERZBERG, F. (1966). *Work and the nature of man.* Cleveland, OH: World.

[2]HISE, P. (1994, February). The motivational employee-satisfaction questionnaire. *Inc.*, pp. 73–75.

[3]O'REILLY, B. (1994, June 13). The new deal: What companies and employees owe each other. *Fortune*, pp. 44–47, 50, 52 (quote, p. 45).

[4]MEYER, J. P., & ALLEN, N. J. (1991). A three-component conceptualization of organizational commitment. *Human Resource Management Review, 1*, 61–89.

[5]LEE, T. W., ASHFORD, S. J., WALSH, J. P., & MOWDAY, R. T. (1992). Commitment propensity, organizational commitment, and voluntary turnover:

A longitudinal study of organizational entry processes. *Journal of Management, 18,* 15–32.

[6]ROSEN, R. H. (1991). *The healthy company.* New York: Jeremy P. Tarcher/Perigee (quote, pp. 71–72).

[7]MARTINEZ, M. N. (1993, June). Recognizing sexual orientation is fair and not costly. *HRMagazine,* pp. 66–68, 70–72 (quote, p. 68).

[8]YANG, C. (1993, June 21). In any language, it's unfair: More immigrants are bringing bias charges against employers. *Business Week,* pp. 110–112 (quote, p. 111).

[9]STEINBERG, R., & SHAPIRO, S. (1982). Sex differences in personality traits of female and male master of business administration students. *Journal of Applied Psychology, 67,* 306–310.

[10]THOMAS, R. R., JR. (1992). Managing diversity: A conceptual framework. In S. E. Jackson (ed.), *Diversity in the workplace* (pp. 306–317). New York: Guilford Press.

[11]See Note 6 (quote, p. 236).

CHAPTER 5

[1]FELDMAN, J. C. (1976). A socialization process that helps new recruits succeed. *Personnel, 57,* 11–23.

[2]WANOUS, J. P., & COELLA, A. (1989). Organizational entry research: Current status and future directions. In G. Ferris & K. Rowland (eds.), *Research in personnel and human resources management* (Vol. 7, pp. 59–120). Greenwich, CT: JAI Press.

[3]KRAM, K. E. (1985). *Mentoring at work: Developmental relationships in organizational life.* Glenview, IL: Scott, Foresman.

[4]ROTHMAN, H. (1993, April). The boss as mentor. *Nation's Business,* pp. 66–67 (quote, p. 66).

[5]MARTIN, J. (1992). *Cultures in organizations.* New York: Oxford University Press.

[6]DEAL, T. E., & KENNEDY, A. A. (1982). *Corporate cultures.* Reading, MA: Addison-Wesley (quote p. 63).

[7]FALSEY, T. A. (1989). *Corporate philosophies and mission statements.* New York: Quorum Books.

[8]MANLEY, W. W., II. (1991). *Executive's handbook of model business conduct codes.* Englewood Cliffs, NJ: Prentice Hall (p. 5).

[9]ARMSTRONG, L. (1994, April 11). Knowledge Adventure's trickiest game: Success. *Business Week,* pp. 102, 104.

[10]SCHEIN, E. H. (1978). *Career dynamics: Matching individual and organizational needs.* Reading, MA: Addison-Wesley.

[11]"The 25 hottest careers." (1993, July). *Working Woman,* pp. 41–51.

[12]Adapted from: MORRISON, E. K. (1994). *Leadership skills.* Tucson, AZ: Fisher Books.

[13]GALEN, M. PALMER, A. T., CUNEO, A., & MAREMONT, M. (1993, June 28). Work and family. *Business Week,* pp. 80–84, 86, 88 (quote, p. 83).

CHAPTER 6

[1]ROBERTS, K. H. (1984). *Communicating in organizations.* Chicago: Science Research Associates (quote, p. 4).

[2]WEICK, K. E. (1987). Theorizing about organizational communication. In F. M. Jablin, L. L. Putnam, K. H. Roberts, & L. W. Porter (eds.), *Handbook of organizational communication* (pp. 97–122). Newbury Park, CA: Sage.

[3]LEVEL, D. A. (1972). Communication effectiveness: Methods and situation.

Journal of Business Communication, 28, 19–25.

[4]DAFT, R. L., LENGEL, R. H., & TREVINO, L. K. (1987). Message equivocality, media selection, and manager performance: Implications for information systems. *MIS Quarterly, 11,* 355–366.

[5]KIECHEL, W., III. (1990, June 18). How to escape the echo chamber. *Fortune,* pp. 129–130 (quote p. 130).

[6]WALTON, E. (1961). How efficient is the grapevine? *Personnel, 28,* 45–49.

[7]MORRISON, E. K. (1994). *Leadership skills.* Tucson, AZ: Fisher Books.

[8]HINKIN, T. R., & SCHRIESHEIM, C. A. (1989). Development and application of new scales to measure the French and Raven (1959) bases of social power. *Journal of Applied Psychology, 74,* 561–567.

[9]MULDER, M. DE JONG, R. D., KOPPELAAR, L., & VERHAGE, J. (1986). Power, situation, and leaders' effectiveness: An organizational field study. *Journal of Applied Psychology, 71,* 566–570.

CHAPTER 7

[1]FORSYTH, D. L. (1983). *An introduction to group dynamics.* Monterey, CA: Brooks/Cole.

[2]GEEN, R. (1989). Alternative conceptualizations of social facilitation. In P. B. Paulus (ed.), *Psychology of group influence,* 2nd ed. (pp. 15–51). Hillsdale, NJ: Lawrence Erlbaum Associates.

[3]ZAJONC, R. B. (1965). Social facilitation. *Science, 149,* 269–274.

[4]AIELLO, J. R., & SVEC, C. M. (1993). Computer monitoring of work performance: Extending the social facilitation framework to electronic presence. *Journal of Applied Social Psychology, 23,* 537–548.

[5]SHEPPERD, J. A. (1993). Productivity loss in performance groups: A motivation analysis. *Psychological Bulletin, 113,* 67–81.

[6]LATANÉ, B., & NIDA, S. (1980). Social impact theory and group influence: A social engineering perspective. In P. B. Paulus (ed.), *Psychology of group influence* (pp. 3–34). Hillsdale, NJ: Lawrence Erlbaum Associates.

[7]MILES, J. A., & GREENBERG, J. (1993). Using punishment threats to attenuate social loafing effects among swimmers. *Organizational Behavior and Human Decision Processes, 56,* 246–265.

[8]WELLINS, R. S., BYHAM, W. C., & DIXON, G. R. (1994). *Inside teams.* San Francisco: Jossey-Bass.

[9]LAWLER, E. E., III, MOHRMAN, S. A., & LEDFORD, G. E., JR. (1992). *Employee involvement and total quality management.* San Francisco: Jossey-Bass.

[10]HACKMAN, J. R. (Ed.) (1990). *Groups that work (and those that don't).* San Francisco: Jossey-Bass.

[11]WELLINS, R. S., BYHAM, W. C., & WILSON, J. M. (1991). *Empowered teams.* San Francisco: Jossey-Bass.

[12]OSBURN, J. D., MORAN, L., MUSSELWHITE, E., & ZENGER, J. H. (1990). *Self-directed work teams.* Burr Ridge, IL: Irwin.

[13]PEARSON, C. A. L. (1992). Autonomous workgroups: An evaluation at an industrial site. *Human Relations, 45,* 905–936.

[14]DUMAINE, B. (1994, September 5). The trouble with teams. *Fortune,* pp. 86–88, 90, 92 (quote, p. 86).

[15]KATZENBACH, J. R., & SMITH, D. K. (1993). *The wisdom of teams.* Boston: Harvard Business School Press.

[16]CAUDRON, S. (1994, February). Teamwork takes work. *Personnel Journal,* pp. 41–46, 49.

[17]See Note 16 (quote, p. 43).

[18]See Note 16 (quote, p. 41).

[19]STERN, A. (1993, July 18). Managing by team is not always as easy as it looks. *The New York Times,* p. B14 (quote, p. B14).

[20]See Note 14 (quote, p. 88).

[21]See Note 14 (quote, p. 90).

[22]See Note 14 (quote, p. 88).

[23]The facts of life for teambuilding. (1994, December). *Human Resources Forum,* p. 3.

CHAPTER 8

[1]YUKL, G. A. (1994). *Leadership in organizations,* 3rd ed. Englewood Cliffs, NJ: Prentice Hall.

[2]KIRKPATRICK, S. A., & LOCKE, E. A. (1991). Leadership: Do traits matter? *Academy of Management Executive, 5,* 48–60.

[3]See Note 2 (quote, p. 58).

[4]BAND, W. A. (1994). *Touchstones.* New York: John Wiley & Sons (quote, p. 247).

[5]BLAKE, R. R., & MOUTON, J. J. (1969). *Building a dynamic corporation through grid organizational development.* Reading, MA: Addison-Wesley.

[6]LEE, C. (1991). Followership: The essence of leadership. *Training, 28,* 27–35 (quote, p. 28).

[7]GRAEN, G. B., & SCANDURA, T. A. (1987). Toward a psychology of dyadic organizing. In L. L. Cum-
mings & B. M. Staw (eds.), *Research in organizational behavior* (Vol. 9, pp. 175–208). Greenwich, CT: JAI Press.

[8]CONGER, J. A. (1991). Inspiring others: The language of leadership. *Academy of Management Executive, 5,* 31–45.

[9]FARNHAM, A. (1993, September 20). Mary Kay's lessons in leadership. *Fortune,* pp. 68–69, 71, 74, 76–77 (quote, p. 74).

[10]See Note 8 (quote, p. 44).

[11]HOUSE, R. J., SPANGLER, W. D., & WOYCKE, J. (1991). Personality and charisma in the U.S. presidency: A psychological theory of leader effectiveness. *Administrative Science Quarterly, 36,* 364–396.

[12]See Note 9.

[13]HOUSE, R. J., & BAETZ, M. L. (1979). Leadership: Some empirical generalizations and new research directions. In B. M. Staw (ed.), *Research in organizational behavior* (Vol. 1, pp. 341–424). Greenwich, CT: JAI Press.

[14]HUEY, J. (1994, February 21). The new postheroic leadership. *Fortune,* pp. 42–44, 48, 50 (quote, p. 44).

[15]See Note 14 (quote, p. 48).

[16]WEBER, J. (1993). Letting go is hard to do. *Business Week Enterprise,* pp. 218–219.

CHAPTER 9

[1]WEDLEY, W. C., & FIELD, R. H. (1984). A predecision support system. *Academy of Management Review, 9,* 696–703.

[2]DENNIS, T. L., & DENNIS, L. B. (1988). *Microcomputer models for management decision making.* St. Paul, MN: West.

[3]MINGO, J. (1994). *How the Cadillac got its fins.* New York: Harper Business.

[4]ROSS, J., & STAW, B. M. (1986). Expo '86: An escalation prototype. *Administrative Science Quarterly, 31,* 274–297.

[5]ROSS, J., & STAW, B. M. (1993). Organizational escalation and exit: Lessons from the Shoreham nuclear power plant. *Academy of Management Journal, 36,* 701–732.

[6]HILL, G. W. (1982). Group versus individual performance: Are N + 1 heads better than one? *Psychological Bulletin, 91,* 517–539.

[7]OSBORN, A. F. (1957). *Applied imagination.* New York: Scribner's.

[8]BOUCHARD, T. J., JR., BARSALOUX, J., & DRAUDEN, G. (1974). Brainstorming procedure, group size, and sex as determinants of the problem-solving effectiveness of groups and individuals. *Journal of Applied Psychology, 59,* 135–138.

[9]JANIS, I. L. (1982). *Groupthink: Psychological studies of policy decisions and fiascoes,* 2nd ed. Boston: Houghton Mifflin.

[10]MOREHEAD, G., FERENCE, R., & NECK, C. P. (1991). "Group decision fiascoes continue: Space shuttle *Challenger* and a revised groupthink framework. *Human Relations, 44,* 539–550.

[11]DALKEY, N. (1969). *The Delphi method: An experimental study of group decisions.* Santa Monica, CA: Rand Corporation.

CHAPTER 10

[1]STEWART, T. A. (1992, May 18). The search for the organization of tomorrow. *Fortune,* pp. 93–98 (quote, p. 93).

[2]BYRNE, J. A. (1993, December 20). The horizontal corporation. *Business Week,* pp. 76–81 (quote, p. 96).

[3]See Note 2 (quote, p. 96).

[4]MORSE, J. J., & LORSCH, J. W. (1970). Beyond Theory Y. *Harvard Business Review, 48*(3), 61–68.

[5]MINTZBERG, H. (1983). *Structure in fives: Designing effective organizations.* Englewood Cliffs, NJ: Prentice Hall.

[6]KIRKPATRICK, D. (1992, July 27). Breaking up IBM. *Fortune,* pp. 44–49, 52–54, 58.

[7]NAKARMI, L., & EINHORN, B. (1993, June 7). Hyundai's gutsy gambit. *Business Week,* p. 48.

[8]GERLACH, M. L. (1993). *Alliance capitalism: The social organization of Japanese business.* Berkeley, CA: University of California Press.

[9]SANKAR, C. S., BOULTON, W. R., DAVIDSON, N. W., & SNYDER, C. A. (1995). Building a world-class alliance: The Universal Card-TSYS case. *Academy of Management Executive, 9,* 20–29.

CHAPTER 11

[1]SHERMAN, S. (1993, December 13). How will we live with the tumult? *Fortune,* pp. 123–125.

[2]REESE, J. (1993, July 26). Corporate Methuselahs. *Fortune,* pp. 14–15 (quote, p. 15).

[3]RICHMAN, L. S. (1993, September 20). When will the layoffs end? *Fortune,* pp. 54–56.

[4]HALF, R. (1986, June). Career 'insurance' protects DP professionals. *Data Management,* p. 33.

[5]MILLER, W. A. (1991, May 6). A new perspective for tomorrow's workforce. *Industry Week,* pp. 7–8, 16 (quote, p. 8).

[6]BARNES, Z. E. (1987). Change in the Bell System. *Academy of Management Executive, 1,* 43–46 (quote, p. 43).

[7]NADLER, D. A. (1987). The effective management of organizational change. In J. W. Lorsch (ed.), *Handbook of organizational behavior* (pp. 358–369). Englewood Cliffs, NJ: Prentice-Hall.

[8]KATZ, D., & KAHN, R. L. (1978). *The social psychology of organizations*, 2nd ed. New York: Wiley.

[9]See Note 7.

[10]HUEY, J. (1993, April 5). Managing in the midst of chaos. *Fortune*, pp. 38–41, 44, 46, 48.

[11]VICARS, W. M., & HARTKE, D. D. (1984). Evaluating OD evaluations: A status report. *Group and Organization Studies, 9*, 177–188.

[12]FISHER, L. (1992, January 12). The latest word on teamwork? 'Mush.' *The New York Times*, p. B16. (quote, p. B16).

[13]See Note 12 (quote, p. B16).

[14]See Note 12 (quote, p. B16).

[15]STEEL, R. P., & SHANE, G. S. (1986). Evaluation research on quality circles: Technical and analytical implications. *Human Relations, 39*, 449–468.

[16]PORRAS, J. I., & ROBERTSON, P. J. (1992). Organization development: Theory, practice, and research. In M. D. Dunnette & L. M. Hough (eds.), *Handbook of industrial and organizational psychology*, 2nd ed. (Vol. 3, pp. 719–822). Palo Alto, CA: Consulting Psychologists Press.

CHAPTER 12

[1]QUICK, J. C., & QUICK, J. D. (1984). *Organizational stress and preventive management.* New York: McGraw-Hill.

[2]COHEN, S., & WILLIAMSON, G. M. (1991). Stress and infectious diseases in humans. *Psychological Bulletin, 109*, 5–24.

[3]TSUI, A. S., EGAN, T. D., & O'REILLY, C. A., III. (1992). Being different: Relational demography and organizational attachment. *Administrative Science Quarterly, 37*, 549–579.

[4]COX, T., JR. (1994). *Cultural diversity in organizations: Theory, research, and practice.* San Francisco: Berrett-Koehler.

[5]ZUBOFF, S. (1988). *In the age of the smart machine.* New York: Basic Books.

[6]HANDY, C. (1994). *The age of paradox.* New York: Morrow (quote, p. 12).

[7]FIERMAN, J. (1994, January). The contingency workforce. *Fortune*, pp. 30–34, 36 (quote, p. 36).

[8]GREENGARD, S. (1994, September). Workers go virtual. *Personnel Journal*, p. 71.

[9]DUBRIN, A. J. (1994). *Contemporary applied management: Skills for managers*, 4th ed. Burr Ridge, IL: Irwin.

[10]GREENGARD, S. (1994, September). Making the virtual office a reality. *Personnel Journal*, pp. 66–76.

[11]See Note 9 (quote, p. 68).

[12]See Note 9 (quote, p. 68).

[13]GHOSHAL, S., & BARTLETT, C. A. (1990). The multinational corporation as an interorganizational network. *Academy of Management Review, 15*, 603–625.

[14]IVANCEVICH, J. M., DEFRANK, R. S., & GREGORY, P. R. (1992). The Soviet enterprise director: An important resource before and after the coup. *Academy of Management Executive, 6*, 42–55 (quote, p. 46).

[15]WALTON, M. (1990). *The Deming management method at work.* New York: Perigree.

[16]STEWART, T. A. (1993, August 23). Reengineering: The hot new managing tool. *Fortune*, pp. 40–43, 46, 48.

[17]The promise of reengineering. (1993, May 3). *Fortune*, pp. 94–97.

[18]HENDERSON, V. E. (1992). *What's ethical in business?* New York: McGraw-Hill.

[19]JANSEN, E., & VON GLINOW, M. A. (1985). Ethical ambivalence and organizational reward systems. *Academy of Management Review, 10*, 814–822.

[20]WOLFE, D. M. (1988). Is there integrity in the bottom line: Managing obstacles to executive integrity. In S. Srivastava (ed.), *Executive integrity: The search for high human values in organizational life* (pp. 140–171). San Francisco: Jossey-Bass.

[21]See Note 8.

Indexes

NAME INDEX

COMPANY INDEX

SUBJECT INDEX